Alina Gromova / Felix Heinert / Sebastian Voigt (eds)

Jewish and Non-Jewish Spaces in the Urban Context

Jüdische Kulturgeschichte in der Moderne
(Jewish Cultural History in the Modern Era)
edited by Joachim Schlör
Volume 4

Alina Gromova / Felix Heinert / Sebastian Voigt
(eds)

Jewish and Non-Jewish Spaces in the Urban Context

Neofelis Verlag

German National Library Cataloguing in Publication Data
A catalogue record for this book is available from the German National Library:
http://dnb.d-nb.de

www.neofelis-verlag.de

Cover Design: Marija Skara
Printed by PRESSEL Digitaler Produktionsdruck, Remshalden
Printed on FSC-certified paper.
ISBN (Print): 978-3-943414-44-8
ISBN (PDF): 978-3-943414-89-9

Contents

Epilogue

Foreword

Jewish Cultural Practice and the Production of Space

All human existence, as Amir Eshel has put it, is „fundamentally connected to and manifested in space“.[1] In the context of Jewish history and culture, this connection contains an additional dialectical tension: "between cosmos and makom",[2] between the places of the material world, manifest in houses, streets, markets, synagogues, and those of the spiritual heritage, in texts, prayers, images, or memories. Life conditions in the Diaspora – among the nations – have brought about a specific poetics of space as a result of this *in-between-ness* and of the physical and mental confrontation between these two worlds. The starting point of Eshel's discussion is Jacob's dream: the awe-inspiring encounter ("ma nora ha-makom ha-zeh!") is expressed in spatial terms; from then on, Jacob's role will be "contingent upon his inhabitating, imagining, depicting, giving meaning to, transgressing – in short, being in – this certain place“.[3]

Jewish topographies emerge from and can be discussed in the framework of such – cultural – activities: to inhabit, to imagine, to depict, to give meaning to, to transgress. To be in a place. The wide variety of cultural practices both among Jews and in their relationship with others is a product of the meeting between "traditions of place" and "visions of space", to use the terms that Julia Brauch, Anne Lipphardt and Alexandra Nocke have chosen for the subtitle of their book,[4] an outcome of the Potsdam-based postgraduate research group *Makom* (2001–2007). Following Lily Kong's assertion „that space is open, contingent and is the outcome of (rather than the container

1 Amir Eshel: Cosmopolitanism and Searching for the Sacred Space in Jewish Literature. In: *Jewish Social Studies* 9,3 (2003), pp. 121–138, here p. 124.

2 Ibid.

3 Ibid., p. 126.

4 Julia Brauch / Anna Lipphardt / Alexandra Nocke (eds): *Jewish Topographies. Traditions of Place, Visions of Space*. Aldershot: Ashgate 2008.

for) complex social processes", and Henri Lefebvre's claim that "space is at once result and cause, product and producer",[5] most researchers agree that enactment and creativity are key notions for our understanding of being in places.

One of the most visible and widely discussed examples of such enacted spaces is the *eruv*, the Sabbath border, a complex network of spatial activities that creates (or produces) – for one day of the week – a *Jewish space*, a kind of private space surrounded by public spaces, within which the law that forbids carrying on a Sabbath is suspended. Inner-Jewish debates about the use and validity of eruvim concern questions of observance and transgression; public debates, as Barry Smith and others have shown, raise questions of ownership and belonging: "Opponents of the eruv argued that public property cannot be designated for the use of a particular group", and non-Jews have expressed their uneasiness about "living in a territory identified with a religion that is not [their] own".[6] In defence of the concept, Manuel Herz argues: "Abstracted from its religious context and analysed upon its urban strategy, the eruv stands for a seeding of an urban realm that nevertheless remains accessible to all groups of society and open to all uses."[7] Justifications of *eruvim*, or of other forms of ritual practices that engage with public space (the temporal building of *sukkot* or the construction of synagogues), require knowledge of "Jewish Conceptions and Practices of Space", as Charlotte Fonrobert and Vered Shemtov have titled their Stanford conference of 2003 and the ensuing publication.[8] Similarly to Eshel, they argue "that neither individual nor community can experience time in this world without claiming, occupying, naming, shaping, negotiating, and losing 'real' space."[9]

This is the context for the present volume that brings together, and into dialogue, research from two of the most innovative fields in current Humanities:

5 Lily Kong: Mapping 'new' Geographies of Religion: Politics and Poetics in Modernity. In: *Progress in Human Geography* 25,2 (2001), pp. 211–233; quoted in Fraser McDonald: Towards a Spatial Theory of Worship: Some Observations from Presbyterian Scotland. In: *Social & Cultural Geography* 3,1 (2002), pp. 61–81, here p. 64; Henri Lefebvre: *The Production of Space*. Oxford: Blackwell 1991, p. 142.

6 Barry Smith: On Place and Space: The Ontology of the Eruv. In: Christian Kanzian / Edmund Runggaldier (eds): *Cultures: Conflict – Analysis – Dialogue*. Frankfurt am Main: Ontos 2007, pp. 406–407.

7 Manuel Herz / Court Jester: The Politics of "Jewish Architecture" in Germany. In: *Jewish Social Studies* 11,3 (2005), pp. 58–66, here p. 58.

8 Charlotte Elisheva Fonrobert / Vered Shemtov: Introduction: Jewish Conceptions and Practices of Space. In: Ibid., pp. 1–8.

9 Ibid., p. 4.

Jewish studies and Urban studies. This collection of papers represents both a continuation of earlier work and an innovative and original contribution: The relationship between Jewish and non-Jewish spaces in the urban context emerges as a useful platform, an arena in which ideas and approaches concerning different historical periods and geographical locations can be discussed.

It is the city, the urban context, that provides both inspiration and information for such an enterprise. This volume also contributes both the material sources and the original thinking that we need to overcome generalisations and essentialist attributions: "Jews have lived in cities for millennia and scholars have consistently studied Jewish urban life."[10] Yes, true – but what does this mean? Is there something like an "urban character", for individuals, for groups and communities, or even for cities?[11] What is the role and function of borders, limits, and margins for the study of Jewish and non-Jewish spaces?[12] What more can we expect from a new publication than productive new questions?

Joachim Schlör
Southampton, June 2015

10 Frankel Institute for Advanced Judaic Studies, Theme for 2007–2008: Jews and the City. https://www.lsa.umich.edu/judaic/institute/themes (accessed 14.06.2015).

11 What is Urban Character? Defining, Constructing and Regulating Urban Place Identity. Chief Investigator: Professor Kim Dovey. Funded by: ARC Discovery-Project Grant 2003–2005. http://www.abp.unimelb.edu.au/research/fund/wuc.html (accessed 14.06.2015).

12 Moritz Föllmer / Habbo Knoch: Grenzen und urbane Modernität. Überlegungen zu einer Gesellschaftsgeschichte städtischer Interaktionsräume. http.//hsozkult.geschichte.hu-berlin.de/index.asp?id=788&view=pdf (accessed 14.06.2015).

Introduction

The concept of space has been widely debated in the fields of history, urban studies, ethnography, literary studies and other related disciplines in recent years. These debates have extended to the realm of Jewish studies, where the term "space" has been applied in various ways.[1] Among the most common theoretical premises for the contemporary discourse on space is Henri Lefebvre's concept of *espace vécu* (lived space).[2]

Yet the discussion of spatialization in Jewish history is far from over; there are still many open questions – and few empirical case studies – about the conception of Jewish space as a *fluid* process, rather than a fixed, closed or complete entity. Such an understanding would imply a conceptualization of Jewish space as an area – and object – of negotiations and controversies, to which the genesis of various discourses and divergent experiences can be traced.

It seems evident that processes of inclusion and exclusion have influenced Jewish and non-Jewish "identity politics" in urban spaces in various epochs and areas. Furthermore, urban space itself can be understood only in relation to adjacent semi-urban and rural environments, which must be taken into account when dealing with the notion of urban space. Hence, space must be understood not just as a physical entity or territoriality, but as a concept constructed and shaped by the discourses surrounding it as well as by the human

1 See among others *Anthropological Journal of European Cultures* 23,2 (2014): Jewish Space Reloaded!, ed. by Eszter B. Gantner / Jay (Koby) Oppenheim; Barbara E. Mann: *Space and Place in Jewish Studies*. New Brunswick: Rutgers UP 2012; Julia Brauch / Anna Lipphardt / Alexandra Nocke (eds): *Jewish Topographies. Visions of Space, Traditions of Place*. New York: Ashgate 2008; Diana Pinto: The Jewish Space in Europe. In: Sandra Lustig / Ian Leveson (eds): *Turning the Kaleidoscope: Perspectives on European Jewry*. New York / Oxford: Berghahn 2008, pp. 27–40; Diana Pinto: A New Jewish Identity for Post-1989 Europe. *JPR Policy Paper* 1 (1996). http://www.jpr.org.uk/documents/A%20new%20Jewish%20identity%20for%20post-1989%20Europe.pdf (accessed 04.05.2015).

2 Henri Lefebvre: *The Production of Space*. Oxford: Blackwell 1997.

beings living in it.[3] Spaces are not just physical and geographical, but also symbolical, mental and social – all aspects which must be analyzed in order to obtain a complete picture of the relevance of space in Jewish and non-Jewish experience.

Taking up this challenge we organized a conference in November 2012, on "Jewish and Non-Jewish Spaces in the Urban Context" at the Institute of European Ethnology and the Georg Simmel Center for Metropolitan Studies at the Humboldt University, Berlin. International scholars from various disciplines gathered to discuss the role of space in Jewish and non-Jewish history, anthropology, cultural sciences, geography, architecture and literature. The central questions behind the conference were: How are Jewish spaces as well as Jewish-non-Jewish spatial relations constructed in various temporal, spatial and discursive contexts? What kinds of overlaps and borders emerge when disparate agents meet simultaneously in Jewish and non-Jewish spaces? Do urban contexts in various times and geographical regions affect the spatialization of the various divergent Jewish forms of self-identification, as well as their perception by the non-Jewish population – and if so, how? A central aim of the conference was to debate the existence of a general theoretical framework linking all the various case studies.

In the brief historiographical introduction that follows this general preface, Felix Heinert suggests one possible framework for historicizing some of the motivating issues behind this volume. Considering the spatial turn as a whole, he polemicizes against certain de-historicized conceptions of this – according to some – revolutionary "turn" in general, and certain influential historiographical traditions of forgetting and reinventing Jewish (and non-Jewish) spatiality in particular.

The articles contained in this volume adopt various methods and disciplinary perspectives. Nonetheless, they all share a common conceptual assumption – namely, that Jewish spaces develop only in relation to non-Jewish spaces. The discussions held during the conference revolved around the following focal points: What spaces are produced by the encounter between Jewish and non-Jewish agents in an urban environment? How is difference marked,

3 Cf. Martina Löw: *Raumsoziologie*. Frankfurt am Main: Suhrkamp 2001; Martina Löw / Georgios Terizakis (eds): *Städte und ihre Eigenlogik. Ein Handbuch für Stadtplanung und Stadtentwicklung*. Frankfurt am Main: Campus 2011, and for a pronounced criticism of some implicitly essentialised conceptualizations of space *within* spatial turn: Jan Kemper / Anna Vogelpohl (eds): *Lokalistische Stadtforschung, kulturalisierte Städte. Zur Kritik einer ‚Eigenlogik der Städte'*. Münster: Westfälisches Dampfboot 2011.

negotiated and, in the end, possibly spatialized? Where and how do spaces of contact as well as spaces of conflict emerge within modern Jewish history? Seeking to address the topic in a broad manner, we invited (cultural) historians, anthropologists, scholars of architecture and literature from Germany, Poland, Hungary, Switzerland, England, the USA, France and Israel. The present volume contains papers delivered during the conference as well as additional contributions intended to round out the broad geographical, epochal and thematic framework.

The first section of the volume, entitled "Historicizing 'Jewish Space', Deconstructing the 'Ghetto' – Early Modern and Modern Perspectives on Jewish Modernity," presents international historiographical analyses of Jewish space in early modern and modern contexts, addressing the controversial role of the ghetto as a Jewish space and depicting the Jewish spaces in the Polish-Lithuanian Commonwealth and Ottoman Algiers.

In his article, "Making Sense of the 'Ghetto'. Conceptualizing a Jewish Space from Early Modern Times to the Present," Jürgen Heyde argues that the term 'ghetto' represents a phenomenon that is easy to exemplify, yet almost impossible to define. Despite – or perhaps because of – the widespread use of the term in various geographical, temporal and cultural contexts, there is no universally accepted definition of the term 'ghetto.' This is all the more striking considering that the origins of the term were firmly established decades ago. The article argues that an understanding of this term requires an investigation into the connotations and meanings ascribed to it in its various settings. This investigation is divided into four parts: The first addresses recent attempts at defining the term from historical and sociological perspectives. The second section analyses two texts fundamental for a modern-day understanding of the term 'ghetto': Louis Wirth's *The Ghetto* and Salo W. Baron's article "Ghetto and Emancipation". In the third part, the focus shifts further back to the time between the French Revolution and World War I, when the early modern ghettos were dissolved but the motif of the ghetto continued to play an important role in the debates about Jewish identity in the modern world. The fourth section focuses on the early modern period itself, when the term 'ghetto' emerged, a period later referred to as "the age of the ghetto". The example of Venice is used to highlight early usages and meanings ascribed to the term. The term 'ghetto,' Heyde argues, has always been an object of debate. Definitions and descriptions of the ghetto have been used to shape specific views of Jewish (and other) history, society and culture. While conceptualizations of the ghetto at any given time were influenced by contemporary interests, they also added to the scope of our knowledge regarding the word's possible meanings. In the course of time, a wide range of connotations unfolded – a symbolic dimension that must necessarily be considered when discussing the ghetto as a Jewish space.

In her article, "Jewish *Shtetl* or Christian Town? The Jews in Small Towns in the Polish-Lithuanian Commonwealth in the 17th and 18th Centuries," Maria Cieśla analyses the social interaction between Jews and their non-Jewish Christian environment in the early modern Polish-Lithuanian Commonwealth, which was home to the largest Jewish community in Europe at the time. Cieśla's analysis centers on the *shtetls*, or small towns where the majority of Jews lived. She argues that the image of the *shtetl*, as depicted in most literature on the subject, is often an oversimplified, idealised vision that ignores the complexity of social life. In order to elucidate that complexity, the author refers to Georg Simmel's concept of space, considering the manifold interactions between Jews and their Christian neighbours, and thereby approaching Christian-Jewish relations from a new angle. Cieśla bases her research mainly on hitherto unanalysed private archives and legal acts. By examining the Jews' economic activity in the market place, in the religious space of the synagogue and in their domestic spaces, she demonstrates the importance of all these areas for social integration between Jews and Christians. Cieśla concludes that the *shtetl* cannot be understood as a Jewish space alone; rather, it is necessary to consider its Christian elements as well.

In "The Nature of Jewish Spaces in Ottoman Algiers," Nora Lafi sets out from the observation that between the end of 15th century and the beginning of the 20th century, the Ottoman Empire appears to have been a safe haven for Jews from various parts of Europe, from Spain to Eastern Europe, the Black Sea and the Balkans. Ottoman cities where local Jewish communities had existed since ancient times – from Salonica to Jerusalem, Istanbul to Medina, Tunis to Bagdad and Sarajevo to Alexandria – welcomed new Jewish populations fleeing European persecutions. The new migrants were incorporated into the framework of the Ottoman policy of tolerance, which was itself rooted in medieval Islamic principles of protection and prescribed precise patterns of communal autonomy. In all these cities, the Jews were a fundamental component of urban life. Lafi analyses the relationship between the Jewish community and the urban space in the city of Algiers, one of the main Ottoman ports of North Africa. In Algiers, the reforms of the 19th century were implemented in a colonial and highly ambiguous form. The issue of the granting of 'equality' to the Jews by the French colonial authorities was central in this respect; indeed, full equality was only given to the colonial settlers, and not to the rest of the Algerian population. The state authorities granted the Jews of Algiers broader access to the civic sphere, while at the same time excluding Algerian Muslims from it. According to Lafi, this biased reform produced a new divide between the Jews and the rest of the Algerian population, with severe consequences for the transformation of lived experiences within the urban space. Many Jewish families moved to the so-called 'European' city that was gradually being constructed on the ruins of part of the old city, which had been destroyed by the French between 1830 and 1832, or beyond the limits of the former walled city. Many small synagogues and workshops of Jewish artisans were destroyed in this first phase of colonial urbanism. It was only in 1845 that the construction of a monumental synagogue initiated a new phase in the relationship between the colonisers and the Algerian Jews. The day-to-day proximity between Jews and Muslims gradually waned, and many shared spaces on the micro-urban level disappeared. Many others, however, remained – based, as Lafi observes, on shared practices of sociability, such as cooking and music – until the exile of 1962, when, in the wake of Algerian independence, most Algerian Jews were forced to leave the country.

In "A Jewish Space in an Extreme Context? German Ghettoes for Jews in Eastern Europe during World War II," Frank Golczewski discusses whether Jewish ghettos built by the Germans in Eastern Europe during World War II can and should at all be labeled as Jewish spaces. He argues that while the ghettos have long been a subject of scholarly interest from the German perspective, the Jewish councils have often been seen merely as dependent auxiliaries. The very possibility of any kind of autonomous action or choice on the part of the Jews, who had been forced to live in special quarters set aside for them, was ruled out. Only in recent years have historians begun to approach these very specific spaces from a Jewish perspective. Through a discussion of the creation of the first ghettos in the General Government – documented in the so-called *Schnellbrief* of Reinhard Heydrich – and an explanation of the various stages of ghettoization on Polish territory, Golczewski shows that there is no single, unified "ghetto world," but rather a conglomeration of many spaces, each with its own characteristics. The picture is further complicated when the ghettos in the German Reich and the occupied Soviet territories are considered. Golczewski argues that the ghettos erected by the Germans were characterized by a certain ambivalence: they included both areas with some form of temporary self-administration as well as areas of clear non-Jewish dominance; the *Judenbann* system as well as open, un-walled or walled ghettos. Even the strictest ghetto regulations were sometimes modified for pragmatic reasons; the question of whether a ghetto can be considered a Jewish space thus cannot be uniformly answered. During the first years of the war, before the Holocaust , many ghettos still possessed a measure of autonomy, and could therefore be classified as Jewish spaces – but this was only a temporary phenomenon. In their later stages, as Golczewski points out – following Tim Cole's terminology, who was the first to apply the notion of the 'spatial turn' to Nazi ghettos – the ghettos in Eastern Europe could no longer be considered Jewish spaces, but rather "waiting spaces for death".

The second section of the volume, entitled "Borderlands, Identity and Interaction," brings together historical analyses of the use and construction of Jewish and non-Jewish spaces in the 19th and 20th centuries. The research it contains on borders and transgressions within Germany and on the Prussian periphery reveals a close interaction between space and identity politics, paving the way toward new theoretical approaches to Jewish space.

Anne-Christin Saß discusses "Transnational and Transcultural Spaces in the Diaspora" as revealed in "The Case of Berlin 1900–1933." Employing the example of Eastern European Jewish migrants, her article examines the creation and alteration of communicative spaces in the urban landscape of Berlin during the first decades of the 20th century. The various communicative spaces established by the spatial strategies of the migrants correspond to particular types of modern urban places such as streets, boarding houses, cafés, union houses and flats, all of which were associated with specific features and experiences of space. The communicative spaces functioned as social and cultural contact zones, which stimulated multifaceted exchanges and transfers. They were, as Saß argues, places of encounter between East and West, between the foreign and the familiar, and were characterized by a deep-seated transnationalism and transculturality. In this way, the article questions the often hastily made assumption that distinct Jewish and non-Jewish spaces existed in the urban context, and refutes the image of Eastern European Jews as a highly segregated and secluded group in Western European cities, highlighting instead the complexity of the processes of differentiation and segregation within a specific urban space and culture.

In "A Border from a Jewish Perspective. Developments on the Prussian Periphery," Ruth Leiserowitz examines an important (trans-)national space for Jews in Eastern Europe. The region between Prussia and the Russian Empire was shaken by the events of the short 20th century, beginning with the end of World War I. From the end of the 18th century until 1914, this area had developed into a key border region between two great powers; it had a high percentage of Jews, who often made up over fifty percent of the population in the small towns. Leiserowitz shows that borders in general, and this border in particular, play an essential role in historical evolution: they could be considered a kind of seismograph, a high-energy zone. Being a "Jewish area," the political vicissitudes of the region affected the Jews most of all. First, in 1916, the German army occupied the area. After Germany's defeat in World War I and its subsequent loss of much of its Eastern territory, the border was shifted and the region became part of the newly established Lithuanian state. But the conflicting territorial claims did not end there; the newly established nation states, with their respective perceptions of ethnicity, often marginalized the Jews. The Soviet invasion of 1940 ended with Nazi Germany's invasion of the Soviet Union, which turned the former border region into the foremost theater of the Holocaust. Some of the first massacres of Jews by the SS-*Einsatzgruppen* were committed on the territory of what had been Lithuania. The prospering Jewish culture there was almost completely destroyed. Leiserowitz demonstrates how political events since the early 19th century influenced the lives of Jews in the Prussian-Russian border region. She also underlines the relevance of borders, as spatial phenomena, as a central historical category within a transnational perspective on Jewish history. The view from the apparent periphery may shed light on fundamental developments, thus upsetting the traditional differentiation between center and periphery.

In "German-Jewish Borderlands. On 'Non-Jewish Jewish Spaces' in Weimar and Nazi Germany," Mirjam Zadoff discusses the notion of Jewish space as the space of 'non-Jewish Jews' (Isaac Deutscher) in the context of the Weimar Republic and Nazi Germany. Her discussion centres on the biography of Werner Scholem, one of the leading Jewish communists in Weimar Germany, whose experience offers insight into the complex and at times dialectic identity of non-Jewish Jews, situated at the interstices of two worlds. These inhabitants of these border spaces were defined by their highly individual experiences as voluntary political and public outcasts from the Jewish community who nevertheless remained linked to it through bonds of family and friendship. At the same time, this 'non-Jewish Jewish space' was shaped by the growing antisemitism in the Weimar Republic, and subsequently in Nazi Germany.

The volume's third section, "Becoming Metropolitan, Reimagining Community," addresses the ways Jews inscribed themselves into the urban spaces, politics (both Jewish and non-Jewish) and practices of daily (Jewish) life in various large cities, in a geographical spectrum extending from Western Europe through Central and Eastern Europe to the Russian Empire.

In her article, "Space for Reflection: Synagogue Building in Nineteenth-Century Urban Landscapes," Saskia Coenen Snyder follows Henri Lefebvre, Michel de Certeau and David Harvey in adopting the assumption that space and location are not neutral categories, but concepts replete with political and ideological meaning. Urban landscapes and buildings contribute to the construction of social relations; yet their significance is often fluid and open to interpretation rather than intrinsic. This shifting meaning is, in turn, continuously contested and called into question, as the author demonstrates using the example of the Oranienburger Straße synagogue in Berlin. While many scholars see the construction of this synagogue as a triumph of Jewish emancipation in 19th century Germany, Coenen Snyder rejects a simplistic perspective, arguing that the history of the synagogue's construction – which lasted nearly two decades, from the first petition to the building's completion in 1866 – was fraught with ambivalence: the synagogue was repeatedly used, by various actors at various times, to (re-)define both Jewishness and Germanness. In addition, the Jewish community had to deal with numerous obstacles placed in its path by the Prussian state regarding every aspect of the building, from its location to its design. The synagogue was constructed at a time when the "Jewish question" was already very much alive within German society, and Jews frequently encountered considerable antisemitic resentment. Coenen Snyder shows that even the synagogue's generally positive reception contained an element of ambiguity: its architecture was seen by many as overly fantastic and "Oriental" – qualities that seemed to underscore the Jews' otherness and foreignness to the German *volk*.

In his contribution, "The Emergence of the First European Jewish Metropolis in Warsaw, 1850–1880," François Guesnet shows the significance of the fact that over the course of a single generation, between 1850 and 1880, the general population of Warsaw doubled, while the number of Jews living in the Polish capital grew threefold, from below 40,000 to over 120,000. The Jews of Warsaw, he contends, outgrew their own capacity to form a community, and morphed into a Jewish metropolis. Guesnet assesses this transformation by looking at the way Jews experienced the Polish metropolis, how they marked spaces as "Jewish," shared and enjoyed "neutral" spaces, and asserted their presence in the face of contestation.

In "Jewish Quarters as Urban Tableaux," Eszter Gantner discusses the concept of the 'Jewish quarter' as it has been applied to Budapest's 8th district in media debates since the beginning of the millennium. This district, which has been under UNESCO protection since 2002, has drawn the attention of various NGOs working to protect its cultural and architectural heritage and to combat the unregulated sale, demolition and construction of buildings in the neighborhood. Gantner analyses the relevant literature on the cultural and architectural reconstruction of Jewish quarters and concludes that the "Jewish nature" of a "Jewish quarter" is generally determined by the Jewish population that used to live or now lives in the given area. With regard to Budapest, however, the author raises the following question: What if the Jewish population, whose relationship to Judaism is heterogeneous, ranging from religious to secular and cultural, does not constitute a distinct group – neither in its appearances nor its practices? Gantner observes that in many cities and towns of continental Europe, including Budapest, the Jewish population tends not to leave clearly recognizable traces in the cityscape. She also stresses the fact that most European cities with historic Jewish quarters no longer have a significant Jewish community; all that remains is a consciousness of memory and an architectural heritage. To describe this Jewishness that exists primarily in relation to architectural heritage and memory, the author suggests the term 'urban tableau,' which she defines as an assemblage of images underlying the perception of 'Jewishness' in European cities and towns bereft of their Jewish communities. Using the examples of Paris, Krakow and Berlin, Gantner discusses the role of urban tableaux and the practices relating to the culture of memory involved in the construction of "Jewishness" and the definition of what constitutes a "Jewish quarter."

In his essay, "Jewish, Urban, Imperial and Other Spaces. The Spatial Momentum in the Historiography of the Russian-Jewish Experience," Alexis Hofmeister discusses the multifaceted relations between Jews and gentiles in the urban environment of the Russian Empire in the 19th and early 20th centuries. Through an examination of several Jewish autobiographies, Hofmeister uncovers various perspectives on the relationship between Jewish and non-Jewish space. Mary Antin remembers her childhood in a small town as having been sharply divided between the Jewish *shtetl* and the unknown, mysterious place called Russia that surrounded it. From her perspective, America is the promised country providing refuge to Jews fleeing persecution in their old home, which becomes, in retrospect, a non-Jewish space. At the same time, Antin sees the *shtetl* as a lost paradise. Osip Mandelstam, by contrast, does not associate Jewish space with small towns and non-Jewish space with urban environments. In his autobiography, written in Moscow, he recalls his childhood in St. Petersburg as having been characterized by "Judaic chaos" as well as anti-Jewish violence. Hofmeister points out that the historicity of spatial perception has been addressed, in historical discourse, in three main fields: the history of Jewish migration, the history of the *shtetl* as a space of life as well as memory, and the history of the pogrom as a history of the fight over public space. Comparing the cases of three different urban spaces – Kiev, Odessa and Yekaterinoslav (Dnepropetrovsk) – Hofmeister argues for revising the notion of a segregated Jewish space in the cities of Imperial Russia. In some parts of the cities, Jews and non-Jews would live and work side by side, while each group also created separate spaces of its own. These parallel processes gave rise to permanent conflicts over the meaning and function of urban space, but also enabled Jews to experiment with Jewish urbanity.

The last section of the volume, "Mapping Jewish and Non-Jewish Spaces of Memory, Narration and Representation," combines historical, cultural and literary approaches to Jewish and non-Jewish space. It shows how memory, imagination and narration charge physical space with symbolic meanings, transforming it into an arena for the negotiation of cultural (and other) possessions.

In "Gypsy Spaces and Jewish Spaces as Hyper-Liminal Spaces of Inversion. Longing for the Shtetl and Gypsy Camp," Monica Rüthers describes Jewish and Gypsy spaces in which people belonging to borderline communities are put on stage at public festivities. These events take place in touristic spaces set apart from the actual living spaces of the minorities, who thus become, simultaneously, performers and "performed." The 1990s saw an upsurge in the interest in Yiddish language, Klezmer music and Chassidism. Starting from the mid-1980s, there has also been a growing fascination with Gypsy music and culture, both in Europe and the United States. The most attractive of these performance spaces are situated in European borderlands and address a heterogeneous public. In light of this fact, the author takes a comparative approach, using spatial concepts to elucidate the structural similarities between Gypsy space and Jewish space. In considering the question of how an exploration of Gypsy spaces can help us better understand Jewish spaces, Rüthers compares two prominent cultural events, the Kraków Jewish Culture Festival and the Gypsy pilgrimage to Saintes-Maries-de-la-Mer. The aggregation of liminal elements seems to promise a transformative experience. In these spaces, Jewish and Gypsy past and present are imagined and exoticized in atemporal enactments whose subjects are dead Jews or "timeless" Gypsies – figures that, collectively imagined, become symbols in popular memory.

Emphasis is placed on tradition and the exotic, pre-modern "other". Locals, visitors and members of minorities are all involved in these "enactments of heritage." Jewish and Gypsy spaces are loci of social inversion that provide the minorities with a precarious temporary status and the "Europeans" with settings in which to negotiate new identities.

In her article, "In the Cellars and Attics of Memory: Mapping Jewish and Non-Jewish Spaces in Contemporary Poland," Magdalena Waligórska discusses the renegotiation of the topographies of 'Jewish' and 'non-Jewish' spaces in contemporary Poland. Analyzing the attempts of local actors to revitalize, commemorate and create Jewish spaces, she identifies two main types of cultural projects: those initiated by Jewish museums, festivals, community centers and other cultural institutions on the one hand, and virtual projects seeking to recover and reconstruct, using digital media, traces of Polish-Jewish architecture on the other. The far-reaching discussion of Jewish spaces that developed in Poland after 1989, as mapped out by scholars, photographers, artists, writers and also tour operators, serves as a backdrop to Waligórska's analysis. She examines the particular case of the Jewish district of Krakow, Kazimierz, as a place in which the "rediscovery" of Jewish space has been closely interwoven with a recent, non-Jewish historical narrative. As a UNESCO World Heritage site, Kazimierz has become one of the main Jewish heritage tourism sites in Central Europe. Since the 1990s, the creation of a tourist infrastructure with cafés, restaurants, concerts and festivals has accelerated the gentrification of the area. It has also provoked protests – both from the quarter's non-Jewish residents, who complain about being driven out of their homes, and the local Jewish inhabitants, who fear an affront to the memory of the historical Jewish community. Waligórska analyses the debates in the media shaped by this recent history, which has led to a heated discussion about "the legitimate and illegitimate uses of a space loaded with conflicting memories and myths". She observes that the fears and hopes of the local Jewish and non-Jewish elements in Kazimierz, together with the change in the local economy and memoryscape, have led to "a new wave of nostalgia about the post-1945 *non-Jewish* Kazimierz" with its proletarian character – sentiments that echo antisemitic stereotypes of Jewish territory appropriation on the one hand and longing for the Communist past on the other. Following de Certeau, Waligórska concludes that the stories and legends attached to a particular place by Jewish and non-Jewish groups are closely interwoven, and that it is from their interconnectedness that the "identity of space" arises. Whether the space is defined as Jewish or non-Jewish depends entirely on the observer.

Diana Popescu's essay, "Between Poetics and Politics. The Eruv and the Wall in Recent Contemporary Artistic Imagination," engages the contradictory nature of two Jewish spatial markers: the historically prevalent eruv, or Jewish ritual enclosure, and the modern and conflict-ridden Israeli wall or security fence. Popescu explores how both spatial markers alternately allow and block contact with the "other"; their ambivalent nature is expressed in artworks such as American Jewish artist Ben Schachter's delicate thread-on-paper maps of *eruvin* (2010), Sophie Calle's *L'Erouv de Jérusalem* (1996) and other recent artistic responses to the wall such as Ravit Cohen Gat and Moshe Gerstel's installation *Next Year in Jerusalem* (2005) and Eyal Weizman's maps, which form part of the group project *Borderlinedisorder* (2002). Popescu shows how artists reflect on the entanglement of the respective spatial politics and poetics of the eruv and the wall, and suggests that these two ambivalent phenomena represent flip sides of the same coin. She also asserts that artistic reflections on spatial practices are important because they force us to reconsider old practices and help us reach a deeper understanding of the effect of such statements on contemporary audiences.

In his article, "Locating Jewish Identities in Naomi Alderman's *Disobedience*", Martin Kindermann analyses various strategies for depicting urban space and its semantic layers as an element of the construction of Jewish identities in Alderman's novel. Based on a relativistic notion of space, he describes space as a relational network in constant motion. He begins by outlining the literary representation of space in general, using the notion of the border as a central element of the spatial network. He then proceeds to establish a correlation between the key concepts of space and the strategies through which Jewish identities are constructed. Kindermann's analysis shows that processes of mutual permeation bring about a hybridization that blurs the seemingly clear-cut borders between the respective semantic sub-spaces. Drawing on Jurij M. Lotman's model of the semiosphere, he aims to observe these semiotic dynamics within the polyvalent space of the semantic border more closely. Alderman's novel constructs urban space as a hybrid structure: Ronit and Esti, the protagonists, are portrayed as hybrid identities, being at once British, Jewish, homosexual and bi-sexual (respectively), secular and orthodox. The literary space of Alderman's text is revealed as a highly polyvalent network of relations that evidences conflict rather than coherence. Mediated by three distinct narrative voices that create a complex narrative framework, the text establishes a polyphonic context that mirrors the intratextual spatial structure of the narrative itself. The author outlines the complex processes of the construction of meaning inscribed in the spatial framework of the city. As the setting for the negotiation of various attempts to construct Jewish identities, urban space is also a space of articulation: conflicting semantic spheres give rise to processes of hybridization, thereby questioning bi-spatial notions with regard to locating Jewishness. The seemingly straightforward conflict between Britishness and Jewishness is thus eventually discarded in favor of much more complex notions of space and identity that lead us, by means of multiple perspectives and a narrative mobility capable of elucidating the conditions for the perception and formation of space, toward a richer understanding of the ambivalent construction of Jewish identity.

Wolfgang Kaschuba, former director of the Institute of European Ethnology at the Humboldt University of Berlin, concludes the volume with the epilogue, "'Jewish Quarter' and 'Kosher Light'. On the 'Migrantisation' of Jewish Urban Space." He investigates how the collective memory of the Holocaust in Germany, and particularly in Berlin, has changed in comparison to previous decades. The young generation – the children of those born soon after World War II – have no direct connection to the Holocaust, and must therefore "immigrate" into the relevant memorial landscape, similarly to those who have immigrated to Germany over the past decades, and who do not share the 'German' memory-*topos*. Instead of a "morality"-bound collective remembrance and "national heritage" – as Jewish history and Jewish life were defined in previous decades – we are now dealing with a confused concept of memory that is fragmented, variable and detached from its concrete historical context. Particularly in urban environments characterised by cultural and ethnic diversity, the Jewish *topos*, which incorporates not just the Holocaust but also religion, music and food, becomes not only 'foreign,' but exotic and even 'stylish'. Terms such as 'Jewish quarter', 'Klezmer' or 'kosher-burger' have become new labels promoted by the German capital as a way of presenting the Jewish *topos* to new groups and new generations in Germany.

We hope that the various contributions in this volume demonstrate the fertility of the interdisciplinary and transnational approaches to Jewish space(s). In addition we also want the book to encourage further research by raising questions and providing new perspectives from international scholars. Stimulating critical research is in our opinion the best effect a book can have.

Alina Gromova, Felix Heinert, Sebastian Voigt
Berlin / Marburg / Munich, March 2015

Jews of This World – Historicizing Jewish and Non-Jewish Spaces in the Urban Context
Blueprint for a Historiographical Thesis

Felix Heinert

The concept of space in general, and of Jewish spaces, spatial constructions and experiences in particular, has been the subject of much historiographical discussion in recent years.[1] "History has its venues"[2] – with this simple yet influential rhetorical figure, Karl Schlögel summed up this "return of space" in the realm of (German) historiography.

Actually, space had been there all along. What Schlögel suggested was a new "technique of seeing" or *Augenarbeit* – a renewed sensitivity, in the realm of cultural studies, to the fundamental spatial dimension of (all) history. Schlögel was particularly interested in a new kind of "map-reading," and a historical reassessment of Europe at the close of the era of its geopolitical division. These and numerous other programmatic and theoretical stimuli – many relating to the politics of memory – from the end of the "Cold War" in Europe have become important points of reference for the "spatial turn" as well as for much recent research on urban development.

Prominent among these general theoretical references is Henri Lefebvre's concept of "lived space" (*espace vécu*), popularized by the 1991 English edition of his *The Production of Space* (1974),[3] which heavily influenced the international interdisciplinary debate, among historians as well. This same period also saw

1 See some reading suggestions in the general preface to this volume.

2 See Karl Schlögel: *Im Raume lesen wir die Zeit. Über Zivilisationsgeschichte und Geopolitik*. München: Hanser 2003, p. 9, as well as Schlögel's preliminary space-related works from the 1980s and 1990s.

3 Henri Lefebvre: *The Production of Space*. Oxford: Blackwell 1991.

the emergence of Pierre Bourdieu's influential procedural and symbolic concept of space,[4] which was to serve as another point of orientation for several subsequent contributions to the field. In the realm of Jewish Studies, Diana Pinto's 1996 paper on the politics of memory and identity has become one of the most quoted programmatic reference points.[5] The research projects initiated by the Graduiertenkolleg Makom, a doctoral program established by the University of Potsdam, on the concept of place and space in European Jewry since the Enlightenment, have objectified the academic debate both empirically and conceptually, channeling it in new, productive directions.[6] These and other reference points of the "spatial turn"[7] also inspired, each in its own way and from its own perspective, several of the interdisciplinary contributions in this volume.

The "spatial turn" cannot be credited with the discovery of either space or *spatiality* as a precondition for human action and perception. Yet its renewed sensitivity to the spatiality of cultural phenomena, cultural attributions and their constructive principles was to prove enriching for cultural and historical studies, as well as for Jewish and Urban studies on the whole – even if the prevalent rhetoric of the innovation-revolutionary turn can now be viewed, from a historical distance, with a certain critical caution.[8]

4 Pierre Bourdieu: Social Space and Symbolic Power. In: *Sociological Theory* 7,1 (1989), pp. 14–25. The argument first appeared in his French lecture in Pierre Bourdieu: *Leçon sur la leçon.* Paris: Éd. de Minuit 1982.

5 Diana Pinto: A New Jewish Identity for Post-1989 Europe. *JPR Policy Paper* 1 (1996). http://www.jpr.org.uk/documents/A%20new%20Jewish%20identity%20for%20post-1989%20Europe.pdf (accessed 31.01.2015).

6 A good overview of this research context offers Michal Kümper / Barbara Rösch / Ulrike Schneider / Helen Thein (eds): *Makom. Orte und Räume im Judentum. Real. Abstrakt. Imaginär.* Hildesheim: Olms 2007.

7 Also seminal for the "spatial turn" in Jewish Studies: Julia Brauch / Anna Lipphardt / Alexandra Nocke: Exploring Jewish Space: An Approach. In: Iid. (eds): *Jewish Topographies – Visions of Space, Traditions of Place.* Ashgate: Aldershot 2008, S. 1–23; Joachim Schlör: Jews and the Big City. Explorations on an Urban State of Mind. In: Ibid., pp. 223–240; Petra Ernst / Gerald Lamprecht: *Jewish spaces: Die Kategorie Raum im Kontext kultureller Identitäten.* Innsbruck: Studien-Verlag 2010, as well as more recently and summarizing the state of debate: Barbara E. Mann: *Space and Place in Jewish Studies.* New Brunswick: Rutgers UP 2012.

8 See for this point an instructive general discussion in Doris Bachmann-Medick: *Turns* und Re-Turns in den Kulturwissenschaften. In: Michael Gubo (ed.): *Kritische Perspektiven: ‚Turns', Trends und Theorien.* Berlin: Lit 2011, p. 128–145, esp. p. 137.

The writings of early twentieth century German-Jewish authors such as Georg Simmel[9], Walter Benjamin[10] and Siegfried Kracauer[11] on urban theory and phenomenology offer good templates in this regard, anticipating numerous historico-cultural and cultural-sociological figures of contemporary Urban Studies repeatedly referred to in this volume.

The above-mentioned intellectuals were not the only ones who, in their writings around the turn of the century, attempted to express the urban and metropolitan experience, then perceived as novel, in theoretical, sociological, philosophical and everyday terms. Against this backdrop, they created a correlation between (metropolitan) urbanity and modernity. In other words, they equated the former – which they distinguished, disputably, from rural, semi-urban, suburban and small-town conceptions of space – with the latter. These historical definitions of urbanity, which presuppose universality and neutrality and which are still, in part, upheld today, have become permeated by numerous contemporary debates, experiences and phantasms.[12] This is particularly true for the varied debates on Judaism and urbanity.[13]

As the contributions to this volume demonstrate, these narratives and the conceptualizations of the peculiar nature of both generic and Jewish urbanity derived from them can exhibit a powerful cogency. Yet these theoretical conceptualizations remain essentially historical narratives, emerging from and situated in a particular space and time – and must be regarded as such.

By no means were all or even most Jews urban, even if they are frequently labeled as such in modern discourse and its paradoxical alternative conceptions.[14] Yet it is precisely in images such as these that urban discourses,

9 Programmatic and often quoted: Georg Simmel: Die Großstädte und das Geistesleben. In: Karl Bücher / Georg von Mayr / Theodor Petermann / Friedrich Ratzel / Dietrich Schäfer / Georg Simmel / Heinrich Waentig (eds): *Die Großstadt. Vorträge und Aufsätze zur Städteausstellung.* Dresden: Zahn & Jaensch 1903, pp. 185–206.

10 See Walter Benjamin's phenomenological 'city texts' from the 1930s in Walter Benjamin: *Gesammelte Schriften*, Bd. V: Das Passagen-Werk. Frankfurt am Main: Suhrkamp 1991.

11 See Siegfried Kracauer's 'street texts' from the 1920s in Siegfried Kracauer: *Straßen in Berlin und anderswo.* Frankfurt am Main: Suhrkamp 1964.

12 See a short but instructive discussion on Simmel's 'big city' concept in Elfi Bendikat: Städte der Moderne. In: Themenportal Europäische Geschichte, 2006. http://www.europa.clio-online.de/2006/Article=105 (accessed 31.01.2015).

13 See Joachim Schlör: *Das Ich der Stadt. Debatten über Judentum und Urbanität, 1822–1938.* Göttingen: Vandenhoeck & Ruprecht 2005, as well as on 'urbanity as stigma' the discussion in Nicolas Berg: *Luftmenschen: Zur Geschichte einer Metapher.* Göttingen: Vandenhoeck & Ruprecht 2008, pp. 120–126.

14 Juri Slezkine has recently used this image with his provocative figure of Jewish mercurian and also has sought to characterize the 'paradox' of the Zionist colonization project from this

practices and self-dramatizations become crystallized. From this perspective, the overly clear-cut conceptual and historical distinction between small-town[15], semi-urban and suburban[16] or rural[17] spatial constructions is called into question – another issue addressed in some contributions to this volume – as it does not necessarily correspond to reality and to the wide spectrum of historical experiences and negotiation processes.

In conclusion: the above reflections are here combined with two theses – one historical, the other pertaining to the history of historiography – and loosely linked around the concept of space:

1. The often proclaimed notion of the exodus from the ghetto, frequently presented, by Jews and non-Jews alike, as the Jews' passage into modernity, is largely or at least often enough illusory. The abandoned "ghetto" was for the most part constructed retroactively, after the purported exodus. Several of the socio-historical contributions and essays on the history of discourse contained in this volume can be read with this in mind. In addition, this caveat can serve as a backdrop for a renewed consideration of the question of the degree to which the National Socialist ghettos of Eastern Europe represented a relapse into the often discussed notion of "pre-modern barbarism." The first point to consider here is that these ghettos were not in their entirety spaces of death and extermination. Rather, as Frank Golczewski shows in his contribution to this volume, they initially continued to offer, albeit with extreme limitations, lived spaces for the Jews, who adopted and

perspective: Juri Slezkine: *The Jewish Century*. Princeton: Princeton UP 2004, p. 102: "Eternal urbanites were to turn themselves into peasants [...] Zionism was the most radical and revolutionary of all nationalisms."

15 On small-town urban contexts, see e.g. the following contributions on East European *shtetlakh*: Yohanan Petrovsky-Shtern: *The Golden Age Shtetl. A New History of Jewish Life in East Europe*. Princeton: Princeton UP 2014; Jeffrey Veidlinger: *In the Shadow of the Shtetl: Small-Town Jewish Life in Soviet Ukraine*. Bloomington: Indiana UP 2013. See also a stimulating discussion extending far beyond Eastern Europe in Jeffrey Shandler: *Shtetl: A Vernacular Intellectual History*. New Brunswick: Rutgers UP 2014.

16 On suburban spaces in Jewish context, see Hannah Ewence: The Jew in the Eruv, the Jew in the Suburb: Contesting the Public Face and the Private Space of British Jewry. In: *Jewish Culture and History* 12,3 (2010), pp. 477–486.

17 On rural Jewry and Jewish-non-Jewish spaces in rural areas, see e.g. a recent work by Stefanie Fischer: *Ökonomisches Vertrauen und antisemitische Gewalt. Jüdische Viehhändler in Mittelfranken 1919–1939*. Göttingen: Wallstein 2014. On projects and practices of Jewish agrarianization in modern times (between 1805 and 1945) and global contexts see the contributions in this instructive special double issue: *Jewish History* 21,3–4 (2007): Jewish Agrarianization, 1804–1945, edited by Israel Bartal / Jonathan Dekel-Chen. On rural and urban Zionist colonization in Palestine/Israel, see e.g. S. Ilan Troen: *Imagining Zion: Dreams, Designs, and Realities in a Century of Jewish Settlement*. New Haven: Yale UP 2003.

appropriated them as such. Secondly – and significantly for my present argument – these spaces were modern spaces.[18] It was not "pre-modernity" that resurfaced here, in the National Socialist projects of ghettoization and the "Final Solution."

As part of and in the wake of discourses on emancipation, the Jews' passage into modernity, often conceived as an exodus from the ghetto, has been variously expressed, time and again, in spatial terms, and thereby spatialized.[19] These (autobiographically documented) narratives are worthy of serious attention as ideas, but not as mere reflections of reality. Nevertheless, the moment the concept of emancipation began to be radically called into question, the idea of the ghetto resurfaced, tellingly, as the preliminary stage of the "Final Solution".

2. A critical analysis of the use of the metaphor of space in the aforementioned Jewish and non-Jewish narratives of modernity implies a new understanding of urban spatial constructions. This understanding can be summed up, with a hint of irony, as follows: Jews had always belonged to *this* world,[20] both after as well as before the advent of modernity. And if they moved in urban contexts, the conclusion to be drawn from this is not the bland observation that they had always – long before breaching the threshold of modernity – positioned themselves in both time *and* space,[21] but rather that spatiality – both sacral *as well as* downright profane – constituted, in addition to sacral and profane temporality,[22] an important dimension of their self-conceptions. As banal as this observation may sound, it is still far from evident for certain parts of Jewish historiography.

18 Though not necessarily in terms of Zygmunt Bauman's modernity thesis: Zygmunt Bauman: *Modernity and the Holocaust.* Ithaca: Cornell UP 1989; id.: *Modernity and Ambivalence.* Ithaca: Cornell UP 1991.

19 See e.g. the spatial imagery in the title of Jacob Katz' historiographical master narrative: Jacob Katz: *Out of the Ghetto: The Social Background of Jewish Emancipation, 1770–1870*, Cambridge, MA: Harvard UP 1973. This is also the case in regard to other complementary or synonymous spatial metaphors for the Jewish passage into modernity, for example: Port and court, *shtetl* and *shtot.* See on this issue an instructive historiographical subchapter "Becoming Modern: Port and Court, *Shtetl and Shtot*" in Mann: *Space and Place in Jewish Studies*, pp. 124–127.

20 Stimulating for this point are the following works: David Biale: *Not in the Heavens: The Tradition of Jewish Secular Thought.* Princeton: Princeton UP 2010; id.: *Power and Powerlessness in Jewish History.* New York: Schocken 1986.

21 A brief, problem-oriented overview of different urban Jewish life forms and spatial practices in various epochs and regions in Mann: *Space and Place in Jewish Studies*, pp. 116–133.

22 Cf. Sylvie Anne Goldberg: *La Clepsydre: essai sur la pluralité des temps dans le judaïsme.* Paris: Michel 2000, and the German translation: Ead.: *Zeit und Zeitlichkeit im Judentum.* Göttingen: Vandenhoeck & Ruprecht 2009.

This state of affairs has almost certainly to do with the intellectualized perception of history, as shaped by the *Wissenschaft des Judentums* (the Science of Judaism)[23] – a "dematerialized" approach to history as a chronological sequence of events – which still today is not yet completely overcome in parts of Jewish Studies. On the one hand, the Science of Judaism recasted Jewish history as the post-biblical history of Judaism.[24] From this historiographical perspective, with the advent of modernity, the Jews suddenly became part of *this* world again, recounting and reflecting their own history as well.[25] On the other hand, it was precisely the Science of Judaism (or at least its influential master narrative) that seems to have implicitly perpetuated the tendentially "de-spatialized" image of Judaism[26] by falling back on the pre-modern, eschatological roots of historiographical and other (mostly elitist) Jewish and non-Jewish *representations* of Judaism. This was evidently a selective representation of modern as well as pre-modern, generic as well as urban Jewish spatial experiences and perceptions of spatiality – of which the latter were also enacted in taverns, on the street or before the rabbinical court, where they were reflected, time and again, in both sacred *and* profane forms.

Classical urban modernity was not, as is often claimed, expressed exclusively in temporal terms. It was usually, if not always – as in the great philosophical debates – also constructed and delineated spatially. Prominent Jewish historians of the 19th and 20th centuries, together with their less-known local and regional spiritual brethren, participated, both implicitly and explicitly,

23 Research on the *Wissenschaft des Judentums* is abundant. See e.g. a good general discussion in Michael Brenner: *Prophets of the Past: Interpreters of Jewish History*. Princeton: Princeton UP 2010, pp. 17–52.

24 See also Ismar Schorsch: *From Text to Context. The Turn to History in Modern Judaism*. Hanover: Brandeis UP 1994.

25 Dan Diner has eloquently encapsulated this problem when discussing the process of "diffusion of historical thinking among Jews" and speaking about the "entering of a profane temporality into the sacral text-worlds of the Jews". (Dan Diner: Ubiquitär in Zeit und Raum – Annotationen zum jüdischen Geschichtsbewusstsein. In: Id. (ed.): *Synchrone Welten. Zeitenräume jüdischer Geschichte*. Göttingen: Vandenhoeck & Ruprecht 2005, pp. 13–36, here p. 19, 21.) At the same time Diner points out in his reflections on general history that Jews have been all the while "also of this world", since they are "not only subjects to the sphere of the sacral, but are at the same time connected to the non-Jewish contexts" (ibid., p. 16). (Translation F. H.)

26 For perceptions of Jewish history, see e.g. Amos Funkenstein: *Perceptions of Jewish History*. Berkeley: University of California Press 1993. See therein especially the chapter "Reform and History: The Modernization of Western European Jews" (ibid., pp. 247–256). For a counterpoint in the controversy over the character of modern Jewish historiography, see also a classical study by Yosef Hayim Yerushalmi: *Zakhor: Jewish History and Jewish Memory*. Seattle: University of Washington Press 1982.

in processes of spatial construction by inscribing Jews in imperial, national, regional and, above all, urban contexts.[27] Neither were global[28] and transnational urban constructions of community, spatial relationships or representations of spatiality by any means postmodern phenomena of *liquid modernity*[29].

Nor was it Zionism that had helped the Jews toward a "renewed" spatial consciousness and spatial mental action. It would be more correct to speak of a Zionist self-dramatization in which Zionism itself was imagined – often with anti-urban undertones,[30] but at the same time, with new urbanist visions[31] – as an exodus from the (urban) ghetto. The vision of the "novelty" of Zionism in Jewish spatial discourse or the amnesia inscribed in certain revolutionary turn-formulae of the "spatial turn" resulted in the frequent creation of a very selective *historiographical* or *historico-historiographical* image of Jewish historical experience. This historical experience was perceived as situated in relation to the Holy Scriptures, playing out in them and about them, beyond the profane space of the city and, tendentially, outside non-Jewish horizons of interaction and experience. At the same time, numerous influential non-Jewish master narratives and urban histories frequently excluded – and continue to exclude until the present day – Jews and other *national* "minorities", portraying them as foreign or exotic or relegating them to secondary importance, as if they were of a different world or as if non-Jews and Jews were living in distinct,

27 See for this point e.g. the instructive contributions in François Guesnet (ed.): *Zwischen Graetz und Dubnow. Jüdische Historiographie in Ostmitteleuropa im 19. und 20. Jahrhundert.* Leipzig: AVA 2009, oder Benjamin Nathans: On Russian Jewish Historiography. In: Thomas Sanders (ed.): *Historiography of Imperial Russia: The Profession and Writing of History in a Multi-National State.* Armonk: Sharpe 1997, pp. 397–432.

28 See e.g. Rebecca Kobrin: *Jewish Bialystok and its Diaspora.* Bloomington: Indiana UP 2010; Anna Lipphardt: *Vilne. Die Juden aus Vilnius nach dem Holocaust. Eine transnationale Beziehungsgeschichte.* Paderborn: Schöningh 2010.

29 For the sociological diagnosis of *liquid* modernity, see Zygmunt Bauman: *Liquid Modernity.* Cambridge: Polity 2000.

30 On pre-, proto-, non- and Zionist projects and practices of Jewish agrarianization in modern times (since the influential non-Jewish and Jewish enlightened discourses on Jewish productivization), see *Jewish History* 21,3–4 (2007): Jewish Agrarianization, 1804–1945.

31 See e.g. Joachim Schlör: *Tel Aviv: From Dream to City.* London: Reaktion 1999; Barbara Mann: *A Place in History: Modernism, Tel Aviv, and the Creation of Jewish Urban Space.* Stanford: Stanford UP 2006; Maoz Azaryahu: *Tel Aviv: Mythography of a City.* Syracuse: Syracuse UP 2007; Anat Helman: *Young Tel Aviv: A Tale of Two Cities.* Waltham: Brandeis UP 2010; Hizky Shoham: *Carnival in Tel Aviv: Purim and the Celebration of Urban Zionism.* Boston: Academic Studies Press 2014.

adjacent urban worlds.[32] Several influential modern and anti-modern Jewish historical blueprints and master narratives also portrayed Jews – until the advent of modernity and beyond – either as victims, as belonging to another world, or as living in their own separate (urban) world.[33]

This *intellectual* dematerialization of the representation of the Jewish in both non-Jewish and Jewish discourse has a century-long tradition. It can be traced, ultimately, to both intra-Jewish eschatological concepts and complementary Christian representations of Judaism – to "a historical phenomenon that did exist not only in the Middle Ages, namely: a primarily polemical Christian discourse on Judaism, without any substantial Jewish interlocutor – at times even without any 'actually existing' Jews."[34] Controversial representations and public debates over "virtual" versus "authentic" Jewish and other spaces persist until the present day;[35] they are also addressed in the present volume.

The following empirically saturated contributions and case studies reveal a mosaic of possible Jewish and non-Jewish spatial practices, spatial debates and spatial constructions in various urban contexts. They do not aspire to offer a "representative" overview – something which, if possible at all, would only be misleading.

32 See in contrast an integrative empirical approach with a programmatic agenda in Till van Rahden: *Juden und andere Breslauer. Die Beziehungen zwischen Juden, Protestanten und Katholiken in einer deutschen Grossstadt von 1860 bis 1925*. Göttingen: Vandenhoeck & Ruprecht 2000, and the English translation: Id.: *Jews and Other Germans: Civil Society, Religious Diversity and Urban Politics in Breslau, 1860 to 1925*. Madison: University of Wisconsin Press 2008.

33 For Eastern Europe and its small-town Jewish lifeworlds, see e.g. the influential historiographic master narrative published after the Holocaust in Mark Zborowski / Elizabeth Herzog: *Life is With People: The Jewish Little-Town of Eastern Europe*. New York: International Universities Press 1952.

34 Michael Toch: Mehr Licht: Eine Entgegnung zu Friedrich Lotter. In: *Aschkenas. Zeitschrift für Geschichte und Kultur der Juden* 11 (2001), pp. 465–487, here p. 477 (Translation F. H.). For the premodern times, these imaginations can be also depicted in iconographical terms as well as in historiographical terms of the history of art. See the discussions in Eva Frojmovic (ed.): *Imagining the Self, Imagining the Other: Visual Representation and Jewish-Christian Dynamics in the Middle Ages and Early Modern Period*. Leiden: Brill 2002. I am grateful to Alexis Hofmeister for this bibliographical reference.

35 See an influential time-diagnostic intervention in the aftermath of the Cold War by Ruth Ellen Gruber: *Virtually Jewish: Reinventing Jewish Culture in Europe*. Berkeley: University of California Press 2002, as well as the revision or the update of her diagnosis barely ten years later: Ead.: "Non-Jewish, non Kosher, yet also Recommended": Beyond "Virtually Jewish" in Post-millennium Central Europe. In: Jonathan Karp / Adam Sutcliffe (eds): *Philosemitism in History*. Cambridge: Cambridge UP 2011, pp. 314–335.

Historicizing Jewish Space, (De-)Constructing "the Ghetto"

–

(Early) Modern Perspectives on the Spacialization of Jewish Modernity

Making Sense of "the Ghetto"

Conceptualizing a Jewish Space from Early Modern Times to the Present

Jürgen Heyde

"What is *a ghetto*?" – At a first glance the answer to this might appear obvious: Any encyclopaedia presents its readers with an etymology of the word and provides examples of places described as ghettos. Examples are derived from the past as well as from the present and may be found almost on any continent of the world, but despite such variety there are distinct similarities these places share. Dictionaries however, present a different picture, focussing not on common historical, social or topographical characteristics, but on showing the linguistic variety of the term. They are less concerned with determining the factual meaning of a certain term, but with the way people ascribe meanings to words, to explore the values, contexts and connotations attributed to them. Here, "ghetto" appears much less unambiguous, because the term carries a variety of emotional connotations, such as "exclusion", "marginalization" or "isolation". Apart from that the term is taken out of the realm of historical/topographical description and transferred to other levels: attitudes of mind ("ghetto-mentality") or even objects of everyday use ("ghetto-blaster").

"What is *the ghetto*?" Given the variety of places and times, of connotations and evaluations, is it really possible to draw a definition, which would encompass everything that is commonly denominated as "ghetto" or allow for a distinction between "real" ghettos and similar phenomena, for which it would be more suitable to find another expression? The title of this article already hints at such distinctions – marking "ghetto" as a "space" and as "Jewish" and setting it in a certain time-frame. The notion of ghetto as a *Jewish space* is indeed a dominant narrative, but it does not fulfil the connotations the term carries, in other words, the sense ascribed to it. In order to understand "the ghetto" it is necessary to trace these connotations back to the debates about ghetto and the various usages of the term in earlier times. The article analyses various debates about "ghetto", starting with recent attempts back to the beginning of the 19th century, and adds some comparative notes on the usage of the term in early modern times.

The first part refers to recent attempts at definitions in historiography (Benjamin Ravid, Feliks Tych) and sociology (Loïc Wacquant). In the second section, two fundamental texts for today's understanding of "ghetto" will be presented, both of which have been published in 1928: Louis Wirth's book *The Ghetto* and Salo W. Baron's article "Ghetto and Emancipation". The third part goes back to the time between the French Revolution and the First World War, to the period where the early modern ghettos were dissolved, but the motif of "the ghetto" got to play an important role in the debates about Jewish identity in the modern world. Lastly it is necessary to have a look at the early modern period itself, the time when the term "ghetto" was shaped and the time that later has been called "the age of the ghetto". The example of Venice will be used to highlight early usages and meanings ascribed to the term "ghetto".

The article argues that "ghetto" at all times has been the object of debates. Definitions and descriptions have been used to shape specific views of Jewish (and others) history, society and culture. While the conceptualizations of "ghetto" at any given time have been influenced by current interests, they have also added to the scope of knowledge about what "ghetto" *could* mean. In the course of time a wide range of connotations has unfolded, a symbolic dimension that has to be taken into account when talking about ghetto as a Jewish space.

Defining the Ghetto

Historiographical definitions concentrate on periods and regions when the term "ghetto" was present in the historical sources of the time as a sort of "official denomination" – be it the Jewish quarters in early modern Italian towns or the compulsory quarters created by the German occupants in Eastern Europe during World War II. The sociological debate, on the other hand, refers to historical examples, but it develops its terminology from systematic comparisons restricted neither to Jewish quarters nor to Europe. All attempts at defining "ghetto" are likewise embedded into broad and lively scientific debates that have led to a huge increase of knowledge within the last decades.

Research on the ghettos in Early Modern Italy during the last two decades has changed the conceptions about the living conditions of the Jewish population profoundly. In his studies Robert Bonfil has shown clearly that the early modern ghetto was not an isolated space, but a place of close everyday interaction between Jews and non-Jews despite the strictly observed segregation of living quarters.[1] David Ruderman has contested the image of the ghetto as a place of exclusion by focussing on the discussions accompanying the institution of segregated living quarters for Jews in that time. These discussions, he points out, clearly show that the institution of a ghetto has to be seen as an alternative to expulsion of the Jews. Therefore the ghetto provided "a legal and natural residence within the economy of Christian space", in which "Jews did belong in some way to [the Christian's] extended community"[2].
Based on his studies on the Jews of early modern Venice, Benjamin Ravid has attempted to define "ghetto" as a special form of Jewish quarter and to establish criteria for a differentiation between "ghettos" and other Jewish quarters. In various articles he looks into the etymology of the term, into the legal acts and the socio-economic factors that set the background for the institution of the ghettos,[3] as well as into the usage of the term since the early modern period.[4] He has drawn up a typology of "the ghetto" in comparison to other Jewish quarters[5] and written about the history of the word and the history of historiography about "ghetto".[6]
In his article "From Geographical Reality to Historiographical Symbol" from 1992 he differentiates between three types of Jewish quarters:

1 Robert Bonfil: *Jewish Life in Renaissance Italy*. Berkeley / London: University of California Press 1994.

2 David B. Ruderman: The Cultural Significance of the Ghetto in Jewish History. In: David N. Myers / William V. Rowe (eds): *From Ghetto to Emancipation; Historical and Contemporary Reconsiderations of the Jewish Community*. Scranton, PA: University of Scranton Press 1997, pp. 1–16, here p. 7.

3 Benjamin Ravid: The Religious, Economic and Social Background of the Establishment of the Ghetti of Venice. In: Gaetano Cozzi (ed.): *Gli Ebrei e Venezia. Secoli XIV–XVIII. Atti del convegno internazionale, Venezia, Isola di San Giorgio Maggiore, 5–10 giugno 1983*. Milano: Ed. Comunità 1987, pp. 211–259.

4 Benjamin Ravid: From Geographical Realia to Historiographical Symbol. The Odyssey of the Word "Ghetto". In: David B. Ruderman (ed.): *Essential Papers on Jewish Culture in Renaissance and Baroque Italy*. New York: New York UP 1992, pp. 373–385.

5 Benjamin Ravid: All Ghettos Were Jewish Quarters but Not All Jewish Quarters Were Ghettos. In: *Jewish Culture and History* 10,2–3 (2008), pp. 5–24.

6 Benjamin Ravid: On the Diffusion of the Word "Ghetto" and its Ambiguous Usages, and a Suggested Definition. In: Fritz Backhaus / Gisela Engel / Gundula Grebner / Robert Liberles (eds): *Frühneuzeitliche Ghettos in Europa im Vergleich*. Berlin: Trafo 2012, pp. 15–38

> (1) Voluntary Jewish Quarters; (2) quarters assigned to Jews, either for their convenience or for their protection, as an inducement to settle in an area, without however establishing a legally exclusive Jewish quarter; (3) The compulsory segregated Jewish quarter in which all Jews were required to live and in which no Christians were permitted to live.[7]

He emphasizes the need to confine the term "ghetto" to the early modern period, since in later times the term became charged with negative connotations that lead to a misunderstanding of Jewish life in the early modern ghettos:

> Thus the word *ghetto* has become a value concept with negative connotations rather than a descriptive word indicating a particular legal, residential system under which Jews lived. The result has been to blur the historical reality of one of the basic aspects of Jewish survival, the Jewish quarter, and thus gives additional urgency to the need for its systematic examination.[8]

In 2008 Ravid returned to this question in an article titled "All Ghettos Were Jewish Quarters but Not All Jewish Quarters Were Ghettos". There he provides an overview of the evolution of Jewish quarters in Europe during the Middle Ages, the distribution of ghettos in early modern Italy, the distinctions against other forms of Jewish quarters and the dissolution of the ghettos in the time of the French Revolution. That leads him to propose a definition of ghettos as "compulsory, segregated and enclosed Jewish quarters".[9] Such a definition, however, would have to be tested through a systematic comparative analysis of Jewish quarters (as well as other residential groups) throughout early modern Europe, based on an extensive set of questions concerning the legal, topographic and economic ramifications as well as the reactions of the people to whom such quarters were assigned.

To Ravid, the non-Jewish authorities are the decisive factor for determining "ghetto", because it was their incentive that led to the erection of compulsory Jewish quarters, which were segregated from the non-Jewish residential areas and surrounded by walls. It was the non-Jewish authorities as well, who maintained the separated living quarters and punished violations against their rules. Therefore the distinction between ghetto as a spatial construct enforced by non-Jewish instances, and the Jewish quarter rooted in voluntary association or inner-Jewish incentives becomes the leading argument in his definition.

7 Ravid: From Geographical Realia, p. 373.

8 Ibid., p. 384; similarly Ravid: On the Diffusion, pp. 33–34.

9 Ravid: All Ghettos, pp. 5–6.

Only several decades after the last of the European ghettos dating back to early modern times had been finally dissolved, the term was introduced again to denote compulsory residential areas for the Jewish population under Nazi occupation, this time mainly in Eastern Europe. Scholarly research on the meaning and definition of "ghetto" in the 20th century is thriving as well. The last years have witnessed copious publications on the ramifications and the internal life within these new compulsory Jewish quarters.[10] From the perspective of the non-Jewish authorities, i.e. the Nazi leadership, they were not intended to replicate early modern ghettos. They were not meant to serve as permanent residential institutions, as Dan Michman has recently shown, but just as an intermediate solution.[11] For the Jews however, the identical naming of the "old" and "new" ghettos symbolized the possibility to create a living space for the inhabitants and not just a temporary stop on the way to the extermination camps in the East.

In his article "Ghettos in Polen"[12] from 2001, Feliks Tych firmly emphasized that before the Nazi occupation there had been no real ghettos in Poland. However, he continued, in the older literature one could find references to ghettos, which denote, in his words, a "Quasighettoisierung" of Polish Jews in the pre-emancipation period. These "quasi-ghettos" were characterized not by stone walls and legal boundaries but by "mental walls", erected and fortified again and again by "clergy of both confessions" ("die Geistlichen beider Konfessionen"), meaning Catholic priests as well as Jewish rabbis.

His distinction between "real ghettos" and "quasi-ghettoization" is aimed at different understandings of ghetto. The "real ghetto" is a compulsory space, erected by an outward authority and assigned to the Jewish population as the only remaining place for them to live. The "quasi-ghetto" indicates a space of increased density and isolation, not just as a result of physical segregation, but foremost owing to the fact that the inhabitants of the ghetto turned their backs to the events and developments on the outside of the ghetto-walls. In

10 Cf. Markus Roth / Andrea Löw: *Das Warschauer Ghetto. Alltag und Widerstand im Angesicht der Vernichtung*. München: Beck 2013; Andrea Löw (ed.): *Alltag im Holocaust. jüdisches Leben im Großdeutschen Reich 1941–1945*. München: Oldenbourg 2013; Klaus-Peter Friedrich / Andrea Löw / Susanne Heim (eds): *Die Verfolgung und Ermordung der europäischen Juden durch das nationalsozialistische Deutschland 1933–1945,* vol. 4: Polen September, 1939–Juli 1941. München: Oldenbourg 2011.

11 Dan Michman: *The Emergence of Jewish Ghettos during the Holocaust*. Cambridge: Cambridge UP 2011, p. 3, 149.

12 Feliks Tych: Ghettos in Polen. In: *Wiener Jahrbuch für jüdische Geschichte, Kultur und Museumswesen* 1 (2001), pp. 69–75.

the first case, it is just external pressure; in the second case it is mostly inner factors, the attitude of the Jews themselves, that erect the – physical and mental – walls und determine the patterns of existence in the ghetto. In the case of Poland Tych proposes a two-fold differentiation: between the "outer" and the "inner" ghetto, and between the modern "real ghetto" (imposed by the German occupying forces during World War II) and the early modern "quasi-ghetto", erected not by external force but by social conventions and ignorance (on both sides of the walls).[13] Like Ravid, he views the ("real") ghetto as a legal space, defined by an outward authority and assigned unilaterally to the Jewish population. He differs, however, on the time-frame, because in Poland it is not the early modern Jewish quarters that warrant being called a ghetto, but the compulsory residential areas introduced by the Nazis.

Sociological studies have to deal with yet a different time-frame and an ever greater variety of places that are called "ghettos". Loïc Wacquant has done extensive research on this topic and tried to find a sociological concept of "ghetto". In the introduction to his influential article "Ghetto", published in the *International Encyclopedia of the Social and Behavioral Sciences* in 2004, he deplores: "while the social sciences have made extensive use of the 'ghetto' as a descriptive term, they have failed to forge a robust analytical concept of the same."[14] In historiography, sociology and anthropology

> the term 'ghetto' variously denotes a bounded urban ward, a web of group-specific institutions, and a cultural and cognitive constellation (values, mind-set, or mentality) entailing the sociomoral isolation of a stigmatized category as well as the systematic truncation of the life space and life chances of its members.[15]

The great variety of connotations accompanying the term makes it futile to use it as an analytical tool; "ghetto" can be defined only approximately: "all ghettos are segregated but not all segregated areas are ghettos"[16]. As a way to make it usable for research, Wacquant proposes to introduce terminological

13 Tych: Ghettos in Polen, p. 70.

14 Loïc Wacquant: Ghetto. In: Neil J. Smelser / Paul B. Baltes (eds): *International Encyclopedia of the Social and Behavioral Sciences*. London: Pergamon 2004, pp. 1–7, here p. 1. According to Wacquant's homepage the article has been translated into nine languages and reprinted several times: http://loicwacquant.net/papers/urban-marginality/ (accessed 19.11.2013).

15 Ibid.

16 Ibid.; Loïc Wacquant: A Janus-Faced Institution of Ethnoracial Closure: A Sociological Specification of the Ghetto. In: Ray Hutchison / Bruce D. Haynes (eds): *The Ghetto. Contemporary Global Issues and Controversies*. Boulder, CO: Westview 2011, pp. 1–31.

variations that can be defined narrowly and thus be made analytically unambiguous (e.g. Wacquants concept of "hyper-ghetto" and "anti-ghetto").[17]
The attempts at defining ghetto presented here propose ways to conceptualize the term as an expression for a topographical unit, but all three show significant discomfort with regards to the temporal dimension of the phenomenon as the biggest obstacle to analytic clarity. To clarify this discomfort, I would like to discuss in the following section two important texts marking the beginning of the contemporary sociological and historical debates about "ghetto". To this day both texts are explicitly or implicitly present in almost every contribution to the discussion.

Interpreting the Ghetto

In 1928 two studies were published, which up to this day have significantly influenced the scientific debate about "ghetto": Louis Wirth's book *The Ghetto*[18] and Salo W. Baron's article: "Ghetto and Emancipation. Shall we revise the traditional view?"[19] Both works argued from different angles and pursued different goals: Wirth analysed "ghetto" under a sociologic perspective, in order to trace the development of ethnically imprinted immigrant quarters in the USA. His work laid the foundations to the Chicago School of Sociology. Baron, on the other side, was looking into the historical dimension of Jewish life in the diaspora; he was mainly interested in the idea that earlier centuries, especially the early modern period, constituted an age of exclusion, isolation and marginalizing of the Jewish population that had come to an end only with Modernity and the emancipation of the Jews.
Both authors referred to early modern Jewish quarters, which they addressed as "ghettos". They asked about the living conditions of the Jewish population, their interaction with the non-Jewish authorities and the significance of the time-frame: the early modern period as the "age of the ghetto". Both described ghetto not as a specific place, but as a set of connotations; they did not base their observations on the appearance of the term in the sources,

17 Cf. Loïc Wacquant: Urban Desolation and Symbolic Denigration in the Hyperghetto. In: *Social Psychology Quarterly* 20,2 (2010), pp. 1–5 (with further references); id.: Ghettos and Anti-Ghettos: An Anatomy of the New Urban Poverty. In: *Thesis Eleven* 94 (2008), pp. 113–118.

18 Louis Wirth: *The Ghetto. With a New Introduction by Hasia R. Diner*. New Brunswick: Transaction 1998 [1st ed.: Chicago 1928]; Wirth chose Frankfurt as an example of an early modern ghetto, pp. 41–62.

19 Salo W. Baron: Ghetto and Emancipation. Shall We Revise the Traditional View? In: *The Menorah Journal* 14 (1928), pp. 515–526.

but on a contemporary comprehension of "ghetto" and could assume their readers to be acquainted with it. In fact their analyses neglected those Jewish quarters that had been called ghettos in early modern sources; to them, ghetto constituted a technical term for early modern Jewish quarters in general. Wirth based his observations on the Jewish quarter in Frankfurt, whereas Baron did not address any particular town for reference. From his arguments one can conclude that his idea was rooted far more in the Eastern European (Polish-Lithuanian) experience than in examples from the Italian peninsula.

Wirth emphasized specific traits of the ghetto and then applied them to the contemporary immigrant quarters in the metropolises especially on the American continent. In his introduction to the 1998 edition of Wirth's book, Hasia R. Diner wrote:

> The Ghetto fused the sociological trends of the early twentieth century with the history of the Ashkenazi (European) Jewry. The Ghetto analysed the history of the zone of Jewish residence, as it shifted from being an area of Jewish self-segregation in late antiquity, to the early Middle Ages, when Jews became to be compelled by law, proclaimed by non-Jewish authorities, to live in a marked off area, separated from the rest of the population.[20]

To Wirth "ghetto" represented not just a physical fact, but also a "state of mind".[21] He considered isolation to be the most important feature of the ghetto and asked how far separation had influenced the character of its inhabitants.[22] Wirth chose the Jewish quarter in Chicago as an example of a "modern ghetto", and used it as a starting point for his observations on similarly constructed non-Jewish immigrant quarters, paving the way to separate the notion of "ghetto" from the Jewish experience in the public debate. He kept, however, the connotations: isolation, control from the outside, backwardness and poverty.

He located the "origin of the Ghetto" (chap. 1) in Jewish settlement in the diaspora itself, already building a bridge from there to the immigrant quarters of the New World. The second chapter deals with ecclesiastical and secular legislation concerning the separation of Jews and Christians in the Middle Ages, leading over to the institution of the ghetto in Rome by Pope Paul IV as an example for the general introduction of compulsory settlements within the Christian world. In chapter 4, however, he chose not Rome but the Jewish quarter in Frankfurt (erected in 1462) as an example of a "typical ghetto".

20 Hasia R. Diner: Introduction. In: Wirth: *The Ghetto*, pp. ix–lxiii, here p. x.

21 Wirth: *The Ghetto*, p. 8.

22 Ibid., pp. 75–96 ("The Jewish Mind").

The following chapters analysed the consequences of that kind of settlement and the isolation from the Christian environment closely linked with it, before Wirth described Zionism and assimilation as ways to overcome "the ghetto" (chap. 7). Both were rooted in the emancipation movement that had led to the dissolution of compulsory quarters and granted equal rights to the Jews in most European countries. Even though no longer enforced from the outside, he claims that there was a continuing isolation preventing the Jews from overcoming the ghetto – and it was everywhere, where Jews had settled in greater numbers. Chapters 8 to 13 mirror the first chapters of the study, dealing with the recent history of Jews in the United States and Chicago as their centre.

In his book Wirth constructed a narration of development using "ghetto" as a metaphor for everything that prevented the Jews from participating in fruitful social development: their dispersion in the diaspora and at the same time the tendency to concentrate locally and to separate (themselves) from their non-Jewish environment; the exclusion by non-Jewish authorities, who at the same time prevented the Jews from returning to their ancestral country; mental isolation and economic backwardness, which would not be overcome even though the exclusion had been abolished. Thus "ghetto" became a transtemporal phenomenon, bound to repeat itself even in the modern world as long as the diaspora-situation continued to exist. At this point, Wirth's study transcended specific Jewish experience: the society in the United States constituted the archetype of a "diaspora-society", formed by immigrants from all over the word, with local communities mirroring all those factors Wirth had described as typical for "the ghetto" in pre-modern Europe.

Salo W. Baron, by contrast, pursued a very different approach. He perceived "ghetto" as a metaphor of Jewish history in the early modern period, conceived as an era of suffering that had been overcome by Emancipation: "Prisoner in the Ghetto, denied access to the resources and activities of Western society, distorted intellectually, morally, spiritually by centuries of isolation and torture, the Jew was set free by the Emancipation"[23].

He challenged the picture of Enlightenment as a "new day after a nightmare of the deepest horror"[24], created by modern Jewish history, from Heinrich Graetz to Simon Dubnow, in several points: legally, a diversified legal system like the early modern one was not tantamount to discrimination, and within

23 Baron: Ghetto and Emancipation, p. 515.

24 Ibid., p. 516.

Christian society there were several groups with a lesser legal standing (e.g. the peasants); demographically and economically Jews had in fact been better off than large parts of Christian society. Persecutions had not been restricted to the Jews, but affected parts of Christian society as well (witches, apostates, heretics).

In its bleak view of Jewish history, modern historiography assigned a crucial role to the ghetto, because it constituted "a phase [...] generally regarded by emancipated Jewry as an unmitigated evil"[25]. Baron differentiates between the ghetto in a "technical sense" and a "non-technical sense". The "technical" ghetto could be linked to the Counter-Reformation and the bull "cum nimis absurdam [!]", forcing all the Jews to live in a secluded district, which "in this extreme application [...] was, of course, obnoxious"[26]. But "in the non-technical sense" he identified ghetto with any Jewish quarter, arising from the tendency of people of mutual interest to live together, just like the neighbourhoods of shoemakers or bakers; the proximity of the synagogue as a social as well as religious centre had played an additional role. Therefore the ghetto (= Jewish quarter) had been existent long before compulsion came, and it enabled the Jews to enjoy autonomy.

To Baron, ghetto as a Jewish space did not constitute anything special. Jewish quarters existed long before non-Jewish authorities erected compulsory residential areas. As a "phase" it was tied to the early modern period, but it became meaningful only as a symbol of past oppression, within the "lacrymose theory of pre-Revolutionary woe".[27] In his opinion it would be pointless to distinguish between "early modern Jewish quarter" and "ghetto". It was especially the notion of Jewish autonomy that contradicted the negative connotations of the term "ghetto", which Baron – like Wirth – used as synonymous to "early modern Jewish quarter". When he emphasized that legal inequality in an early modern society was not tantamount to discrimination, and neither discrimination nor persecution (which he did not deny) were exclusively aimed against Jews but also against groups within Christian society, he put the evolutionary narration into perspective that used the early modern era as a negative background in order to make the achievements of Modernity shine even brighter. To him the "early modern ghetto" constituted an era of Jewish history that had to be analysed in itself – and these studies offered positive impulses for Jewish historical consciousness as well.

25 Baron: Ghetto and Emancipation, p. 519.

26 Ibid.

27 Ibid., p. 526.

The Symbolic Ghetto

Both Wirth and Baron published their texts before "ghetto" acquired new political relevance due to the politics of the Nazis. Both treated "ghetto" not as a relic of bygone times, but as a *lieu de memoire*, which belonged to the early modern period but still held importance for Jewish identity in their times. It is remarkable that neither of them related to early modern Italy nor discussed "ghetto" as a source term. In fact the separation between the term and the places that had been called "ghetto" in the 16th to 18th centuries was not recent but had developed gradually since the times of the French Revolution and the Jewish struggle for emancipation everywhere in Europe.

The first step toward a new definition of "ghetto", from a topographic to a symbolic sense, took place during the Napoléonian era. When French revolutionary troops marched into Italy in the 1790s, they celebrated the destruction of the ghetto-walls as an act of liberation. Thus, in August 1797 the new magistrate of Padua decreed that Jews ("Hebrews") in this town were free to take residence in any street they wished, and added immediately "that the barbarous and meaningless name of Ghetto, which designates the street which they have been inhabiting hitherto, shall be substituted by that of Via Libera".[28] The removal of the ghetto walls was meant to end the social separation of Jews and Christians. The Jewish quarter as a markedly Jewish place was considered outdated, the thought of equality rendered old social group demarcations superfluous. In order to convey that message to the population, the revolutionary government decided on a demonstrative public act:

> [T]he municipal police committee shall carry out the solemn levelling to the ground of the Gates, Arches and simple precinct Walls of the ex-Ghetto in such a manner that no vestige shall remain of the ancient separation from other neighboring streets.

Similar acts were to be performed

> in all the communities of the department where Ghettos did exist.[29]

Admittedly these revolutionary ideals were far from uncontested in their time. Jewish settlement rights used to be restricted intermittently up to ca. 1870; depending on political cycles restrictions were lifted or introduced anew. Even though the factual living conditions were less and less determined by

28 Padova, 28 August 1797. In: Paul Mendes-Flohr / Jehuda Reinharz (eds): *The Jew in the Modern World. A Documentary History*. New York / Oxford: Oxford UP 1995, p. 122.

29 Padova, 15 September 1797. In: Ibid., p. 123; Ariel Viterbo: Da Napoleone all'Unità d'Italia. In: Claudia De Benedetti (ed.): *Gli Ebrei e Padova*, vol. II: Il cammino della speranza. Padova: Edizioni Papergraf 2000, pp. 1–52.

these rules, as symbolic acts those restrictions had an impact. Increasingly "ghetto" became a symbol – in more than one sense. On the one hand it stood for political repression as a whole; Ludwig Börne asked during the Restoration after 1830: "Isn't Germany nowadays the ghetto of Europe? Doesn't every German wear a yellow mark on their hat?"[30] On the other hand the term became a symbol of unfinished emancipation. Stepping "out of the ghetto" and into society: attending non-Jewish schools, taking part in the social life of the non-Jewish society, acquiring "general education" – those were the demands of the early assimilationists in the second half of the 19th century, who saw themselves as the true heirs of the Jewish Enlightenment. Their demands were no longer directed at the non-Jewish authorities or the non-Jewish society in general, but at the Jews themselves.

A popular expression of these demands can be found in the so-called ghetto literature. In this genre "ghetto" was used as a representation not of an urban space – the Jewish quarter –, but a Jewish space per se, dominated by tradition and social constraints, culturally isolated from the non-Jewish environment and therefore hopelessly backward. The heroes of the early ghetto literature experience a moment of revival and leave the ghetto, the place of the past, in order to win the future.[31] These stories were situated not in those places, which in earlier times had been called "ghetto", but very often in rural areas, where in the opinion of the authors old, traditional Jewish social structures still prevailed. One of the most popular regions to host these "ghetto stories" in the second half of the 19th century was Habsburg Galicia.

In Galicia, too, at the end of the 19th century one of the most intensive debates about "ghetto" and its importance for the Jewish population in the modern world took place. It began around 1880 in the Polish-language assimilationist press and was aimed at a public consisting of "modern" Jews living in the urban centres as well as non-Jewish readers. Several years later, Zionist writers took up the connotations introduced in the assimilationist press

30 "Ist nicht Deutschland der [*sic*!] Ghetto Europas? Tragen nicht alle Deutschen einen gelben Lappen am Hute?" Ludwig Börne: Menzel der Franzosenfresser. In: Id.: *Sämtliche Schriften*, vol. 3, ed. by Inge Rippman / Peter Rippmann. Düsseldorf: Melzer 1964, pp. 871–984, here p. 889; Rainer Erb / Werner Bergmann: *Die Nachtseite der Judenemanzipation. Der Widerstand gegen die Integration der Juden in Deutschland 1780–1860*. Berlin: Metropol 1989, pp. 86–96.

31 Jonathan M. Hess: *Middlebrow Literature and the Making of German-Jewish Identity*. Stanford: Stanford UP 2010; Kenneth H. Ober: *Die Ghettogeschichte. Entstehung und Entwicklung einer Gattung*. Göttingen: Wallstein 2001; Gabriele von Glasenapp: *Aus der Judengasse. Zur Entstehung und Ausprägung deutschsprachiger Ghettoliteratur im 19. Jahrhundert*. Tübingen: Mohr 1996.

publications, and polemicized against them or developed their own interpretation of what ghetto meant for Jewish identity.

The Polish assimilationist press strongly emphasized the contrast between "ghetto" and emancipation, especially since the beginning of the 1880s, when orthodox leaders in Galicia succeeded in convincing the government to leave the "Cheder" schools as the principal form of Jewish elementary school. The assimilationist camp had failed to dominate the public discussion about education, and now their writers felt the need to find an explanation for it by examining the state of development in the Jewish society as a whole.

On August 1st, 1883 *Ojczyzna*, the monthly journal of the association Agudas Achim or: "Society of Brothers" published an article that illustrates how the notion of "ghetto" was woven into the analysis of current political issues:

> Since the walls of the ghetto have been torn down, since the light of day shines onto these dark relicts, who hold such a lot of misery, so many miserable consequences of the violently broken development of the Jewish population, just since that time one thought is dominating – the thought of improving the abnormal structures of Jewish society and education. That thought is dominant not only among the more enlightened Jews, but also among the friends of mankind and the patriots of the other confessions. The question of equal rights for the Jews, not just in the word of the law, but also in real life and under every circumstances, that is what every man ever wished and still is striving for, every man who desires the well-being of the land and the improvement of the nation.[32]

In this text, ghetto is presented as the center-point of the argument. "Ghetto" symbolizes darkness, misery and violence against the Jews, and it was emancipation that brought an end to the "ghetto". To achieve this, one had to correct the "abnormal structures of society" – by formally acknowledging equal rights. But there was also the need to correct the "abnormal structures of education". In order to complete emancipation it was necessary to educate the Jewish population in a new spirit. Such a new education was the goal not only for the "more enlightened Jews", but also for the "friends of mankind and patriots of the other confessions", because emancipation served not only the Jews but also the improvement of the nation.

Therefore education was an essential mission, but it was severely handicapped by the traditional school-system, especially by the further existence of the community schools, the so-called "chajder", as the assimilationist authors put it. They fought for the abolition of the "chajder" and wanted to introduce a secular, Polish-language-based school system for Jews and non-Jews alike. To perpetuate the "chajder" as a religious parochial school, *Ojczyzna* argued in

32 [Lwów, 31 lipca 1883 r.]. In: *Ojczyzna* 15, 01.08.1883, pp. 59–60, here p. 59.

1882, would be the same as voluntarily moving back into the ghetto – not in a topographical sense, but spiritually:

> Should we ourselves erect the walls of the moral ghetto and confine ourselves within it, when the world has at last unlatched the rusted bolts of what had been our prison for centuries, and opened the doors wide, when the world expects us to actively take part in the works and efforts for the fulfilment of the great task of mankind? Should we prove ourselves to be unworthy of their trust, should we get away from them und lock ourselves up in the narrow circle of just religious needs?[33]

The assimilationist authors considered a close connection between Jews and non-Jews to be the necessary fundament for the development of the Jewish population. Only through such a link emancipation could really be brought to life. Any deviation from that path would lead the Jews back to the ghetto, which they imagined as a prison, the embodiment of spiritual and intellectual isolation, economic and moral backwardness and altogether misery. "Ghetto" served as a negative matrix to highlight the goals of the assimilation movement. In these texts "ghetto" appeared not as an institution that was forced upon the Jews by their non-Jewish environment, but as an inner-Jewish tradition. If there were any hints to an involvement of non-Jewish authorities at all, as a rule they remained very unspecific: even in articles about the ghetto in Rome neither the Catholic Church nor the Pope were mentioned, but the authors located the roots of the ghetto in ancient times.

In the first phase, at the beginning of the 1880s, the articles about ghetto were oriented exclusively towards a polemic with Jewish tradition. The waves of anti-Jewish violence in the Russian empire in 1881 and 1882 were registered and deplored, but not associated with the notion of "ghetto". Only several years later, around 1890, articles in *Ojczyzna* linked ghetto and anti-Semitism: through the rise of anti-Semitism, they wrote, the walls of the ghetto were brought up again, the violent riots reminded of the age of the ghetto.[34] That was a time, when assimilationist circles in Galicia loudly lamented the crisis of their movement; the last number of *Ojczyzna* was published in 1892. But anti-Semitism, and the danger it posed to the Jewish population appeared to be just an irritating remnant of an era long gone by. Much more important was the struggle about concepts for the future and therefore the conflict with Zionism who presented a different view than the assimilationist camp.

33 S. Margulies: O naszych stosunkach wyznaniowych. In: *Ojczyzna* 9, 01.05.1882, pp. 35–36.

34 For example: Enefde: Z chwili (Nowy rok – Smutne echa – Położenia żydów w kraju naszym). In: *Ojczyzna* 18, 15.09.1890, pp. 141–142; Jürgen Heyde: Miejsce czy symbol? "Ghetto" w europejskiej historii (XVI–XX w.). In: *Czasy nowożytne* 26 (2013), pp. 17–34, here p. 26.

At the beginning of the 20th century, there was a new attempt to establish an assimilationist journal in Galicia, the weekly *Jedność*. In their editorials, Tobias Aschkenase and Bertold Merwin often proclaimed that anti-Semitism and Zionism were more or less the same, for both were representations of the "ghetto":

> [T]he natural outcome of the historical revolution, the historical imperative – the unbreakable link of the Jews to their ancestral fatherland Poland, the enlightenment, education and cultivation of the Jewish people in that spirit, who has always been the substance and the basis of its existence in this land, in the name of the great idea of brotherhood – that won't please those, whose work – is destruction, whose striving – their own career, whose motto – going back to the ghetto, and whose idea – the Zionist mandate.[35]

The Zionist press in Galicia, especially the two-weekly journal *Przyszłość* (Cracow 1892–1897) and its successor, the weekly *Wschód* (Lwów 1900–1911) reacted to the accusations of the assimilationist camp, but only seldom directly. Zionist authors argued against the nonsense and the moral bankruptcy of the assimilationist ideas, which were not accepted by the non-Jewish society and would just lead to the dissolution of the Jews in the non-Jewish ocean. Their writers picked up the motif of "ghetto" and attached new connotations to it.

In Zionist publications in Galicia, "ghetto" was characterized by pressure from the outside and misery on the inside, but, as the authors pointed out, that had never been able to destroy the Jewish culture. In 1896 Salomon Schiller argued in *Przyszłość* in an editorial titled "Our national existence":

> They locked us up in ghettos, but it was just the fact that they kept us away from themselves, this prison autonomy, which strongly supported the development of independent national and socio-cultural characteristics. No less important for our national psyche was the contempt we had for the Arians. Because that way our consciousness of superiority grew stronger, and we were filled with the thought, that we are the chosen nation.[36]

These words already indicate a re-interpretation of the "ghetto"-memory. In the works of Israel Zangwill, the British Zionist who was acclaimed "Dickens of the Ghetto", and whose works were enthusiastically received in the Galician Zionist press, this re-interpretation is taken even further. Zangwill loved to write about Jews who had "left the ghetto" in order to live in the modern world among non-Jews. But there they sensed an inner emptiness and a longing for Jewish company and community. Therefore they set off again and

35 His: Syon, a… "Dilo". In: *Jedność* 7, 19.04.1907, pp. 1–3, here p. 1.

36 Salomon Schiller: Nasz byt narodowy (ciąg dalszy). In: *Przyszłość* 18, 20.06.1896, pp. 137–140, here p. 139.

returned for a while to the ghetto. But that is not the end of their journey; it is just the right starting point for the real passage – the way to the Jewish land (which did not necessarily need to be Palestine).[37]

In this interpretation "ghetto" ceased to be just a symbol of the past, of former exclusion and marginalization against the Jews. "Ghetto" gained value as a link to a new Jewish life in a future Jewish land. But as the way to the own Jewish country turned out to be long and difficult, life in the diaspora still appeared to be a necessity for a long time. In this situation Zionist writers reflected about the global historical significance of "ghetto" as an – albeit temporary – alternative to the modern world like the one, which the assimilationists imagined.

In *Wschód*, in 1901, the author reflected about the relation between Herzl's Zionist program and "ghetto". He quotes – albeit not literally – Max Nordau:

> Let us discard the old ghetto, let us free ourselves from its atmosphere, which is characterized by servant-like submissiveness and lack of self-esteem, and let us build a new ghetto, a ghetto of mutual support, of mutual refinement, a hotbed of Jewish science, a cradle of Jewish arts. In a word, let us concentrate locally, let us collect our inborn mental strength, and we will rise up, and we will impress the world with the power of the Jewish mind. 'Hej, shoulder to shoulder' – onwards to our common work, and by the time, when this ghetto of spirit, of Jewish thinking will become reality, then the Jews will cease to be inhabitants of the ghetto.[38]

In this conception as well, ghetto symbolized a life in isolation from non-Jews. But in contrast to the "old ghetto", where non-Jews had dictated the conditions of life, and the Jews had had to adapt, this "new ghetto" arose from the Jews' own initiative. It enabled them to outlast the time of the diaspora until a new Jewish state was built. This "new ghetto" did not need a place; it was not a segregated quarter, but an attitude of mind. That way, Zionist authors took the "spiritual ghetto" or the "moral ghetto" that the assimilationists had often deplored, and attributed a new meaning to it – no longer as a symbol of

37 Meri-Jane Rochelson: Zionism, Territorialism, Race, and Nation in the Thought and Politics of Israel Zangwill. In: Eitan Bar-Yosef / Nadia Valman (eds): *"The Jew" in Late-Victorian and Edwardian Culture. Between the East End and East Africa.* Basingstoke: Palgrave Macmillan 2009, pp. 144–160; Nadia Guth Biasini: Der Traum von der Moderne. Literarische Verarbeitungen zionistischer Ideen bei Israel Zangwill und Theodor Herzl. In: Heiko Haumann / Peter Haber (eds): *Der Erste Zionistenkongress von 1897. Ursachen, Bedeutung, Aktualität. … in Basel habe ich den Judenstaat gegründet.* Basel: Karger 1997, pp. 161–165.

38 Listy z Wiednia. In: *Wschód* 37, 18.06.1901, pp. 10–11, here p. 10. Nordau's article appeared in: *Die Welt* 50, 14.12.1900, pp. 1–5; the quotation refers to p. 4.

repression and backwardness, but as the expression of Jewish self-determination and as a link between past and future.

The debates of the 19th century focused entirely on the symbolic dimension of "ghetto" whereas the connection with the early modern place name became barely visible anymore. In discussing what might be called the heritage of the (early modern) ghetto, the questions of agency of the Jewish inhabitants and responsibility of the non-Jewish authorities were linked to interpretations of the term "ghetto". Any such interpretation – as a place of isolation and backwardness, a prison or a place of Jewish unity – derived from the connotations attributed to the term from the inside as well as from the outside of the ghetto.

The 19th century debates seem remarkably disconnected from the early modern reality. Only very rarely were historical facts brought up, and if for example, the erection of the ghetto in Venice in 1516 or the bull "cum nimis absurdum" issued by Pope Paul IV in 1555 were mentioned, they were not analysed but invoked as symbols, whose meaning was assumed to be clear to everyone.

In fact, the following paragraph argues that from the very beginning "ghetto" possessed a symbolic quality. It was because of that symbolic character that the term, which originated in a specific place name, could quickly get adopted to denote Jewish quarters in other places as well. I will try to show that by discussing two of the earliest documents dealing with "ghetto" – the Venetian decrees of 1516 and 1541 – and highlighting the use of the term by contemporaries in Venice and beyond.

The Topographic Ghetto: the Term and the Place

The foundation of the Venetian Ghetto in 1516 is well established in historiography as one of the turning points in Jewish history. The events leading to the establishment of the Jewish quarter in Venice are well known, just as the main provisions of the documents issued by the Venetian Senate in 1516 and later on. However, the historiographic narrative is almost exclusively focused on the relations and negotiations between the Venetian authorities and the Jews. Inner-Christian and inner-Jewish agendas show up only on the margins, but they are not used to broaden the focus. The following short re-narration of the events accompanying the establishment of the ghetto as well as the main provisions of the documents of 1516 and 1541 tries to overcome the traditional binary picture by emphasizing the complexity of agendas in the process. It argues that the use of a newly coined term – "ghetto" – allowed for an amount of vagueness as to the character of the newly formed location that enabled all interested parties to project their own agendas onto it. Therefore from the very beginning, "ghetto" was more of an interpretative frame than a technical term, as it has been traditionally regarded.

The Venetian ghetto founded in 1516 was not based on a pre-existing Jewish quarter or a similar compact settlement area from which the Jews would have been relocated. Since the late Middle Ages Jews had lived on and off in Venice, but never had a permanent residence within the city walls been established. Long-term settlement developed however on the Venetian *terraferma*, with Mestre becoming the most important Jewish centre on Venetian territory. At the beginning of the 16th century the Venetian Senate issued a privilege to three Jewish bankers from Mestre, allowing them to settle in the city if the *terraferma* would be struck by war.[39] Even after the military conflict with the league of Cambrai ended, the Senate prolonged the bankers' permission to stay, arguing that the revenues from the Jews were needed to rebuild the town. The Venetian clergy was opposed to these measures; especially around Easter 1515 and 1516 tensions within the city's population rose, and demands for an expulsion of the Jews were raised. Due to ongoing military tensions a return to the *terraferma* did not seem appropriate; therefore the magistrate looked for a place that would allow the Jews to stay in the town.[40]

From the very beginning the propositions revolved around a separate living area for the Jewish population, even though Jewish representatives voiced concern about their security should they be segregated from the Christians. After a first proposition – the island of Giudecca – was turned down in 1515 because of Jewish protests, in 1516 the walled – and therefore in the opinion of the Senate secure – area of the *ghetto nuovo* was established as the new residence for the Jews living in Venice.[41]

39 Benjamin Ravid: The Venetian Government and the Jews. In: Robert C. Davis / Benjamin Ravid (eds): *The Jews of Early Modern Venice*. Baltimore / London: Johns Hopkins UP 2001, pp. 3–30, here pp. 3–8; id.: The Legal Status of the Jews in Venice to 1509. In: *Proceedings of the American Academy for Jewish Research* 54 (1987), pp. 169–202; Reinhold C. Mueller: Les Prêteurs Juifs du Venise au Moyen Age. In: *Annales. Histoire, Sciences Sociales* 30,6 (1975), pp. 1277–1302.

40 Elisabeth Crouzet-Pavan: Venice between Jerusalem, Byzantium, and Divine Retribution: The Origins of the Ghetto. In: Alisa Meyuhas Ginio (ed.): *Jews, Christians, and Muslims in the Mediterranean World after 1492*. London: Cass 1992, pp. 163–179; Robert Finlay: The Foundation of the Ghetto. Venice, the Jews and the War of the League of Cambrai. In: *Proceedings of the American Philosophical Society* 126 (1982), pp. 140–154.

41 On the negotiations Ravid: The Religious, Economic and Social Background, pp. 213–222.

A segregated living quarter for non-citizens was in itself not a new concept: The German (north-Alpine) merchants resided in Venice in the *fondaco dei Tedeschi*, a walled building complex that was closed for the night, much like it was intended for the Jewish quarter as well. The *Tedeschi* however were not allowed to bring their families to Venice; the temporary character of their residence was clearly emphasized, even if the *fondaco* was a permanent institution.[42]

If we examine the negotiations and compare the provisions for the *ghetto* with the regulations of the *fondaco*, the foundation of the new Jewish quarter looks indeed like a measure of inclusion, facilitating a permanent Jewish residence close to the city itself (as opposed to the *terraferma*). The vocal opposition to such a step explains, why the decree issued by the Venetian Senate in 1516 is worded very differently, portraying the new institution as a means of exclusion.[43]

The document states that it aims to re-institute the old custom according to which Jews could not stay in the city of Venice. Recently it had been bypassed by "Hebrew perfidiousness" as well as necessity and the conditions of the time. To end such disorder and inconvenience it had been decreed that all Jews were to live together in the court lying in the ghetto by the church of San Girolamo ("san hieronymo"). In order to keep the Jews from wandering around noisily the whole night, very much to the displeasure of the Lord Jesus Christ, two gates were built at the border to the *ghetto vecchio* (which was not included into the Jewish quarter yet) and on the other side, by the bridge. Those gates were to be closed at night and reopened in the mornings. High walls should be erected between them and all other entrances closed up. If Jews were found outside the gates at night, they were to be punished, the penalties rising with every new offence. The guards at the gates had to live there day and night, furthermore two boats had to patrol the walls; the guards were nominated by the Venetian authorities but should be paid for by the Jews.

A good example of the ideologically loaded atmosphere, in which the document was issued, is the next paragraph, dealing with synagogues. It stated it was shameful and a very bad example that the Jews possessed synagogues everywhere on the Venetian territory, which were visited by Christian men

42 Olivia Remie Constable: *Housing the Stranger in the Mediterranean World. Lodging, Trade, and Travel in Late Antiquity and the Middle Ages.* Cambridge: Cambridge UP 2003, pp. 308–328.

43 The text of the document is edited in Ravid: The Religious, Economic and Social Background, pp. 248–250.

and women, and where they chanted their prayers loudly. In order to end such abuse, the Jews should not be permitted to have a synagogue anywhere in the town, not even in the aforementioned place (= the ghetto), but only in Mestre, just as it had been before the war.

The document of 1516 argued on two levels and addressed two different target-groups: On the one hand it was directed at the Jews in Venice. It assigned an area of residence and marks the legal ramifications under which they were allowed (and forced) to settle there. On the other hand it refused to acknowledge the introduction of a new element within the Venetian townscape. It aimed at correcting an abuse, at ending disorder and inconvenience, at re-instituting the old order, such as it had been before the war. The new area of residence was not named as "Jewish quarter" or (potentially) as "fondaco degli ebrei" – it just went by the name the place had been called beforehand. The argumentation was not urban, it was religious, and as such it described a "non-space" – isolated from the Christian population, separated by walls and patrolled by guards. Even though the Jews were supposed to reside in the "ghetto behind [the church] San Hieronymo", they should not build a synagogue there, but only in Mestre, just as it had been before the war. Such an argumentation was aimed at the critics of the Venetian government, especially the clerics, whose sermons about the wrath of God being conjured by the politics of the government towards the Jews, had stirred up emotions and insecurity within the population. The criticism of the Jewish presence in Venice had been first and foremost a criticism of the Senate, whose politics had caused the decline of the Republic evident in the turmoil of the war.[44] The document of 1516 provided a clear message in answer to that: The evils you have addressed have been corrected and the former (=good) state reinstituted – the danger to the Republic therefore averted. The exclusionary rhetoric of the document had fulfilled its purpose already at the end of 1516, when the political situation around Venice visibly calmed down. The Senate had shown that it took its critics seriously; the institution of a Jewish residential area in the *ghetto nuovo* appeared as a measure of exclusion even though it fell far short of what the clerics had demanded.[45]

44 Cf. Crouzet-Pavan: Venice between Jerusalem, Byzantium, and Divine Retribution.

45 On the performative dimension of early modern legal acts Jürgen Schlumbohm: Gesetze, die nicht durchgesetzt werden – ein Strukturmerkmal des frühneuzeitlichen Staates? In: *Geschichte und Gesellschaft* 23 (1997), pp. 647–663; Jürgen Heyde: Polemics and Participation – Anti-Jewish Legislation in the Polish Diet (Sejm) in the 16th Century and Its Political Contexts. In: Yvonne Kleinmann / Stephan Stach / Tracie Wilson (eds): *Religion in the Mirror of Law. Eastern European Perspectives from the Early Modern Period to 1939*. Frankfurt am Main: Klostermann 2015, in press.

From the very beginning the living conditions in the new residential area were difficult. It was declared that only Christians were supposed to be owners of the land – even in the *ghetto nuovo.* Christian owners should erect houses at their own expense and then rent them out to Jews. The houses built in the first years after 1516 provided not enough space for all the Jews living in the ghetto. Jews complained about speculation by the Christian house owners and built additional floors at their own cost to enlarge the living space. Only after 1530 the conflicts about housing in the ghetto diminished. The Venetian courts strengthened the position of the Jewish inhabitants of the ghetto. They could sell and buy apartments without asking the owner of the ground; in practice the Jews were treated as the owners of the houses they had built with their own money, even if the ground on which they were built belonged to a Christian. The Venetian courts even adopted a new term for that: "jus gazaga" (or: casaca) – from the Hebrew "hazakah" – expressing just the hereditary entitlement to the apartments and houses erected by Jews regardless of the land on which they were built.[46]

In the same time, one of the most discriminating points in the document of 1516 was tacitly abolished: the prohibition to build a synagogue anywhere but in Mestre. In 1528/29 the *Scuola Grande Tedesca* was built in the *ghetto nuovo*, in 1532 the *Scuola Canton*, and in the next decades several other synagogues followed.[47]

In 1541 the Venetian Senate issued another document concerning the Jewish residential area.[48] Jewish Levantine merchants had approached the Board of Trade (*Cinque Savi alla Mercanzia*) asking for a place to settle in the city. Rhetorically the Senate's answer to them differed profoundly from the 1516 decree, reverting to the line of argumentation used in the documents of 1503 and 1509. In a lengthy introductory note the Venetian Senate emphasized the importance of Jewish Levantine trade for the city before introducing the request of Jewish merchants for a place of residence in Venice. They had approached the Board of Trade, because due to the narrowness in the ghetto they had not been able to find a suitable place. The board declared its willingness to provide lodging for them, and if there was nothing suitable available in the ghetto, then the board would provide space in the *ghetto vecchio.* There

46 Ennio Concina: Owners, Houses, Functions. New Research on the Origins of the Venetian Ghetto. In: Meyuhas Ginio (ed.): *Jews, Christians, and Muslims in the Mediterranean World*, pp. 180–189.

47 Donatella Calabi: The "City of the Jews". In: Robert C. Davis / Benjamin Ravid (eds): *The Jews of Early Modern Venice*, pp. 31–49, here pp. 41–45.

48 Ravid: The Religious, Economic and Social Background, pp. 222–228, the text of the document on pp. 250–251.

the Jewish merchants should reside under the same conditions as in the *ghetto nuovo* – it was a priority to "keep these Jews always locked and guarded" ("restando sempre ditti Hebrei serrati et custoditi"). Therefore not topography decided, where the ghetto was, but the conditions of residence.

The text of the document shows that negotiations were already far advanced; the Levantine merchants and the Board of Trade seemed to agree that there was no appropriate room for them in the *ghetto nuovo*, and they had a concrete alternative in mind. Visible as well were negotiations within the Venetian authorities, indicated by the sentence on keeping the Jews always locked and guarded. The phrase reminds of the rhetoric of 1516, which was invoked later to specify the ramifications under which the merchants could take residence in the city. Like in 1516, in the document of 1541 the Senate did not admit to creating something new: the Levantine merchants were supposed to reside in the ghetto, as usual, although not in the *ghetto nuovo*, but in the *ghetto vecchio* – a place, which yet had not been included in the walls that surrounded the ghetto since 1516, and a place, where up to then, Christians lived. Therefore the demand that the lodging of the merchants in the *ghetto vecchio* had to match the conditions of the *ghetto nuovo* at the same time masks and reveals the fact that a new Jewish space was to be created in Venice.

Several weeks later, on July 20th, 1541 the council issued another document. The investigation of the Board of Trade had confirmed, it emphasized, that the Jewish Levantine merchants could not take up residence in the *ghetto nuovo* because of its narrowness. They were to lodge in the *ghetto vecchio*, but under the condition that everything be arranged in the same way as in the *ghetto nuovo*. The document specified the walls that had to be erected, the gates within them (and the closing of three already existent gates), the evacuation of the Christian inhabitants and the compensation payments for the house-owners, because their property had been assigned to the Jews. Moreover it decreed that these merchants were not allowed to bring their families; they were only supposed to engage in trade and had to leave Venice after four months. This demand had no precedent in the legal ramifications of the *ghetto nuovo*, but referred to the conditions of the merchants in the *fondaco dei tedeschi* – so the new residents had to face restrictions concerning Jews *and* foreign merchants alike.

Again, inclusive regulations were "balanced" by demonstratively excluding requirements; this time concerning the duration of residence. In contrast to 1516, when it took several years before the first synagogue could be opened in the ghetto, almost immediately negotiations began between the merchants and the Venetian authorities in order to rearrange the terms of residence to make them acceptable for the merchants. Still in 1541 the permitted duration of residence was prolonged to two years, and after 1543 the permit was renewed regularly (even though in some years only for one year). In 1589 the Levantine merchants were accepted as Venetian (and no longer Ottoman) subjects.[49]

Jewish presence in Venice, as I have tried to show, appears as a constant process of negotiations. At the same time the decrees and charters regulating Jewish settlement constituted a sort of ritualized, performative act; their repetitive and largely predictable formula essentially expressed both the permanent and the temporary character of that presence. Such double character originated in the fact that the documents addressed a dual audience: on the one hand Jewish bankers and merchants were to be integrated into the economic, and to a certain extent also social order of the city, on the other hand influential groups within Venetian society pressed for far reaching exclusion.

Such ambiguity led to different appropriations of the term "ghetto", with different meanings ascribed to it: The Venetian authorities avoided to acknowledge that the ghetto formed a new entity, a Jewish space within the city. The document of 1516 expressively underlined its aim to re-institute the pre-war status, in 1541 the authorities offered plainly to "accommodate the said travelling Jewish Levantine merchants in the ghetto". Around 1530 "ghetto" already appeared in Venetian sources as a generic term, even though the *ghetto vecchio* at that time still was part of Christian Venice.[50] It took more than one and a half century until the notion that the ghetto constituted in fact a Jewish space was mirrored in terminology. Visitors in the 16th and early 17th had sometimes mentioned the ghetto as the place of the Jews or located them as part of the urban setting in general; in 1688 Maximilian Mission, an English traveller, for the first time called the Ghetto a Jewish quarter ("Jewry"), in 1765/66 Joseph Jerome de la Lande called the ghetto a "Juiverie".[51]

49 Benjamin Ravid: The Legal Status of the Jewish Merchants of Venice 1541–1638. In: *The Journal of Economic History* 35,1 (1975), pp. 274–279; id.: The First Charter of the Jewish Merchants of Venice 1589. In: *AJS Review* 1 (1976), pp. 187–222; id.: An Introduction to the Charters of the Jewish Merchants of Venice. In: Id.: *Studies on the Jews of Venice 1382–1797*. Aldershot: Ashgate 2003, pp. 203–246 [first published in: Elliott Horowitz / Moises Orfali (eds): *The Mediterranean and the Jews II: Society, Culture and Economy in Early Modern Times*. Ramat-Gan: Bar Ilan UP 2002].

50 Curt Sigmar Gutkind: Ghetto. In: *Zeitschrift für Romanische Philologie* 52 (1932), p. 731.

51 Benjamin Ravid: Christian Travelers in the Ghetto of Venice. Some Preliminary Observations. In: Id.: *Studies on the Jews of Venice*, pp. 111–150 [first published in Stanley Nash (ed.): *Between History and Literature. Studies in Honor of Isaac Barzilay*. Tel-Aviv: Ha-Kibbutz Ha-Me'uhad 1997], p. 133 (Maximilien Misson: *A New Voyage to Italy*. 5th enlarged ed., 2 vols. in 4 parts. London: Bonwicke 1739, vol. I/ii: pp. 476, 484); p. 134 (Joseph Jerome de la Lande: *Voyage en Italy*. 2nd ed., 9 vols. Paris: Desaint 1786, vol. 8: pp. 425, 577).

Among the Jewish population the term "ghetto" appeared early as well.[52] The appropriation of the area as a Jewish space, however, is evident from the practice of the "jus gazaga" (and its acceptance by the authorities) and later during the negotiations on the second enlargement of the ghetto by the *ghetto nuovissimo* in 1633.[53]

From the very onset on, it appears, "ghetto" has been first and foremost a narrative frame, designed to host differing, even seemingly mutually exclusive expectations. The ghetto in Venice offered Jews a permanent place of residence, while claiming to restore a former state, when Jews did not have the opportunity to live in the town. It was strictly confined by walls and guards, but flexible in its topographical structures. The documents, which outlined the legal and topographical ramifications of the Jewish residential area, were directed not only at the Jews (as the direct addressee), but also at a Christian Venetian public aiming for the exact opposite. So, from the very beginning, "ghetto" became an umbrella term masking the character of the new area by allowing to avoid a clear definition: on the one hand, clearly a Jewish place had been instituted, a place of permanent (if constantly negotiated) residence, where structures of autonomy developed and Jewish representatives became partners in negotiations with the Venetian authorities. On the other hand, the ghetto could always be understood as a Christian dominated space of marginalization and symbolic exclusion. Therefore, even in the earliest references, the term "ghetto" was used not as a topographical expression – up to 1541 next to the "Jewish" *ghetto nuovo* there was the "Christian" *ghetto vecchio* –, but as a generic term.

By comparison the Frankfurt "Judengasse", taken by Wirth as reference for an early modern ghetto, with all its legal similarities to Venice, was never questioned in its character as a Jewish space – and as long as it existed it was never called "ghetto" in official documents.[54] In Rome, however, where a "vicus judeorum" as a clearly defined Jewish space had existed well before 1555,

52 David Reubeni, 1523–1527. In: Nathan Elkan Adler (ed.): *Jewish Travelers.* London: Routledge 1930, pp. 251–328, here p. 269; Ravid: On the Diffusion of the Word "Ghetto", p. 22.

53 Benjamin Ravid: The Establishment of the Ghetto Nuovissimo of Venice. In: Haim Beinart (ed.): *Jews in Italy. Studies Dedicated to the Memory of U. Cassuto on the 100th Anniversary of his Birth.* Jerusalem: Magnes 1988, pp. 35–54.

54 Fritz Backhaus: Die Einrichtung eines Ghettos für die Frankfurter Juden im Jahre 1462. In: *Hessisches Jahrbuch für Landesgeschichte* 39 (1989), pp. 59–86; Isidor Kracauer: *Geschichte der Juden in Frankfurt a. M. (1150–1824).* Frankfurt am Main: Keip 1987 [1st ed. Frankfurt 1925–1927]; on "ghetto" remembrance in the 19th century Christhard Hoffmann: From Heinrich Heine to Isidor Kracauer. The Frankfurt Ghetto in German-Jewish Historical Culture and Historiography. In: Fritz Backhaus / Gisela Engel / Robert Liberles (eds): *The Frankfurt Judengasse. Jewish Life in an Early Modern German City.* 2nd ed. Edgware: Vallentine Mitchell 2010, pp. 41–58.

in the second half of the 16th century "ghetto" competed with other newly introduced and markedly Christian dominated expressions like "seraglio". The new legal ramifications introduced by Pope Paul IV in 1555 warranted a new terminology, and "ghetto" (or in its Roman version "ghet") proved to be open enough to carry Christian as well as Jewish, exclusionary as well as inclusive interpretations.[55]

Ghetto – Spaces and Narratives

Over the centuries, one of the most striking features of the term "ghetto" has been its openness to differing interpretations and its reluctance to let itself be moulded into one commonly accepted definition. Modern debates on "ghetto" have tried to appropriate more than a technical term. Any attempt to make sense of the ghetto had to provide its own answer to a whole set of connotations: living conditions within the area marked as "ghetto"; relations between "ghetto" and its surroundings: legal, social, cultural relations between Jews and non-Jews; the existence – and meaning – of a Jewish space within a Christian environment. Marginality and isolation vs. proximity and contact, exclusion vs. inclusion – any of these connotations can be "true" with regards to "ghetto", depending on the message "ghetto" is supposed to convey.

A ghetto – be it Venice, Warsaw or even Soweto – can be analysed in its topographical structure, located in its timeframe, studied in its legal, social, economic and cultural ramifications. A study of "the ghetto", however, leads to different aspects. It has to discover the preconceptions and connotations associated with the term. They can be negative: isolation or backwardness, as well as positive: closeness or empowerment. A common denominator may be found in the aspect, that "ghetto" always discusses the relation between a group and its environment. Apart from that, the inherent ambiguity of "ghetto" has always offered opportunities to appropriate the term, and by doing so, to shape perceptions and realities behind it. "Ghetto" as a narrative framework has facilitated debates on identities and social relations not in spite of, but because of this very ambiguity.

55 Adriano Prosperi: Incontri rituali. Il Papa e gli ebrei. In: Corrado Vivanti (ed.): *Storia d'Italia. Annali 11: Gli ebrei in Italia*, vol. 1: Dall'alto Medioevo all'età dei ghetto. Torino: Einaudi 1996, pp. 497–522; Kenneth Stow: *Theater of Acculturation. The Roman Jews in the Sixteenth Century*. Seattle / London: University of Washington Press 2001; id.: The Consciousness of Closure. Roman Jewry and Its Ghet. In: Ruderman (ed.): *Essential Papers on Jewish Culture in Renaissance and Baroque Italy*, pp. 386–400; Sandra Debenedetti-Stow: The Etymology of "Ghetto". New Evidence from Rome. In: *Jewish History* 6,1–2 (1992), pp. 79–85.

Jewish Shtetl or Christian Town?

The Jews in Small Towns in the Polish-Lithuanian Commonwealth in the 17th and 18th Centuries

Maria Cieśla

The early modern Polish-Lithuanian Commonwealth was home to the biggest Jewish community in Europe. The majority of these Jews lived in small towns, the shtetls – the mythical Eastern European places where Jews lived were indeed small towns in which, as it has been indicated in the latest research, the Jews constituted only a part of the inhabitants.[1] An idyllic picture of the East European shtetl known from literature is different from the picture gained from the latest research. My paper describes the patterns of Christian-Jewish coexistence in the shtetls in the early modern Polish-Lithuanian Commonwealth.

In the beginning of the analysis a definition of a small town has to be formulated. It is worth noting that Polish-Lithuanian small towns differ a great deal from their West European equivalents. In previous research a small city was defined in many ways; however the most important factors were firstly the number of inhabitants and secondly the town's function in the economic system. Thus by this research the number of inhabitants a small town should have was estimated to be about 1,050–1,705 persons, or about 300 chimneys.[2] The local market was described as dealing mostly with agricultural products, and other ones – for instance, luxury goods – were less significant. Thus one

1 About the Shtetl see Antony Polonsky (ed.): *The Shtetl Myth and Reality*. Oxford: Littman 2004.

2 Stanisław Alexandrowicz: Zaludnienie miasteczek Litwy i Białorusi w XVI–XVII w. In: *Roczniki Dziejów Społecznych i Gospodarczych* 27 (1965), pp. 35–69, here p. 38; Jerzy Ochmański: W kwestii agrarnego charakteru miast WKsL w XVI. In: *Studia Historica w 35 lecie pracy naukowej H. Łowmiańskiego*. Poznań: Państwowe Wydawnictwo Naukowe 1960, pp. 277–395, here p. 294.

of the most important functions of those towns was to connect rural areas with bigger towns and cities. They were the so-called farm market towns.[3] In the case of Polish-Lithuanian small towns, the jurisdictional independence and the use of the so-called Magdeburg Law cannot be counted as a typical feature. One has to bear in mind that many small towns, especially in the Lithuanian part of the Commonwealth, had no Magdeburg right.[4] Nevertheless, the towns constituted administrative and religious centres.[5]

Another characteristic feature of the small towns was their multi-ethnicity. In almost every small town in the Polish-Lithuanian Commonwealth lived both Jews and Christians. It is very difficult to assess the precise number of Christian and Jewish inhabitants in the early modern period. In previous research the proportion of Jews living in small towns was estimated to be at least 40 % of the total population.[6] However, facts and dates speak against this assumption; it seems that the Jewish communities were only in some places that large; on average, the percentage of Jews was smaller. Let us consider some examples of places which are the subject of the forthcoming analysis. In Dawidgródek[7] Jews possessed only around 15 % of all houses in the town in 1720; from this we can assume that Jews constituted about 25–30 % of the total population.[8] Or Nieśwież[9], where Jews also constituted 25–30 % of

3 Andrzej Wyrobisz: Typy funkcjonalne miast polskich. In. *Przegląd Historyczny* 72 (1981), pp. 25–51, here p. 37.

4 Zofia Klujewska-Topolska: Oznaczenia i klasyfikacje miast w dawnej Polsce (XVI–XVIII w.). In: *Czasopismo Prawno – Historyczne* 8,2 (1956), pp. 253–269, here p. 267.

5 Stanisław Alexandoriwcz: Miasteczka Białorusi i Litwy, jako ośrodki handlu w XVI i w połowie XVII wieku. In: *Rocznik Białostocki* 1 (1961), pp. 63–131.

6 Adam Teller: The Shtetl as an Arena for Polish-Jewish Integration in the Eighteenth Century. In: Polonsky (ed.): *The Shtetl: Myth and Reality*, pp. 25–41, here p. 39.

7 Dawidgródek (now Davyd-Haradok) a town in the southwestern part of the Grand Duchy of Lithuania. For more about the town see: Dawidgródek. In: *Słownik Geograficzny Królestwa Polskiego*, ed. by Filip Sulimierski / Bronisław Chlebowski / Władysłąw Waliszewski. Warszawa: Nakładem Filipa Sulimierskiego i Władysława Walewskiego 1880, vol. 1, p. 914.

8 Central Archive of Old Acts in Warsaw, The Radziwiłł Family Archive (hereafter AR) XXV, s 680, Inwentarz Dawidgródka, 1720.

9 Nieśwież (Nesvizh) a town in the White Russian part of the Grand Duchy of Lithuania, which was one of the main residences of the Catholic part of the Radziwiłł family; for more about the town, see *Nieśwież – Historia – Kultura – Sztuka. Materiały konferencji naukowych w Nieśweżu*. Warszawa / Mińsk: Przegląd Wschodni 1998. The Jewish community was founded in the end of the 16th century, see Jacob Goldberg: *Jewish Privileges in the Polish Commonwealth. Charters of Rights Granted to Jewish Communities in Poland-Lithuania in the Sixteenth to Eighteenth Centuries* (hereafter JPP). Jerusalem: Israel Academy of Sciences and Humanities 1985–2001, vol. II, no. 93–94.

the town's total population.[10] Data from previous demographic studies are similar;[11] on the basis of the above mentioned facts it is possible to conclude that on average the Jews constituted about 20–30 % of the total population of a small town.

Additionally, the Christian population was heterogeneous as well. Thus in small towns lived Catholics, Greek-Catholics, Orthodox Christians, Protestants and Armenians. What is more, Muslim inhabitants have to be noted. It is almost impossible to compile the demographic data. Nevertheless, some basic information (unfortunately only about bigger towns) which shows this tendency can be cited. For instance, in Zamość in the middle of the 17th century, 21 houses belonged to Germans and Scots, 32 houses to Armenians and 23 to Jews, and last but not least the majority of the houses belonged to Roman and Greek Catholics; however, the numbers are not known.[12] Another example is provided by Słuck[13] which housed 13 or 14 Orthodox parishes, 1 Protestant (Calvinist), 1 Lutheran, and 1 Catholic. In the Protestant Calvinist parish were 4 priests – this parish was one of the biggest in the Grand

10 AR XXV, s 2672/1.

11 Examples are numerous; see Jakub Goldberg: Społeczność żydowska w szlacheckim miasteczku. In: *Biuletyn Żydowskiego Instytutu Historycznego* 59,3 (1966), pp. 3–28; Maria Bogucka: The Jews in Polish Cities in the 16th–18th centuries. In: Adam Teller (ed.): *Scripta Hierosolymitana XXXVIII, Studies in the History of the Jews in Old Poland in Honor of Jacob Goldberg*. Jerusalem: Magnes Press 1998, pp. 51–57; Danuta Molenda: Ludność żydowska w Olkuszu w okresie przedrozbiorowym. In: *Biuletyn Żydowskiego Instytutu Historycznego* 4, 116 (1980), pp. 3–25; Tomasz Opas: Sytuacja ludności żydowskiej w miastach szlacheckich województwa lubelskiego w XVIII w. In: *Biuletyn Żydowskiego Instytutu Historycznego* 67 (1968) pp. 3–37; Rafał Mahler: Żydzi w Nowym Sączu w XVII–XVIII w. In: *Biuletyn Żydowskiego Instytutu Historycznego* 55 (1965), pp. 3–32; Janina Morgerstern: O osadnictwie Żydów w Zamościu XV–XVII w. In: *Biuletyn Żydowskiego Instytutu Historycznego* 42–43 (1962) pp. 3–17; Ireneusz Ihnatowicz: *Głębokie miasteczko na Białorusi w XVIII w.* In: *Miasto region, społeczeństwo. Studia ofiarowane Prof. Andrzejowi Wyrobiszowi w sześćdziesiątą rocznicę Jego urodzin.* Białystok: Dział Wydawniczy Filii UW 1992, pp. 93–100.

12 Janina Morgerstern: O osadnictwie żydowskim w Zamościu na przełomie XVI i XVII w In: *Biuletyn Żydowskiego Instytutu Historycznego* 43–44 (1962), pp. 3–17, here p. 4.

13 Słuck is one of the most important cities belonging to the Radziwiłł family and is located in the East parts of the Grand Duchy of Lithuania; it was one of the main trade centers in the White Russian part of the Grand Duchy of Lithuania and one of the main Jewish communities in GDL. For more about the town, see Anatol Hryckiewicz: Torgovyje svjazi Slucka s gorodami Polshyi Pribaltiki v XVII–XVIII viekach i ih rol vinnosiemnoi torgovlie goroda. In: *Acta – Baltic – Slavica* 6 (1969), pp. 51–73; Barbara Pendzich: The Jewish Community of Słuck After the Polish-Muscovite War of 1654–1667. In: *Proceedings of the 11th World Congress of the Jewish Studies.* Jerusalem: World Union of Jewish Studies 1997, pp. 173–180; Rafał Degiel: *Protestanci i prawosławni w Słucku. Patronat wyznaniowy Radziwiłłów birżańskich nad cerkwią prawosławną w księstwie słuckim w XVII w.* Warszawa: Neritron 2000; Tomasz Gromelski: *Struktura zawodowa i socjotopografia Słucka w drugiej połowie XVII i w XVIII w.* MA Thesis, University of Warsaw 2001.

Duchy of Lithuania. Some estimations, which are not very precise, determine that around 50–70 % of the Christian dwellers were Orthodox.[14] The situation in Lwów was similar: 50 % Poles (Latin Catholics), 20 % Ruthenians, and about 16–20 % Jews.[15]

The issue of Jewish-Christian coexistence in small towns has been discussed in previous research. Historians such as Janina Morgerstern, Anatol Leszczyński, Jakub Goldberg, Stefan Gąsiorowski and lately Adam Teller have described the situation of the Jews in such places as Zamość, Kraśnik, Wieruszów, Lutomiersk, Żółkiew and so on.[16] However, in none of these studies was the concept of space discussed.

My aim is to investigate the question of Christian-Jewish coexistence using the concept of space. In this paper I apply the definition of space formulated by Georg Simmel. Following his explanation, I am assuming that "the socially constructed spatial configurations influence the emergence of certain forms of social interaction and the character of social associations varies depending on whether their participants are spatially in touch or are separated from each other".[17]

Following Simmel's space definition, I have divided my paper in two parts. In each of them I will look at the Jews from a different perspective. In the first one I investigate their legal position. The question of how the Jewish living space was defined and the privileges given by the Christian authorities will be discussed. Special attention will be paid to the methods that were applied by the definition of the Jewish space in Polish-Lithuanian small towns. In the second part the legal situation will be compared with social practices. The

14 Tomasz Gromlewski: *Struktura zawdodowa i socjotopografia Słucka w drugiej połowie XVII i w XVIII wieku*, M.A thesis, University of Warsaw, p. 45.

15 Maurycy Horn: Społeczność żydowska w wielonarodowym Lwowie. In: *Biuletyn Żydowskiego Instytutu Historycznego* 157,1 (1991), pp. 3–15, here p. 3.

16 Jacob Goldberg: Poles and Jews in the 17th Centuries. Rejection or Acceptance. In: *Jahrbücher für Geschichte Osteuropas* 22 (1974), pp. 248–282; Teller: The Shtetl as an Arena for Polish-Jewish Integration in the XVIII Century, pp. 25–40; Stefan Gąsiorowski: *Żydzi i chrześcijanie w Żółkwi w XVII I XVIII wieku.* Kraków: Polska Akademia Umiejętności 2001; id.: Żydzi w Kiejdanach w XVII i XVIII wieku. Rekonesans badawczy. In: Anna Michałowska-Mycielska / Marcin Wodziński (eds): *Małżeństwo z rozsądku. Żydzi w społeczeństwie dawnej Rzeczypospolitej.* Wrocław: Wydawnictwo Uniwersytetu Wrocławskiego 2007, pp. 73–87.

17 Andrea Glauser: Pionierarbeit mit paradoxen Folgen? Zur neueren Rezeption der Raumsoziologie von Georg Simmel. In: *Zeitschrift für Soziologie* 35,4 (2006), pp. 250–268, here p. 257: "die sozial konstruierten räumlichen Konfigurationen sich auf die Entstehung bestimmter Formen von sozialen Wechselbeziehungen auswirken und dass der Charakter von sozialen Vereinigungen variiert, je nachdem ob ihre Teilnehmer sich räumlich berühren oder voneinander getrennt seien" (translation Alina Gromova).

question of how the Jews created their living space by themselves and to what extent this new social space connects with their privileges will be discussed. In this paper an attempt will be made to consider Christian-Jewish relations from a new angle.

The majority of these small towns were private at the time that is being discussed, and thus the majority of my reference material comes from private archives. A special focus was put on one of the best-preserved family archives – the Warsaw Radziwiłł Family Archive. Due to the fact that the majority of the Radzwiłł properties were located in the Grand Duchy of Lithuania, my paper concentrates on this part of the Commonwealth; however, some material from the Crown of Poland was used as well. I used legal documents, inventories, and court material and diaries of Christian burghers. It is worth noting that the majority of my reference material are court acts, which means that the picture of social contact between Jews and Christians depicted in those acts is very negative because the court acts describe only conflicts; nevertheless, one has to bear in mind that the daily life of those people was shaped not only by conflicts.

Let us start the analysis with a quotation from a privilege given by King Władysław to a small town called Wojń[18]: "So that the mentioned Jews of the town of Wojń buy houses, squares in the very market and streets, gardens, fields and these administer on them entry houses and whatever they want to build."[19] Thus the living space of the Jews was not determined by the Christian authorities. A comparison with other Jewish privileges has shown that this was a marked tendency. There are multiple examples: Bychów, Chęciny, Dobromil, Kazimierz, Leżajsk, Buczacz Lubartów, Janowiec, etc.[20] According to Jurgita Siauciunaite-Verbickiene's research, the lack of limitation was a characteristic feature of small towns in the 16th century; it seems, however, that this tendency was typical of later centuries as well.[21] What's more, it

18 Wojń was a small town on the West border of the Grand Duchy of Lithuania; it belonged to the royal properties, about Wojń see *Słownik geograficzny Królestwa Polskiego iinnych krajów słowiańskich*, vol. 13, p. 736.

19 "Aby pomienieni Żydzi miasteczka Wojnia domów, placów w samym rynku i ulicach ogrodów, grontów włócznych i sianorzętych nabywać i onymi dysponować na nich domy wjezdne i jakie chcą budować" (JPP 2, No. 127).

20 JPP I, No. 3, JPP I, No. 4, JPP I, No. 6, JPP I, No. 15, JPP I, No. 21, JPP II, No. 68, JPP II, No. 88, JPP II, No. 78.

21 Jurgita Siauciunaite-Verbickiene: The Jewish Living Space in the Grand Duchy of Lithuania: Tendencies and Ways of its Formation. In: Jurgita Siaucinaite-Verbickiene / Lara Lempertiene (eds): *Jewish Space in Central Eastern Europe. Day to Day History*. Cambridge: Cambridge Scholars 2007, pp. 7–27, here p. 11.

seems to be stronger in the second half of the 17th century. A lot of Jewish communities were founded during times of economic crisis; the invitation of Jews was one of the applied methods of crisis prevention. No wonder that under such circumstances owners allowed Jews to settle all over their town.[22] In this context there is special meaning given to a market square and a main street, which, as will be argued below, were strongly connected to Jewish economic activity.

In this connection one has to mention the issue of religious space. On one hand Jewish religious spaces were determined very precisely. In the majority of privileges space for a synagogue and a cemetery were included, and sometimes places for a house of study and a Jewish ritual bath were determined. It seems that Christian authorities tried to concentrate all Jewish religious institutions in one close space. Uncertainty still prevails as to whether the factor behind it was a religious or a fiscal one; it has to be considered that the Jewish religious institutions paid different taxes. It is worth noting that the Christian authorities allowed Jews to mark the eruv; an example is provided by the privilege given to the community in Lubraniec: "They will have freedom to build a synagogue and kierhof [cemetery] school and put strings according to Jewish custom"[23]. On the other hand, Jews were excluded from Christian religious spaces.[24] This tendency can be seen in many privileges; nevertheless, different methods were used. Firstly, Jews were not allowed to be in the street during the most important Christian holy days, such as Good Friday or Corpus Christi. In some places where a Jewish quarter was created, the Jews were forced to close the gate of their quarter.[25] However, as it will be recalled, such places were very rare. Other differences were seen in regulations describing the way in which a synagogue should be built; usually the Jews were reminded that the building should not look like a church or that it should not be in the same shape as a church. Eventually in some places, Jews were not allowed to build houses close to a church; an example is provided

22 Such privileges were given to: Chęcin (JPP I, No. 4), Kazimierz Dolny (JPP I, No. 15).

23 "wolność będą mieli budowania sobie bożnicy i szkoły kierhofu i ciągnienia sznurków podług zwyczajów żydowskich" (JPP I, No. 23).

24 About the Catholic Church and the Jews in the early modern Polish-Lithuanian Commonwealth, see Judith Kalik: *Haknesia katolit wehayehudim bemamlechet Polin-Lita bemea 18*, Phd thesis, Jerusalem 1998.

25 JPP I, No. 27 (Łask), JPP II, No. 76 (Gnin), JPP II, No. 93 (Nieśwież).

by the privilege for Radzonów, where it states that "Jewish houses should be distant from the parish church for 82 elbows"[26].

An analysis of the privileges shows some exceptions from the general rules. Let us take the example of Nieśwież: "And we have given to Jews a separate street, so that in one place they have dwellings and houses, yet we add that the street so should be built, that it be closed, and that it be always locked for the night, and that they hold the keys."[27] In the privilege given by Mikołaj Sierotka Radziwiłł in 1589, in contrast with other documents, the Jewish living space was determined very precisely. Moreover, the Jewish gate had a significant practical and symbolic meaning, which, as we read in the privileges, should be closed every day in the evening. One can ask: why were those regulations introduced in Nieśwież? It seems that one of the reasons can be found in the biography of the owner. Mikołaj Sierotka Radziwiłł was a newly converted Catholic who tried to introduce the doctrine of the Holy See in his properties.[28] The example of Nieśwież represents one of the privileges that introduced one of the most restrictive regulations. Similar to it are privileges given to Gnin and Kępno; some privileges speak about a Jewish street or "their privileged street"; however, as Siauciunaite-Verbickiene's research has shown, Christians were allowed to settle in those streets as well.[29]

Further research shows that the Jewish living space was determined not only in the privileges given to its communities, but also by many different factors. Let us examine the issues of jurisdictional dependence and the taxation of the Jews. As will be argued below, they played a crucial role in the choice of Jewish living space.

"The Jews should obey only the King and his officials within their jurisdiction."[30] This is a crucial statement taken from the General Privilege for the Lithuanian

26 "Dmostwa zaś żydowskie na łokci 82 oddalone być mają od kościoła farnego" JPP II, p. 117.

27 "A iżeśmy osobliwą ulicę Żydom dali, abyw jednym miejscu mieszkanie i domy swe mieli, tedy tego wprzód dokładamy, iż ta ulica tak się budować ma, żeby zamczysta była aby ją na noc zawsze zamykali, a klucze u nich bywać mają" JPP II, No. 93; Other examples: JPP I, No. 27 (Łask), JPP II, No. 76 (Gnin).

28 About Mikołaj Sierotka Radziwiłł see Tomasz Kempa: *Mikołaj Krzysztof Radziwiłł Sierotka (1549–1616) wojewoda wileński*. Warszawa: Wydawnictwo Naukowe 'Semper' 2000.

29 Siauciunaite-Verbickiene: The Jewish Living Space in the Grand Duchy of Lithuania, p. 12.

30 "Którzy Żydowie nie pod inszą władzą i urzędami ieno pod zwierzchnością królewską wojewodów, starost naszych pod którymi kto z nich mieszka." (*Akty izdavaemye Vilenskoiu Komisieiu dla razbora drevnikh aktov* (hereafter AVAK), Vilna; B Typografy Guberskyego Pravlenya 1871, 5, p. 300.)

Jewry. Thus Jews, in contrast with other townspeople, had the status of free people with jurisdictional dependence only on the king and his officials. The same principle was sanctioned in every document given to Jewish communities in the Polish-Lithuanian Commonwealth; seldom or if ever did Jews depend on the jurisdiction of the town's courts.[31] The one difference between the royal and private towns was that in the latter Jews answered directly to the court of the town owner and his representatives. This rule was introduced by a general privilege given to the nobility in 1539 that is seen as one of the most important privileges for the development of the Jewish legal position in the Polish-Lithuanian Commonwealth.[32] Due to this privilege Jews were not answerable to the so-called Magdeburg Law; what's more, they should never have been cited by the town's court. Most of the privileges state that cases between two Jews should be solved in a rabbinical court, by way of analogy, the cases between a Jew and a Christian burgher had to be solved in the court of the owner. For instance in the privilege given to the Jewish community in Orla, Janusz Radziwiłł declared: "Firstly all those Jews who live and will live in the town Orla of mine shall be tried before my Orlan governor; whoever will be accused by Christians in all cases he shall judge and the guilty will however have an appeal to me over mayoral courts free we make".[33] Due to this regulation Jews constituted a separate group within the townsfolk or, to take the analogy further, the quarters inhabited by the Jews constituted a separate space where usual town laws were not in force.[34]

The different tax relations could be seen as a practical consequence of the privileges described above. In general, the Jews paid different taxes than

31 Adam Kaźmierczyk, *Żydzi w dobrach prywatnych w świetle sądowniczej i administracyjnej praktyki dóbr magnackich w XVI–XVIII w.* Kraków: Księgarnia Akademicka 2002, p. 176–185. The dependence on the town's court was more seldom in the Grand Duchy of Lithuania, see Maria Cieśla, *Żydzi w Wielkim Księstwie Litewskim 1632–1764. Sytuacja prawna. Demografia. Działalność ekonomiczna,* PHd. Warszawa 2010, p. 55.

32 Adam Teller: Telling the Difference Some Comparative Perspectives on the Jewish Legal Status in the Polish-Lithuanian Commonwealth and the Holy Roman Empire. In: *Polin* 22 (2009), pp. 109–142, here p. 119.

33 "Na przód wszscy ci Żydzi, którzy w tym mieście moim orlańskim mieszkają i mieszkać będą sądzić się mają przed namiestnikiem moim orlańskim kótrzy by obżałowani byli od chrześcijan we wszstkich sprawach swoich sądzić ma i powinen będzie z wolną jednak apelacyją do mnie nad sądów wójtowskich, burmistrzowskich wolnych ich czynimy" (AR XXIII, t. 105, p. 1).

34 About the Jewish citizenship in the towns see Maria Cieśla: The Other Townsfolk. The Legal Status and Social Positions of the Jews in Cities of the Grand Duchy of Lithuania in the 17th–18th Century. In: Yvonne Kleinmann / Stephan Stach / Tracie L. Wilson (eds): *Religion in the Mirror of Law. Eastern European Perspectives from the Early Modern Period to 1939*. Frankfurt am Main: Klostermann, in press.

the Christian townspeople. The general privileges stated that the Jews were exempt from obligations to pay any town's taxes – such as taxes connected to their trade activities, housing etc. In lieu thereof, Jews were legally obligated to pay a poll tax – the so-called pogłówne. It seems, however, that in many towns Jews paid a part of the town's taxes together with Christian townspeople. The general privilege did not introduce any binding principle; hence, Jews paid different taxes in every town, and sometimes the individual system even changed over time. In cases when a Jewish community was powerful and Christian burghers weak, the Jews often succeeded in receiving tax exemptions. In cases when they had to pay the taxes –especially ones connected to their economic activity – two general principles were introduced. Firstly, in some towns Jews paid part of all taxes, proportional to the number of Jews living in the town. In Słuck, for instance, the Jews in the first half of the 17th century constituted about one-third of all city inhabitants, ergo they paid one-third of all city taxes and duties. In the second half of the 17th and in the 18th century a rapid demographic growth of the Jewish population contributed to a conflict with Christian burghers, who tried to increase the Jewish share of the general taxes.[35] The second principle was that instead of paying taxes the Jews paid a fixed contribution to the city council, which delivered tax money from the whole city to the state treasury.

Broadly speaking, the houses in which Jews lived always constituted a special space within the town; they were not a subject of the Magdeburg Law and were not obliged to pay any town's taxes. Moreover, the Jewish houses had practically brought no income into the town's treasury.

According to most of the privileges, Jews had the right to settle anywhere in the whole town, despite this the Jewish houses were always separated from other parts of the town. Thus, the position of Jews was ambiguous.

All the regulations discussed above were parts of the foundation privileges given by a town's owner, and thus they reflected his wishes. Undoubtedly, they were never exactly observed. Generally, shortly after the foundation of a new community, conflicts with Christian townspeople would break out. The reason behind these was firstly the jurisdiction and secondly the special tax regulations. The latter was the main reason, especially in the second half of the 17th century, as a sharp demographic growth in Jewish communities was noted. Thus, the Christian burghers argued against the special taxation of Jews, because the Jewish houses hadn't brought any income into the town's

35 AR XXIII, t. 134, p. 1; AR XXII, t. 154, p. 5.

coffer. In general the conflicts ended with a new definition of the Jewish living space. An example is provided by Mir.[36] In the founding privilege the Jewish living space was not limited. Nevertheless, in the second half of the 17th century, a significant demographic growth in the Jewish community was noted. It was no wonder that soon after controversy broke out centred around the taxation of the new Jewish houses. As a result a new privilege for the Jewish community was issued in 1703. It is not surprising that this privilege limited the number of the Jewish houses in the town's market to 11 houses.[37] Such examples are multiple, and thus exactly the same regulation was introduced in Druja[38] where the number of Jewish houses was limited as well.[39] Another such example was the situation in Pyzdry[40], where the Jews and Christian burghers signed a contract in which the Jewish living space was limited.[41]

It is worth noting that the pursuit of a new definition of Jewish living spaces was significant for the Jewish community as well. In general Jews made an effort to receive a privilege granting a close Jewish settlement in a town. The powerful communities could receive a privilege, which in the older Jewish historiography was unfortunately called – *de non tolerandis Christianis*[42]. According to this document the Christians were not allowed to settle in the Jewish parts of the town. The first example is provided by the privilege given to the

36 Mir is a small town in the center of the white Russian part of the GDL, which belonged to the Radziwiłł family; it housed a Jewish community since the middle of the 17th century. Mir was an important trade center (a yearly marked) and it was one of the meeting places of the Lithuanian Vaad. About Mir see *Słownik geograficzny Królestwa Polskiego*, vol 6, p. 488.

37 AR XXIII, t. 92, p. 7, "Przywilej Karola Stanisława Radziwiłła dla Żydów mirskich", 06.04.1703.

38 Druja was a town in the northern part of the Grand Duchy of Lithuania; in the time under discussion the town belonged to the Sapieha family, see Otto Hendeman: *Dzisna i Druja magdeburskie miasta.* Wilno: Towarzystwo Przyjaciół Nauk: Skład Główny w Księgarni św. Wojciecha 1934.

39 Hendeman: *Dzisna i Druja magdeburskie miasta,* p. 459.

40 Pyzdry was a royal town in the Wielkopolska region it was a well-known economic center. About Pyzdry see: *Słownik geograficzny Królestwa Polskiego,* vol. 9, pp. 332–333.

41 JPP I, 43.

42 Majer Bałaban, one of the most important Jewish historians, invented the name. The term would suggest that the privilege was a Jewish answer to the so called de non tolerandis Iudaeis privileges; however one has to bear in mind the differences between the Jewish and Christian privileges. Barbara Klein: Obrigkeitliche und innerjüdische Quellen: ein untrenbares Miteinander. In: Rolf Kießling / Peter Rauscher / Stefan Rohrbacher (eds): *Räume und Wege jüdischer Geschichte im Alten Reich 1300–1800*, pp. 252–283. For more about the de non tolerandis Judaeis privilege see Jacob Goldberg: De non tolerandis Judaeis. On the Introduction of the Anti-Jewish Laws into Polish Towns and the Struggle against them. In: Shmuel Yeivin (ed.): *Studies in Jewish History. Presented to Professor R. Mahler on his 75th birthday*. Merhavia 1974, pp. 5–51.

Jewish community in Kazimierz (Cracow), which was issued in 1568.[43] By the same token was the privilege given to the community in Vilnius in 1646, which became an integral part of the general privilege for the Lithuanian Jewry several years later.[44] In the light of previous research the privilege was a consequence of some economic and social development. As Sauciunaiute-Verbickiene argued, it was introduced in a time of growing economic crisis that led many Jews to bankruptcy. Thus the Jews were afraid of their Christian debtors, who might have claimed their money in a violent way; therefore, Jews wanted to be safe in their living quarters.[45] However, further reflection casts doubt on this, and thus the economic argumentation seems not to be sufficient. One has to bear in mind the religious regulations as well. It would appear that a close Jewish quarter was significant in the determination of the eruv.

So much can be said in terms of the legal analysis, it has to be stressed that the legal definition of the Jewish living space was ambiguous. It follows that the foundation privileges of Jewish communities very rarely limited Jewish living space. In contrast, both Jews and Christian authorities tried to define a close Jewish quarter. Moreover, sometimes in one place there were contradictory regulations. That brings us to the question of which of the privileges were observed in the daily life of a Jewish community in the small towns of the Polish-Lithuanian Commonwealth. The answer to that is provided by an analysis of inventories of towns. Let's take the example of Biała;[46] in the market square (Rynek) 20 houses belonged to Jews and 18 to Christians. The Jews lived in other streets of the town as well; for instance, there were 6 Jewish houses in Międzyrzecka Street, 14 in Łosicka Street, 7 in Zańcuska Street, and 5 in Zaszkolna Street and Brzeska Street.[47] In all those streets the

43 Heidemarie Petersen: Selbstverständnis einer polnischen Judengemeinde des 16. Jahrhundert: Die Taqanot Qraka aus dem Jahr 1595. In: Christhoph Cluse / Alfred Haverkamp / Israel Yuval (eds): *Jüdische Gemeinden und ihr Christlicher Kontext in kulturräumlich vergleichender Betrachtung.* Hannover: Hahnsche Buchhandlung 2003, pp. 505–512.

44 Maria Cieśla: *Żydzi w Wielkim Księstwie Litewskim*, p. 73.

45 Sauciunaute-Verbickiene: *The Jewish Living Space in the Grand Duchy of Lithuania*, pp. 12–13.

46 Biała (now Biała Podlaska) was one of the main towns in the Radziwiłł estate; it was located in the west part of the Grand Duchy of Lithuania, close to the border with the Kingdom of Poland. A significant number of Jews lived in the town. For more about Biała see Andrzej Rachuba: Biała pod rządami Radziwiłłów w latach 1568–1813. In: Tadeusz Wasilewski / Tadeusz Krawczak (eds): *Z nieznanej przeszłości Białej i Podlasia.* Biała Podlaska: Podlaskie Towarzystwo Społeczno Kulturalne 1990, pp. 37–65. There is no separate research about the Jewish community in Biała.

47 AR XXV, s. 123 "Rewizja generalna placów, gruntów, miasta Białej" 1725.

Jews lived together with Christians; the Jewish houses constituted less than 50% of all houses in each street. By the same token, one can describe the situation in Mir. Here 18 from 44 houses on the main market square (Rynek) were inhabited by Jews in 1720. The majority of Jews lived in other streets together with Christians.[48] It emerges that there was no separated Jewish street in Mir; surprisingly, Cerkiewna Street (sic!), where a synagogue and a Jewish ritual bath stood was only partly inhabited by Jews. As it stands, only 10 of the 21 houses there belonged to Jews in 1747.[49]

Upon closer investigation of different source materials it emerges that Jews shared with Christians not only streets but houses as well. In this connection one has to mention Christian servants, who worked in Jewish houses and inns rented by Jews, etc.[50] It is obvious that in almost all cases Jews shared their houses and flats with Christian servants. At the same time, however, Christian townspeople rented rooms and flats to Jews, and in this way a shared Christian-Jewish living space was created.[51]

Summing up, it must be stressed that in ordinary daily life a distinguishable Jewish living space was not in evidence in the small towns of the Polish-Lithuanian Commonwealth in the 17th and 18th century. The Jews shared their living space with Christians. Following the space definition by Georg Simmel one has to ask whether this living space contributed to the creation of shared social spaces as well.

For the sake of this analysis one has to distinguish several spaces in which Christians and Jews met and were active together. Firstly, it seems that most important were daily neighbourhood contacts. It transpires that close neighbours visited each other and spent evenings together. Often from the depictions of the documented conflicts a picture of normal contact emerges, a case in point being a blood libel trial from Nieśwież from the beginning of the 18th century. In this context one has not to analyse the accusation of someone killing a young woman but concentrate on the testimonies given by the

48 AR XXV, 2448 "Inwentarz Hrabstwa Mirskiego" 1720.

49 AR XXV, 2455/1 "Inwentarz Hrabstwa Mirskiego" 1747.

50 See Jacob Katz: *The "Shabes Goy". A Study in halakhic flexibility.* Philadelphia: Jewish Publ. Society 1989; Jacob Goldberg: *Poles and Jews in the 17th Century*, pp. 248–282; Adam Kaźmierczyk: The Problem of Christian Servants as Reflected in the Legal Codes of the Polish-Lithuanian Commonwealth during the Second Half of the Seventeenth Century and in the Saxon Period. In: *Gal – Ed* 15–16 (1997), pp. 23–40; Judith Kalik: Christian Servants Employed by Jews in the Polish-Lithuanian Commonwealth in the Seventeenth and Eighteenth centuries. In: *Polin* 14 (2001), pp. 259–270; Józef Gierowski: Chrześcijanie a Żydzi w Rzeczypospolitej Obojga Narodów. In: Andrzej K. Link-Lenczowski (ed.): *Na szlakach Rzeczypospolitej w nowożytnej Europie.* Kraków: Księgarnia Akademicka 2008, pp. 617–624.

51 Stefan Gąsiorowski: *Żydzi w Kiejdanach w XVII i XVIII wieku. Rekonesans badawczy*, p. 80.

Christian townspeople; the fact that the accused Jews were neighbours was significant for the Christians. They spoke about visiting their neighbours.[52] It is worth noting that Jews and Christians visited each other surprisingly often. In many court trials or in diaries we can read about Jews and Christians and how they would drink and eat together. An example is provided in a case from Orla where Zelman Beniaminowicz, a local Jew, was at his home together with Antoni Dziesiączuk a local Christian burgher; they drank and spent time together.[53] It is worth noting that the events are described in such a way that it is obvious to the present reader that the people saw this as normal and common.

The second shared space was the market. In order to explain it one has to analyse the professional structure of the Jews. It emerges that the Jews monopolised trade in small towns. For instance in Kleck[54] the Jews possessed 17 of 33 market stalls in the market square in 1694. The Jewish trade dominance was felt much more strongly in the second half of the 18th century; so that in 1760 19 out of 27 market stalls belonged to Jews. A similar development is noted in Dawodgródek; in 1760 the Jews possessed all the market stalls in the town.[55] To take the argument further, one has to pay attention not only to trade but also to lease holdings as well. An interesting picture is gained from the inventory of Birże,[56] where almost 70% of the Jews were active in trade and lease holding in the second half of the 18th century. Finally, there is Kopyl,[57] where,

52 AR XV, t. 6, p. 20, p. 19: "Symon Woroniecki rymarz sąsiad bliski mieszkający u Wolfa często bywający u niego żadnej niewiasty przebywającej i mieszkającej nigdy nie widział"; p. 22: "Pan Andrzej Hermanowicz także akademik pod sumieniem zostający zbierając się do juramentu zeznał, iż na przód będąc niejednokrotnie u Wolfa".

53 AR XXIII, t. 105, p. 1.

54 Kleck was a private town in the Grand Duchy of Lithuania; it belonged to the Radziwiłł family and was known for regular fairs. See *Słownik Geograficzny Królestwa Polskiego,* vol. 4, pp. 122–123.

55 Anatol Hryckiewicz: *Частновладельческие города Белоруссии.* Minsk: Nauka i Tehnika 1975, p. 138.

56 Birże (now Biržai) was located in the northeast part of the Grand Duchy of Lithuania; it was an important trade center on the way to Ryga. About Birże see Eustachy Tyszkiewicz: *Birże. Rzut oka na przeszłość miasta, zamku i ordynacji.* Petersburg 1869. There was a Jewish and a Karaite community; for more about it see Juliusz Bardach: Żydzi w Birżach radziwiłłowskich w XVII–XVIII wieku. In: *Przegląd Historyczny* LXXXI,1–2 (1990), pp. 199–220; Jacob Mann: Texts and Studies in Jewish History and Literature, vol. II. In: *Karaitica.* Philadelphia: Hebrew Press / The Jewish Publication Society in America 1935.

57 Kopyl (now Kapyl) is located in the central part of the Grand Duchy of Lithuania; for more about the city see Kopyl. In: *Słownik Geograficzny Królestwa Polskiego*, vol. 4, p. 386; about the Jewish community see Adam Teller: *Kesef Koach Wehashpaa. Yehudim beahuzot Mishpahat Radziwiłł be Mea 18.* Jerusalem: Merkaz Zalman Shazar 2005, pp. 64–66.

similar to Birże, about 68 % of the Jewish population worked as merchants and leaseholders. It is important to stress that Jewish merchants were the only ones from small towns who reached international markets.[58]

The second very important Jewish profession was lease holding, which meant the running of inns and the selling of alcoholic beverages. A good example is provided by Nieśwież; it appears that more than 50 % of the Jewish population of the town was active in the production and selling of alcoholic beverages in 1628.[59] The tendency was even stronger in the 18th century, although exact data is only available from bigger towns such as Słuck; however, it seems that they are representative for smaller towns as well. Almost all breweries in the town belonged to Jews in 1698[60]; what's more, the Christian townspeople very often complained that all the inns in town belonged to Jews.[61] Last but not least, it is worth mentioning that artisans were less important in the professional structure of the Jewish communities in small towns. It seems that these small groups of artisans produced only for internal Jewish needs. Unsurprisingly, the most significant groups of artisans were butchers and tailors who had to work in accordance with some religious regulations.[62]

The Jewish dominance in the economic life of the small town contributed to the creation of a special space. Due to the fact that Jewish trade activity was concentrated in the main market square and in the main streets of the town, spaces for social integration between Jews and Christians were created. In this context several space levels of contacts can be distinguished.

The first one is the level of merchant-client contact. It is obvious that a Christian had to buy in Jewish shops, and that the Jewish merchants were the only ones who provided some goods. The concentration of Jewish trade activity in the main areas of towns thus meant that trade activity was oriented towards a Christian client. One may suspect that the source materials depicting this kind of contact would be very rich. Nevertheless, it is very difficult to find any information about such contacts. Due to the special features of the sources, those of court records, one is confronted only with descriptions of conflicts. Thus we know that drunken Christians didn't want to pay for their

58 Cieśla: *Żydzi w Wielkim Księstwie Litewskim*, p. 343.

59 AR XXV, s. 2666, "Inwentarz zamku, miasta, dworu, folwarków, ziemian, bojar wszystkiej włości", 1628, 1629.

60 AR XXIII, t. 137, p. 4, s. 115, "Notatia browarów miejskich słuckich", 13.01.1698.

61 AR XXIII, t. 134, p. 1, 349.

62 Cieśla: *Żydzi w Wielkim Księstwie Litewskim*, pp. 366–379.

goods; sometimes they were aggressive and hit Jewish merchants.[63] However, in the majority of cases, transactions were completed without any problems; needless to say that they were not noted in court sources. Only rarely can one find in other kinds of sources a description of positive contact. Such a case is described in the memoirs of Bazyli Rudomicz, a burgher in Zamość. He notes in his diary many times that he bought some goods in Jewish shops; his shopping list is very diverse, starting with food and spices through to clothes, cows and horses. What's more, he recalls a dream of his wife in which her mother told her not to buy anything in Jewish shops.[64]

The second level was the cooperation of Jewish and Christian merchants. It could be reasonably argued that such co-operations were typical of small towns. As opposed to cities where it was less common that Jews and Christians were business partners.[65] However, in small towns different kinds of Jewish-Christian cooperation were depicted. Firstly, Jews and Christians shared trade companies, for instance the cooperation between Filip Kozielicz, an Orthodox priest, and Leyba Izraelowicz, a Słuck Jew. According to an agreement the Jew who possessed a horse had to go to Lwów with a wagon which belonged to the priest and buy some goods. However during the trip Leyba Izraelowicz had a lot of unexpected troubles, resulting in the fact that he finally came home without any products, not to mention the debts he collected on his way.[66] The second characteristic is the cooperation between Jewish merchants and Christian artisans or drivers. An example is provided by a Jew, also from Słuck, who cooperated with Leon Marcinowicz, a Christian who possessed a horse and a wagon.[67]

Mutual trust was the principal factor behind the cooperation of Jews and Christians. As has been argued in previous research, the trust was much more significant than religion or nationality; thus, Jews chose Christians as their partners because they trusted them.[68] One can recall the blood libel

63 Jan Siedlecki: O osadnictwie Żydów w Brańsku i starostwie brańskim. In: *Biuletyn Żydowskiego Instytutu Historycznego* 1–2 (1988), pp. 125–131, p. 129.

64 Bazyli Rudomicz: *Emfemeros czyli diariusz prywatny pisany w Zamościu w latach 1656–1672*, transl. from Latin by Władysław Froch / Marian Lech. Lublin: Klementowski 2002, vol. 1, pp. 68, 106–107.

65 Gershon David Hundert: *Security and Dependence. Perspectives on Seventeenth Century Polish-Jewish Society Gained through a Study of Jewish Merchants in Little Poland*, Phd, Columbia University 1978.

66 LVIA, f. 1280, s. 2070 Księga sądu zadwornego słuckiego, No. 64.

67 LVIA, f. 1280, s. 2070, nr. 11, "Dekret w sprawie Leona Marcinowicza mieszczanina i obywatela słuckiego z Bunimem Szlomowiczem Żydem także słuckim", 06.09.1695.

68 Cornelia Aust: *Commercial Cosmopolitans: Networks of Jewish Merchants between Warsaw and Amsterdam 1750–1820,* PhD thesis, Philadelphia 2010, pp. 126–127.

trial in Nieśwież; it follows that Jews asked their Christian business partners to protect them because, as they argued, they knew one another and they trusted one another.[69] Similar sentences can be found in Christian diaries. For instance Roch Sikorski – a burgher from Bielsk Podlaski[70] – wrote about his friend, somebody who was trustworthy – a Jewish merchant who had a shop in the Market Square in Bielsk.[71]

It has to be borne in mind that, stemming from professional cooperation, mutual trust gave rise to private contacts as well. Doing business meant spending a lot of time together, and speaking and sharing a lot of significant life experiences led in turn to the sharing of their private lives. Let's return to the previously described case of Leyba Izraelowicz; this example can shed new light on the issue of Christian-Jewish economic cooperation. According to the contract that he made with the Orthodox priest at the time when he was travelling to Lwów, his Christian partner had to take care of his wife, who stayed in Słuck. He had to pay her a certain amount of money every week, so it means that he visited her; unfortunately, in the reference material, there is no depiction of such a visit. Nevertheless, it is obvious that the social component was very important in the economic cooperation between Jews and Christian.

Thus the third space level of contact included spending free time together. One of the places for private contacts between Jews and Christians were inns run by Jews. Inn-keeping in towns, as may be recalled, was one of the most important occupations in the professional structure of Jews. It must be taken into consideration that the majority of inns were located in shared Christian-Jewish spaces – for instance, in market squares or on main streets. Surprising as it may seem, there were no inns on the so-called Jewish street. The Christians constituted the majority of clients in Jewish inns; however, Jews went there to spend their evenings as well. Taking into account that in many small towns an inn run by a Jew was the only place where people could meet in the evening, it is not surprising that both Jews and Christian came to the inns. The characteristic features of the reference materials, as may be recalled, allow us

69 Lietuvos Valstybės Istorijos Archyvas (Vilnius), f. 1280, s. 2070, Nr. 11, "Dekret w sprawie Leona Marcinowicza mieszczanina i obywatela słuckiego z Bunimem Szlomowiczem Żydem także słuckim", 06.09.1695.

70 Bielsk Podlaski was a royal town in the border region between the Kingdom of Poland and the GDL. For more information see *Słownik Geograficzny Królestwa Polskiego*, vol. 1, pp. 214–215.

71 Roch Sikorski: *Łyk i kołtuny. Pamiętnik mieszczanina podlaskiego (1790–1816)*. Warszawa: Nakładem Księgarni J. Czarneckiego 1917, p. 35; Teller: *The Shtettel as an Arena for Integration*, p. 37.

to learn about the conflicts in the inns. Nothing could be easier than to demonstrate that Jews and Christians argued in the inns and that conflicts were very brutal. However, it is not surprising that people after consuming alcohol were aggressive. But it seems to be more interesting in this context that Jews and Christians sat and spent time together. It is significant that in the majority of the known court trials, both Jews and Christians were witnesses to the incidents in the inns, and remarkably it is not important what the subject of the conflict was. Jews and Christians equally gave evidence about robberies, rows, and theft.[72] Nevertheless Jews were witnesses and participated in many more sophisticated cases, as for instance in Orla, where some Christians were accused of casting a spell in the inn. It follows that Jews participated in the sorcery.[73] Analysing the conflicts in the inns, one has to pay attention to descriptions of events that led to them. It emerges that before fights Jews and Christians played cards or music together.[74] It is very difficult to gain some information about what Jews and Christians talked about in the inns. Only rarely are such conversations noted in protocols of court trials. An example is provided by a famous case from Rzeszów, described in a previous research by Yvonne Kleinmann; it shows that a serious subject was raised. It follows that a conversation between a Jew and a Christian started with a discussion about local politics and ended with a struggle about Jesus Christ.[75] It seems that local politics and events significant for Jews and Christians, were often discussed in the inns; a similar example is provided by a court trial in which a Christian burgher was accused by Jews of cooperating with the enemy during the Polish-Russian war in the middle of the 17th century. A vibrant discussion depicting the events of the war was held in an inn in Słuck.[76]

It could be reasonably argued that a Jewish innkeeper had a special position in the local community. Due to his work he had an opportunity to get to know all the people living in the town, and thus he was familiar with all events occurring in the Christian community as well as in the Jewish community. The special position of the Jewish innkeeper can be seen in the story told by Roch Sikorski, who was searching for his relatives in another town. Needless

72 LVIA f. 1240, Nr. 55, Dekret z Rozią Izraelówną, 26.11.1697.

73 AR XXIII, t. 105, p. 1, Wyrok sądu zadwornego orlańskiego, 25.02.1733.

74 AR XXIII, t. 105, p. 1, Wyrok sądu zadwornego orlańskiego, 03.03.1739.

75 Yvonne Kleinmann: "Blasphemie" wider den katholischen Glauben? Der Fall eines jüdischen Schankwirts in Polen 1726. In: Dan Diner: *Synchrone Welten. Zeiträume jüdischer Geschichte*. Göttingen: Vandenhoeck & Ruprecht 2005, pp. 37–66.

76 AR XXIII, t. 134, p. 2, p. 211.

to say, his most important advisor and helper was the local Jewish innkeeper. From the story it emerges that he knew everybody in town, and what is more, he used to spend time together with the local elite.[77] It seems that in some cases close contact with a Jewish innkeeper led to friendship. Such a case is described in the diaries of Bazyli Rudomicz, who often spent time in the inn ran by a Jew called Pszczółka. They spoke about different subjects, and in difficult times helped each other. What's more, Rudomicz praised the knowledge and characteristics of his Jewish friend.[78]

To sum up, it needs to be stressed that the mutual economic space led to the creation of different shared spaces. Thus the professional activity of the Jews cannot be seen only from the economic angle. It is important to stress that it had a very significant social component. Therefore the economic activity of Jews led to the creation of shared social Christian-Jewish spaces, and the definition of space formulated by Georg Simmel is then applicable to the situation of the Jews in the early modern Polish-Lithuanian Commonwealth.

One can ask whether the shared Christian-Jewish space in the towns had a special meaning for contemporaries. In order to answer this question, one has to analyse the crisis situations and conflicts. One of the characteristic features of Jewish privileges is that the Jews were responsible for defending the town together with the Christian burghers. This meant that in the case of a war Jews had to participate in the defence in an active way – or by paying a part of the contribution or by participating in fights. In this connection the most common resolution was for the Jews to pay a part of the military tax. In general the tax was divided into two parts – one paid by Christians and the second by Jews; examples are provided by Międzyrzec Podlaski, Opole, Zółkiew and so on.[79] Nevertheless in some places the Jews were members of the town's defending guard, and their duties were different in every town; for instance in Słuck they had to take part in organised military exercises. Furthermore, there was Jewish participation in the fire-fighting guard. As with Christians, they were responsible for protecting the town against fire. For the sake of the present analysis it is more significant that the Jews indeed participated actively in a town's defence. The examples are multiple; for instance it is known that Jews participated actively in the defence of Witebsk in the first half of the

77 Sikorski: *Łyny i kołtuny*, p. 125.

78 Bazyli Rudomicz: *Emfemeros czyli diariusz prywatny*, vol. I, p. 277.

79 JPP I, 31; JPP I, 37; JPP II, 129. In general for more about the Jewish military duties see Maurycy Horn: *Powinności wojenne Żydów w Rzeczypospolitej XVI–XVII wieku.* Warszawa: Państwowe Wydawnictwo Naukowe 1978.

17th century, and they built special gates that protected the town.[80] The situation in Bychów was similar, where several years later the Jews took an active part in the defence of the town. Thus there are certain grounds for supposing that the shared Christian-Jewish space was valuable for their contemporaries. Nevertheless it has to be borne in mind that because of the lack of sufficient source material, it is very difficult to confirm this hypothesis.

Summing up, it is hard to escape the obvious conclusion that in the small towns of the Polish-Lithuanian Commonwealth in the early modern period shared Christian-Jewish spaces existed. Thus it is impossible to analyse the history of the Jewish shtetl without taking into consideration the Christian parts of the shtetl. When seen in this light one could argue that the Christians were significant inhabitants of the Jews' shtetls and the Jews of the Christian small towns.

80 AVAK, vol. 5, p. 73.

The Nature of Jewish Spaces in Ottoman Algiers

Nora Lafi

Introduction

The condition of the Jewish population of Ottoman cities is presently the object of a very stimulating historiographical convergence between research within Jewish Studies that has mostly focused on the inner social and religious life of Jewish communities, studies on urban governance in an Ottoman context that focus on patterns of local old regime municipal life,[1] and studies on cosmopolitanism and the governance of diversity that focus on the specific Ottoman imperial approach to this question.[2] This *aggiornamento*, after decades of academic segmentation between these distinct ways of tackling the question of the Jewish condition in Ottoman cities, began at the end of the 1990s.[3] On the one hand, specialists from Jewish Studies now increasingly take into account Ottoman imperial archives, while on the other hand, specialists from Ottoman Studies increasingly take into account the dimension of social life within confessional communities and acknowledge the importance of the archives of such communities in order to understand not only their inner organisation but also the very nature of the Empire. This

1 Old regime is intended here as the governance system that was elaborated by the Ottomans between the 16th and the 18th centuries and that was reformed during the period of the Tanzimat, starting in the 1830s.

2 For reflection on this subject, see Ulrike Freitag / Nora Lafi: Cosmopolitanism and Conflicts: Changes and Challenges in Ottoman Urban Governance. In: Iid. (eds): *Urban Governance under the Ottomans: Between Cosmopolitanism and Conflict*. London: Routledge 2014, pp. 1–19.

3 See, for example, Eyal Ginio: The Administration of Criminal Justice in Ottoman Selânik (Salonica) during the 18th Century. In: *Turcica* 30 (1998), pp. 185–209; M. Ali Shuman: *Al-yahûd fî Misr al-'uthmâniyya hattâ al-qarn al-tâsi''ashr*. [Jews in Ottoman Egypt up to the 18th c.] Cairo: Al-Hay'a al-Misriyya al-'âmma lil kitâb 2000, p. 261.

is why our perception of the Jewish condition in Ottoman cities has been profoundly renewed.
Between the end of the 15th century and the beginning of the 20th century the Ottoman Empire appears to have been a safe refuge for Jews from various parts of Europe, from Spain to Eastern Europe, the Black Sea or the Balkans, where they were the victims of policies of segregation, expulsion, forced conversion, discrimination and persecution. Ottoman cities from Salonica to Jerusalem, from Istanbul to Medina, from Tunis to Bagdad and from Sarajevo to Alexandria, where local Jewish communities generally existed since ancient times, welcomed new Jewish populations fleeing European persecutions. These new elements were inserted into the framework of the Ottoman governance of diversity, which itself derived from medieval Islamic principles of protection and comprised precise patterns of communal autonomy.[4] In all those cities, the Jews were a fundamental component of urban life. Their existence as a community was acknowledged at the level of the Empire.[5] From at least the reign of Mehmed II (1451–1481) there was a Jewish Millet in the Empire, a specific institutional organisation dedicated to non-Muslim populations.[6] The Jews, just like the Armenians and the Greeks, constituted a collective body at the scale of the Empire, headed by the figure of the *Hakham-Bashi*, or Chief Rabbi. This figure was the representative of the Jewish communities of the Empire in front of the Sultan, and was in charge of the coordination of the collection of imperial taxes within the Jewish communities. On the basis of the medieval Islamic concept of *dhimmi*, the Millet took the form of a contract of protection between Muslim rulers and the Peoples of the Book (*ahl al-kitâb*).[7] This contract organised the relationships between confessional communities as well as between such communities that paid a specific tax, and the established power. The term minority was not used at that time. And in many cities and villages of the Empire, the

4 See Abdelwahab Medded / Benjamin Stora (eds): *A History of Jewish-Muslim Relations from the Origins to Present Day*. Princeton: Princeton UP 2013, p. 1152.

5 See Yaron Ben-Naeh: *Jews in the Realm of the Sultans. Ottoman Jewish Society in the 17th Century*. Tübingen: Mohr Siebeck 2008, p. 503; Aryeh Shmuelevitz: *The Jews of the Ottoman Empire in the Late 15th and the 16th Centuries*. Leiden: Brill 1984. See also Robert Olson: Jews in the Ottoman Empire in Light of New Documents. In: *Jewish Social Studies* 41,1 (1979), pp. 41–51, 75–88 ; as well as the classic work by Moïse Franco: *Essai sur l'histoire des Israélites de l'Empire Ottoman depuis les origines jusqu'à nos jours*. Paris: Durlacher 1897.

6 See Bülent Şenay: Communal Autonomy of the Jewish 'Millet' in the Ottoman Turkish Tradition. In: *Studia Hebraica* 6 (2006), pp. 75–86.

7 For an insight on current debates on this concept: Anver Emon: *Religious Pluralism and the Islamic Law: Dhimmis and Others in the Empire of Law*. Oxford: Oxford UP 2012, p. 384.

Muslims were not a majority. Non-Muslim religious practices were authorized, as well as the construction of religious buildings. Confessional communities were given a high degree of autonomy for the governance of their internal affairs.[8] Most topics pertaining to justice were dealt with inside this communal system.[9] Jews were granted a precise legal and fiscal status. This status was in no way a form of equality, a concept not present in the old regime institutional organization in any case. This status comprised a certain number of limitations, pertaining to the symbolical dimension, for example the imposition of specific dress codes[10], the prohibition of riding horses and wearing weapons, and pertaining to the professional sphere, for example in the limitation of their access to certain professions. But this did not prevent Jews from being important figures at the court of the Sultan, sometimes even councillors and ministers. The specific taxation system to which Jews were subject does not show obvious signs of systematic overtaxation.[11] But at various occasions, generally at the scale of specific cities or provinces, Jews were obliged to pay exceptional taxes. Nonetheless, rich Muslim merchants were also regularly submitted to such exceptional taxes.

In spite of the existence of a unique Jewish Millet, one should not have an excessively homogeneous image of the Jewish condition and identity in the Ottoman Empire. At the scale of the Empire there was a great diversity of local Jewish communities. These communities comprised peoples of different ethnic, linguistic and cultural backgrounds. Jews of Germanic, Spanish, Italian, Anatolian, Greek, Berber and Arabic culture, among others, were present in the Empire. There was neither spiritual unity or similarity of worship practices nor spiritual unity. In order to reflect this diversity, the Jewish Millet was constituted of four distinct entities: Rabbinism, Karaism, Askenazim and Sepharadism.[12] The extension of the Empire towards North Africa (and policies of ethnic and religious cleansing in Christian Europe) reinforced this diversity.[13]

8 See Najwa Al-Qattan: Dhimmis in the Muslim Court: Legal Autonomy and Religious Discrimination. In: *International Journal of Middle-East Studies* 31,3 (1999), pp. 429–444.

9 Halil Inalcik: Foundations of Ottoman-Jewish Cooperation. In: Avigdor Levy (ed.): *Jew, Turks, Ottomans: A Shared History*. Syracuse: Syracuse UP 2002, pp. 3–14.

10 Betül Ipsirli Argit: Clothing Habits, Regulations and Non-Muslims in the Ottoman Empire. In: *Journal of Academic Studies* 6,24 (2005), pp. 79–96.

11 See Ben-Naeh: *Jews in the Realm of the Sultans*, pp. 150–154.

12 On the latter dimension: Avigdor Levy: *The Sephardim in the Ottoman Empire*. Princeton: Darwin 1992.

13 See Norman Stillman: *The Jews of Arab Lands*. Philadelphia: Jewish Publication Society 1979.

The object of the present article is to analyse the relationship between the Jewish community and the urban space as illustrated by the case of the city of Algiers, one of the main Ottoman harbours on the North African coast. Algiers was an Ottoman city between 1516 and 1830. It became such after the Greek corsair Barbarossa who had converted to Islam had defeated the Spanish who controlled Algiers and several other ports on the Southern Mediterranean coast. Barbarossa had been a corsair for the Ottoman navy for decades, operating between Izmir, Lesbos and the Italian coasts. He had settled in La Goulette near Tunis a few years earlier and had worked at reinforcing the Ottoman naval presence in the Western Mediterranean.[14] When he seized Algiers, the aim was to insert this city into the Ottoman imperial sphere as well as the territory it was the capital of. The struggle with Spain for the control over the city and the neighbouring waters lasted for another couple of decades, but in 1541, with the defeat of Charles V who had tried to besiege Algiers, Ottoman sovereignty over the city was consolidated. It was to last until French colonisation in 1830.[15]

The Jews of Algiers: Diversity and Identity

The history of the Jews of Algiers before the French colonisation has not been studied in great detail. Most studies address the period of the French colonisation.[16] Moreover, as the majority of available accounts (archives, travellers' reports, enquiries) on the Jewish condition in Algiers date back to the beginning of the colonial era, when systematically negative views on the Ottoman period were published in the framework of the promotion of the new colonial organisation, it is quite difficult to acquire a balanced portrayal of Ottoman times. For such a portrayal, paying greater attention to Ottoman archives, local communal archives and accounts by travellers of the 17th and 18th centuries, as well as by former prisoners who had lived in the city for a certain time, can help scholars to deconstruct or at least critically examine the dominant discourse in historiography that was inherited from the colonial

14 See Sander Rang / Ferdinand Denis (eds): *Histoire de la Régence d'Alger*. Paris: Angé 1837, p. 241.

15 See Henri Delmas de Grammont: *Histoire d'Alger sous la Domination Turque*. Paris: Leroux 1887, p. 461. For a general presentation of the period, see Jamil Abun-Nasr: *A History of the Maghrib in the Islamic Period*. Cambridge: Cambridge UP 1987, p. 455.

16 For a general presentation see: Benjamin Stora *Les Trois Exils des Juifs d'Algérie*. Paris: Stock 2006, p. 240. For the Ottoman period, see: Ali Tabilat: Yahûd al-Jazayir fi al-fitra al-'uthmaniyya (1516–1830). In: *Arab Historical Review for Ottoman Studies* 11,12 (1995), pp. 167–185.

period. Ottoman Algiers in general, not only as for its Jewish history, suffers from this kind of bias. As Joshua Schreier states, the rhetoric of the 'civilizing mission' France claimed to be enacting when colonising the Ottoman province of Algeria insisted on describing local Jews as backward and oppressed.[17] A whole literature describing the Jews as dirty, unorganised and subject to the arbitrary domination of the 'Turks' developed in these times.[18] This vision of the Ottoman past didn't alter significantly during the 130 years of French rule. The Ottoman period in general remained largely unknown or viewed through a very negative lens.[19] The very Ottoman identity of the former imperial province was constantly underestimated. Even after the end of colonisation, most of the nationalist historiography of the new Algerian state reproduced colonial representations of the Ottoman period. For its part, Jewish Studies mainly focused on the colonial period with little attention to the Ottoman one. This inertia of interpretative paradigms inherited from colonial times has long delayed the convergence between Ottoman Studies and Jewish Studies that was becoming more common elsewhere. Contrary to what happened in cities like Salonica, Istanbul, Alexandria or Jerusalem, where this kind of convergence began to produce historiographical results, the case of Algiers has long remained understudied. But new impulses in the practice of the historical profession and in the dialogue between specialists of various themes and periods have now begun to modify this situation.[20]

Just like in numerous cities of the Empire, there were many Jews in Ottoman Algiers: they represented about 20 % of the local population. The strong urban character of the Jewish population of the Algerian province in general (80 % of the Algerian Jews lived in cities, against only 5 % of the Algerian Muslims)[21] resulted in the fact that cities were strongholds of Jewish

17 Joshua Schreier: *Arabs of the Jewish Faith: The Civilizing Mission in Colonial Algeria*. Piscataway: Rutgers UP 2010.

18 For example, Johanny Pharaon / Emmanuel Goldscheider: Lettre sur l'état des juifs de l'Algérie et sur les moyens de les tirer de l'abjection dans laquelle ils sont tombés. In: *Archives Israélites de France* 1 (1840), pp. 477–480.

19 As illustrations of this literature see Walsin Esterhazy: *De la Domination Turque dans l'Ancienne Régence d'Alger*. Paris: Gossilin 1840, p. 325; Delmas de Grammont: *Histoire d'Alger sous la Domination Turque*, p. 458.

20 See Anne Hélène Hoog: Garder la mémoire, montrer l'histoire: Sur les traces du judaïsme d'Algérie. In: Ead. (ed.): *Juifs d'Algérie*. Paris: Skira-Musée d'histoire du judaïsme 2012, pp. 17–25. See also Schreier: *Arabs of the Jewish Faith*.

21 Jacques Taïeb: Les Juifs du Maghreb au XIXe siècle. Aperçus de démographie historique et répartition géographique. In: *Population* 47,1 (1992), pp. 85–103. See also Henri Garrot: *Les Juifs Algériens*. Alger: Relin 1898, p. 71.

identity. In the 18th century, there were communities of at least 4,000 people in Constantine and of 3,000 in Tlemcen as well as important communities in cities like Medea, Mostaganem, Blida, Cherchell and Mascara.[22] The city of Oran was an exception: it remained under Spanish control during most of the Ottoman period in the rest of Algeria.[23] Initially Jews were not expelled, but in 1669 they were forced to leave and took refuge in Algiers, Constantine and sometimes the Tuscan harbour of Livorno.[24]

In Algiers, there were about 1,000 Jews at the time of its integration into the Ottoman Empire. This figure grew to 9,000 during the 17th century, to 12,000 around the year 1700 and possibly 20,000 in 1725.[25] It then declined to 6,500 in 1830, following the economic crisis the city was affected by in the context of the end of the Mediterranean privateering and conflicts with France and the US.[26] The Jewish population of Algiers was very diverse[27] and reflected the diversity of the Jewish population of the Algerian province in general.[28] First, there were the Jews from the continental regions of North Africa: mostly converted Berbers who had been there since ancient times, between the Sahara desert, the Sahel and the mountains of the inner parts of the province. Many of them belonged to the Hanensha tribe and had been connected to trans-Saharian and Mediterranean trade networks since the Middle Age.[29] Although they were also present in the main cities including Algiers, from a demographic point of view, however, this group of Jews was not

22 Taïeb: Les Juifs du Maghreb au XIXe siècle. See also Louis Durieu: *Les Juifs Algériens*. Paris: Cerf 1902, p. 502. On the case of Tlemcen, see Susan Slyomovics: The Geographies of Jewish Tlemcen. In: *The Journal of North-African Studies* 5,4 (2000), pp. 81–96.

23 See Vahran Oran / Mustafa Budak et al.: *Osmanli Belgelerinde: Cezayir*. Ankara: DAGM 2010, p. 30; Richard Ayoun: Les Juifs d'Oran avant la conquête française. In: *Revue Historique* 267,2 (1982), pp. 375–390.

24 Jean-Frédéric Schaub: *Les Juifs du Roi d'Espagne: Oran 1509–1669*. Paris: Hachette 1999, p. 240.

25 Haim Zeev Hirschberg: *A History of the Jews of North Africa. From the Ottoman Conquests to the Present Time*. Leiden: Brill 1981, pp. 7–10. For a compilation of all the available figures on the population of the city in Ottoman times: Federico Cresti: *Alger à la Période Turque: Obervations et Hypothèses sur sa Population et sa Structure Sociale*. In: ROMM *(Revue de l'Occident Musulman et de la Méditerranée)* 44 (1987), pp. 124–133.

26 See Lemnouar Merouche: *Recherches sur l'Algérie à l'Époque Ottomane: la Course, Mythe et Réalités*. Saint-Denis: Bouchène 2007, p. 353. See also Salvatore Bono: *Corsari nel Mediterraneo*. Milan: Mondadori 1993, p. 243.

27 See Hirschberg: *A History of the Jews in North Africa*. See also Richard Ayoun / Bernard Cohen: *Les Juifs d'Algérie: 2000 Ans d'Histoire*. Alger: Rahma 1994.

28 Nora Lafi: Etre juif dans l'Algérie ottomane. In: Hoog (ed.): *Juifs d'Algérie*, pp. 68–81.

29 See Michel Abitbol: *Communautés Juives et Marges Sahariennes du Maghreb*. Jerusalem: Institut Ben Zvi 1982.

dominant. Indeed, the Jewish population of Algiers had been growing considerably towards the end of the Middle Ages under the effect of migrations from Europe. As Laugier de Tassy, a French Officer of the Dutch army, who had been a prisoner in Algiers for some years, stated in a 1725 account, "le plus grand nombre vient de ceux qui ont été chassés de l'Europe: de l'Italie en 1342, des Païs-Bas en 1350, de France en 1403, de l'Angleterre en 1422 et d'Espagne en 1462".[30] The Jews from the Iberian Peninsula represented the most populous group.[31] The number of Jews who took refuge in North Africa following the wave of persecutions in post-Reconquista Spain is still the object of historiographical debates, but what is sure is that in Algiers their arrival transformed the identity of the local Jewish community. Many Jews from Spain belonged to the elite of guilds: they brought their skills and networks to North Africa. They also brought with them the Al-Andalus cultural tradition. Muslims from the Iberian Peninsula also took refuge in the city. At the time of the integration of Algiers into the Ottoman Empire, Andalusian Jews constituted a relatively new group in urban society but they nevertheless had already provided the local Jewish community with a new cultural identity.[32]

With the integration into the Ottoman Empire, a new phase of Jewish migrations into the cities of the coast, including Algiers, took place. Belonging to the Empire was seen as a guarantee of security, as well as of insertion into dynamic commercial networks. Numerous Moroccan Jews came to Algiers during this period. Jews from the Mzab region in southern Algeria also reinforced their presence in Algiers. Yet there was also a further category of Jews during the Ottoman period: those coming from Livorno.[33] Most of them were descendants of those Algerian Jews who had migrated to Tuscany following their expulsion from Oran by the Spanish crown in 1669, and Algiers had always been part of their commercial horizons. During the Ottoman period, a whole Mediterranean network of Italian Jews developed in North

30 Laugier de Tassy: *Histoire du Royaume d'Alger*. Amsterdam: Du Sauzet 1725, p. 74. "Most of them had been expelled from Europe. From Italy in 1342, from the Netherlands in 1350, from France in 1403, from England in 1422 and from Spain in 1462".

31 See Michel Abitbol: Juifs d'Afrique du Nord et expulsés d'Espagne après 1492. In: *Revue de l'Histoire des Religions* 210,1 (1993), pp. 49–90.

32 Henri Kamen: The Mediterranean and the Expulsion of Spanish Jews in 1492. In: *Past and Present* 119 (1998), pp. 30–55. For a comparison with the Tunisian case: Ahmad al-Hamrouni: *Al-hijrât al-Andalousiyya ilâ al-balâd al-tûnisiyya* [The Andalusian Migration in Tunisia]. Tunis: Mediyacom 2009.

33 On this category: Jean-Pierre Filippini: Les négociants juifs de Livourne et la mer au XVIIIe siècle. In: *Revue Française d'Histoire d'Outre-mer* 87,326–327 (2000), pp. 83–108.

Africa, sometimes with the consequence of becoming French or British *protégés* in order to escape Ottoman fiscality. This diversity of the local Jewry was visible in all aspects of urban life. As Laugier de Tassy stated, "chaque nation a ses tribus et ses synagogues".[34] There were also huge social and cultural differences between all parts of the Jewish population. But they all participated in the constitution of a civic sphere which was both distinct from that of other confessional communities and simultaneously integrated into the general Ottoman system of local governance.

Communal Governance and Commercial Activities

In Algiers, as in all other cities of the Ottoman Empire, the Jews were granted a status of communal civic autonomy. The Ottoman imperial system not only tolerated this communal autonomy, but also used it as one of its basic structures of local governance. Jewish communal institutions were both fully integrated into the imperial system and yet genuinely autonomous. There was little interference with communal affairs and a great respect for communal identity. The city itself was governed not only by a local ruler embodying with a certain degree of autonomy the prerogatives of the central Ottoman state, but also by a series of local institutions of old regime nature emanating from the local notability. Just like in Tunis and Tripoli, a chief of the city (*sheikh al-balad*), generally a notable from one of the most powerful Muslim families, headed the various institutions of local governance. He chaired the council of notables and had competence over markets, urban space, street security, local taxes and in general all urban affairs pertaining to the Islamic concept of good governance, the *Hisba.*[35] The Ottoman Empire reinforced these prerogatives of medieval origins by integrating them into the general scheme of imperial governance under the form of a kind of pact of imperiality between urban notables and the central government. There were also local institutions of governance at the scale of the streets, neighbourhoods and professional guilds. In this framework, Jews were fully integrated. They had their own chiefs in their streets and neighbourhoods and their chief was part of the council of notables. This figure, as urban chronicles testify, took part

34 De Tassy: *Histoire du Royaume d'Alger*, p. 74. "Each nation has its own tribes and its own synagogues".

35 See Michael Cook: *Commanding Right and Forbidding Wrong in Islamic Thought.* Cambridge: Cambridge UP 2000; Ellis Goldberg: Private Goods, Public Wrongs and Civil Society in Some Medieval Arab Theory and Practice. In: Ellis Goldberg / Reşat Kasaba / Joel S. Migdal (eds): *Rules and Rights in the Middle-East: Democracy, Law and Society.* Washington: University of Washington Press 1993, pp. 248–271.

in all deliberations of urban nature and his seal can be found along with those of Muslim notables on numerous petitions that the urban civic body sent to Istanbul in case of conflict with the local ruler.[36] Jewish individuals, just like all Ottoman subjects of all faiths, could also send individual petitions to the Sultan. The Jewish institutions of communal autonomy were placed under the responsibility of a *Muqaddam*. This figure had civic, judicial, deliberative and religious functions. As Laugier de Tassy states for the year 1725, "dans chaque ville, ils ont des juges de leur nation pour leurs affaires particulières et de peu de conséquence. Mais lorsque les parties ne sont pas contentes des décisions de leur juge, elles portent leur cause devant la justice turque, qui décide souverainement et fait exécuter les jugements".[37] Communal justice represented both, an internal chamber of social regulation dealing with worship practices, family, property and commercial affairs inside the community, and a lower grade of criminal justice for the members of the community. But recourse to the general system of justice was always possible. In fact, it was mandatory as soon as a Muslim was part of the dispute.

The fiscal status of the Jews was specific and different from that of the rest of the population: the Jewish community had to pay taxes as a collective body whereas Muslim subjects were taxed individually. It was the task of the communal institutions to distribute the fiscal burden among its members. This status however was not necessarily discriminatory as such. The Jews represented about 20% of the population and paid about 25% of the taxes, a figure which, as it comprises the taxes of some of the most important trade companies of the city, is not evident of fiscal discrimination.[38]

As for their activities, the Jews were mostly involved in trade and commerce. Indeed, recent historiography invites a more nuanced reconsideration of the stereotype of Jews involved predominantly in money lending.[39] For religious

36 *See* Nora Lafi: Petitions and Accommodating Urban Change in the Ottoman Empire. In: Elisabeth Özdalga / M. Sait Özervarlı / Feryal Tansug (eds): *Istanbul as Seen from a Distance: Centre and Provinces in the Ottoman Empire, Istanbul.* Istanbul: Swedish Research Institute 2011, pp. 73–82.

37 De Tassy: *Histoire du Royaume d'Alger*, p. 75. "In each city they have judges of their own nation for their private affairs. But when one of the parts involved does not agree with the decision of the judge, it can bring its cause in front of the Turkish justice that decides in full sovereignty and has decisions implemented".

38 See Miriam Hoexter: La Taxation des Corporations Professionnelles d'Alger à l'Époque Turque. In: *ROMM* 36 (1983), pp. 19–39. See also Abraham Cahen: Les Juifs dans l'Afrique Septentrionale. In: *Recueil des Notices et Mémoires de la Société Archéologique de Constantine* 11 (1867), pp. 102–207.

39 Haim Gerber: Jews and Money-Lending in the Ottoman Empire. In: *The Jewish Quarterly Review* 72,2 (1981), pp. 100–118.

and cultural reasons, this activity was of course specific of the Jews, but often limited compared to the main activities of their houses of commerce. What remains true however is the fact that Jews, at the scale of the Empire and at the local scale in Algiers, were the actors of a huge development of the field of investment. They were also very active in the administration of the Ottoman customs as well as in the farming of some imperial and local taxes.

The Jews of Algiers also played an important role in the organisation of commerce.[40] They constituted one of the main elements of the dynamic of commercial growth Algiers experienced in Ottoman times and took part in all the aspects of this growth, including slave trade and the exploitation of the benefits of privateering.[41] They often shared houses of commerce with Muslim traders.[42] But their network was specific: they were in contact with other Jewish houses of commerce in the Empire and beyond. The example of the intercontinental trade of ostrich feather between the Sahara, various Ottoman provinces, Europe and then America illustrates this dynamic.[43] Feather was the main export material for the port of Algiers. Jewish trade networks did not only represent the continuation of medieval trade routes: they were part of the invention of new imperial Ottoman trade routes after the inclusion of the Ottoman West into the Empire. This imperial Ottoman dimension of the trading activities of the Jews of Algiers is central to understanding their role in commerce.[44]

The Jews of Algiers were also very active in the effort to insert Ottoman trade into Mediterranean networks, predominantly in Livorno, but also Marseille, the Black Sea, Scandinavia and the Atlantic. The same families often had representatives in various Mediterranean ports like Salonica, Livorno, Istanbul or Alexandria[45]. They later extended these networks to Great Britain, the

40 See Mohamed Amine: Les commerçants à Alger à la veille de 1830. In: *Revue d'Histoire Maghrébine* 77–78 (1995), pp. 11–112.

41 See Raed Bader: L'esclavage dans l'Algérie coloniale (1830–1870). In: *Revue d'Histoire Maghrébine* 26 (1999), pp. 57–69.

42 Mohamed Amine: Rapports entre commerçants musulmans et *dhimmis* dans le commerce d'Alger (début XIXe s.). In: Daniel Panzac (ed.): *Histoire économique de l'Empire ottoman et de la Turquie*. Louvain: Peeters 1995, pp. 99–105. See also Rachida Yacine: The Economic and Political Roles of the Jewish Minority in Algiers at the Beginning of the 19th Century. In: *Arab Historical Review for Ottoman Studies* 5,6 (1992), pp. 123–133.

43 Sarah Abrevaya Stein: Mediterranean Jewries and Global Commerce in the Modern Period: On the Trail of the Jewish Feather Trade. In: *Jewish Social Studies* 13,2 (2007), pp. 1–39.

44 See David Cesarani (ed.): *Port Jews: Jewish Communities in Cosmopolitan Maritime Trading Centers (1550–1950)*. London: Cass 2002.

45 On the Jews of Alexandria, see: Gudrun Krämer, The Jews in Modern Egypt. London: I. B. Tauris 1989 p. 319.

U.S. and South America. Marriage strategies were central to this collective building of a trade network. But the Jews of Algiers were not only active in commercial and financial professions such as trade, investment and money lending. Many of them were also members of multi-confessional guilds of artisans.[46] A few guilds were dominated by the Jews. There was a great social differentiation within the Jewish community. But contrary to the image that was given during colonial times for the sake of the promotion of the new system of communal organisation, there was an intense communal life inside the Jewish community, or more precisely inside its various components. The Jewish community had strong institutions of charity, teaching and sociability.[47] All these institutions played an important role in the fashioning of a distinct Jewish space in Ottoman Algiers.

Jewish Spaces: The *Hara* and the City

The urban morphology of Algiers in Ottoman times was that of a walled old regime city built on a hill, in which the medieval structure had been partly transformed by several programmes of Ottoman urbanism. This urbanism had multiple effects on the built environment and city landscape, for example by enlarging the main market areas and the area of the harbour.[48] New administrative buildings were built during the period, as well as numerous new structures designed to fortify the city.[49] The city had about 100,000 inhabitants at the beginning of the 18th century. Laugier de Tassy indicates there were about 5,000 Jewish houses in 1725: "L'on compte environ 100,000 habitants dans la Ville, y compris 5,000 maisons ou familles juives originaires de Barbarie".[50] Jews had the right to own property. They could also use the system of the endowment (*waqf* and *habus*) in order to retain and preserve properties in the

46 Hoexter: La Taxation des Corporations Professionnelles d'Alger à l'Époque Turque.

47 See Najwa Toubal: *Tâ'ifât al-yahûd bi-mujtama' madînat al-jayzâ'ir mâ bayn 1700–1800* [The Jewish Community in the Cities of Algeria (1700–1800)]. Cairo: Dâr al-Churûq 2009.

48 See Tal Shuval: *La Ville d'Alger à la Fin du XVIIIe Siècle: Population et Cadre Urbain*. Paris: Centre National de la Recherche Scientifique 1998. *For a comparison with the case of Tunis: Ahmed Saadaoui: Tunis Ville Ottomane: Trois Siècles d'Urbanisme et d'Architecture. Tunis: Centre de Publications Universitaires 2001*. On the medieval structure see: Patrice Cressier / Mercedes Garcia Arenal (eds): *Genèse de la Ville Islamique en al-Andalus et au Maghreb Occidental.* Madrid: Casa Velazquez 1998.

49 See Federico Cresti: Description et iconographie de la ville d'Alger au XVIe siècle. In: *ROMM* 33–34 (1982), pp. 1–22.

50 De Tassy: *Histoire du Royaume d'Alger*, p. 166. "There are about 100,000 inhabitants in the city, including 5,000 Jewish households or families originating from Barbaria".

long term[51]. With the exception of those perceived as Jews from Livorno, they were theoretically required to live in the Jewish neighbourhood, the *hara*: "Les Juifs Maures ont un quartier assigné pour leur demeure et il ne leur est pas permis de se mêler parmi les Mahometans, comme il est libre aux autre Nations. Mais les Juifs européens peuvent se loger où ils veulent: aussi se distinguent-ils des autres, et ne demeurent-ils jamais dans leur quartier".[52] The *hara* was the heart of Jewish life in the city. It was situated inside the city walls and was in no way a closed space. It was fully integrated to the urban fabric. Some streets had doors that were closed at night, but this feature of security regulation was also present in all other neighbourhoods. The medieval *hara* was extended several times during the Ottoman period, responding to the needs of a growing population. It was said to have only about 150 houses in the 1520s, a figure that grew up to 5,000 two centuries later. A new Ottoman Jewish neighbourhood in the Mellahin quarter, near Bab-el-Oued, was also established. There were also numerous mixed quarters in which Jews lived. The rich merchants lived in neighbourhoods also inhabited by rich Muslim merchants. In contrast, there were also poor Jews working and living in the houses of richer Muslims. Each quarter had its own synagogue. Very often such buildings were the expression of the euergetism of rich Jewish notables within a given community.

The Jews of Algiers were entitled to take part in all urban activities and were fully part of urban society. They were subject, however, to a specific and discriminatory dress code. As Laugier de Tassy states, "Ils sont obligés d'être habillés de noir depuis les pieds jusqu'à la tête, pour les distinguer par une couleur que les turcs méprisent".[53] During most of the Ottoman period, however, the dress code was not enforced strictly and the Jews who dressed in black were mostly those of strong religious observance. It seems that most merchants and artisans had a looser interpretation of the dress code. Meanwhile, Jews from Livorno could dress freely: "Il leur est aussi permis d'aller habillez à leur manière, et on les nomme ordinairement les Juifs francs. Le peuple les appelle communément les Juifs chrétiens, à cause de la conformité

51 See Tal Shuval: La pratique de la mu'awada à Alger au 18e siècle. In: *Revue du Monde Musulman et de la Méditerranée* (*REMMM*) 79 (1996), pp. 55–72.

52 De Tassy: *Histoire du Royaume d'Alger*, p. 77. "Moorish Jews are obliged to reside in their own neighbourhood. They are not allowed to live in the middle of the Mahometans as other Nations can do. But European Jews can reside wherever they wish: that's why they never live in their quarter".

53 Ibid., p. 75. "They have to dress in black, from the feet to the head. This colour, that the Turks despise, is their mark".

de leurs habits. Les femmes juives sont habillées comme les Maures des villes et aussi proprement qu'elles veulent".[54]

If there were distinct Jewish spaces, such as within the *hara*, in front of the main synagogues and Jewish schools and around the seats of the main Jewish houses of commerce, there was nonetheless a pattern of constant interactions in daily life between the Jewish and the Muslim population. They used the same urban amenities, largely fountains, ovens and public baths, and they shared many common activities. They also shared the same language, Arabic, as well as the same kind of habitat. Studies have illustrated how Jewish domestic interiors were not fundamentally different from Muslim ones.[55] In the mixed neighbourhoods it was not uncommon that Jews and Muslims share the same building for a house.[56] Many Jewish children attended Quranic schools in order to secure a high competence in the writing of the Arabic language. There were also common female sociabilities on the roofs and terraces of the city and in the yards, as Jewish and Muslim women socialised while cooking, washing and beautifying themselves. Jews were generally invited to all Muslim religious festivals, including weddings. The same was true vice versa, as most Jewish religious festivals ended with a meal shared with Muslim neighbours and colleagues. Many professional sociabilities were common, particularly in the world of guilds.[57]

However, there were, of course, many tensions in the urban space involving the condition of Jews, in this society of old regime which was ordered with respect to difference and did not promote equality. Symbolic vexations were not uncommon, like the fact of having to give priority to 'Turks' in the line in front of a fountain for example, as well as during occasions of conflict. But this dimension was carefully regulated, in the framework of what appears to be a genuine expression of Ottoman cosmopolitanism: not only the coexistence of different confessional communities, but also the participation of non-Muslims to the sphere of civic governance. In the case of Algiers, the crucial issue was whether this manifestation of old regime Ottoman regulation could be reformed so as to promote equality. But this was never given

54 Ibid. "They can dress the way they want. People call them the Frank Jews. People also call them commonly the Christian Jews, because they dress like Christians. Jewish Women are dressed like urban Moorish women and in the most appropriate way they want".

55 Jacques Taïeb: *Être Juif au Maghreb à la veille de la colonisation*. Paris: Albin Michel 1994, p. 113.

56 See Sakina Missoum: *Alger à l'époque ottomane: la Médina et la maison traditionnelle*. Alger: INAS 2003.

57 See Jean-Louis Miège: *Les Relations entre Juifs et Musulmans en Afrique du Nord (XIXe–XXe s.)*. Paris: Centre National de la Recherche Scientifique 1982.

the chance to be addressed, contrary to what happened in cities that remained under Ottoman control until the 20th century. In Algiers, colonisation happened as early as in 1830, before the advent of the imperial reformist effort of the next decades.

Conclusion

This renewed perception of Jewish urban life in Ottoman times invites a revision of judgments about the colonial period, which in Algiers started with the 1830 French conquest of the city. The rhetoric of the 'civilizing' mission of French colonisation tended to alter the perception of Ottoman times. So too did the necessity of promoting the new system of ordering Jewish communities that was introduced by the French, on the consistorial model.[58] The fact that in Ottoman times Jews were not only part of the imperial framework of governance, but also an essential element of the economic vitality of the region, invites us to reflect on the transition to what is perceived as modernity. In Algiers, the reforms of the 19th century came under a colonial and highly ambiguous form. The question of the granting of a status of 'equality' to the Jews by French colonial authorities is central in this respect. Indeed, equality was with the colonial settlers, and not the rest of the Algerian population.[59] It granted the Jews of Algiers a more extensive access to the civic sphere, while at the same time excluding Algerian Muslims from this very sphere. This biased reform introduced a new fracture between the Jews and the rest of the Algerian population. It had severe consequences with respect to the transformation of live experience within urban space. Many Jewish families joined the so-called 'European' city, which was progressively built on the ruins of part of the old city, destroyed by the French between 1830 and 1832, on the one hand and beyond the limits of the former walled city on the other.[60] André

58 See Morton Rosenstock: The Establishment of the Consistorial System in Algeria. In: *Jewish Social Studies* 18,1 (1956), pp. 41–54.

59 See Martine Cohen: Les déclinaisons historiques du franco-judaïsme et ses critiques contemporaines. In: *Archives des Sciences Sociales des Religions* 144 (2008), pp. 141–161; André Chouraqui: *Les Juifs d'Afrique du Nord*. Paris: Puf 1952, pp. 99–101. See also Joëlle Allouche-Benayoun: Les enjeux de la naturalisation des Juifs d'Algérie. In: Jean-Pierre Luizard (ed.): *Le choc colonial et l'Islam*. Paris: La Découverte 2006, pp. 179–195. As an illustration of the debates of the 1860s that led to the decision: C. Frégier: *Les Juifs Algériens: Leur passé, leur présent, leur avenir juridique, leur naturalisation collective*. Paris: Lévy 1863.

60 See André Raymond: Le centre d'Alger en 1830. In: *Revue de l'Occident Musulman et de la Méditerranée* 31,1(1981), pp. 73–84. See also: Zeynep Çelik: *Urban Forms and Colonial Confrontations: Algiers under French Rule*. Berkeley: University of California Press 1997, and Hélène Vacher (ed.):

Raymond states that among the first buildings that were destroyed by the French during the very first weeks and months of their occupation were the 'barracks' of Jewish artisans.[61] Many small synagogues were also destroyed. The Jewish *hara* was deeply damaged by this first phase of colonial urbanism. It was only in 1845 that a new phase began in the relationship between the colonizers and Algerian Jews, with the construction of a monumental synagogue.[62] The proximity of daily life between Jews and Muslims tended to be less common, and many shared spaces at the micro-urban scale gradually disappeared. But many others remained, however, still revolving around shared practices of sociability, such as cooking and music, until the exile of 1962, when after the Algerian independence most Algerian Jews had to leave the country.[63]

Villes Coloniales aux XIXe-XXe Siècles: d'un Sujet d'Action à un Objet d'Histoire (Algérie, Maroc, Libye et Iran). Paris: Essais et guide bibliographique. Maisonneuve & Larose 2006.

61 André Raymond: Le centre d'Alger en 1830. In: *Revue de l'Occident Musulman et de la Méditerranée* 31,1 (1981), pp. 73–81.

62 Valérie Assan: Les Synagogues dans l'Algérie coloniale du 19e siècle. In: *Archives Juives* 37,1 (2004), pp. 70–85.

63 On the history of the Algerian Jews in the 20th century: Michael Laskier: *North-African Jewry in the Twentieth Century: The Jews of Morocco, Tunisia and Algeria.* New-York: NYU Press 1994, p. 400. On the importance of shared cooking traditions: Joëlle Bahloul: *Le culte de la table dressée: rites et traditions de la table juive algérienne.* Paris: Métailié 1983, p. 304.

A Jewish Space in an Extreme Context? German Ghettoes for Jews in Eastern Europe during World War II

Frank Golczewski

Intro

When talking about Jewish spaces usually we do not have in mind the quarters set aside for Jews by the Germans in Eastern Europe during World War II. If we connect a 'space' with an adjective marking a specific group of people, we normally connote that the said group was able to shape, define and organize this 'space' on its own conditions, on its own responsibility. This was definitely not the case with the Jewish "living quarters" (*Jüdischer Wohnbezirk*) as some of these temporary ghettoes were called. Their documentary base was the *Schnellbrief* sent by Reinhard Heydrich, the Head of German Security Police, on September 21, 1939[1] to the Heads of his *Einsatzgruppen* ordering the Jews to be concentrated in larger cities close to railway tracks in order to segregate them from the 'Aryan' population and prepare for their deportation 'to the East' – whatever that might have meant at that time.

This order was not executed immediately. In the General Gouvernement (GG) created by the Germans from what had remained of pre-war Poland after Germany, Lithuania and the Soviet Union had annexed substantial parts, it depended on the local German administrative authorities how they would deal with the Jews. The first ghetto was created by the new German mayor

1 Schnellbrief Heydrich to Chefs der Einsatzgruppen, 21.09.1939, Nürnberg Document PS-3363. Printed in: Tatiana Berenstein / Artur Eisenbach / Bernard Mar / Adam Rutkowski (eds): *Faschismus – Getto – Massenmord.* Berlin (GDR): Rütten & Loening 1960, Doc. 1, pp. 37–41; also http://www.lsg.musin.de/geschichte/geschichte/natsoz/heydrichs_bildung_Ghettos.htm (accessed 20.07.2011); English translation: http://users.stlcc.edu/rkalfus/PDFs/086.pdf (accessed 17.06.2013).

of Piotrków at the beginning of October 1939, probably mainly due to the bombardment effects and the desire to make use of Jewish homes. This first ghetto, liquidated in some stages until mid-1943, did not correspond to our regular imaginations. There was no wall, no guards were present, just signs on the roadside marking the borders of this 'open ghetto' as such installations became to be called. Nevertheless, the area was off limits to non-Jews (if not on German duty) and the Jews were not allowed to remain outside of it if not in possession of a special permit. During the following two years many more ghettoes were created in occupied Poland, including areas directly integrated into German Reich territory like in those of Zichenau/Ciechanów, Eastern Upper Silesia and the Reichsgau Wartheland with Łódź, where one of the largest ghettoes, second only to Warsaw, was walled. These ghettoes differed from each other, some were quarters segregated by walls and guard, others were just designated areas, in some cases whole villages or industrial compounds were set aside as ghettoes. The creation of ghettoes continued in 1941 in the occupied Soviet territories – in the Baltic countries, western Belorussia and the western and southwestern districts of Ukraine. Further to the east ghettoes – if one still can call them so – were just temporary installations waiting for the German execution squads (*Einsatzgruppen*, *Einsatzkommandos*) to murder all Jewish inmates indiscriminately. In 1944, when the Hungarian government decided to deliver the Hungarian Jews to the Germans, a set of short-lived ghettoes was established in some provincial towns and in Budapest. By summer of 1944 even the longer existing ghettoes of Şiauliai in Lithuania and Litzmannstadt were liquidated. An exception were the numerous ghettoes in the Romanian administrative area in Ukraine (Transnistria) and the large ghetto of Theresienstadt/Terezín in Bohemia – these were the only ghettoes that were finally liberated by the Allies. Though there exist quite many published memoirs on Transnistrian ghettoes, they are still not evaluated scholarly.

On the other hand, there are many scholarly works on ghettoes – at least about the larger ones – but for a long time practically all of them concentrated on the dominant German factor that shaped the ghettoes and treated the Jewish Councils (*Judenräte*), established in the same Heydrich *Schnellbrief*, as nothing more than dependant transmission tools to administer them. Basically, this perspective is fully justified, of course. But the question arises if the ghettoes can only be seen through German eyes; shouldn't we take into account the small autonomous pockets existing in these terrible creations?

Even if we do not accept the ghettoes as 'Jewish space' – ghettoization created a 'non-Jewish space' by evicting people considered to be Jews out of the non-ghetto parts of towns. Still we would have a problem naming the ghetto counterpart.

To state it clearly – Jewish everyday life in the ghettoes has been something eye witnesses, scholarship and pedagogical projects have treated. In Yad Vashem's Educational Materials, compiled by its International School for Holocaust Studies, there is a lesson plan with the title 'Compassion within the Ghetto walls' dealing with the "self help" moves, soup kitchens, smuggling and the youth movement. The objective is to show how organizations worked that were "established by Jews imprisoned in the Warsaw Ghetto in order to help other Jews in the ghetto." The result had to be to show how those acted who "were able to maintain their humanity in the face of unprecedented inhumanity".[2]

Whereas the first publications on the Shoah understandably concentrated on the outside relationship, with the German extermination efforts in the first place, followed by Jewish fighting and martyrdom,[3] Trunk's book on the Jewish Councils was an important early one to discuss activities of Jewish institutions (though, of course, they were imposed on the Jews by the Germans).[4]

As already visible from Yad Vashem's focus, Warsaw, the largest ghetto – in fact, a city-sized installation – attracted earlier views on the interior situation: Ruta Sakowska dealt in her doctoral dissertation that was then published in Polish and German, with the internal situation in the Warsaw ghetto, giving a first insight into the self-organizing efforts, self helping organizations and the social structures that developed in this forced community. Her work uses the famous Ringelblum Archive, a repository of official and unofficial sources produced independently of and in secrecy from the Germans.[5] Earlier memoirs offered an insight into minds and acts of ghetto inhabitants,[6] but only

2 See http://www.yadvashem.org/yv/en/education/lesson_plans/ghettos.asp (accessed 01.01.2014).

3 With titles like Natan Eliasz Szternfinkiel: *Zagłada Żydów Sosnowca*. Katowice: Centralna Żydowska Komisja Historyczna 1946; Ministerstwo Obrony Narodowej (ed.):*Męczeństwo, walka, zagłada Żydów w Polsce 1939–1945*. Warszawa: Wydawnictwo MON 1960.

4 Isaiah Trunk: Judenrat: *The Jewish Councils in Eastern Europe under Nazi Occupation*. New York: Macmillan 1972.

5 Ruta Sakowska: *Ludzie z dzielnicy zamkniętej*. Warszawa: PWN 1975 (German: *Menschen im Ghetto. Die jüdische Bevölkerung im besetzten Gebiet, 1939–1943*. Osnabrück: Fibre 1999).

6 Cf. Michel Mazor: *La cité engloutie*. Paris: Éditions du Centre 1955 (English: *Vanished City. Everyday Life in the Warsaw Ghetto*. New York: Marsilio 1993) – for Warsaw, or the known *Dziennik Dawida Sierakowiaka*. Warszawa: Iskry 1960 (German: *Das Ghettotagebuch des Dawid Sierakowiak*. Leipzig: Reclam 1993).

during the past decade more and more authors developed interest in Jewish life as opposed to death in the Nazi ghettoes. Again, it is the large ghettoes that became the primary focus of scholars' interest. One of the most prolific pioneers in this field is the German historian Andrea Löw who wrote a groundbreaking study on Łódź and other titles (with a collaborator) on Warsaw and Cracow.[7] And at last a collective work on some smaller ghettoes like Chmielnik, Otwock, and some Volhynian towns was published.[8] Other titles are the books by Eric Sterling and Ruby Rohrlich,[9] the latter due to the article by Sterling on the dilemma of resistance in Vilna, and by the formation of new social groups by Ami Neiberger.

If there is a 'Jewish space', there is also a 'non-Jewish space' and vice versa. We have some constructions of the 'non-Jewish space' that seem to support our point. Two books by serious scholars on the cities mentioned before were written without ever taking more than a passing reference to the Jews who at that time still lived there.

Tomasz Szarota worked exceptionally well on everyday life in Warsaw during the war – and excluded the ghetto but for some general remarks from his study. This might have been for censorship reasons at that time – later Szarota wrote about "anti-Jewish incidents" in wartime Warsaw, indeed.[10] There cannot, however, be a similar excuse for Anna Czocher who wrote a book about occupied Cracow, writing about the non-Jewish Poles only. She motivated her "narrow focus on the Polish population" being "dictated by the occupying power's racial policies" and "racial segregation". But until March 1941 Jews lived in all of Cracow and until early 1943 they were in the ghetto, but many if not most of them passed the ghetto gates daily to work in 'Aryan' Cracow.[11]

7 Cf. Andrea Löw: *Juden im Ghetto Litzmannstadt. Lebensbedingungen, Selbstwahrnehmung, Verhalten.* Göttingen: Wallstein 2006; Andrea Löw / Markus Roth: *Juden in Krakau unter deutscher Besatzung 1939–1945.* Göttingen: Wallstein 2011; Andrea Löw / Markus Roth: *Das Warschauer Ghetto. Alltag und Widerstand im Angesicht der Vernichtung.* Munich: Beck 2013.

8 Christoph Dieckmann / Babette Quinkert (eds): *Im Ghetto 1939–1945. Neue Forschungen zu Alltag und Umfeld. Beiträge zur Geschichte des Nationalsozialismus.* Göttingen: Wallstein 2009.

9 Eric Sterling (ed.): *Life in the Ghettoes during the Holocaust.* Syracuse, NY: Syracuse UP 2005; Ruby Rohrlich (ed.): *Resisting the Holocaust.* Oxford: Berg 1998.

10 Tomasz Szarota: *Okupowanej Warszawy dzień powszedni.* Warszawa: Czytelnik 1973 (German: *Warschau unter dem Hakenkreuz. Leben und Alltag im besetzten Warschau 1939–1945.* Paderborn: Schöningh 1985); Tomasz Szarota: *U progu zagłady. Zajścia antyżydowskie i pogromy w okupowanej Europie.* Warszawa: Wydawn Sic! 2000.

11 Cf. Anna Czocher: *W okupowanym Krakowie. Codzienność polskich mieszkańców miasta 1939–1945.* Gdańsk: Wydawn Oskar 2011.

Ghetto as a 'Jewish Space'?

To approach these ghettoes in the context of 'Jewish Spaces' is probably very controversial. Ghettoes were not intended as spaces for Jewish life, but my thesis is that in kind and partly they developed into that.

It is not an absolutely unfounded approach to see the ghettoes not only as a 'waiting room' to death, but as an area where Jewish life developed, because people did not know (at least in the beginning) that they would be killed. Samuel Gringauz who spent the war in the ghetto of Kovno/Kaunas wrote in 1949:

> From the historical-sociological point of view the ghetto is a significant instance of enforced Jewish national concentration. From this standpoint the ghetto is an interesting case of a sudden and arbitrary ejection of a Jewish group from the social condition of extra-national diffusion and the enforced transfer of the group into the social status of inner-national concentration. The ghetto was a sociologically relevant experiment of a Jewish community under specifically abnormal and extraordinary living conditions.[12]

The 'resettlement' option many people believed in the beginning, might even have motivated Zionist minded Jews to prepare for some kind of resettlement in a 'productive' context.[13] When we look at the kibbutzim organized in some of the ghettoes, e.g. in Marysin, a 'rural' part of the Łódź ghetto, we realize that one of the major aims of these Hakhsharah institutions was preparation for a future agricultural life in Palestine. In the Łódź ghetto other political groups as well organized training camps and youth groups that were not just agents of escapism (though this might have played a role as well) but institutions that planned for something considered to be realistic in the future.[14]

At present some scholarly projects deal with the construction of values and living rules in the ghettoes, with planning – not for the gas chambers but for either some new form of afterlife or an extension of the regular pre-ghetto life. One of them is that by Hanna Schmidt Holländer: Her doctoral dissertation, finished in 2014, does not only concentrate on the 're-education' of intellectuals, judges, musicians into artisans (that were both needed in the ghetto and in a future community and whose new professions were expected

12 Samuel Gringauz: The Ghetto as an Experiment of Jewish Social Organization (Three Years of Kovno Ghetto). In: *Jewish Social Studies* 11 (1949), pp. 3–20, quotation: p. 4.

13 This term, antisemitic in contents (as Jews were not less 'productive' in their traditional occupations), was nevertheless adopted by the Zionist terminology.

14 See for this topic Löw: *Juden im Ghetto Litzmannstadt*, pp. 195–207; Sheva Glas-Wiener: *Children of the Ghetto*. Fitzroy, VIC: Globe 1983, pp. 73–74.

to offer an option of survival due to their usefulness), but also on the development of Jewish pedagogical and spiritual life (both religious and secular) as an effort to continue some sort of Jewish life.[15]

The German persecution even supported a re-orientation towards Jewishness. What sounds strange and immoral at a first glance, nevertheless describes a discernable fact. Comparable to the Jewish Cultural Union (*Jüdischer Kulturbund*) in Germany the exclusion from the inter-cultural contacts and assimilation resulted in added importance of more Jewish forms of cultural and everyday life.

The *Jüdischer Kulturbund* (until 1935 under the name of *Kulturbund Deutscher Juden* – Cultural Union of German Jews) had been created in Berlin in July 1933 as a reaction to the earlier layoffs of Jewish artists from the state funded cultural life. At its height in 1935 it had about 70,000 members organized in 36 regional sections. Its activities included theatre productions, concerts, lectures etc. Non-Jews were banned from attendance (though there were exceptions) and only occasionally works written by non-Jewish authors were granted permission by a close censorship by Goebbels's Propaganda Ministry. After 1938 only the Berlin section was allowed to continue until 1941, mainly for propaganda purposes.[16]

In the first years, this Nazi creation did not at all reflect the desires of German Jews – but in time it became the only agency where Jews could profess arts and scholarship. The normative results of reality created – against the earlier will of the people affected – a closer relationship between them and 'Jewish' works of art and scholarship.[17] Though the creation of a 'ghetto culture' was critically discussed by the remaining German Jews, many of the participants saw this fig leaf created by the Nazi Propaganda Ministry as a way (the only one) to save at least a surrogate of their former cultural life.

15 See also her article Hanna Schmidt Hollaender: Reinstating Normality: the Stabilizing Function of School for Children in Jewish Ghettos. In: *Zeitschrift für Genozidforschung* 13 (2012), pp. 82–101. The dissertation with the title *Ghetto Schools. Jewish Education in Nazi-Occupied Poland* is still unpublished.

16 For literature see Eike Geisel / Henryk M. Broder: *Premiere und Pogrom. Der Jüdische Kulturbund 1933–1941. Texte und Bilder.* Berlin: Siedler 1992; Barbara Müller-Wesemann: *Theater als geistiger Widerstand. Der Jüdische Kulturbund in Hamburg 1934–1941.* Stuttgart: M&P 1996; Rebecca Rovit: *The Jewish Kulturbund Theatre Company in Nazi Berlin.* Iowa City: University of Iowa Press 2012.

17 I put the word 'Jewish' in quotation marks because the definition of 'Jewish' was a Nazi construction.

Another approach to our problem was introduced by Tim Cole[18] to whose credit goes the first effort to apply the 'spatial turn' in historiography to this Jewish context. Cole characterized the Nazis as an agency that allocated space both to Jews, to Germans and to others. Their objective was overall control: Cole compares the 'controllable' camps to barracks and organized 'Aryan' cities where control was also the main objective. We could also point to his division between 'spaces of life' and 'spaces of death' in his "spatial questions of Holocaust Ghettoization" where the author examines "just where the doctors of space charged with implementing ghettoization planned and located ghettoes".[19] However, there is not only the question of Nazi planning, but also the desire to figure out how ghettoes developed and how they were viewed and organized by the inmates. And a second question: what can we define as 'ghettoes' within this concept of 'spatial' questions.

In our context, I would rather concentrate on the structural form of forced segregation, because this can be compared to many other segregating societies, making the Jewish case one that can be compared in the historical context (and not isolated as an a priori moribund entity). This is a way not to exclude the Jewish fate from history as something 'unique', but to historicize it.[20]

If we agree that forced segregation was a fundamental issue in a situation when the outcome was not completely clear yet (and it became clear only in the end of 1941 when, except for Eastern Upper Silesia, ghetto creation activities were replaced by their liquidation that took another two years) we can now approach the central topic of my paper – the *forms* of ghettoization in Eastern Europe – having in mind that forms and contents have a dialectic relationship.

18 Tim Cole: *Holocaust City*. New York / London: Routledge 2003.

19 Ibid., p. 25.

20 Of course, this implies that I do not subscribe to the concept of a complete 'historical uniqueness' of the Jewish case which seems to me be more of a political than a historical categorization. I am highly aware of the fact that this is a step in the direction of diminishing the singularity factor of the Shoah, but apart from the by now really singular 'industrial' killings in the Nazi death factories comparative approaches by historians (as different from equating ones) are a necessary undertaking in order to define the historical place of what the Germans did to the Jews in World War II.

Stages of Ghettoization on Former Polish Territory

Ghettoization in occupied Poland and the other German occupied territories was until late 1941 a part of the policy to segregate the Jewish from the non-Jewish population. It depicted a different legal or political approach to the segregated groups of people, thus illustrating legal inequality in the space. In the first year of German occupation, Jews were only in exceptional cases selected for immediate murder – one of them was the burning of Jews in the Będzin synagogue on September 8, 1939. Most of the German acts had in mind future deportations as indicated in Heydrich's *Schnellbrief* (see footnote 1), humiliating Jews and winning cheap forced labor. The deportation's destination was not yet set, so there are still discussions on how realistic projects like the Madagascar plan really were. Part of this picture were the deportations of Jews from Upper Silesia across the Bug and San to the Soviet occupied zone and the expulsion of Jews (but also of non-Jewish Poles) from directly annexed areas in Central Poland to the GG. The refusal of the GG administration to accept more expellees stopped this procedure in early 1940 and lead to the creation of ghettoes in the annexed Wartheland areas, one of the first being that of Łódź in April 1940.

Preparing for the segregation process and a future deportation, the Germans "excluded the Jews from economic life" handing their enterprises and shops over to German, Ukrainian, and sometimes Polish "trustees" (*Treuhänder*) – who now acted as subjects of a "commissarial management". In most cases these enterprises retained the names of the earlier Jewish owners (as these had acquired a certain reputation), but were officially and visibly marked as belonging to a new "national" space and marketed in this way to potential customers.

Being excluded from economic activity meant also the creation of mobility: without a place to work (except in cases of being forced to work by the occupiers) the Jews could be moved around without economic considerations. By restricting their mobility to cases permitted by the Germans, the Jews were at the same time excluded from using public transport at will, changing their place of living without permission and from independently leaving the area of their local community. Thus separation, concentration and legal restriction were implemented even before formal ghettoes were installed.

A remarkable step in that direction was the requirement for Jews to mark themselves by a white armband with a hexagonal star, issued in the GG on November 23, 1939,[21] followed by a ban on voluntary changes of the place

21 Verordnung über die Kennzeichnung von Juden und Jüdinnen im Generalgouvernement, 23.11.1939. In: *Verordnungsblatt für das Generalgouvernement* (VOBlGG) 8, 30.11.1939, p. 6.

of residence in the executive order from December 11.[22] Concentration had to follow according to the earlier Heydrich order.[23]

But whereas the above orders were applied immediately, the 'concentration' and formal ghettoization followed only gradually, non-coordinated and inconsistently. After the first Piotrków ghetto, there followed ghettoes in the small towns of Puławy and Radomsko in December 1939, but most ghettoes came into being later in 1940 or 1941 only.

In the largest city of Warsaw after the temporary installation of closed areas due to the fear of epidemics, the formation of a 'Jewish quarter' was ordered by the head of the district administration Ludwig Fischer on October 2, 1940. It was closed on November 16, 1940, and in the following time Jews from smaller towns in the area were transported into it, crowding it horribly and building up the largest ghetto ever created in World War II with a population of more than 400,000 people.[24]

The ghetto in the city of Łódź, renamed Litzmannstadt, was closed on April 30, 1940, after it had become clear that a complete deportation of the Jews from the territories annexed to the Reich into the GG would not work out. Smaller ghettoes and some more liberal areas were created around this central town, like in Brzeziny in July 1940 or in Łęczyca in February 1941 – they were liquidated in the spring of 1942, when most of the inhabitants were killed by exhaust fumes in Kulmhof (Chełmno), whereas some qualified workers had a chance to stay alive temporarily by being deported to the remaining ghetto of Łódź.

Whereas in most cases Jews were, indeed, concentrated in towns, this was not an iron rule either. Cracow, the capital of the GG, was imagined by the new rulers as becoming '*judenfrei*' – cleared of Jews. After Hans Frank had issued a statement along these lines on April 12, 1940, a resettlement order was issued in May 1940, and from mid-August on Cracow Jews were directed to smaller regional towns like Bochnia, and about 5,000 to the district of Lublin.[25] Only about 15,000 Jews were issued a permit to remain in Cracow – they were deemed necessary as a specialized working force. Until March 1941 they could live in all city areas – only then Podgórze, a run-down area south of

22 1. DurchführungsVO zur VO vom 26.10.1939 über die Einführung des Arbeitszwangs, 11.12.1939. In: *VOBlGG* 13, 21.12.1939, pp. 231–232.

23 See fn. 1.

24 Best described in Barbara Engelking-Boni / Jacek Leociak: *Getto warszawskie. Przewodnik po nieistniejącym mieście*. Warszawa: Wydawnictwo IFiS PAN 2001 (English: *The Warsaw Ghetto. A Guide to the Perished City*. New Haven: Yale UP 2009).

25 Cf. Andrzej Chwalba: *Dzieje Krakowa*, vol. 5. Kraków: Wydawnictwo Literackie 2002, pp. 107–108.

the Vistula river was declared a ghetto for Jews and closed – i. e. segregated from the outer world – by March 21, 1941. In the larger towns of Lublin and Częstochowa ghettoes were installed only in March 1941, too.

The Warsaw ghetto was in fact a metropolis with many facilities (even entertainment establishments, theatres etc.) that belonged to such a big city. Many of the smaller ghettoes were likewise intended to resemble a Jewish town with an administration (the *Judenrat*), workshops, soup kitchens. The horrible population density, terrible sanitary conditions, hunger, illness and death contributed to a highly controversial picture which German soldier 'tourists' and propaganda film teams gladly presented as 'typical' for the 'subhuman' Jews. Ghettoes like that of Cracow were in a slightly better position – when practically all inhabitants had to work during the day, they had a chance to be better fed and the overcrowding was not as appalling as in other places.

When Germany attacked the Soviet Union in June 1941, in the former Polish territories of Galicia, Volhynia and Belarus'[26] ghettoes were created as well. Mass murder by the *Einsatzgruppen* killed many male elite and workforce Jews in the first weeks of German occupation and those unfit for work, now including women and children, were murdered later in 1941. Separate Jewish quarters were marked out in the second half of 1941, and many if not most of them were liquidated during 1942. In the Galician capital of L'viv (Galicia was annexed to the GG) the ghettoization was interrupted in December 1941 due to the administrative chaos it created and only resumed in the fall of 1942 after the first large deportations of Jews into the extermination camps had reduced their numbers.

There are different ways to define ghettoes. In the course of my own research I have identified about 500 ghettoes and other similar areas (not counting labor camps) in the GG in January 1942.[27] The United States Holocaust Memorial Museum established "at least 1,000 ghettoes in German-occupied and annexed Poland and the Soviet Union alone".[28] Whichever count you accept, these installations were ubiquitous and diverse – in contrast to labor camps or prisons they retained at least in theory remnants of privacy (like families living together) and self-administration (though the *Judenrat* organs

26 Only rarely ghettoes were built east of the 1939 Polish eastern border – Minsk being such an exception.

27 Frank Golczewski: Polen. In: Wolfgang Benz (ed.): *Dimension des Völkermords*. Munich: Oldenbourg 1991, pp. 452–457.

28 Encyclopedia of the Holocaust. http://www.ushmm.org/wlc/sp/article.php?ModuleId=10007445 (accessed 10.06.2013).

had to follow German orders and were autonomous only to a very small extent). Practically all of the occupied territories were divided into areas set aside for Germans, locals or Jews.

Though there are signs that ghetto inhabitants hoped for a continuation of living after the war (supported in kind by the Germans who up to the end led them to believe that they would be 'resettled' [*ausgesiedelt, umgesiedelt*] somewhere where they would have to work), constant killing actions (in the beginning more visible in the eastern new ghettoes of Galicia than in the 1939 GG) and omnipresent death by starvation marked the ghettoes as highly dangerous places. But as it was the case with the establishing of ghettoes, their liquidation did not follow a perceptible plan either.

The ghetto landscape moved constantly. Smaller ghettoes were liquidated, with some or all of their inhabitants moved to larger ones – the non-specialists (but this was not a clear rule either) being 'resettled' to unknown places. Only the brave ones realized that this was nothing but a camouflage for extermination. Still nobody had any direct knowledge of thc death sites established between 1941 and 1942.

Starting in late 1941 (in the Warthegau) the ghettoes were liquidated in 'actions'. But even when in their course children, old and sick people were killed on the spot, this could support a last hope that those fit for work would still have a chance to start a new life somewhere. The system that provided for a 'privileged' class (members of the *Judenräte*, Jewish policemen, specialist workers and their families) saw to it that those were deported last – until then they had to support the Germans who seemed to provide for their survival. As a tragic result, those elites in numerous cases selected those who were to be sent to their deaths by themselves (like in Vilnius) or their members committed suicide when they realized the dead end quality of their actions (like Adam Czerniaków in Warsaw).

How does this relate to the concept of 'Jewish space'? We see clearly that the Germans were the masters of everything – but within their context of disinformation and fraud the way to hold up discipline was founded on the illusionary perception by some Jews that they could still shape their future.

Nevertheless, in 1943 nearly all ghettoes were liquidated (the exceptions were Łódź, Şiauliai and the Hungarian ghettoes [until 1944], Transnistria and Theresienstadt) and only those who were sent to work in a labor camp (now without family members and without any influence on their existence) had a small chance to survive.

This makes it clear that the allocation of a 'Jewish space' was at best a temporary phenomenon. We have already mentioned that ghettoization was one way to mark spaces as (temporarily) destined for Jewish use. As these ghettoes still possessed some remnants of autonomy they can on my opinion be interpreted in this way – without forgetting, however, that they had this function in the eyes of the victims only; the Germans never saw them as a real haven for Jews.

Reich Territory

Much more controversy might be reached by defining other 'Jewish spaces'. In the German Reich area the establishment of ghettoes for Jews was not planned. We have already registered that this happened nevertheless in the 'Warthegau' (and in the often neglected districts of Zichenau/Ciechanów and Białystok [in 1941] that were annexed as well) when the deportation of the Jews came to a halt after the winter of 1939/40. The ghettoes created in Łódź and some smaller towns were, however, similar to those in the GG – that is why we discussed them in that context. The situation in Upper Silesia which was also directly incorporated into the German Reich, was different. Here also the creation of ghettoes had not been part of the general plan in the beginning.[29]

In Germany proper – from 1939 on – we find a different measure, repeated later in Budapest. In order both to segregate Jews and to win attractive housing for non-Jews, Jews were made to move to designated Jewish houses (*Judenhäuser*). Following a housing law, Jews could be stripped of their housing by the local administration and Jewish house-owners were obliged to accept Jewish tenants in their possessions, transferred to them by the local administration.[30]

Into these 'Jewish houses', Jews were transferred from their previous housing, freeing the latter for non-Jewish use. A high tide of this 'moving movement' ('*Umzugsbewegung*') rose in the summer of 1939. Though this action was completed only in a few larger cities – this process of housing segregation (still not accompanied yet by a marking of Jews) designated materialized separate

29 Some aspects of Jewish life in Nazi Germany can be found in Andrea Löw / Doris L. Bergen / Hájková Anna (eds): *Alltag im Holocaust. Jüdisches Leben im Großdeutschen Reich 1941–1945*. Munich: Oldenbourg 2013.

30 Gesetz über Mietverhältnisse mit Juden, 30.04.1939. In: *Reichsgesetzblatt* I, 1939, p. 864.

spaces for Jews and non-Jews.[31] Whereas in the beginning this separation was confined to invisible dividing lines – with separate culture institutions, separate physicians etc. – now separate spaces were allocated to the two politically defined groups. Still the segregating 'final' objective of such a division – to deport these people – was not self-evident, and the 'Jewish houses' were scattered all over the towns.

One could also define the marking requirement (*Kennzeichnungspflicht*), introduced in the GG in 1939, in the Reich and the Protectorate Bohemia and Moravia in September 1941, as a form of ghettoization – Jews became visible outside their housing and bore their 'portable' ghetto with them.

A specific space was created in Eastern Upper Silesia, i.e. the Eastern Strip (*Oststreifen*) that had not been part of Prussia before 1918. Though the area was directly incorporated into the Reich, it was still divided from former Prussian territories by a police border (*Polizeigrenze*). The territory where Auschwitz developed into the most known murder site introduced a marking requirement for Jews on December 21, 1939[32] that was implemented in the following weeks. First the marking was an armband with the Star of David, but in September 1941 the marking procedure introduced in the Reich (a yellow star with a black inscription) was extended to this area as well.

The Upper Silesian Jews were in the beginning supposed to leave for the East, the crossing over to the Soviets was favored and supported by the Germans. When this did not appeal to larger numbers and the deportations from the Warthegau had stopped too, the Germans reacted to the expected larger length of stay of the local Jews.

With some exceptions for specialists, in the first half of 1940 Jews from the German side of the police border (from cities like Bielitz/Bielsko, Kattowitz/Katowice, Königshütte/Chorzów, Myslowitz/Mysłowice or Teschen/Cieszyn) were dislodged to the Eastern Strip, where they had to resettle in places like Będzin, Dąbrowa, Olkusz and Sosnowiec. Thus the small Eastern Strip was used as an 'entrepot' where Jews should be concentrated up to the 'final solution'. Steinbacher qualifies it as a provincial dumping region („*provinzinterne Abschubregion*").[33]

31 Angela Schwarz: Von den Wohnstiften zu den ‚Judenhäusern'. In: Angelika Ebbinghaus / Karsten Linne (eds): *Kein abgeschlossenes Kapitel: Hamburg im ‚Dritten Reich'*. Hamburg: EVA 1997, pp. 232–247, term quoted: p. 239.

32 Sybille Steinbacher: *‚Musterstadt' Auschwitz. Germanisierungspolitik und Judenmord in Ostoberschlesien*. Munich: Saur 2000, p. 166.

33 Ibid., p. 120.

Until 1943, there were no 'closed ghettoes' here. In some cases quarters were earmarked for Jews, but what was prominent (in the central towns) were continuous mixed Jewish-non-Jewish towns. Jews were marked, but they were only partly constrained in their movement. In some cases, in theory the whole city was open to Jewish housing; one of the first authors on Sosnowiec, Natan Eliasz Szternfinkiel, described the situation as a "moral ghetto".[34]

The practice was that certain central streets were closed to Jews so that they lived in the "underdeveloped quarters", "quite often without canalization and electric lighting". But as no clear ghetto borders were established the Jews could maintain contacts with the non-Jewish population and even travel from one town to another in special streetcars.[35] Thus solely travel between Będzin, Dąbrowa, Sosnowiec and Strzemieszyce was possible, whereas Jews could not cross the police border into Mysłowice or Katowice. Street cars between Dąbrowa, Sosnowiec and Będzin and the line between Będzin and Czeladź first had 'Jewish' areas segregated by chains, then Jews were restricted to the platforms and were not allowed to enter the cars themselves,[36] in 1941 – as people did not observe the restrictions – a special car 'For Jews only' ran as the last one at the end of the tram-train.

The Jews of the area were administered by a *Central Office of the Jewish Councils of Elders* (*Zentrale der Jüdischen Ältestenräte in Ost-Oberschlesien*), sometimes also called 'Central Council of Elders', having its seat in Sosnowiec and responsible for the Jews of the whole area. Parallel administrations – reminding of the Austro-Marxist plans for 'cultural autonomy' – organized the population of this strip and created an exceptional situation of separation and mixture.

The closure of some streets and places was called '*Judenbann*' (ban on Jewish presence). In Sosnowiec as early as around the turn of the years 1939/40 a first resettlement action was implemented. Jews were evicted from flats in the principal streets like *Hauptstraße* and *Rathausstraße*. After some weeks Jews were even banned from walking through these streets so that they had to walk detours in order to reach their permitted quarters.[37] This '*Judenbann*' was

34 Szternfinkiel: *Zagłada*, p. 12.

35 Steinbacher: *‚Musterstadt' Auschwitz*, p. 121.

36 Report des Polizeireviers 42, 20.05.1940. In: Aleksandra Namysło (ed.): *Zagłada Żydów Zagłębiowskich*. Będzin: IPN Katowice 2004, p. 87.

37 Szternfinkiel: *Zagłada*, S. 19–20; the suggestion comes from a report by the V. Police precinct, 11.06.1940, cf. Namysło (ed.): *Zagłada*, S. 89. The implementation is documented in the report of June 24, 1940, ibid., p. 90.

formalized in municipal ordinances in 1941, when it was extended to the use of parks and sports grounds.

According to Sybille Steinbacher, one of the reasons for the '*Judenbann*' were Germanizing plans for Eastern Upper Silesia. As the mayors were heads of German Reich municipalities, they undertook efforts to dislodge the Jews from the townscape of their realms in order to present their Germanizing achievements to their superiors.

Taking this into account, we see a correspondence between the politically desirable definition of German spaces (difficult in an area where the overwhelming majority of the population was Polish or Jewish) and the restriction of Jews to less visible marginal 'Jewish spaces'. As much of the eastern strip was perceived as being accessible for Jews (who faced here less restrictions than in the GG and enjoyed a better supply, supported by owners of commercial firms who used their labor), the supporters of Germanizing the strip (mayors, police etc.) constantly fought for restricting the Jews to 'real' ghettoes – finally succeeding early in 1943, when closed ghettoes were established in the strip and the Jews were forced to move into them. This was for the last 5–6 months only, in the summer of 1943 the Jews of the Eastern Strip were deported to Auschwitz for extermination or to labor camps. Spatial segregation and space organization were practiced here in a different way, but in the end this had no influence on the destiny of the people.

Occupied Soviet Territory

Whereas ghettoes in the occupied Soviet territory were modeled on the GG variation in pre-1939 Polish towns in Ukraine and Belorussia, there were some peculiarities to the Soviet area cases. As mass killing was prominent from the beginning of the 1941 campaign (though along different lines at first) ghettoes were not the first priority. Instead, forced labor and restrictions of different kinds were practiced, motivating Shmuel Spector to write on Volhynia:

> As a matter of fact, the formation of ghettoes was neither vital nor necessary, as the residence and movement restrictions imposed on the Jews with the onset of the occupation amounted to ghettoization de facto.[38]

Il'ja Al'tman defined "open ghettoes" in these areas in a similar way:

38 Shmuel Spector: *The Holocaust of Volhynian Jews 1914–1944*. Jerusalem: Yad Vashem 1990, pp. 117–118.

> Without physical isolation of the Jews in guarded quarters or buildings they had a provisional character […]. People living in an 'open' ghetto remained in their houses or flats. Sometimes they were transferred to another (unwalled) part of the locality. […] The necessary mark of such a ghetto was the establishment of a Jewish Council or the appointment of an Elder. […] The second most important mark of a ghetto of this type was the partial isolation of the Jewish inhabitants. In comparison to the remainder of the local people it was expressed by the visible restriction of movement within the locality. […] The way to ensure the isolation was the visual marking of the Jews (notations in documents, markings on clothes, markings on houses and residences). Altogether this allows us to speak of a ghettoization.[39]

The special ordinance no. 1 (*Besondere Anordnung Nr. 1*) of the (military) *Gebietsleiter* of July 10 ordered the marking of Jewish shops and firms.[40] This meant that even before ghettoes were established Jewish houses were marked with different signs (a yellow rectangle, a blue star of David [in Sarny] or a yellow circle), which served as an indication that both Germans and locals could rob those houses without having to fear punishment.[41]

According to Spector, the creation of ghettoes in towns where 70–90% of the inhabitants were Jewish was not considered to be sensible. This is to comment on the order by the commander of the Rear Army Area South that ghettoes should only be created where this would be desirable. The army was not necessarily interested in ghettoes as she was prepared to hand over the territory to civilians who would have to deal with the administration.[42] That is why in Volhynia (differing in that from e.g. Minsk) formal ghettoization started in October 1941 only, after the transfer to the civilian *Reichskommissariat Ukraine* – and it did so, too, in small towns like Kostopol, Stepan, Deražno, Berezno, Ludvipol, Horochiv, and Berestečko.[43] Some villages were completely declared to be 'Jewish Land Settlements' – like Osova, Sofiïvka, Selišče north of Rivne.[44]

During the final stage of ghetto existence in some towns more than one ghetto was established. In these cases – Kolomea is an example – there was a division between 'useful', i.e. working, Jews and the others, indicating that working was an important issue. The ghettoes for non-working Jews were as a rule much worse than those for the workers. And they were liquidated earlier,

39 Il'ja Al'tman: *Žertvy nenavisti.* Moskva: Soveršenno Sekretono 2002, pp. 72–73.

40 Spector: *Holocaust,* p. 80.

41 Ibid., pp. 89–90.

42 Cf. ibid., p. 117.

43 Ibid., p. 118.

44 Ibid., pp. 118–119.

the one in Kolomea in April 1942 after just one month of existence – killing the inhabitants on the spot or in extermination sites like Bełżec.[45]

Only in the western part of the occupied Soviet territory ghettoes sometimes can be described as temporary 'living areas' for Jews, as rudimentary 'Jewish spaces'. East of the former Polish-Soviet border places where Jews were kept – though still registered in the ghetto category by present-day scholars like Martin Dean and Il'ja Al'tman – served just as collecting points for complete extermination. Following Tim Cole's terminology I would not call them Jewish spaces anymore – but in fact 'waiting spaces for death'. Unfed and killed at will, the inmates could not have any hope for salvation – that is why they did not think of organizing their life, a necessary prerequisite to assume something like a 'Jewish space'.

Conclusions

Of course, one can discuss in lengthy terms, if the German ghettoes were in fact 'Jewish spaces'. In Tim Cole's terms they were and in the interest of historicizing the Nazi times it bears fruit to discuss them as such, because with this perspective one can compare them with other voluntary and non-voluntary forms of living (like DP camps after the war, where national social life of Ukrainians, Poles and future Israelis developed in a very specific way). With a different approach to the Jewish councils than the one introduced by Hannah Arendt,[46] we learn that the relationship between these administrations and the administered Jews was diverse and that these bodies sometimes indeed served as organizers of a rudimentary Jewish life.[47] Of course, this variant of Jewish life developed due to German persecution, first in the Reich and later in some of the ghettoes, but nevertheless I deem it fruitful to look at the situation from this angle – notwithstanding the forced quality of this social organization. Defining spaces does not demand voluntary action – one looks at a specific use of space.

Not the least result would be the appreciation of Jewish efforts not to give up hope – efforts to prepare for a possible survival of those who were doomed to die.

45 Cf. Chana Weinheber-Hacker: Churbn. In: Shlomo Bickel (ed.): *Pinkas Kolomei*. New York: Kolomeyer Memorial Books 1957, pp. 325–356. http://www.jewishgen.org/yizkor/kolomyya/kol425.html (accessed 01.10.2007).

46 Hannah Arendt: *Eichmann in Jerusalem*. Munich: Piper 1964, p. 209.

47 Svenja Bethke will prove this in her just finished dissertation: *‚Kriminalität' und ‚Recht' in den jüdischen Ghettos Warschau, Litzmannstadt und Wilna im Zweiten Weltkrieg*. Phil. Diss Hamburg 2013.

As a result of German antisemitism, of the Nuremberg laws and, finally, the murderous activities of the Germans confronting the European Jews, we find very different forms of social reactions to segregation and rightlessness. There was not a unified ghetto world, but a mixture of areas with very different qualities. We encounter

- areas with some kind of temporary self-administration and areas of clear non-Jewish dominance
- the *Judenbann* system and
- open, unwalled or walled ghettoes.
- In some cases the theoretical regulations were modified for pragmatic reasons:
- 'closed ghettoes' were partly 'opened' to make work possible
- ghettoization was replaced by marking of houses and people.

On the other hand – abolition of the marking was a 'privilege' in 'privileged' mixed marriages in Germany only. In some cases physicians were exempted from the ghetto order.

In the final analysis of this short transitory stage, we observe a manifestation of administration by an administrative and spatial structure that has the single person as a unit. In the perspective of the SS and the German 'ideologues', these 'units' were only understood as collectivities: ghettoes were intended only as intermediary stops on the way to death. In practice, they developed, however, sometimes for months or years into 'Jewish Spaces' in the urban context.

Let us not stop here: When mixed societies were segregated due to the expulsion of the Jews, not only 'Jewish spaces' developed. The result of the segregation was also the creation of non-Jewish spaces in countries, where Jews had for centuries played an important social, commercial and intellectual role. The transformation of Eastern and Central Europe into a mainly non-Jewish space changed it tremendously. Some of the economic difficulties of the later years resulted from the drain of the Jews much in the way German intellectual life suffered by the departure of Jewish and non-Jewish emigrants and the killing of those Jews who stayed. This aspect of segregation and the vanishing of the segregated population remains hitherto underresearched.

Borderlands of Identity and Interaction

Transnational and Transcultural Spaces in the Diaspora The Case of Berlin 1900–1933[1]

Anne-Christin Saß

The city is commonly regarded as a social space where strangers meet each other. But cities also enable "transitions between the known and the unknown, the familiar and the unfamiliar, the native and the foreign".[2] In this regard, many sociologists have shown a great interest in exploring one of the focal points for social life: the neighbourhood.[3] They have highlighted that the neighbourhood functions as a focal point for processes of social transition, in particular for migrants, who are confronted with a foreign city, a different culture and an unknown society. Thus, the question of the construction and function of ethnic neighbourhoods has long been at the core of historical and sociological migration research. The classical sociological and historical studies on the immigration of Eastern European Jews to the big cities of Western Europe and the United States during the course of the 19th and early 20th century focussed very much on the infrastructure, the economics and cultural implications of Jewish neighbourhoods.[4] Due to the partial refusal of

1 The following article is based on my PhD-thesis *Berliner Luftmenschen. Osteuropäisch-jüdische Migranten in der Weimarer Republik*. Göttingen: Wallstein 2012.

2 Markus Schroer: *Räume, Orte, Grenzen. Auf dem Weg zu einer Soziologie des Raums*. Frankfurt am Main: Suhrkamp 2006, p. 244.

3 One of the first classical studies is Louis Wirth: *The Ghetto*. Chicago: University of Chicago Press 1928. For the German discussion since the 1970s see the influential article by Ulfert Herlyn: Wohnquartier und soziale Schicht. In: Id. (ed.): *Stadt- und Sozialstruktur*. München: Nymphenburger Verlagshandlung 1974, pp. 16–41. For recent discussions see for example Loic Wacquant: *Das Janusgesicht des Ghettos und andere Essays*. Gütersloh: Bauverlag 2006; Linda M. Lobao / Gregory Hooks / Ann R. Tickamyer (eds): *The Sociology of Spatial Inequality*. Albany: State University of New York Press 2007.

4 Among others this is true for Selma Cantor Berrol: *East Side East End. Eastern European Jews in London and New York (1870–1920)*. Westport, CT: Praeger 1994; Joseph Green: *A Social*

the majority society and the religious and economic need for living at close quarters, these studies consider the group of Eastern European Jews to have been highly segregated and secluded. However, the implicit assumption of the Jewish migrants as a homogenous group with well-defined religious and ethnic characteristics is highly problematic. Moreover, these studies are often shaped by a normative understanding of segregation as a phenomenon of crisis and social inequality, which is set in opposition to the integrative ideal conception of socially and ethnically mixed living quarters.[5]

In contrast to this normative approach, this article takes a somewhat different perspective and tries to explore the spatial strategies of the migrants in close connection to specific places in the urban landscape. The approach adopted here is based on the premise that one of the main characteristics in urban life is the simultaneity of establishing and avoiding contacts. In this perspective, the city offers its inhabitants the opportunity to encounter each other, but leaves the choice up to them how far they make use of it.[6] Against this background, tendencies of segregation will not just be understood as expressions of social inequality and religious or ethnic difference, but also as active strategies of individual actors. Employing the example of Berlin, this article examines the different spatial strategies of Eastern European Jews during the first decades of the 20th century. How did the migrants adjust to the opportunities and challenges of urban life in Berlin? How did they engage with specific urban places? Which kinds of communicative spaces were created?

The concept of "communicative spaces" includes geographically defined social spaces in the urban landscape, which are characterised by intensive communicative relationships between the city inhabitants. Furthermore, these spaces correspond with particular types of modern urban places such as streets, boarding houses, cafés, union houses, and flats, which were connected to specific features and experiences of space.[7] The different types of places

History of the Jewish East End in London (1914–1939). Lewiston: Edwin Mellen 1991; Irving Howe, with the assistance of Kenneth Libo: *World of Our Fathers. The Journey of the East European Jews to America and the Life They Found There.* New York: Simon & Schuster 1976. For more comprehensive studies, which include a detailed analysis of the relations between the immigrants and the local Jewish community see Tobias Brinkmann: *Von der Gemeinde zur "Community". Jüdische Einwanderer in Chicago 1840–1900.* Osnabrück: Rasch 2002; David Feldman: *Englishmen and Jews. Social Relations and Political Culture 1840–1914.* New Haven / London: Yale UP 1994, pp. 139–257.

5 For a detailed discussion of this problem see Schroer: *Räume*, pp. 244–248.

6 See ibid., p. 245.

7 For the inherent features and functions of specific urban spaces see Alexa Geisthövel / Habbo Knoch (eds): *Orte der Moderne. Erfahrungswelten des 19. und 20. Jahrhunderts.* Frankfurt am Main: Campus 2005.

will provide the structure of the following analysis, which will show that the communicative spaces of Eastern European Jews in Berlin were characterized by a deep-seated transnationalism and transculturality. They functioned as social and cultural contact zones which stimulated multifold exchanges and transfers among the migrants themselves, between foreigners and locals, Eastern European Jews and German Jews as well as Jews and Gentiles.

Streets

After their arrival, the majority of the several tens of thousands of Jews who came to Berlin after the collapse of the Russian and Habsburg Empire at the end of World War I already knew where to go in Berlin. Most of them had heard of a certain place in the capital of the Weimar Republic: Grenadierstraße. The "main street" of Jewish immigrants in the Scheunenviertel district near Alexanderplatz housed several kosher restaurants, bakeries, greengrocer's shops, bookstores, boarding houses, and orthodox prayer rooms. Business was not limited to the shops but took place on the street. Orthodox migrants, although in the minority, formed an especially visible element of street life and contributed much to the contemporary perception of the quarter as an East European 'shtetl' or 'ghetto'.[8] However, this perception is somewhat misleading and does not adequately reflect the different functions and meanings of Grenadierstraße for the migrants.

During the immediate post-war years Grenadierstraße played an important role as information and contact market. Nowhere else one could come into contact with other Jewish migrants so straightforwardly and nowhere else could one pick up loads of information about the wide range of local institutions and organizations run by the migrants and the Jewish community as easily. On the street, the migrants shared news about their home countries, discussed options for further migration and the possibilities of obtaining a permanent residence status in Germany. Addresses of landlords and -ladies, guesthouses and emergency shelters, welfare and employment offices were passed from one to the other and experiences with state authorities were shared. In the small restaurants and cafés around Grenadierstraße the

8 To the contemporary perception of the Scheunenviertel as "shtetl" or "ghetto" see Jeffrey Wallen: Migrant Visions – The Scheunenviertel and Boyle Heights, Los Angeles. In: Verena Dohrn / Gertrud Pickhan (eds): *Transit und Transformation. Osteuropäisch-jüdische Migranten in Berlin 1918–1939*. Göttingen: Wallstein 2010, pp. 320–334; Joachim Schlör: *Das Ich der Stadt. Debatten über Judentum und Modernität 1822–1938*. Göttingen: Vandenhoeck & Ruprecht 2005, pp. 111–113; Anne-Christin Saß: Ein ‚ostjüdisches' Quartier? Jüdische Migranten vor und nach 1918 im Berliner Scheunenviertel. In: *Trajekte* 10,19 (2009), pp. 48–51.

migrants continued with their conversations and deepened their relations. A small café at the corner Alte Schönhauser/Linienstraße was called Café New York, because of the many stranded transitory migrants, who met there and dreamt of a better future in the United States.[9]

But also for migrants who lived in Berlin for a while, Grenadierstraße remained an important place. Morris Gruenberg, who grew up in Scheunenviertel in the 1920s, remembers that his mother's weekly shopping tours through Grenadierstraße "were often accompanied by personal talk about their families, as well as some local gossip, which were all traditional rituals at this Jewish street market."[10] Moreover, the actual political developments in the young nation-states in Eastern Europe and the Weimar Republic with its implications for the living conditions of the migrants and their status as foreigners were heatedly discussed. The Grenadierstraße was a lively meeting point and could function as a substitute for home. Even for those who like Markus Rebhuhn, who originally came from a Galician shtetl and made a career from a peddler to the owner of two men's clothing shops – which were frequented almost exclusively by gentile customers – the Grenadierstraße continued to be their "social, cultural and religious hinterland"[11].

However, several shops such as the lending library and bookstore of David Rosenberg in Grenadierstraße developed into spaces of intense intellectual and spiritual exchange. Abraham Tobias, who was born in Chrzanów (Galicia), described the Rosenberg bookstore in retrospect as "a kind of intellectual meeting point and reading circle in the style of the book stores one could find today in some Eastern European Jewish centres of Western Europe"[12]. The bookstore was devoted half to Modern Hebrew literature, half to religious publications and ritual objects. Recent rabbinical responses, state of the art magazines and the latest novels laid side by side on shelves and tables. This is a small, but excellent example of how spaces, which are today labelled as typically *ostjüdisch*, were indeed spaces of modernism, characterised by the intertwining of secularisation and sacralization of everyday life.

Simultaneously, Grenadierstraße was also a place where migrants came into contact with German society. Contemporary sources and autobiographical

9 See Morris Gruenberg: *Berlin N–54. A Story about Life in Berlin, Germany. From the 1920's through World War II.* Maitland, FL: Romex International 2000, p. 83.

10 Ibid., pp. 19–20.

11 Horst Helas: *Juden in Berlin-Mitte. Biografien – Orte – Begegnungen.* 2nd rev. Edition. Berlin: Trafo Weist 2001, pp. 68–69.

12 Abraham Tobias: Grenadierstraße. In: M. M. Sinasohn: *Die Berliner Privatsynagogen und ihre Rabbiner 1671–1971.* Jerusalem: Author's edition 1971, pp. 50–53, here 51.

memoirs of Jewish migrants and non-Jewish inhabitants of the Scheunenviertel present the picture of a multifaceted network of relationships and contacts between both groups. Contacts and interactions in everyday life took place in the house, the yard, on the street and in the shops. Jewish and non-Jewish residents met each other in different social roles as strangers, business partners, neighbours and friends.[13] According to Morris Gruenberg, the general attitudes of the non-Jewish neighbours towards the migrants ranged from "polite coolness to open hostility"[14]. Many migrants, such as Alfons Weber, report friendly relationships with individual neighbours.[15] The high population density in the quarter and the fact that only one third of the residents in Grenadierstraße were of Jewish origin made it impossible – for ultra-orthodox Jews as well – not not come into contact with German society.[16] Even Mischket Liebermann, the daughter of Rabbi Pinchus Elieser Liebermann, who in her autobiography stresses the tendency of orthodox Jews to separate from their German neighbours, refers to the lengthy discussions between her father and the warden of the synagogue. In the evenings both men discussed day-to-day political matters and the contradictions, which arose from urban everyday life for observant Jews.

The proletarian and urban environment of Grenadierstraße caused conflicts between parents and their children not only in the home of the Liebermanns, but also in many orthodox families. Some children and young people, such as Mischket, were more interested in entertainment, theatre and cinema, than in observing religious laws. Under the impression of the political tensions and violent conflicts between radical left and right wing groups at the nearby Bülowplatz many young migrants developed an interest for social questions. In some cases this interest led to a membership in Jewish or German socialist and communist groups.[17]

The diverse functions of Grenadierstraße and the large variety of experiences described by the migrants refer to the street as a transcultural and

13 For a detailed description of the neighbourly relations in Scheunenviertel see Saß: *Berliner Luftmenschen*, pp. 377–384.

14 Gruenberg: *Berlin N–54*, p. 56.

15 Alfons Weber: A Brief History of the Weber Siblings. Jewish Museum Berlin, 2010/77/0, pp. 6–7.

16 See: Die Siedlungs-, Wohnungs- und Bevölkerungsverhältnisse in der Dragoner-, Grenadier-, Linien-, Rücker- und Mulackstraße. In: *Mitteilungen des Statistischen Amts der Stadt Berlin* 5,5 (März 1929), pp. 1–12.

17 See for example Mischket Liebermann: *Aus dem Ghetto in die Welt*. Berlin (GDR): Verlag der Nation 1977; Max Fürst: *Talisman Scheherezade. Die schwierigen zwanziger Jahre*. München / Wien: Hanser 1976.

transnational social space in the urban landscape of Berlin. It was neither a Jewish ghetto nor an idyllic shtetl, but rather a "transitional zone of condensed communication"[18] between gentile Germans, Galician, Polish, Russian, and German Jews. The manifold encounters between different cultures, religions and nationalities opened up a wide range of Jewish and non-Jewish, religious and secular, political and cultural alignments. As hub between East and West, it provided the migrants with guidance and orientation in a foreign city, but could also convey feelings of home and security.

Boarding Houses

In contrast to the streets, boarding houses and hotels were first of all spaces of transition and an emblem for the cultural uprootedness and homelessness of the Jewish migrants in Weimar Berlin. As an intermediary space the boarding house is characterized by the contradictions of its social structure and the temporal intimacy in the communal life of its inhabitants. People with various backgrounds, different fates and divergent expectations for the future lived together in a very confined space, in which the boundaries between private and public gradually became fuzzy. For most of the Jewish migrants the boarding house was a first place of refuge. This place of refuge was embedded in an urban, metropolitan culture, in which the migrants were strangers. In the boarding house the migrants found themselves – both physically and mentally – in a space of transition between Eastern and Western Europe, between the past and the future, between the loss of their homes and a new unfamiliar environment, not knowing whether the new place would ever become a home.

In the literary treatment of the migration experience boarding houses play an important role, too. They are often used as a synonym for the migrant's existence. One of the most famous descriptions is David Bergelson's short story *Among Refugees*, in which he sheds light on the experiences of exile and homelessness in Berlin at the precarious moment after World War I.[19] In the centre

18 The article's understanding of transnational social spaces is primarily shaped on Johannes Paulmann: Grenzüberschreitungen und Grenzräume. Überlegungen zur Geschichte transnationaler Beziehungen von der Mitte des 19. Jahrhunderts bis in die Zeitgeschichte. In: Eckart Conze / Ulrich Lappenküper / Guido Müller (eds): *Geschichte der internationalen Beziehungen. Erneuerung und Erweiterung einer historischen Disziplin.* Köln: Böhlau 2004, pp. 169–196.

19 See David Bergelson: Tsvishn Emigrantn. In: *Shturemteg.* Kiev: Kooperativer Farlag "Kultur-lige" 1927 / Vilna: B. Kletskin 1928, pp. 165–192. Bergelson wrote the story before the assassination of the Ukrainian nationalist Simon Petljura in 1926 by Scholem Schwarzbard, but revised the story after the incident. For a detailed discussion see Delphine Bechtel: Bergelsons Berliner Erzählungen. Ein vergessenes Kapitel der jiddischen Literatur. In: Walter

of attention stands the divided character of a young Jewish migrant, who is obsessed with the idea to assassinate a *pogromchik*[20] living next door in the same Berlin boarding house. The complaints of East European Jewish workers about the director of the shelter of Jüdischer Volksverein (Jewish People's Association) in Berlin Mitte, Sally Kirschstein show, that this constellation was not only a literary arrangement, but actually became reality for some migrants.[21] Due to the acute housing shortage following World War I and the rapid increase in the number of refugees from Eastern Europe to Weimar Germany the Jüdischer Volksverein gave shelter not only to Jewish migrants, but also to non-Jewish Polish workers. This brought about the heated protest of Polish Jews living in the shelter. According to them, some people had found refuge there, who – after their return to Poland – would immediately take part in anti-Semitic violence.[22]

Depending on the facilities and the residency structures boarding houses were also places of community building. This was especially true for the Logirhaus Centrum in the Scheunenviertel and the Pension Struck in the Western part of Berlin, which provided a temporary home for all kinds of Jewish migrants from Eastern Europe.[23] The Pension Struck at Uhlandstraße, which was run by a distant relative of the German-Jewish painter Hermann Struck, served as a meeting point for migrants of different origin. Gershom Scholem, who was the only German among the Eastern Europeans, emphasized in his memoirs the mix of Russian, German, Yiddish and Hebrew spoken at the dinner tables and the lively debates about the major upheavals and political developments in Soviet Russia, Poland, and Romania.[24]

Röll / Simon Neuberg (eds): *Jiddische Philologie. Festschrift für Erika Timm*. Tübingen: Niemeyer 1999, pp. 252–272, here pp. 262–263.

20 Yiddish term for a person, who is responsible for leading and/or carrying out anti-Semitic pogroms.

21 The Jewish People's Association was founded by around thirty German Jewish Zionists in 1904 and aimed to help the growing number of Eastern European Jews, who had been heading west to flee the pogroms in Imperial Russia.

22 Minutes of a meeting by the Arbeiterfürsorgeamt jüdischer Organisationen Deutschlands, 21.11.1918. Centrum Judaicum Archive, 1,75A C Ge1 Nr. 907.

23 A vivid description of the Logirhaus Centrum is given by Joseph Roth: Flüchtlinge aus dem Osten. In: Michael Bienert (ed.): *Joseph Roth in Berlin. Ein Lesebuch für Spaziergänger*. Köln: Kiepenheuer & Witsch 1996, pp. 76–79. For the Pension Struck see Gershom Scholem: *Von Berlin nach Jerusalem. Jugenderinnerungen*. Frankfurt am Main: Suhrkamp 1977, pp. 110–112.

24 Scholem: *Berlin*, p. 111. In his diary Gershom Scholem takes a much more critical stance and criticizes the superficiality and the petite bourgeois squareness of some of the lodgers. Gershom Scholem: *Tagebücher nebst Aufsätzen und Entwürfen bis 1923*, vol. 2: 1917–1923, ed. by Karlfried Gründer / Herbert Kopp-Oberstebrink / Friedrich Niewöhner. Frankfurt am Main: Jüdischer Verlag 2000, p. 18.

In spite of the religious, cultural and political differences the migrants were connected with each other by the collective experiences of war and violence and their transitory émigré existence in Berlin. In this reading, the boarding house was a transitory space, where the foreignness of the migrants was highlighted. Moreover, the shared experiences of being a stranger in Weimar Germany helped to establish a sense of togetherness among the very heterogeneous group of migrants.

Cafés

In view of the cramped living conditions, it comes as no surprise that many of the Eastern European Jewish writers and intellectuals were attracted by the local urban café culture, which especially during the 1920s served as an emblem of Berlin's modernism and modernity. Since the 1910s cafés in Berlin were spaces of leisure, consumption, and representation as well as spaces, in which significant literary, cultural and societal activities have occurred.[25] Berlin's 'literary café', as Shachar Pinsker with reference to Edward Soja has convincingly pointed out, has to be understood as a 'thirdspace': "a site of negotiation between inside and outside, public and private, mass consumption and the avant-garde, men and women, Jews and Gentiles, 'the local' and the immigrant."[26] Writers, journalists, politicians, and activists met at the Café Monopol near Friedrichstraße in the city centre, at the Café des Westens, the Café Leon, and above all the Romanisches Café in West Berlin. These cafés were not only "key locations on the spatial map of Hebrew and Yiddish modernism in the metropolis",[27] but also a central interface for the development and coordination of humanitarian aid projects and the regulation of Jewish emigration on a global scale.

According to Yeshayahu Klinov, an Ukraininan Journalist, a unique situation had come to existence during the 1920s:

25 For the Berlin café as a Jewish space see Sarah E. Wobick-Segev: German-Jewish Spatial Cultures: Consuming and Refashioning Jewish Belonging in Berlin, 1890–1910. In: Gideon Reuveni / Nils Roemer (eds): *Longing, Belonging, and the Making of Jewish Consumer Culture*. Leiden: Brill 2010, pp. 39–60.

26 Shachar Pinsker: Deciphering the Hieroglyphics of the Metropolis. Literary Topographies of Berlin in Hebrew and Yiddish Modernism. In: Gennady Estraikh / Mikhail Krutikov (eds): *Yiddish in Weimar Berlin. At the Crossroads of Diaspora Politics and Culture*. London / Leeds: Modern Humanities Research Association Maney 2010, pp. 28–53, here p. 32.

27 Ibid., p. 33.

> Berlin is perhaps the only Jewish city in the world where, for years, an atmosphere has been created in which Jews could congregate, live together, get closer and learn from each other – without that hatred and the conflicts that are ever present in even our smallest communities. Is this because a bizarre curiosity has brought them here, to the banks of the Spree River, Jews who think alike and share the same goals, and belong to the same school of thought? Certainly not! […] Often, it is not the narrow table at the Romanisches Café or the Café Trumpf that separates our worldviews, but a deeper ideological chasm. But this is the reality – we understand each other – and I even dare say we have respect for our competitors…[28]

This "luxury", Klinov was convinced, one was not be able to afford everywhere, but only in Berlin, where the Eastern European Jewish intellectuals were not involved in daily party routine and struggles with their political opponents. From this point of view, the café appears as *klal* or community idyll, which played an important part in building networks and in overcoming linguistic, cultural and political boundaries among the intellectual elite of the migrants. But, and this was the main point of the contemporary critique by Jewish intellectuals in Eastern Europe, these encounters and transfers remained restricted to the comparatively small group of intellectuals in Berlin and had only little impact on the bulk of Jewish migrants in Berlin and abroad.[29]

A further ambivalence can be found in the relations of East European Jewish intellectuals to modern Weimar culture and society. On one side, Eastern European Jewish writers, artists, and journalists met most of the prominent figures of Berlin's modernism in the Romanisches Café, and these experiences left strong marks on their works and their intellectual development.[30] On the other side, the café experience of the Eastern European Jewish intellectuals refers very clearly to their simultaneous participation and marginalization

28 Yeshayahu Klinov: A Briv tsu Daniel Tsharnin. In: Moishe Shalit (ed.): *Daniel-Tsharny-Bukh*. Pariz: Tserata 1939, pp. 165–170, here p. 166.

29 For a detailed discussion see Heather Valencia: Yiddish Writers in Berlin 1920–1936. In: Edward Timms / Andrea Hammel (eds): *The German-Jewish Dilemma from the Enlightenment to the Shoah*. New York: Mellen 1999, pp. 193–207. For the heavy disputes between workers and intellectuals among the group of migrants in Berlin see Saß: *Berliner Luftmenschen*, pp. 180–189.

30 See among others Shachar Pinsker: *Literary Passports. The Making of Modernist Hebrew Fiction in Europe*. Stanford: Stanford UP 2011; Heather Valencia: Else Lasker-Schüler und Nochem Stencl. Eine unbekannte Freundschaft. Frankfurt am Main: Campus 1995; Delphine Bechtel: The Russian Jewish Intelligentsia and Modern Yiddish Culture. In: Michael Berkowitz (ed.): *Nationalism, Zionism and Ethnic Mobilization of the Jews in 1900 and Beyond*. Leiden: Brill 2004, pp. 213–226; Gennady Estraikh: Vilna on the Spree: Yiddish in Weimar Berlin. In: *Aschkenas* 16,1 (2006), pp. 103–127.

in modernist Berlin culture.[31] Their marginal position became also spatially apparent in the strict separation between "Yiddish" and "Hebrew" tables on the one hand and German tables on the other. Sitting on a "Jewish" table in the Romanisches Café allowed the writers and intellectuals to become part of Berlin's modernist culture. Simultaneously, they could maintain a critical distance to the modernist enterprise. In this respect, the café functioned as a main communicative space for East European Jewish intellectuals in Weimar Berlin and a place at which the migrants positioned themselves in German society.

Reading Rooms, Union Houses, and Meeting Halls

Another, equally important meeting point was the correspondence office of the American Yiddish Daily *Morgen-Zhurnal*. Since autumn 1922 the office was located at Breite Straße, not far from Berlin's newspaper district. The bureau functioned as major communication centre for the twenty-two European correspondents and the Berlin-based employees. At the same time, the office served as a contact point between travellers with US-American citizenship and Jews from Berlin, who maintained their social, family or business contacts to the United States. Within a short period of time, the reading room developed into an influential space of communication. Students, journalists, writers, and social activists from Lithuania, Russia, Ukraine, and Poland visited the reading room to study the major American and Yiddish newspapers displayed here. The visitors often stayed several hours because of the "familiar atmosphere".[32]

The multifunctional usage of the bureau, where travellers from the United States felt at home as well as migrants from Eastern Europe, refers once again to the relevance of Berlin as important intersection between East and West. Its mediating function was manifested in the transnational networks of the migrants, but also at concrete places in the urban landscape. To this end, Weimar Berlin was an interspace, characterised by the relations between elements of mobility, the familiarization in a foreign city, and a transnational structured Jewish environment.

In contrast to this group of several thousand intellectuals, the tens of thousands of Jewish workers gathered in their own union houses and club restaurants. With the foundation of the so-called Arbeter-Kultur-Fareyne (Cultural

31 See Pinsker: Deciphering the Hieroglyophics, pp. 32–33.

32 See A grus fun dem »Morgen-zshurnal's« eyropeisher biuro. In: *Morgen-Zshurnal*, 08.06.1923.

Workers Union) and tea kitchens they built on forms of communitarization which were very common in their former home countries. The description of the worker's home Ber Borochow by the Galician social worker and member of the socialist worker's party Poalei Zion Salomon Adler-Rudel illustrates their central functions as places of refuge and a "home in transit":

> The workers home of the Poalei Zion in Berlin: There is a peculiar and strong feeling of fellowship of a certain group. Jewish workers from several cities in the East can get together and create their own home. Uprooted and far away from their former home countries, they spend here a few hours in the week as if they were at home.[33]

As sites of exchange and contact the union houses strengthened not only feelings of solidarity among the Jewish workers. Discussing the political developments in Eastern Europe, the relations between the Jewish, German and international labour movements as well as the social and political position of Jewish workers in German society, challenged the workers to rethink their political opinions and provided opportunities for new orientations.

In contrast to the union houses, migrants with different social, political and cultural backgrounds congregated in meeting halls, for example at the Logenhaus in Kleiststraße (Charlottenburg district) or the Ressource Saal in Oranienburger Straße (Berlin Mitte district). In 1927, the Ressource Saal saw among others a meeting of the Berlin committee of the Central Yiddish School Organization (CISZO), which was attended by workers, craftsmen and intellectuals, who were all followers of divergent political currents. But at this point, they were united in the idea of supporting Yiddish language and Yiddish culture in Poland.[34] On these occasions, the migrants often continued with the discussions and confrontations, which were already set up in their former home countries. An intriguing example is the foundation of the Berlin kultur-lige (cultural league), which represented all groups of workers as well as well-known personalities such as the writer David Bergelson and the prominent statistician Jacob Lestshinsky. In 1921, representatives of the three Jewish labour parties, the Bund, the Poalei Zion, and the Hapoel Hazair, heavily disputed at Ressource Saal the question whether the aim of the kultur-lige should be the promotion of Yiddish culture, secular Jewish culture, or

33 Salomon Adler-Rudel: Berlin. Notizen eines Durchreisenden. In: *Freie Tribüne* (Vienna), August 1919.

34 For a detailed discussion see Saß: *Berliner Luftmenschen*, pp. 255–260.

simply proletarian culture. In the absence of an agreement, the kultur-lige finally ceased its activities.[35]

Meeting halls were not only places in which different political ideas clashed with each other, they also opened up the possibility of creating new alliances, as demonstrates the case of the Verband der Ostjuden (Union of Eastern Jews). Founded in 1919, the association pursued the aim to represent the political, social, and cultural interests of the Eastern European Jews in Germany and to defend them against anti-Semitic attacks. After initial difficulties between class-conscious workers and several founding members, the Verband der Ostjuden succeeded in gaining members from all fractions of the heterogeneous migrants group: Yiddishists, Hebraists, Bundists, Zionists, intellectuals, craftsmen and members of the middle class.[36] They all were united by the general objective of the association to build "a combination of the traditional Jewish lifestyle, the spirit of the new milieu and the requirements of the current economic and cultural life".[37]

Reading Rooms, Union Houses, and Meeting Halls functioned as spaces of retreat, leisure, education, and political debates. The relative closeness of the Meeting Halls und Union Houses turned them into Eastern European Jewish enclaves where issues of Jewish politics and class as well as questions of integration and participation were renegotiated continuously. The conflicts and disputes often led to the formation of new alliances between the different political factions.

Apartments

The already mentioned urban spaces – streets, boarding houses, cafés, union houses, and meeting halls –were strongly connected with specific types of usage, spatial functions, and strategies of appropriation. In contrast, the apartment was a communicative space which was generally open to different forms of use. Although the fewest rooms or flats in which Eastern European

35 See Estraikh: Vilna on the Spree, p. 114.

36 To the formation and politics of the Verband der Ostjuden see Trude Maurer: *Ostjuden in Deutschland 1918–1933.* Hamburg: Christians 1986; Anne-Christin Saß: Vom *Mizrekh-Yid* zur *Jüdischen Welt.* Die Publikationsorgane des „Verbands der Ostjuden" als Dokumente ostjüdischen Selbstverständnisses im Berlin der Weimarer Republik. In: Eleonore Lappin / Michael Nagel (eds): *Deutsch-jüdische Presse und jüdische Geschichte*, vol. 1. Bremen: edition lumière 2008, pp. 273–290.

37 Benzion Fett: Unsere Konferenz. In: *Jüdische Welt*, 16.01.1931.

Jews lived in Weimar Berlin met the bourgeois ideal of familial intimacy, they offered at least a certain degree of privacy and different ways of using.

This was especially true for the flats of Eastern European Jewish migrants in the more prosperous districts in the Western part of the city. The rooms were often used as meeting rooms for individual groups. The Berlin Bundists for example met in the flats of leading party members on the occasion of working meetings or anniversary celebrations. The flat of the historian Elias Tsherikover was used as a regular meeting point for scholarly sessions and workshops. Members of the historical section of the YIVO and the working group of the Mizrekh Yidisher Historisher Arkhiv (Eastern European Jewish Historical Archive) met regularly at his place.

In comparison, the representative flat of the family Grüngard near the town hall in Schöneberg district, served as a gathering place for Jewish intellectuals with Zionist background.[38] The aim of the Grüngard Salon was twofold: Promoting the Zionist cause through conversation, lectures, readings, and entertaining. Especially members of the Hebrew speaking Jewish society attended the meetings. This site of social, cultural, and political exchange is an impressing instance of how the German-Jewish salon culture of the 19th century was taken up and transformed by Jewish migrants from Eastern Europe. With its Eastern European style and Zionist orientation this transcultural communicative space offered a counter model to the middle class way of life and the liberal culture of the German Jews, as it was expressed especially by the Central-Verein deutscher Staatsbürger jüdischen Glaubens (Central Association for German citizens of the Jewish faith).[39]

In contrast, less affluent migrants were often forced to use their rooms simultaneously as living room and working space and had to share their room with other lodgers. The flowing transition between private, professional, and public spheres created completely different communicative spaces than the middle class flats in Charlottenburg and Schöneberg. The institution of "Privater Mittagstisch" (Private Dinner table) is a very good example for the overlapping of the different spheres. Couples or, more often, single mothers offered regularly lunch and dinner in their homes. In the flat of Rosa Gruenberg, for example, traditional Russian and Jewish dishes were served

38 The history of the Grüngard Salon is for the first time explored by Anat Feinberg: "Wir laden Sie höflich ein" – The Grüngard Salon and Jewish-Zionist Sociability in Berlin in the 1920s. In: Dohrn / Pickhan (eds): *Transit und Transformation*, pp. 234–256.

39 For the objectives, culture and politics of the Centralverein see Avraham Barkai: *„Wehr Dich!" Der Centralverein deutscher Staatsbürger jüdischen Glaubens 1893–1938*. München: Beck 2002.

to migrants from Eastern Europe. If required, transit migrants were offered a place to sleep, too. The guests, who frequented Rosa's Little Russia, were mostly of Jewish origin. In addition, there was "a small, but steady clientele from the substantial Russian émigré colony in Berlin"[40], who had heard about the fine cuisine and found the way to Rosa Gruenbergs flat on Rückerstrasse in Scheunenviertel.

To eat traditional Jewish and Eastern European dishes in Berlin produced not only a sense of home. To have lunch or dinner with initially unknown migrants in an intimate social atmosphere also had a symbolic meaning. Against the background of a foreign city and the increasing alienation from religious and cultural traditions such an experience was able to mediate a sense of togetherness and feelings of cultural solidarity. Above that, many households of Eastern European Jewish migrants in Berlin carried on the tradition of inviting the needy to the Jewish Shabbat dinner. In this way, contacts were tied between newcomers and migrants who had been living in Germany for a longer time. These meetings reminded the established migrants of their own first experiences in Berlin and strengthened feelings of community among the group as a whole.

In contrast, the studies of the rabbis in Scheunenviertel were spaces of retreat and intense studying as well as central places of mediating conflicts between the migrants. Orthodox rabbis, like Pinchus Elieser Liebermann, held their weekly court in the study and arbitrated familial and business conflicts, especially marital disputes. Often, he and his wife had to give practical everyday information to newcomers and their families.[41] Therewith an orthodox Eastern European practice was carried on in Berlin, but the contents of the disputes referred to the contradictions which orthodox migrants had to face in a modern metropolis.

The manifold use of the apartments demonstrates their important function as communicative spaces in the daily life of the migrants. Whereas the apartments of Eastern European Jewish intellectuals played a crucial role in creating political, cultural and scholarly networks among this social group, the apartments of the poorer and often religious migrants functioned as contact zones between migrants of diverse social, religious and cultural backgrounds. These encounters helped significantly to establish a sense of community among the migrants.

40 Gruenberg: *Berlin N–54*, p. 20.

41 See Liebermann: *Ghetto*, pp. 40–43.

From Jewish Spaces to Transcultural and Transnational Spaces

In contrast to the still prevalent picture of Eastern European Jews as a segregated minority in Western European countries, this article has highlighted different spatial strategies and practices of Jewish migrants and has asked how they adjusted to the challenges of urban life during the first decades of the 20th century. The different communicative spaces which were set up by the strategies and practices of the migrants were intrinsically linked with specific urban places in Weimar Berlin. They were embedded in the metropolitan culture of the city and shaped the identifications of the migrants in different ways. The transcultural and transnational social space of Grenadierstraße could help to insure one's origin, but functioned also as starting point of getting into contact with German society. In contrast, boarding houses stressed experiences of homelessness and transition. Union houses and meeting halls were both places of communitarization and conflict. Even the flats were no enclosed places but were characterized by the overlapping of public and private, Jewish and non-Jewish spheres. What connects these diverse and sometimes contradictory experiences with each other, is the perception and description of Berlin as a unique place of encounter between East and West, the foreign and the familiar, Eastern European Jews and German Jews as well as Jews and Gentiles.

In this way, the concept of communicative spaces helps us to deconstruct the rush assumption of the existence of distinct Jewish and non-Jewish spaces in the urban context. The analysis of the formation and alteration of communicative spaces goes beyond the study of certain urban districts with a high proportion of migrants and the related questions of ghettoization, deprivation, and cultural self-assertion. Rather, it emphasizes the heterogeneity and variety of the migrant experiences, the interrelation, and overlapping of mutual rapprochements between locals and newcomers as well as the complexity of cultural transfers, processes of differentiation and segregation within a specific urban space and culture.

A Border from a Jewish Perspective
Developments on the Prussian Periphery

Ruth Leiserowitz

1.

Borders play an essential role in history; however, they are rarely the focus of historical reflection. The border at the center of attention here was the eastern part of the long common stretch where Prussia and the Russian Empire first encountered one another. This period began with the partitioning of Poland at the end of the 18th century and came to an end after the First World War. Thus one can justifiably speak of a "long" 19th century on the border. Today, this former boundary is located in Lithuania. It is no longer a border and therefore *de facto* no longer exists. Following it, one finds the remnants of old customs houses; one can still clearly recognize the abrupt endings of both the planted trees along the avenues and the old paved streets that were previously on the Prussian side. The old buildings in the locales on either side of the former border are really not much different from one another. What does stand out is the dilapidated synagogues and large Jewish cemeteries in the towns that once belonged to the sphere of influence of the Russian Empire. The landscape itself proves to be virtually an archive of a society whose culture and experiences were inseparable. This border region is easily recognizable as what would have been understood as a Jewish area. It was here that Prussia bordered on the old *Lite* or *Lita*, the region in which Lithuanian Jews (who were also referred to as Litvaks) lived from the end of the 14th century to the beginning of the Second World War. In studying the history of this border region, it quickly becomes apparent that Jews played a seminal role on the border in the 19th and the first half of the 20th century.

The Jewish aspect of the Prussian periphery will be described in this article, filling a gap in the research on the Jews in Germany and Lithuania by describing not the urban centers but the border region from the perspective of the *longue durée*. The question of Jews on the German borders has been primarily studied for the period 1880–1914[1], and research is mainly concerned with questions of national identity rather than actors on the border or transnational actors, although Tobias Brinkmann partly covers this when describing transnational Jewish NGOs around the turn of the century.[2] I will show that the German-Lithuanian border was a fluid one for over a century, constituting a transnational "Jewish space". Both the phenomenon of the creating of this special space and its transnational character can be analyzed only by using a long-term perspective, also taking into account the important decades between the Crimean War (1853–1856) and the construction of cross-border railway lines (1869) when the border region was reduced to a mental line. The hypothesis of the article is that the Jewish inhabitants, as a consequence of their transnational orientation, were able to play an integral role in the region. To prove this, it is necessary first to consider the border and its development from both sides. I will describe how Jews experienced their environments and engaged with the border region. I will then analyze how "Jewish spaces" emerged, how they were contested, performed, used and finally misused by those who hated the Jews. The article is therefore about the border as a transnational space and the transnationality of those who crossed the border.

2.

Let me start with a few specifics about this mostly unfamiliar, unspectacular, but nevertheless interesting region: Nimmersatt was the most northerly border and post station in Prussia at the beginning of the 19th century. This tiny outpost lay adjacent to the Baltic Sea, about 12 kilometers north of Memel. Starting there, the Prussian border stretched out, at first dropping gently to the south, then running about 100 kilometers in an easterly

1 See Elizabeth A. Drummond: On the Borders of the Nation. Jews and the German-Polish National Conflict in Poznania, 1886–1914. In: *Nationalities Papers* 29,3 (2001), pp. 459–475; Mathias Seiter: Multiethnische Grenzgebiete: Deutsche Juden und die Grenzregionen Posen und Elsass-Lothringen 1871–1914. In: *Tel Aviver Jahrbuch für deutsche Geschichte* 40 (2012), pp. 78–94; Tobias Brinkmann: *Points of Passage: Jewish Transmigrants from Eastern Europe in Scandinavia, Germany, and Britain 1880–1914*. New York: Berghahn 2013. In contrast, there is a good study covering the entire 19th century for Jews on the Galician border: Börries Kuzmany: *Brody. Eine galizische Grenzstadt im langen 19. Jahrhundert*. Wien / Köln / Weimar: Böhlau 2011.

2 Tobias Brinkmann: Why Paul Nathan Attacked Albert Ballin. The Transatlantic Mass Migration and the Privatization of Prussia's Eastern Border Inspection, 1886–1914. In: *Central European History* 43,1 (2010), pp. 47–83.

direction from the market town of Heydekrug. Shortly before the little river Šventa it made an abrupt turn to the south, meeting up with the Memel River. In the year 1812, this border line separated the Kingdom of Prussia from the Russian Empire (stretching from Nimmersatt to the Memel at the level of Schmalleningken). During that time, the Grand Duchy of Warsaw (created in 1807) bordered Prussia south of the Memel. This relatively short stretch had maintained its course for centuries. Neighboring Lithuania, which since the Lublin Union of 1569 was joined with Poland into the kingdom of the two countries, had a truly homogenous structure, both economically and socially. There were ethnic and cultural differences between Poland and Lithuania, which were obscured by the shared Roman Catholic religion. With the third partition of Poland in 1795, Russia occupied Lithuania, giving Prussia a new neighbor. This partition brought substantial changes, some of which were to have quite long-term consequences. For its part, Russia saw the border first and foremost as a buffer zone. It quickly began renaming many places. In the Lithuanian Governorate, numerous locales received Russian names. A regional reform in December 1842 by the tsarist administration separated the Governorate of Kaunas from the Governorates of Wilna and Šiauliai. Kaunas now ran along the Russian side as the direct neighbor of East Prussia (up to the bank of the Memel). While Prussia previously had a variety of neighbors (such as the Duchy of Kurland, the Lithuanian territory of the United Kingdom of Poland, and then the Kingdom of Poland), their neighbor on the border now was clearly Russia. For the most part, the population living in the countryside was Lithuanian or Polish. The Jews lived in the small towns on the border, often comprising up to 50% of the population, with the result that people called the towns *Shtetl.* They were called Litvaks because this was the Yiddish term for a Jew of the historical Lithuania including large swaths of northeastern Poland (notably the Białystok and Suwałki regions), northern and western Belarus, and southern Latvia. These Jews had a distinctive Yiddish dialect and were defined by their widespread opposition to Hasidism.[3]

The further developments along the border can be described as follows: the Russian Empire began to isolate itself from its new neighbors and for decades sealed its border. After the Russian ports were blockaded during the Crimean War (1853–1856), the government had to finally open up its border

3 Allan Nadler: Litvak. http://www.yivoencyclopedia.org/article.aspx/Litvak (accessed 13.10.2014).

for foreign trade, giving a major boost to the border region. Shortly afterwards, the construction of cross-border railway lines made the border tremendously porous, allowing the region to flourish. In the middle of the 1880s, ten years after the foundation of the German Empire, the Prussian government limited and bureaucratized border crossings. During World War I armies of both Empires crossed the border more than once: in 1914, Russian soldiers attacked East Prussian cities, and in 1916 the German army occupied the Lithuanian region. As a result of this war and the subsequent peace treaty, the border was shifted for the first time in centuries, because Germany lost most of the northern part of East Prussia. In 1924, this area was designated as the Memel region and given to the newly re-constituted Lithuanian state by the League of Nations. The characteristics of the region changed, as it lost its specificity as the imperial periphery. Adjacent nation states strove for ethnic homogeneity and harbored territorial claims against each other. Yet they still protected people's freedom of movement for some time. However, in 1939 the border was forcefully revised to make it easier for the Hitler regime to occupy the Memel region. After being occupied in the summer of 1940 by the Red Army, it was in Lithuania that the National Socialist and Stalinist regimes now confronted each other directly. The newly founded Lithuanian Soviet Republic was hermetically sealed off. In June 1941, the Wehrmacht crossed the border by force. In 1944, the Red Army pushed towards East Prussia and occupied the region. As a consequence of the Second World War, East Prussia was divided among the Lithuanian Soviet Republic, the USSR, and Poland. The former national border either disappeared or was turned into an internal border between the Lithuanian Soviet Republic and the Kaliningrad region. Since 1992, one part once again forms a national border, but in this case between the Republic of Lithuania and the Kaliningrad Region of the Russian Federation.

3.

Border regions can generally be considered as a kind of seismograph, as zones of enormous dynamism. Although borders have been established and regions with differing characteristics and structures have been separated for a long time, there is still no general and coherent theory of borders.[4] The

4 Markus Bauer / Thomas Rahn (eds): *Die Grenze. Begriff und Inszenierung.* Berlin: Oldenbourg 1997, p. 8. More recently: Bernhard Struck: Grenzregionen. http://www.ieg-ego.eu/struckb-2012-de URN: urn:nbn:de:0159-2012120307 (accessed 01.10.2013); Etienne François / Jörg Seifarth / Bernhard Struck: *Die Grenze als Raum, Erfahrung und Konstruktion. Deutschland, Frankreich und*

border examined here over a period of 130 years was sometimes a barrier, sometimes a conflict zone, but mostly an area of contact. Did the border have only a political dimension, or was there also a cultural one? It must have done, since one could clearly experience here what Lucien Febvre described for the Western part of Germany after 1945: "A border first comes into existence […] when on the other side of a line, a different world begins, a nexus of ideas, feelings, and enthusiasms which surprise and confuse the stranger."[5] However, it must also be carefully questioned whether a fixed border line really existed during those 130 years. Had the other world already begun in the land around the border, far in advance of the actual boundary?

A cultural border can only be conceived when one links together the metaphorical images used to express the cultural differences with the threads of concrete interaction that are acceptable to the historian.[6] Cultural borders are more specifically experienced in language use, religious practices, celebrations, rituals, in public communication, yet also in the patterns of settlements and architectural styles. But over and above that, the phenomenon of this particular border engenders a special interest. As Georg Simmel wrote back in 1908: "The border is not a spatial reality with sociological effects, but rather a sociological reality which takes its form spatially."[7] Indeed it is exactly these sociological realities that need to be described in order to grasp the situation of the Jews in the region as a whole.

4.

Other population groups also lived on both sides of the border in the 19th and 20th century, but the Jews will be the focus here. Beginning in the 18th century, Jews had in rising numbers settled on the Lithuanian side of the border. They had barely moved to the region when they began crossing over the border regularly as traders and merchants. Following Elfi Haver, one can argue: "Border always presupposes an 'on the other side'. Border cannot be thought without a knowledge and image of the other side. It is a dialectical

Polen vom 17. bis 20. Jahrhundert. Frankfurt am Main: Campus 2007; David Laven / Timothy Baycroft: Border Regions and Identity. In: *European Review of History – Revue Europeenne d'Histoire* 15,3 (2008), pp. 255–275.

5 Lucien Febvre: *Der Rhein und seine Geschichte.* Frankfurt am Main: Campus 1994, pp. 163–164.

6 Jürgen Osterhammel: Kulturelle Grenzen in der Expansion Europas. In: *Saeculum* 46 (1995), pp. 101–138, here p. 108.

7 Georg Simmel: Soziologie. Untersuchungen über die Formen der Vergesellschaftung. In: Id.: *Gesamtausgabe*, vol. 11, ed. by Ottheim Rammstedt. Frankfurt am Main: Suhrkamp 1999, pp. 687–790, here p. 689.

concept."[8] He also points out that the awareness of a border, with its inescapable notion of a limit to one's own living area, is only possible when people think of a 'beyond'.

Of greater interest than the border itself are the border region and the outbound communication across the border; in other words, the sociological facts as Simmel puts it. In general, the cultural diversity of life found in the border region (in addition to Lithuanians, there were Germans, Poles, Russians, and Roma living on both sides) was marked at the beginning of the 19th century by a relative disregard for the border itself. The collective consciousness of the national groups on both sides of the border did not have a territorial connection. Their consciousness was more static, and linked above all with the ownership of their parcels of land. It was not until after 1863 that border-crossing activities started among the Lithuanians, primarily because of the nationalist movement. Jews, who crossed the border with higher frequency, caused them to stand out among the general population.

From the Jewish perspective, the developments in the region can be outlined briefly: After the issuance of the Edict of Tolerance in 1812, Jews increasingly left Lithuania and migrated to Prussia, founding settlements. Around 70 years later, after 1881, the Jewish immigrants on Germany's Eastern border came into political focus for the first time when Prussian legislation for the so-called "cross-overs" (*Überläufer*) was made stricter. The Jewish way of life now had to receive an explicit permission from the German bureaucracy.[9] During the same period, because of pogroms in Russia, a large Jewish migration over the border began, primarily to the United States of America, but also to South Africa. Barely 60 years later, in June 1941, the first mass extermination of Jews was committed on this exact section of the border. The Tilsit *Einsatzkommando* crossed the border and killed almost the entire Jewish population.

8 Elfi Charlotte Haver: *Der geographische Raum in der Vorstellungswelt des Menschen. Über die Beziehungen sozialer Gruppen zu ihrer geographischen Umwelt.* Ph.D., Münster 1974, p. 102.

9 From 1812 onward, the Prussian government dealt with the "question of the Polish cross-overs" (*Überläufer*) (Geheimes Staatsarchiv Preußischer Kulturbesitz (GStA), XX. HA, Rep. 77, Tit. 1176, No. 2a, vol. 5, pp. 143–156), meaning Poles and Jews. Among the Jews this meant primarily merchants, agents, and traders who had settled in Prussia near the Russian border. (It was especially in the 1880s that the term 'cross-over' was used. It is interesting that on 9 February 1886 Ludwig Windhorst spoke out in the Prussian House of Representatives against the use of this term: "Ich nenne sie Einwanderer, Überläufer ist ein ganz verkehrter Name. Die Leute sind ja nicht übergelaufen, eingeschlichen, sondern sie sind eingewanderte Männer. Sie sind eingewandert aus verschiedenen Gründen: weil ihnen unsere Gegend angenehmer ist, weil ihnen unsere Gesetze bequemer sind als [die] in Russland." (*Stenographische Berichte des preußischen Abgeordnetenhauses* 1886, vol. 1, p. 422).

5.

Until the 19th century, there was still a kind of 'no man's land' between the settlements on both sides of the border. The border region extended from the last horse-relay and post station and the local customs station prior to the border through to the next post station and customs house on the other side.[10] However, hardly anyone knew the actual border line, assuming they had not crossed it as a trader or traveler. The border experience was unique. Post coachmen, people travelling a long distance, and merchants were the ones who most frequently travelled past the sentry boxes. Jews crossed the border regularly as well, primarily as merchants, but also for additional reasons: Jews did not have the permission to stay in a market town (such as Memel) overnight, or they may have had to take a body for burial to a Jewish cemetery.[11] But the majority of citizens seldom came into the direct vicinity of the border during this period. In the first half of the 19th century, most inhabitants did not often come close to the border and thus experienced it not as a line of demarcation, but rather as an alien zone. Political awareness of the border did not play a role in the minds of the general population. Maps were not widely available and were only used by those travelling. Exact maps were not drawn and disseminated until the development of the *Chaussee* system (in East Prussia after 1816).[12] An awareness of the border was revived most frequently during the great market fairs, which took place on both sides of the border several times a year. During these events wares and purchasing patterns could be compared. In addition, one could closely study the large number of foreigners. Marketplaces with many foreigners were strongly associated with the border by the local residents, even when the locale did not lie immediately on the border line. Thus Tilsit was for a long time generally considered a border town, although the actual border ran 25 kilometers further to the north.[13]

The political events at the turn of the 19th century, the partitions of Poland, and the hostilities in East Prussia in the course of the Napoleonic wars meant the citizens experienced a shifting of borders. As a consequence, crossing the

10 Leopold Zedlitz-Neukirch: *Polen: Ein historisch-geographisch-statistisches Taschenbuch für Reisende, Geschäftsmänner und Zeitungslesende.* Berlin: Duncker & Humblot 1831, p. 22.

11 GStA, XX, Rep. 2I, Tit. No.16, No.1, Acta wegen der sich im Lande aufhaltenden unbefugten Juden 1808–1810; XX, Rep. 9, No. 294 (1801–1807) Fortschaffung der jüdischen Propinationspächter, Krüger und Schänker, auch Fährenpächter aus den Domänen.

12 The construction of chausses (extra-urban roads with a solid pavement designed by engineers) created a basis for improving the flow of trade during the early industrial period.

13 Otto Glagau: *Littauen und die Littauer.* Tilsit: J. Reyländer 1869, p. 34.

border became increasingly normal. For the first time in 1812, a border crossing on a huge scale took place when Napoleon's Grande Armée moved into Russia. Many Jewish traders sensed the business opportunity of a lifetime and trekked with the baggage train or followed it. The troops left considerable traces and, of course, much war damage on the Prussian-Lithuanian border. The cities were ransacked, and even the private coffers were emptied. However, flexible Litvak traders were able to earn a fortune through clever business dealings during the war; as registered military suppliers for the Napoleonic troops, they gained favorable spots in the East Prussian border region.[14] The trade in wood and grain in particular allowed them to make a good living in peacetime. Jewish merchants in the first half of the 19th century crossed the border very frequently. The number of Litvaks who conducted trade with the neighboring country (legally, semi-legally, and illegally) increased enormously despite the Russian restrictions.

6.

At the end of the 1860s, life on the border changed very quickly. The newly constructed rail lines did not just run up to the border, they crossed it. Border agents, customs houses and transport companies sprouting up were no longer surrounded by a 'no man's land', but were instead integrated into the infrastructure of the newly developing communities. Border traffic now took place effectively in public view. The border line that people were not generally aware of at the beginning of the 19th century had now become something clearly obvious on both sides. On the basis of an agreement with the Russian empire, border traffic was only allowed for the residents of the 10 kilometer wide strip of land on either side of the border, with border certificates being issued to the locals. This possibility of a relatively flexible existence led to a massive Jewish settling of places close to the border which previously had not held any attraction at all. The increased border traffic needed an infrastructure, which also blossomed into its own culture with the attendant restaurants, shops, cartage companies, and currency exchanges. It was primarily Jews who invested in providing services, opening businesses, hotels, and transport companies and marketing new goods and consumer products even in the smallest villages. Between 1860 and 1880, an incredibly liberal naturalization policy toward Jewish emigrants was in effect in East Prussia. In 1871,

14 GStA, XX. HA, Rep. 77, Tit. 1021, Memel, No. 2 wegen der von den Juden in Memel acquirierten Häuser und Grundstücke, Armee-Lieferant Meierowitz.

after the founding of the German state, the number of applications for naturalization grew significantly. Becoming a German citizen was now attractive. The visible border, that is the international border, was something the Jews perceived as being relatively negotiable. From this attitude arose the hope that the invisible internal border, that is, the one between local people and strangers, could be managed just as easily.

7.

However, this progression ended abruptly and in a manner completely unexpected by the residents in the region. In 1881, significantly stricter immigration regulations were introduced by the Prussian government, giving expression to clearly anti-Slavic and anti-Semitic policies. Issues such as border patrol, pass control and registration, citizenship, issues of asylum, immigration and emigration, as well as legislation concerning foreigners were re-written or applied more strictly. The empire's border in the East began to take on a clear shape. The border showed itself to be a peripheral organ of the state, as proposed by 19th century geographer Friedrich Ratzel. Numerous Russian and Polish citizens were expelled at short notice. The numbers varied from 10–15,000 for all of Prussia. Only someone who could show himself to be "useful" was permitted to stay. In that sense, the living situation of the Litvaks was now marked by huge contradictions. They played an essential role in the economy, but became victims of anti-Semitic policies toward foreigners, which were focused purely on economic exploitation and were clearly directed against integration. On the other hand, the East Prussian province was dependent on the Russian and Polish hinterlands (as were all the Eastern provinces). The deportations disrupted the towns' international trading business: for example, the Königsberg grain trade proved to be irreparably damaged. Further emigration was permanently stopped by these policies.

8.

Nevertheless, the Jews on the border still played a role in the decades to follow, albeit from a different perspective. While the border crossings of Russian citizens without identity papers a few years prior to this had been handled very rigidly by the gendarmes, the Prussian authorities now decided to deal with such cases differently, mainly for economic reasons. The immigrants from Russia, primarily Lithuanians, Poles, and Jews, were permitted to transit through Prussia only when they either had the required pass and a ticket for a berth on the Hamburg American Line or North German Lloyd or some other cabin berth, as well as a certain sum of money. Emigration agents shot up like mushrooms in the 1860s. Agents of many foreign companies travelled through Russia and offered their services: speedy transportation over the border as well as passage on a ship. The German authorities wanted to earn the lion's share of this enterprise. Money could be made at different levels. The smuggling agents, that is, Jews or Lithuanians who organized the transportation from inside the country out to a meeting point near the border, raked in huge commissions. A further (considerably smaller) profit was earned by the Jewish owners of the drinking establishments where those future emigrants often had to wait for days until there was a good opportunity to cross over. The Lithuanian and Prussian waggoners or the Lithuanian and Jewish guides who took the emigrants – who in smuggling jargon were called "golobki" (little pigeons) – across the border line and brought them to a travel agent also profited. Naturally, the Russian border patrol also held out its hand. The supervising and support agents of the shipping lines (who were in part German, but also German Jewish) were waiting near the border – Memel, Insterburg, Schwirwindt, Tilsit, and Eydtkuhnen – and held the reins of this large-scale trans-border business in their hands. To demonstrate the magnitude of this operation: In Eydtkuhnen alone, a total of 13,232 Russian emigrants arrived between November 1895 and November 1896. In Tilsit during the same time, over 4,000 people purchased passage on a ship. During this phase, Jews were present in quite divergent and differentiated positions: they made up part of the migrants, but also comprised important elements of the network for crossing the border. In addition, on the German side there was a line of Jewish aid organizations which developed numerous services for provisioning and helping their fellow brothers and sisters.

The Jewish immigrants who travelled across this section of border (from 1881 until World War I) represented only a small part of the total migration. The awareness of the Jewish aspect was significantly more pronounced because of the many facets of Jewish presence. The Jewish immigrants on the Eastern German border came into political focus for the first time when the Prussian legislation against what were called the "cross-overs" was made more stringent, and Jewish existence required the clear acknowledgement and approval of the German nation. Russian and Lithuanian Jews began crossing the border *en masse* with the intention of emigrating to America. At this time, the border region underwent a major change into a transit area, now primarily being passed through by collective streams of people, a state of affairs that was to last until 1914. Israel Bartal has commented extensively on the year 1881 as a "significant milestone" in the history of the East European Jews.

Bartal focuses on this specific moment with reference to the official anti-Semitism in the policies of the Russian Empire and the politicizing of Jewish nationalism.[15] 1881 represents a crest or turning point in light of the initiation of the expulsion policies in Prussia and their implementation in 1885 and thereafter. This was not a construction aimed primarily at East European Jews; rather it emerged from the harshening policies of the Prussian Interior Ministry.[16] The effects of these events on both sides introduced a new phase in the border's history.

9.

The role of the Jews on the East Prussian border expanded during the 19th century. First they were the ones able to cross over the border and distinguished themselves by doing so. Later they became active as investors and represented an economic leadership in the trading taking place around the border. In addition, they built up transnational networks offering migrants essential aid stations. For decades, Jews recognized the border area as an opportunity and thus it had a formative impact on them. The importance of the Jewish involvement in the region became clear in 1941. Members of the state police in Tilsit, in the first days of Operation Barbarossa in June 1941, shot and killed the Jewish residents of the *Shtetl* near the border. The perpetrators considered the Lithuanian strip of border in the first eight weeks of the war as an extraterritorial area in which they could carry out any actions. They were aware that they were engaged in a border violation in a double sense – both territorially and morally. However, they tried to ignore this breaking of taboos by representing their actions as a special task during which they committed irreversible deeds. German border police and customs agents participated voluntarily in the firing squads. They saw in them a part of their duty: bringing "peace and order" to the border area and ridding the region of its national stains (*national zu entflecken*), thereby preparing it for annexation to East Prussia. The border region, in which up to that point the Jews had formed a constitutive element, was fundamentally changed in the summer of 1941, because the Jewish population was completely annihilated.

15 Israel Bartal: *Geschichte der Juden im östlichen Europa 1772–1881*. Göttingen: Vandenhoeck & Ruprecht 2010, pp. 13, 167.

16 The fact that both phenomena of anti-Semitism occurred simultaneously needs further analysis, which I can mention here only in passing. See also Helmut Walser Smith: *The Continuities of German History, Nation, Religion, and Race Across the Long Nineteenth Century*. Cambridge / New York: Cambridge UP 2008, p. 111: "Historians are just now beginning to put this story together".

10.

The border as a spatial phenomenon should be taken as a central historical category of transnational history.[17] To that extent, the concept of transnationality should and must be plumbed again, especially since the scholarly landscape contains numerous different approaches to it and it is frequently overworked at present.[18] Transnationality is understood here as a process in which migrants, through their daily activities and their social, economic, and political connections, create cross-border social realms and have access to information and goods from another country. In the ways they live their lives, they configure their social realm so they are virtually at home and grounded in two national realms.[19] Their position in the public sphere is defined on the basis of these various affiliations.[20] What emerges from their plural social contextualization is a bipolar coupling such that the events in the land of their origin also influence life in their new homes, and what happens in the places where the immigrants now live is reflected in their old home.[21] Through the circulation of people, money, possessions, and information the spheres become intertwined. Migrants with transnational ways of living are also referred to as *transmigrants*. The transmigrants of the 19th century, in the course of their cross-border lives, were confronted with various processes

17 Nancy Foner: *In a New Land. A Comparative View of Immigration.* New York / London: New York UP 2005; Ayse Çalar / Nina Glick Schiller: Towards a Comparative Theory of Locality in Migration Studies. Immigrant Incorporation and City Scale. In: *Journal of Ethnic and Migration Studies* 35,2 (2009), pp. 177–202; Linda Basch / Nina Glick Schiller / Cristina Szanton Blanc: From Immigrant to Transmigrant: Theorizing Transnational Migration. In: *Anthropological Quarterly* 68,1 (1995), pp. 48–63; Josh DeWind / Peggy Levitt / Steven Vertovec: International Perspectives on Transnational Migration. An Introduction. In: *International Migration Review* 37,3 (2003), pp. 565–575; Ewa Morawska: Disciplinary Agendas and Analytic Strategies of Research on Immigrant Transnationalism: Challenges of Interdisciplinary Knowledge. In: *International Migration Review* 37,3 (2003), pp. 611–640; Kiran Klaus Patel: *Nach der Nationalfixiertheit. Perspektiven einer transnationalen Geschichte. Antrittsvorlesung, 12. Januar 2004.* Berlin: Humboldt Universität 2004, esp. p. 3.

18 Çalar / Glick Schiller: Towards, pp. 185–186; Foner: *In a New Land*, p. 56.

19 The definition of "transnational social space" from Ludger Pries concerns a space that stretches over plural localities and between different dwelling places and living areas. Yet this social space is not coextensive with unified surface areas on this or that side of the border line, but rather is a product and creation of elements from the regions of origin and residence that provide identity and social structure. On the one hand, this space is configured through the life practices of the migrants. On the other hand, the migration (a transmigration) brings the relationship between a stretch of land and social spaces into a new balance. Ludger Pries: *Die Transnationalisierung der sozialen Welt. Sozialräume jenseits von Nationalgesellschaften.* Frankfurt am Main: Suhrkamp 2008.

20 Basch / Glick Schiller / Szanton Blanc: From Immigrant, p. 48.

21 DeWind / Levitt / Vertovec: International Perspectives, p. 567.

of *nation-building* in their respective countries and in some cases became involved in these processes. Their identities and practices were also defined through hegemonic categories such as "race" and "ethnicity," which were deeply rooted in the country.[22] During the 19th century, transmigrants were also aware of the possibility of assimilating into a nation; in that period the homogenization of very different subjects as citizens of a country and sharing a national culture simply required acculturation.[23] Immigrants to a society which increasingly expressed itself in national gestures had at that time ultimately forfeited a claim to a social option from earlier centuries, under which strangers experienced positive discrimination or privileges.[24] For a long time Jews had an interesting relationship with space, and their transnational practices had already endured for a long time in the border area under discussion.[25] Ultimately, the border region developed into an important transit area for the refugees coming out of the tsarist empire, with most of them emigrating abroad after 1881. What role did the transmigrants play in this context? They were the ones who essentially organized the first pulses of traffic coming through this transit area, for these men (and women) were the ones who knew their way around emerging intercultural incompatibilities, functioning as virtual translators and mediators. They were also involved in setting up "support networks". Their role became all the more important the more the border region evolved from a pluralistic to a national space.

11.

How was the Jewish world shaped? The Jewish community is often depicted as a network community.[26] Indeed, networks did play an essential role. This phenomenon has already been described and analyzed multiple times, particularly its range and scope.[27] The image of the network is still in vogue today, even though Jürgen Osterhammel reminds us that the visual metaphor

22 Morawska: Disciplinary Agendas, p. 611–640.

23 Dirk Hoerder: *Cultures in Contact. World Migrations in the Second Millennium.* Durham: Duke UP 2002, p. 361.

24 Ibid., p. 362.

25 Basch / Glick Schiller / Szanton Blanc: From Immigrant, p. 48.

26 Dan Diner: Geschichte der Juden – Paradigma einer europäischen Historie. In: Gerald Stourzh (ed.): *Annäherungen an eine europäische Geschichtsschreibung.* Vienna: Österreichische Akademie der Wissenschaften 2002, pp. 85–103.

27 Susan K. Wierzbicki: *Beyond the Immigrant Enclave. Network Change and Assimilation.* New York: LFB 2004; Charles Tilly: Transplanted Networks. In: Virginia Yans-McLaughlin (ed.): *Immigration Reconsidered. History, Sociology, and Politics.* New York: Oxford UP 1990, pp. 78–95.

of a network can be deceptive, because the structural gaps among the configurations have to be seen from repeated relationships or interactions.[28] Furthermore, Osterhammel emphasizes the two-dimensionality of the network. Nevertheless, it becomes apparent in the analysis of the diverse contacts presented here that contemporaneous networks also existed in hierarchies through which a third level could selectively emerge. The modifications through modernization or the phenomenon of new connections with already existent non-Jewish structures are of interest as well.[29] Among these, for example, would be the inter-Jewish contacts within the German army.[30] Modernization was a further factor playing an essential role for the whole border region. The resulting acceleration of life in general, of sending and receiving messages, of a person's ability to move around, and of the advance in setting up of networks was immense in the second half of the 19th century.[31]

Quite different forms of cross-border migration can be held up for review from within the long period being investigated here. The complex process of Litvaks relocating into Prussia (for the 19th century) is one. Another would be the important role of the movement through the East Prussian border area by emigrants from the tsarist empire who were heading toward America (from the end of the 1880s up to the outbreak of the First World War). A third is the flight of the Jews from the NS regime. Although migration was extensive, these examples all represent a major challenge to the individual and inherently share an ambitious goal: to reach a new life on the other side of the border. All processes of migration rest heavily on cumulative causes.[32] Marriage customs and family relationships were essential, and social capital specific to the intended destination was also a determining factor.[33] The

28 Jürgen Osterhammel: *Die Verwandlung der Welt. Eine Geschichte des 19. Jahrhunderts.* Munich: Beck 2009, p. 1010.

29 Tilly: Transplanted, p. 85.

30 Ruth Leiserowitz: *The German Army as a Matchmaker. Litvak Families in East Prussia and Their Network*, unpublished manuscript.

31 Osterhammel: *Verwandlung*, p. 1010.

32 This concept of a "cumulative causation" states that the migrations as first initiated caused complex processes of change both in the areas of origin and eventual residence that then made probable a stabilization and expansion of the migration. Regarding this, reference should be made primarily to Tilly: Transplanted, pp. 78–95, but also to the works of Douglas Massey; see, e. g., Douglas Massey: An Evaluation of International Migration Theory: The North American Case. In: *Population and Development Review* 20 (1994), pp. 699–751.

33 According to Pierre Bourdieu, social capital is the totality of resources that come with membership in group. Exchange relationships, which are based on this capital, have material and symbolic connections and have a multiplier effect on actual capital at hand and that which

importance of the home community, of shared heritage, should also not be underestimated.[34]

12.

Overall, approaching the Jewish history of the 19th and 20th centuries from the perspective of the border has proven fruitful. On the one hand, the development of 'border' emerges as a phenomenon and with it the border region. In addition, approaches to Jewish history from this perspective are sharpened. Third, the potential of the periphery can be pulled into focus.

The career of "border as a peripheral organ of the state"[35] began in the 19th century. Its form and the weight of attention given to it changed several times over the subsequent 130 years. All the phenomena of that time, the modernization and the nationalism, left their traces, leading to a change in importance. The essential changes on the border were always consequences of political processes. Significant political changes found their spatial expression on the border.

These changes had an impact on the Jewish minority on the border, whose history can be interpreted primarily as internally connected processes of mobilization and migration. The border never represented a strict divide between the experiences of the Jews from the East and the German Jews. A far-reaching east-west dialogue and a cultural interconnection existed instead. Central locales were available in the compacted border area as well as in the border towns. The extent to which the political and cultural movements around the border coincided with those of the German minority on the border is an area for further research.

is convertible into other forms of capital. The reproduction of social capital requires a constant nurturing of relationships. Pierre Bourdieu: *Die verborgenen Mechanismen der Macht.* Hamburg: VSA 1992, pp. 49–79; Dirk Hoerder / Yvonne Hébert / Irina Schmitt: Transculturation and the Accumulation of Social Capital. Understanding Histories and Decoding the Present of Young People. In: Iid. (ed.): *Negotiating Transcultural Lives. Belongings and Social Capital among Youth in Comparative Perspective.* Göttingen: V&R Unipress 2005, pp. 11–38, here pp. 17–19.

34 Common origin – from the same place – can also be classified as an "ascriptive friendship relationship", similar to an ambiguous status of one's kinship group. Social relationships of migrants and potential migrants determined the scale and the course of migration processes which brought about the translocation of the networks.

35 Fiedrich Ratzel: *Politische Geographie oder die Geographie der Staaten, des Verkehres und des Krieges.* 2., rev. ed. Munich / Berlin: Oldenbourg 1903, p. 123.

Although the border region was reduced to a mental line for a certain time, it was able to form transit areas; however, after a short period these always dissipated because of nationalization processes.

To summarize: Jews on the East Prussian border were a constitutive factor in the border region for the entire period under study. While in the 19th century they distinguished themselves on the border primarily within the economic sphere, their role from the end of the century onward was increasingly reduced. As time passed, experience of the border became common knowledge for all and all the actors on the border wanted to profit from it. In 1941, when offensive forces brought geopolitical change, the sphere of life which for decades had been seized by the Jews as an opportunity was transformed. It now became the place of their annihilation. Their territoriality became their fate.

German-Jewish Borderlands
On 'Non-Jewish Jewish Spaces' in Weimar and Nazi Germany

Mirjam Zadoff

Introduction: The 'Non-Jewish Jewish Space'

At the age of only seven years, Werner Scholem made his first appearance as an actor and as a revolutionary. Together with his brothers he acted in a play called *Ex oriente lux*, which had been written by his gifted mother and was performed at his uncle's wedding party. He entered the stage in a long curly wig and sandals, with a shepherd's crook and a small leather-bag containing phylacteries. Although his disguise resembled that of a Biblical shepherd, the child was supposed to be impersonating a Jew from Zionist Palestine and the central figure in a play to honor and mock his uncle's passion for the national Jewish revival.[1] Betty Scholem had given the role of the Jew to her most rebellious and probably most difficult son – not expecting that it would be her youngest, Gerhard, who would leave for Palestine 19 years later, in 1923, while his brother Werner allegedly uttered the following words: "Schade, daß ein junger Mensch wie du seine Kraft an eine solche Sache verschwendet, statt sich in den Dienst der Weltrevolution zu stellen, die vor der Tür steht."[2] By that time he was about to become one of Germany's most influential communist politicians and revolutionaries.

1 Betty Scholem: Ex Oriente Lux. In: Paul Mendes-Flohr: *Divided Passions. Jewish Intellectuals and the Experience of Modernity.* Detroit: Wayne State UP 1991, pp. 109–116.

2 Gershom Scholem: *Von Berlin nach Jerusalem. Jugenderinnerungen.* Rev. ed. Frankfurt am Main: Suhrkamp 1994, p. 201. ("Too bad a young person like you wastes his energies for such a cause instead of putting that energy in the service of the world revolution that is knocking at the door.")

Although Werner Scholem constantly tried to leave behind what suggested his Jewish origin, like many other Jewish leftists, he was always considered a Jew, a revolutionary Jew. Short, with dark hair and dark eyes and a nose repeatedly described as an '*Adlernase*,' an aquiline nose, occasionally wearing glasses, he resembled every stereotype of the Jewish intellectual he refused to be.[3] In that sense, he perfectly fit Isaac Deutscher's definition of a non-Jewish Jew, just as his idols Rosa Luxemburg and Leon Trotsky did. Deutscher, a British-Polish historian, was among the first to deal with the complexity of the communist Jews when he presented his concept of the 'non-Jewish Jew' to the World Jewish Congress in 1958.[4] He refused to accept the then widespread view in Jewish historiography according to which communist Jews had consciously crossed over the line beyond the Jewish world, and for that reason could not be a subject of inquiry in Jewish history. Deutscher, whose own biography had led him from being a Jewish Jew to a non-Jewish Jew, was fascinated by this movement out into an exposed and vulnerable public space, motivated by the longing for universal solidarity.

The space of the revolutionary non-Jewish Jew – located on the borders of Jewish identity and Jewish culture, yet within the networks of Jewish families and friends – stands at the center of this article. By focusing on the exemplary biography of the German-Jewish revolutionary Werner Scholem, I suggest an alternative approach towards Jewish spatial history: to inscribe an individual experience into the public spaces and focal points of modernity that became the whereabouts of and for many non-Jewish Jews – urban neighborhoods, political venues and concentration camps.

I. In Search of Revolutionary Spaces

Born in 1895, two years before his famous brother, Werner Scholem grew up to be the enfant terrible of his family. At the age of 12, sent away because of his difficult nature, he spent several years in a provincial Jewish boarding school, where he, as Gershom Scholem described it, "encountered a considerable amount of religious hypocrisy and false patriotism, which he found quite repulsive."[5] After a few years in the depressing atmosphere of the Samson

3 Hermann Weber: *Die Wandlung des deutschen Kommunismus*, vol. 2. Frankfurt am Main: EVA 1969, p. 286.

4 Isaac Deutscher: *The Non-Jewish Jew and Other Essays.* London: Oxford UP 1968; Marci Shore: Children of the Revolution. Communism, Zionism, and the Berman Brothers. In: *Jewish Social Studies* 10 (2004), pp. 23–86, here p. 61.

5 Gershom Scholem: *From Berlin to Jerusalem. Memories of My Youth.* New York: Schocken 1980, p. 32.

School in Wolfenbüttel, he convinced his parents to bring him back to Berlin, then a sizzling center of a variety of Jewish cultures. In the immediate vicinity of his parents' home in Berlin-Mitte, he quickly became involved with Zionism, to which he introduced his younger brother Gerhard. His own interest soon turned towards another direction, and when his father, the Berlin printer Arthur Scholem, learned that his son had become a member of the socialist youth movement, he was again sent to boarding school. In Hanover, Werner Scholem was getting prepared for his Abitur in a private boarding school, yet he also found his first political stage: soon after his arrival he left the bourgeois city center behind and crossed the bridge to Linden. This suburb was Hanover's solution for industrialization: 80,000 people lived here in four-storied tenement blocks, in-between no parks or trees but shabby backyards, the whole area surrounded by a belt of fuming factories. In this anti-bourgeois counter-world, entirely different from everything he had experienced before, he not only found a lively labor movement, but also the love of his life: Emmy Wiechelt, a young employee and activist in the Social Democratic Party of Germany (SPD), whom he regarded as his way out of the bourgeois German-Jewish world of his parents, a milieu he – just like his brother Gerhard – regarded as hypocritical and rotten.[6]

After a few months of their acquaintance he eventually decided to move in with Emmy, who shared a tiny flat with her parents. This decision in favor of the proletarian space caused a terrible row with Arthur Scholem, who disliked Emmy's social status even more than the fact that she was not Jewish. When Werner Scholem married his fiancée several years later, he described it as "crossing the Rubicon," a move into a world beyond, which would not allow him to return.[7] This move had its roots in the years 1913 and 1914, when his physical transition of crossing the bridge to Linden had been followed by a drastic ideological and spiritual shift: In the summer of 1914, the outbreak of World War I changed Werner Scholem's life, just as it had changed the lives, future and world views of countless young men all over Europe. Unlike his classmates – among them Ernst Jünger – he did not welcome the war with enthusiasm.[8] He found himself within a minority group of war-opponents

6 Renee Goddard / Robin Glendinnig: *Reni and the Brownshirts. The Childhood of Renee Goddard.* Audio Play, TX Radio 4, 18.06.2002. Transcript Bristol 2002, p. 9. Renee Goddard (Renate Scholem) is the daughter of Werner and Emmy, born in 1923.

7 Werner Scholem to Gerhard Scholem, 12.08.1917. Israeli National Library, Archive G. Scholem, Arc. 4°1599.

8 Mirjam Zadoff: *Der rote Hiob. Das Leben des Werner Scholem.* Munich: Hanser 2014, pp. 40–47; Ernst Jünger to Gershom Scholem, 20.04.1975. Israeli National Library, Archive G. Scholem,

following Karl Liebknecht and together with his younger brother Gerhard. From then on until the end of the war, the two brothers became not only ideologically but also emotionally very close, as is reflected in an intensive unpublished correspondence. They shared not only the enmity against their father – who expected them to enlist in the army and resented them for their refusal – but also the quest for a utopian world that would solve the problems of their German-Jewish existence: either by offering a way into Judaism, by becoming a Zionist, or a way out of it, by becoming a socialist. Both ideologies promised their followers a new and better world, an unexplored territory beyond the restrictive and disenchanted landscapes of German Jewry.

The intensive debate between the two Scholem brothers reveals that during the first years of the war, their political convictions were not as well defined as it seemed in retrospect.[9] Thus, for a certain period of time Gerhard was deeply influenced by his radical and uncompromising elder brother: disappointed by what he described as shallowness and indecisiveness in German Zionism, Gerhard came to regard socialism as a form in which to express his urge for clear commitments. And so Werner introduced him to the counterworlds of revolutionary socialist Berlin. In Neukölln, they joined meetings of the revolutionary underground-group around Luxemburg and Liebknecht, and were both among the few to distribute the forbidden ultra-left and pacifist journal *Die Internationale*.[10] Werner, on the other hand, felt a need to discuss Judaism and Zionism with his younger brother. To him he confessed that he still believed in Judaism, even intended to raise his future children as Jews and considered getting involved in the Zionist movement after the war.[11]

The reality and experience of the war drove the two brothers apart, however, as much as it had brought them together in the first place. Considerably different everyday lives and experiences played a big part in this development. Despite his pacifism, Werner Scholem had been drafted into the army as early

Arc. 4°1599; Gershom Scholem: *Walter Benjamin. The Story of a Friendship*. London: Jewish Publication Society of America 1961, p. 6.

9 For the correspondence, see: Israeli National Library, Archive G. Scholem, Arc. 4°1599, and a few published letters in: Gershom Scholem: *Briefe I: 1914–1947*, ed. by Itta Shedletzky. Munich: Beck 1994, pp. 3–15.

10 Zadoff: *Der rote Hiob*, pp. 56–57; Gershom Scholem: *Tagebücher*, vol. 1: 1913–1917, ed. by Herbert Kopp-Oberstebrink / Karlfried Gründer / Friedrich Niewöhner. Frankfurt am Main: Suhrkamp 1995, p. 79, fn. 18, p. 133, fn. 46; id.: *From Berlin to Jerusalem*, pp. 51–52; id.: *Walter Benjamin*, pp. 7–8.

11 Werner Scholem to Gerhard Scholem, 07.07.1916. Israeli National Library, Archive G. Scholem, Arc. 4°1599.

as the winter of 1915, whereas Gerhard successfully managed to postpone his draft and later on was disqualified due to a simulated nervous disease. When Werner returned wounded to Berlin, a cursing and boozing soldier, his brother had already completed his first three semesters at university and just spent a summer vacation in the Swabian Alps.[12] Werner's estrangement from the world of his parents, which had begun years before, when he was first sent to boarding school, had increased tremendously on the battlefield. This alienation deepened while he, just released from military hospital, spent almost a whole year in prison. Anonymous witnesses had reported him to the police when he had joined an anti-war demonstration of the extreme left in January 1917 – in uniform and on the Emperor's birthday.[13] It was when he was finally released from prison that he reached the decision to break all ties with his family and marry Emmy Wiechelt. At the age of 22, Werner Scholem left behind the bourgeois-Jewish world of his parents and relatives and entered the space of revolutionary socialism. Neither his charge of treason nor his political involvement had upset his father as much as the marriage with the non-Jewish girl, who did not own a penny. Consequently, Arthur Scholem disinherited his son and refused to ever meet him again.[14]

Soon after the wedding, the radical pacifist was sent back to the trenches, and it might have been his worst experience – among the many bad experiences he eventually had in his life – that he missed the revolution in Germany. While the country was turned into a republic, he was trapped in a two-month military retreat from France. He finally reached Hanover on Christmas 1918 and was welcomed by his wife – and his daughter, Edith, who had been born three months earlier.[15] While Berlin was experiencing the Spartacist uprising in January 1919, he found himself still in Hanover and in urgent need of finding a way to support his family. He was unable to resume his studies of history and took up the life of a journalist and politician. As he told his brother Gerhard, he not only had become the central figure of the Independent Socialists

12 Scholem: *Briefe I: 1914–1947*, p. 480.

13 Werner Scholem to Gershom Scholem, 05.02.1917. Israeli National Library, Archive G. Scholem, Arc. 4°1599.

14 Marriage certificate. University of Hanover, Archive Emmy and Werner Scholem, File nr. 171231; Emmy Scholem to Gerhard Scholem, 05.02.1918. Israeli National Library, Archive G. Scholem, Arc. 4°1599; Last Will Arthur Scholem, 24.09.1921. University of Hanover, Archive Emmy and Werner Scholem, File nr. 250218.

15 Werner Scholem to Gerhard Scholem, 26.12.1918. Israeli National Library, Archive G. Scholem, Arc. 4°1599.

(USPD) in Hanover but also his own correspondent: in the morning he was writing articles on the speeches he had given the evening before.[16]
By that time, the contact between the brothers had almost come to an end – their lives, languages and interests had changed too drastically. Gerhard had discovered the world of Jewish mysticism as his field of interest and as a way of translating his political convictions into scholarly terms, and he came to regard his brother as a mere populist orator and lurid journalist. Yet he advised his friend Werner Kraft in Hanover to go and meet him.

> Personally, I would counsel you to go and see how he behaves one of these days – that is whether he disappears into a cloud of pure phraseology. [...] Incidentally, you should know of him through the press. He's supposed to be the roaring lion of the Independents for the entire province. He is (at twenty-three!!!) the chairman of the Linden Independent Socialist faction and of the workers council in Hanover to boot, and editor of the 'Volksstimme' in Braunschweig.[17]

Regardless of his disapproval, even Gerhard Scholem couldn't help being impressed by his brother's achievements. Without any help or support from the family, Werner Scholem was soon making a remarkable career in the German Communist Party. In the winter of 1921, at the age of only 25, he was elected the youngest member of the Prussian State Parliament and appointed a member of the editorial board of the party journal *Rote Fahne.*[18]
In 1924, he became the central figure in the ultra-leftist leadership of the German Communist Party (KPD) next to Ruth Fischer and was elected to the German Reichstag.
Werner Scholems transformation into a radical revolutionary and politician, who was known and hated all over Germany, had a strong spatial component. Since he had crossed the bridge to Hanover's proletarian quarters in 1913, his life happened in very different urban settings than before: in auditoriums, street demonstrations, in plenary halls and (whenever the KPD was involved in revolutionary acts) in hiding and in various prisons.
Between 1918 and 1927, he and Emmy chose to live in working-class neighborhoods in Hanover, Halle and Berlin, since the young politician thought it

16 Founded in 1917, this party unified the leftist war-opponents within the German Social democracy. Werner Scholem to Gerhard Scholem, 07.02.1919. Israeli National Library, Archive G. Scholem, Arc. 4°1599.

17 Gerhard Scholem to Werner Kraft, 10.04.1919. In: Scholem: *Briefe I: 1914–1947*, pp. 202–203; Werner Scholem actually worked for the *Braunschweiger Volksfreund*, not the *Volksstimme*, as his brother writes.

18 *Reichstagshandbuch, 2. Wahlperiode 1924*. Berlin 1924, p. 516.

essential to be close to his voting public.[19] As someone who in the ranks of the KPD was regarded as a Jew and an intellectual, he had to be especially concerned about appearances. Therefore he was abandoning every aspect of his life which might be considered as bourgeois or which referred to his past. Instead he carefully gave himself the looks of a modestly dressed "advocate of the people."[20] Only in 1927, after he had left the party, did the family move to a nicer part of Berlin, where they set up a more comfortable lifestyle, albeit nonetheless hidden from the public in the rear part of the building.

II. The German Parliament as a 'Non-Jewish Jewish Space'

Werner Scholem's ready wit and '*Berliner Schnauze*' (Berlin bluntness) made him famous beyond communist circles and all over the country. As a Member of Parliament in Berlin, he became known as a provocative and uncompromising politician. Even the social democrat Carl Severing, Prussian minister of the interior, once asserted that he had considerable respect for the rhetorical talents of the young deputy.[21] Although he acted as a representative of communism and internationalism, he was persistently confronted with antisemitic attacks amongst the deputies of the center-right parties: as a reaction to each and every one of his speeches, he was vilified as a "Jew boy scoundrel" and mocked for his – allegedly typical Jewish – physical appearance.[22] He himself neither denied his being Jewish, nor did he explicitly refer to it. But under the influence of being regarded as the paradigmatic Jewish dissident, he gradually became a defender of the Jewish cause. By presenting his engagement for Jews as a universalist concern for the oppressed, he turned the Prussian parliament as well as the Reichstag into 'non-Jewish Jewish spaces.'

Among the many debates in which Werner Scholem embarked on this difficult strategy was the infamous '*Ostjudendebatte*' during the years of 1921 and 1922.[23] In this long-lasting debate, Prussia negotiated its attitude towards Eastern European Jews who were living within the state's borders since the war without having obtained German citizenship. At the height of the post-war

19 Interview with Edith Capon [undated], private archive Renee Goddard.

20 Betty Scholem to Gershom Scholem, 08.04.1924. In: Betty Scholem / Gershom Scholem: *Mutter und Sohn im Briefwechsel 1917–1946*, ed. by Itta Shedletzky / Thomas Sparr. Munich: Beck 1989 , p. 102.

21 *Sitzungsberichte des Preußischen Landtags*, vol. 10. Berlin 1923, p. 13658.

22 *Sitzungsberichte des Preußischen Landtags*, vol. 11. Berlin 1923, p. 14926, and vol. 12. Berlin 1924, p. 17695.

23 *Sitzungsberichte des Preußischen Landtags*, vol. 10, pp. 13556–13622.

German inflation, this political conflict dealt with the general shortage of resources – apartments, food, jobs – which were not supposed to be shared with 'strangers.' In the discussions, center-right deputies called for deporting the migrants back to their countries of origin and closing the Eastern borders to any future immigration of Jews. The '*Ostjudendebatte*' introduced a rude and aggressive verbal antisemitism in the Prussian parliament, in a time when anti-Jewish rhetoric started to become a central component of political culture in Germany.[24]

During the debate, members of the German National People's Party addressed their accusations not only against an anonymous group of Jewish migrants, whom they described as "degenerate creatures," carrying deadly diseases; they also targeted certain members of parliament itself. For instance, Wilhelm von Kaehler, a professor of economics, claimed that some deputies of the German Communist Party were not only Bolsheviks, but that their family names referred to old and new relations to Eastern European Jews. This was an accusation directed mainly against Werner Scholem, whose family had lived in Germany for several generations, but who, unlike other Communists, had never changed his Jewish last name.[25]

The deputy so addressed joined the debate with an extensive speech, in which he pointed out antisemitic stereotypes and forcefully defended the rights of Eastern European Jews in Germany as members of the international proletariat. He reminded his audience that it had been the Wilhelminian state that had brought these Jews from Poland to work in German ammunition factories; and now the very same people were cursed as war-profiteers by German right wing politicians, who demanded their return to their home countries. But in truth, Werner Scholem continued, these polemics were aimed against the migrants only because people feared and envied their keen intellect.[26] Unsurprisingly, his statement provoked further accusations, claiming that the young deputy always had been and still was a 'stranger' in Germany: a Bolshevist, an Internationalist and a homeless Jew, just like the thousands of Jewish migrants being kept in custody in German detention camps, while

24 Martin H. Geyer: *Verkehrte Welt. Revolution, Inflation und Moderne. Munich 1914–1924*. Göttingen: Vandenhoeck & Ruprecht 1998, p. 280.

25 *Sitzungsberichte des Preußischen Landtags*, vol. 10, pp. 13556–13568.

26 Ibid., pp. 13580–13588; Frank M. Schuster. *Zwischen allen Fronten. Osteuropäische Juden während des Ersten Weltkrieges (1914–1919)*. Vienna / Cologne / Weimar: Böhlau, pp. 236–239; Ludger Heid: *Maloche – nicht Mildtätigkeit. Ostjüdische Arbeiter in Deutschland 1914–1923*. Hildesheim: Olms, p. 129; id.: *Oskar Cohn. Ein Sozialist und Zionist im Kaiserreich und in der Weimarer Republik*. Frankfurt am Main: Campus, pp. 113–115.

the Prussian parliament was debating their fate. And so Werner Scholem was polemically advised by his fellow deputies to return to Eastern Europe together with them.

As a public figure, Werner Scholem was always regarded as a Jew in the eyes of Jews and non-Jews alike, and especially amongst antisemites. He himself only exceptionally referred to his Jewish background and only in defense against antisemitism. Despite his explicit rejection of Jewish culture and religion and despite his self-chosen exile from the social networks of the Jewish world, he always stayed in close contact with Jewish friends or family members. This dialectic identity also defined his position in the Prussian parliament and the Reichstag, where he fought for communist causes and – even if not openly – also for Jewish ones. Consequently, he time and again turned the German Parliament into a stage for the "new Jew" of the Weimar Republic: the radical leftist 'non-Jewish Jew'.

III. Trapped in a Deadly Interspace

In 1924, at the height of his career, Werner Scholem was among the first who vigorously opposed the bolshevization of the KPD. Together with Arthur Rosenberg and Iwan Katz, he turned against the influence from Moscow and Stalin's growing totalitarianism, to which Ruth Fischer as party leader, albeit with reservations, had decided to subordinate the KPD. Consequently, in 1925 he was accused of being the leader of an 'ultra-leftist' opposition inside the KPD, and an attempt was made to frame him with a corruption scandal. He was suspended from the party's Central Committee, defamed as an 'intellectual,' a 'Bohemian' and a 'coffee-house poet.' A year later he was expelled from the KPD and then also resigned from his post as an editor on the staff of *Rote Fahne*. At the young age of 30, Werner Scholem was now a politician out of work, with no other occupation but a persistent belief in the coming revolution. He took up the study of law at Humboldt University and completed his degree in 1931. It was then when Trotsky's son Léon Sedov contacted him: his father, Sedov claimed, regarded him as a very capable politician and as the hope for a Trotskyite opposition in Germany. From that point on, Werner Scholem kept in touch with the exiled Trotsky, and wrote on a regular basis for his journal *Permanente Revolution*, which was published in Germany.[27]

27 Zadoff: *Der rote Hiob*, pp. 187–200.

When the Nazis came to power Werner Scholem was among the first to be arrested. Although released soon after, he was imprisoned again just before leaving the country in the spring of 1933 – this time by the Gestapo and together with his wife. Although having officially resigned from politics years before, he was charged with high treason. In November 1933, Emmy Scholem was released from prison and left the country with their two daughters in order to settle in England. Meanwhile her husband was awaiting his trial, which finally took place in spring 1935. He had been told that the reason for his charge was a love affair he had had during his legal studies with Marie-Luise von Hammerstein, the daughter of the commander-in-chief of the *Reichswehr*. Given the fact that another daughter of the general was accused of espionage for the Bolsheviks, the Gestapo blamed him for being part of a Communist conspiracy. Yet in his lawsuit, the connection to the Hammerstein family remained unmentioned; instead his case had been built up entirely on false evidence. Consequently, even the National Socialist *Volksgericht* could not help but find him not guilty. Nonetheless, immediately after the trial he was deported to concentration camp: first to the Lichtenburg concentration camp in Saxony, then to Dachau and finally to Buchenwald. His famous name and face made life in the camps more difficult for him, and he was exposed to ridicule by SS officers. Stalinist inmates regarded him as a betrayer of the communist cause, and punished him for his political '*Eigensinn*' (waywardness) by isolating him within the camp society. As a Trotskyite and a Jew, he appeared to be the paradigmatic 'other,' and described his fate as being crushed between National Socialism on one side and Stalinism on the other. None of his family's numerous attempts to set him free was successful. It was always at the very last moment that the Gestapo refused to release him without further explanation.[28]

It has been assumed that these somewhat mysterious refusals by the Gestapo to set him free had been based on the Hammerstein case,[29] but this seems to be a doubtful reason. Gershom Scholem offered a different explanation, mentioning that his brother's name had been listed among the enemies of propaganda minister Joseph Goebbels.[30] Although the factual list most

28 Zadoff: *Der rote Hiob*, pp. 203–287.

29 Michael Buckmiller / Pascal Nafe: Die Naherwartung des Kommunismus — Werner Scholem. In: *Judentum und politische Existenz. Siebzehn Porträts deutsch-jüdischer Intellektueller*, ed. by Michael Buckmiller / Dietrich Heimann / Joachim Perels. Hanover: Offizin 2000, pp. 60–81, here pp. 75–76.

30 Gershom Scholem to Walter Benjamin, 19.04.1936. In: Walter Benjamin / Gershom Scholem: *Briefwechsel 1933–1940*, ed. by Gershom Scholem. Frankfurt am Main: Suhrkamp 1980, pp. 216–217.

possibly did not exist, it seems that Werner Scholem had been one of Goebbel's best and most hated enemies: already in 1924, Goebbels had mentioned him in his diary together with Karl Marx as two of the most important advocates of Jewish internationalism within the communist world. And in 1935, in Goebbel's famous Nuremberg speech, Werner Scholem was referred to most prominently as the head of the Berlin Jewish communist press.[31] Finally in November 1937, when the exhibition *Der Ewige Jude* was opened in the Museum of Technical Science in Munich, a plaster mask of Werner Scholem was put on display. The mask had been taken in Dachau and the face was unmistakable, though considerably aged after almost five years of imprisonment and concentration camp. In this huge antisemitic and anti-Bolshevik exhibition, he represented the fate of the Jewish communist dissident – by 1937 an impossible and deadly interspace in Germany just like in Russia. The former Member of Parliament and fallen political leader was now an imprisoned and humiliated Jew and Trotskyist, lacking any lobby or support and exposed to ridicule and persecution. Consequently, in the summer of 1940, after more than seven years in Nazi confinement, he was killed in the notorious stone pit at the Buchenwald concentration camp. Most possibly it was due to the involvement of Stalinist *Kapos* in the camp that he had been transferred to the stone pit, where he was shot by an SS officer. According to several accounts of other Trotskyist inmates, his position had been most vulnerable and isolated: too famous, too Jewish, too intellectual and too dissident.[32]

The highly individualistic and uncompromising space of the 'non-Jewish Jew,' which Werner Scholem had defined for himself during the years of the Weimar Republic, had now turned into a trap. The lack of community and affiliation, which had always marked his independence, created a deadly interspace between Stalinist and National Socialist interests.

Conclusion: Border Lands in Jewish History

Following the biographical experience of the German-Jewish politician Werner Scholem, this article has dealt with the existence of 'non-Jewish Jewish spaces' in Weimar and Nazi Germany. The 20th century provides various such

31 Diary entry, 14.07.1924. In: Joseph Goebbels: *Tagebücher*, vol. I: 1924–1929, ed. by Ralf Georg Reuth. Munich / Zurich: Piper 2008, pp. 102–103; Joseph Goebbels: *Welt-Bolschewismus ohne Maske.* Kernstück der Rede des Dr. Goebbels auf dem Reichsparteitag in Nürnberg 1935. Fichtebundblätter Nr. 791, Hamburg [1935], p. 2; see also id.: Communism with the Mask Off. German Propaganda Archive, Calvin College. http://www.calvin.edu/academic/cas/gpa/goeb58.htm (accessed 03.05.2015).

32 Zadoff: *Der rote Hiob*, pp. 266–295.

exemplary biographies of Jews, whose lives can be understood as permanent religious, ethnic and social boundary experiences. These biographies often are too individual, fractured or incoherent to be clearly assigned to a given group. But they nonetheless opened up certain spaces of experience, located on the borders of Jewish worlds, networks and cultures.

These lives, as border experiences, were often condemned to fall into oblivion. Also Werner Scholem would be long forgotten in Jewish memory and historiography, if it was not for his younger brother. Gershom Scholem kept diaries and correspondences reflecting his relationship with Werner, and dedicated parts of his autobiography to their childhood and youth, when they were united in friendship and mutual political interest.[33] The relationship between the Scholem brothers highlights the strong bonds that existed between 'Jewish Jews' and 'non-Jewish Jews,' and analyzes the latter not only in relation to the world of Jewish thought and experience, but also within the networks of Jewish families, friends, memories and fates.

Werner Scholem's biography is part of a phenomenon that was made possible by the fundamental changes in the first third of the 20th century, when revolutionary upheavals brought into being the 'non-Jewish Jewish spaces' of the radical left. These interspaces were determined on the one hand by a messianic political belief, which opened them towards a utopian future (even if this was temporary and elusive); on the other, they were defined by antisemitism, which limited them towards a past of anti-Jewish resentment and aggression. Therefore it appears that highly modern and archaic tendencies clashed here on the ground of a 'non-Jewish Jewish space,' turning this space in-between into exposed and dangerous territories.

33 Scholem: *From Berlin to Jerusalem*.

Becoming Metropolitan,
(Re-)Imagining Community

Space for Reflection

Synagogue Building in Nineteenth-Century Urban Landscapes[1]

Saskia Coenen Snyder

Since the ground-breaking publications of Henri Lefebvre, Michel de Certeau, and David Harvey on the production of space in the 1970s and 1980s, there has been a growing scholarly interest in space and place as legitimate objects of analysis.[2] Rather than regarding space and location as neutral categories innocent of political or ideological manipulation – "simply inherited from nature"[3] as Lefebvre phrased it – scholars now increasingly accept them as social products actively engaged in the construction of cultural identities. Indeed, some scholars have argued that the more conventional categories of historical analysis such as class, race, ethnicity, and gender can no longer be applied effectively without a careful consideration of the built environment and of more abstract notions of public and private, territorial boundaries,

1 I would like to thank Harvard University Press for granting permission to reprint this essay. Reprinted by permission of the publisher from BUILDING A PUBLIC JUDAISM: SYNAGOGUES AND JEWISH IDENTITY IN NINETEENTH CENTURY EUROPE by Saskia Coenen Snyder, pp. 8–9, 14–16,56–64, 76–78, 259–260, Cambridge, Mass.: Harvard University Press, Copyright © 2013 by the President and Fellows of Harvard College.

2 See, among others, Henri Lefebvre: *The Production of Space*, trans. from the French by Donald Nicholson-Smith. Cambridge: Blackwell 1991; Michel de Certeau: *The Practice of Everyday Life*, trans. from the French by Steven Rendall. Berkeley: University of California Press 1984; Edward W. Soja: *The Political Organization of Space*. Washington: Association of American Geographers, Commission on College Geography 1971; Michel Foucault: *Discipline and Punish: The Birth of a Prison*. New York: Vintage 1979. These works inspired the so-called "spatial turn" in the field of cultural studies, which emphasized the importance of the concept of space as an analytical category as opposed to that of time. Geographical (spatial), rather than historical (temporal), forces became the means to understand social and cultural change.

3 Lefebvre: *The Production of Space*, pp. 193–194.

and transgression. Space and place, in other words, determine "how human interaction occurs, who interacts with whom, and the content of that interaction, [making them] bearers of meaning in their own right."[4] This greater sensitivity to spatiality and locality as active forces shaping human behavior has allowed for a better understanding of how social relations are constructed. It has also illuminated the sometimes highly political and ideological agenda of those involved in the production of space and place. Urban ghettos, gated communities, and middle-class suburbs, for instance, show quite clearly the intent to segregate one ethnic, religious, or economic group from another, significantly influencing people's behavior, the ways in which they identify themselves, and how they are perceived in society at large.

The buildings that adorn our urban landscapes participate in these processes. They are not lifeless structures that silently witness the passing of the ages, merely offering shelter for human activities until they are destroyed or added to a preservation list. On the contrary, they actively shape everyday experiences. Aside from their practical use in the organization of our lives – by providing accommodations for living, work, education, religious services, and cultural activities – buildings play a crucial role in defining who we are, or aspire to be, as people. They communicate to the public cultural preferences and political ambitions, religious heritage, successes and failures. Moreover, people's use (or neglect) of buildings, their attempts to embellish (or vandalize) them, and the desire to reproduce them reveals they are not merely inert objects of reflection, but mediums through which cultural practices are established and reproduced. Buildings, in other words, matter. They have stories to tell – stories about the need for their existence, about the people who use them, and about the events taking place within or around them.

How buildings are seen, treated, and remembered is subject to cultural change; they have no intrinsic, stable meaning. Brian Ladd showed this quite convincingly in his examination of Berlin, in which he linked the city's urban landscape with German national identity. To Ladd, buildings and monuments are "the visible remnants of the past," important not because of their aesthetic value but because "they are the symbols and repositories of memory."[5] Interpretations of and responses to such structures as the Brandenburg Gate, Hitler's bunker, and the Reichstag altered as Germany was transformed from a

4 Mike Parker Pearson / Colin Richards: Ordering the World: Perceptions of Architecture, Space and Time. In: Iid. (eds): *Architecture and Order: Approaches to Social Space.* New York: Routledge 1994, pp. 1–33.

5 Brian Ladd: *The Ghosts of Berlin: Confronting German History in the Urban Landscape.* Chicago: University of Chicago Press 1997, p. 4.

totalitarian state to a divided nation to a reunited capitalist democracy, revealing much about the city's history and Germany's collective identity. It was not the physical form of the buildings themselves, in other words, but the dynamic interaction with human participants within a particular historical setting – what critical theorist Lindsay Jones called the "human experience of architecture"[6] – that produced meaning and that illuminates the inherently fluid, situational, and transient nature of this meaning as historical contexts continually change. The meaning of a building, then, is "not a condition or quality of the thing itself, [but] arises from situations [...] at some specific time in some specific place."[7] Without contextualization, buildings remain silent.

Jones's *The Hermeneutics of Sacred Architecture*, which argues for the need to relate aesthetics with religious rituals and human experiences in order to produce interpretation, is particularly useful when examining Jewish spaces in an urban context, in our case nineteenth-century synagogues. If architectural meaning arises in relation to circumstance, then we need a greater sensitivity to space and place in order to understand the meaning of purpose-built synagogues and their function in the public domain. This requires an examination of the triangular framework consisting of the building in question, the human actors who surrounded it, and the context in which their interaction occurred. How contemporaries talked about the synagogue – in newspapers, building committee minutes, picture postcards – and how Jews utilized the building are central, as are the local conditions that give each place of investigation its own story.

The majority of scholars who have examined well-known, conspicuous houses of worship have concluded they were markers of European Jewry's exodus from the ghetto, "the bearers of the message of the new Judaism of modern times in free and equal societies [...] publicly redefining Jewishness in the new socio-political context [and expressing] a feeling of gratitude toward the government that had liberated them."[8] In fact, argues Dominique

6 Lindsay Jones: *The Hermeneutics of Sacred Architecture: Experience, Interpretation, Comparison*, vol. 1: Monumental Occasions. Reflections on the Eventfulness of Religious Architecture. Cambridge: Harvard UP 2000, p. 29.

7 Ibid., p. 41.

8 L. Scott Lerner: The Narrating Architecture of Emancipation. In: *Jewish Social Studies* 6,3 (2000), pp. 1–30, here p. 1. See also Richard I. Cohen: Celebrating Integration in the Public Sphere in Germany and France. In: Michael Brenner / Vicky Caron / Uri R. Kaufmann (eds): *Jewish Emancipation Reconsidered: The French and German Models*. Tübingen: Mohr Siebeck 2003, pp. 55–73.

Jarrassé, the monumentality of the nineteenth-century synagogue was "a demonstration of successful social integration."[9] Especially in Germany, scholars argue, where the majority of Jews became urban and middle-class in the nineteenth century but emancipation remained incomplete, their communicative function was particularly explicit. Having acquired the financial means and the legal rights to build on a large scale, Jewish communities welcomed the opportunity to erect synagogues in a style that has come to be known as "the architecture of Emancipation." The 1866 Oranienburger Straße synagogue, designed by Eduard Knoblauch (1801–1865), is often presented as the prime example. The building reflected the faith in emancipation quite explicitly: it was a spectacular structure purposefully designed to catch the eye of the city dweller and impress him or her with its sheer scale and grandeur. In fact, one of Knoblauch's earlier designs was rejected because the building was insufficiently visible to the public. The final result was a synagogue that highlighted the contemporary western European attraction to the Orient but that also emphasized the Jews' difference, advertising their confidence about their future in the German fatherland. It became the ultimate expression of the "modern" Jew, that is, the cultivated, prosperous burgher who had successfully acquired *Bildung*.[10]

On closer examination, however, the story of this new urban phenomenon is more complex. If monumental synagogues were simply a visual testimony to European Jewry's successful movement toward integration, then the Oranienburger Straße synagogue should attest to a success story in German-Jewish relations, which is an incomplete reading of the situation indeed. The synagogue, for one, was built at a time when numerous *Judengesetze* (Jewish clauses) limited Jewish liberties and when the question of Jewish political emancipation was still hotly debated. Gratitude, in other words, was not the primary message conveyed by the new synagogue. To better understand what these buildings really meant for Jewish men and women we need to broaden

9 Dominique Jarrassé: *Guide du Patrimoine Juif Parisien*. Paris: Parigramme 2003, p. 65.

10 *Bildung*, for which there is no real English synonym, is an all-encompassing term for cultural sophistication, education, and cultivation, including character formation and moral growth. For Jews, *Bildung* served as an entrée into the culture of the German bourgeoisie and was an affirmation of one's "Germanness." Marion Kaplan argues that *Bildung* was highly appealing to German Jews as one did not have to be born into it. "It could be acquired at the university, in cultured circles, and in a family of good breeding. Moreover, *Bildung* could be joined to Jewish ethnic and religious identities." (Marion A. Kaplan: Part III. As Germans and as Jews in Imperial Germany. In: Ead. (ed.): *Jewish Daily Life in Germany, 1618–1945*. New York: Oxford UP 2005, pp. 173–270, here p. 182.)

our gaze to include not only the buildings themselves but also how they functioned in the wider historical context in which they were built. Synagogues after all, as Jones has argued with respect to all buildings, mean nothing in and of themselves; only through the dynamic interactions that take place between the structure and the contemporaries who interact with them is meaning generated.[11] A proper analysis of synagogues, then, needs to include close attention to space and place.

A greater sensitivity to spatiality and locality suggests that these emerging landmarks tell very different stories about northern European Jewish communities and consequently ask us to be careful with easy generalizations about their meaning. In Berlin, the Oranienburger Straße synagogue was more than a visual declaration of comfort and prosperity. It was used as a political symbol to convince the German public of the Jews' "worthiness" as *gebildete Bürger* – culturally sophisticated, bourgeois citizens loyal to the German state. Jews had kept their end of the bargain: they had discarded the shackles of the medieval ghetto and become "true Germans," and they therefore deserved full legal and social emancipation. More importantly, when we shift our attention away from the building itself and focus instead on the context in which it was built, used, and talked about, then it also becomes a product of the *Gemeinde's* sense of insecurity rather than confidence, of its consciousness of the fragility of its status rather than its conviction that full emancipation was only a matter of time. Berlin, after all, had witnessed a difficult and prolonged process of granting rights to Jews over the course of the nineteenth century, and now that Germany was moving toward unification the question of who "belonged" to the nation became increasingly pertinent. Indeed, the "Jewish question" became a fiercely debated issue in German public discourse and would remain so after unification in 1871, when discussions over what constituted *Deutschtum* and *Judentum* intensified. Building a spectacular synagogue in a time like that, then, was intimately tied to the socio-political status of German Jewry. Much was at stake, and the public aspect of the new building, its size and location, and its interior lay-out became contentious issues. Some were concerned by the hateful comments spewed out by antisemites such as Heinrich von Treitschke, who proclaimed he was not surprised that "the most beautiful prayer house of the German capital [was] a synagogue." For Treitschke, the opulence and centrality of the Oranienburger Straße building was visual evidence of what he had proclaimed all along, namely that

11 Jones: *The Hermeneutics of Sacred Architecture*, Introduction, p. 1–37.

"the Jews in Germany were more powerful than in any other west-European country."[12] Its Oriental style, after all, only confirmed the Jews' inherent foreignness and their unwillingness to conform to German cultural mores. Others were less worried that the "exoticism" of the Oranienburger Straße synagogue would provoke an antisemitic backlash and instead considered the building an absolute necessity in order to display the community's progress. Yet others complained that the obsession with Reform – which manifested itself among other ways in the remodeling of the interior after Christian churches – signaled the downfall of Judaism and the loss of a Jewish identity. In short, synagogues in Berlin, particularly the Oranienburger Straße building, became the medium through which Jews publicly debated their political and ideological ambitions, giving us clues about manifestations of Jewish identity in the German context.

Taking into account the contemporary milieu in which synagogues were constructed and used is *as* important to a proper analysis of European synagogue building as the examination of their interior and exterior appearance. As Jews and non-Jews from a variety of socioeconomic backgrounds voiced their opinions over the emergence of conspicuous synagogues, they inadvertently also commented on their own ideological views. In Berlin, the bold statement of success made by the Oranienburger Straße synagogue is illusive as the debates swirling around the building reveal that Jews were anything but accepted members of the *Bildungsbürgertum.*

Let us look more closely at Berlin. The building history of the synagogue began in 1846, when *Gemeinde* officials first submitted a request to the Prussian *Ministerium des Innern* to build a second house of worship. "The synagogue of the Jewish community that is currently located in the Heidereutergasse," stated the appeal, "no longer suffices to host the large numbers of members on Sabbath and especially on the High Holidays [...] It is therefore an urgent necessity to erect a new synagogue and to commence building one quite soon."[13] In the same year prominent members of the community formed a "committee for the construction of a new synagogue," which included, among others, the well-to-do silk manufacturer Joel Wolff Meyer. With the appeal process started, the committee proceeded and proposed a plan to raise

12 Heinrich von Treitschke: Herr Graetz und sein Judenthum. In: Hermann Simon (ed.): *Die Neue Synagoge Berlin: Geschichte, Gegenwart, Zukunft.* Berlin: Stiftung Neue Synagoge Berlin – Centrum Judaicum 1992, pp. 1–47, here p. 10.

13 Geheimes Staatsarchiv Preußer Kulturbesitz [GSPK]: I. HA, Rep. 77, Ministerium des Innern, Tit. 1021, No. 62, Bd. 2. Letter dated 02.02.1846.

the necessary funds. By selling seats for the new synagogue – the number of which were yet to be determined – it hoped to attract sponsors and to commit community members to the project. "For the time being though," stated the committee, "only between 600 and 800 seats can be purchased, namely first-class seats for 150 thaler and second-class seats for 100 thaler."[14] Unsure about the outcome of their request to the *Ministerium* and about the size and location of the building, the committee erred on the conservative side. It would take more than ten years before the Jews received permission to build and twenty years before the project was completed.

The committee members were initially drawn to a plot of land in the immediate vicinity of the Heidereutergasse synagogue in Berlin Mitte, on which stood an old lumber warehouse. The majority of Jews lived in the surrounding area and it would be convenient to have religious services at a nearby location. King Friedrich Wilhelm IV, however, vetoed this site. The relevant ministries had advised him the place was far too prominent and would make the Jews too visible to the public. The close vicinity of the site to the Christian Garnison (Garrison) church, in particular, was objectionable. A communiqué from the city authorities to the king expressed concern that the presence of Jews might "disturb" Christian worshippers. Attracting more Jews to an already predominantly Jewish area by building a "synagogue in a public, conspicuous place" ("eine Synagoge an einem öffentlichen von allen Seiten in die Augen fallenden Platz") would be disruptive for pious Christians attending Sunday services. On the basis of these obstacles, stated the letter, "[we] have few qualms about dismissing the present appeal made by the [Jewish] Elders."[15] Not only did city officials turn down the choice of location, they rejected the request to build altogether. While Jews had been a constant presence in Berlin since the 1670s, the authorities preferred to keep their visibility to a minimum and to keep the practice of Judaism largely out of sight.

The king, on the recommendation of city officials, consequently denied the appeal, although his statement rephrased the reasons for dismissal: "It appears to me this particular building site is not suitable because of its limited distance from the existing synagogue, which would be inconvenient for

14 Central Archive for the History of the Jewish People, Jerusalem: Moritz Stern Collection, P 17/573, p. 1. Joel Wolff Meyer purchased four A-category seats (two women's and two men's seats) and two B-category seats (one for the women's and one for the male's section) and paid a total of 800 thaler.

15 GSPK: I. HA, Rep. 77, Ministerium des Innern, Tit. 1021, No. 62, Bd. 2. Denkschrift der Minister des Innern und für geistliche Angelegenheiten an den König, 11.01.1847.

Jews living in other areas in the city." In other words Jews, not Christians, would be the ones inconvenienced by a new house of worship built in the middle of the Jewish neighborhood. Wilhelm did, however, propose another option: "Would it not be preferable to execute the intended construction in a remote area of the city, perhaps in Köpenickerfelde. In this case I would not be against a building site located directly on the street."[16] This remark suggests that the king was not against constructing a new synagogue per se, but that he opposed the idea of having two in the city center. By relegating the Jews to Köpenickerfelde (today known as Kreuzberg), the king could satisfy all parties. He could grant Jews permission to build their house of worship, appease the Berlin officials, and keep Christians on their way to the Garnison church from being "disturbed" by encountering an increasing number of Jews. Even better, a new synagogue situated on the outskirts of Berlin would entice Jews to relocate from Mitte to less populated neighborhoods, thereby contributing to the development of the city. According to Harold Hammer-Schenk this tactic suggests that Wilhelm disadvantaged the Jews not merely because he disliked them, but also because he considered the long-term urban development of Berlin.[17] This is, however, speculation. What we can state with certainty is that in the late 1840s Prussian Jews, and building projects proposed by the Jewish *Gemeinde*, were still highly dependent on the goodwill and approval of the king – this in stark contrast to communities in Amsterdam or London, where Jews faced considerably fewer obstacles from state and local authorities.[18]

That the Köpenickerfelde alternative did not please Berlin's Jewish leaders is not surprising. Erecting a new synagogue at a significant distance from where the vast majority of worshippers lived was counterproductive, and the potential barrage of complaints about its remote location was not something to look forward to. The outbreak of the revolution, however, temporarily halted the negotiations. Prussia's ruling order and long-held power relations were challenged and the air was brimming with excitement. King Friedrich Wilhelm and the city authorities had more pressing problems on their hands than

16 GSPK: I. HA, Rep. 77, Ministerium des Innern, Tit. 1021, No. 62, Bd. 2. Edict of January 29, 1847.

17 Harold Hammer-Schenk: Baugeschichte und Architektur der Neuen Synagoge. In: Hermann Simon (ed.): *‚Tuet auf die Pforten'. Die Neue Synagoge 1866–1995*. Berlin: Stiftung Neue Synagoge Berlin – Centrum Judaicum 1995, pp. 1–284, here p. 44.

18 For more on Jewish building practices in Amsterdam and London, see Coenen Snyder: *Building a Public Judaism*, chapters 2 and 3, pp. 87–207.

the construction of a new synagogue. And to Jewish officials, seeking permission to build at a time when Prussia's traditional power structure appeared to be crumbling and a royal consent might soon be obsolete, seemed pointless. Only in the mid-1850s, when it became clear that the counter-revolution was strong in Prussia, did negotiations resume.

Building initiatives were further halted by growing tensions between Jews advocating Reform and those in favor of strictly Orthodox practice. Many feared that a second synagogue would intensify religious divisions in the *Gemeinde* and promote communal fragmentation. Having Reform-oriented members congregate in the new synagogue while the Orthodox met in the existing building was not considered conducive to communal harmony and it made a bad impression on the Christian public. A new executive council therefore voted in July 1852 to put a stop to further construction plans.

"We have come to the conclusion to depart from earlier intentions proposed by the previous community council to build a second synagogue, and to reconstruct and expand the existing synagogue instead." The advocates of Reform, after all, only

> encouraged destructive ideas, which worked to the disadvantage of the political situation [...] A productive means to combat these ideas [...] lies in the preservation of external unity [and] in the collection of everyone in one synagogue for religious services. This is the primary reason [why we are against] the plan to found a second synagogue.[19]

This decision greatly annoyed the building committee member Joel Wolff Meyer, who confessed privately that he, "an honorable man who has been greatly involved in the cause," found himself "deceived and betrayed by the obstinacy of orthodox Jews who prevent anything from happening."[20] Meyer's complaints, however, did little to change the minds of Jewish officials. The latter decided, as an alternative, to enlarge the Heidereutergasse structure at a cost of approximately 9,000 thaler. They engaged the Protestant architect, Eduard Knoblauch, who expanded the building's capacity and repainted the decorative interior in an eclectic classical-Romanesque style, the "simplicity of which linked the synagogue to modern elegance."[21] He also added anterooms, a second gallery, and pews. According to Hammer-Schenk, however, the effect of the reconstruction of the old synagogue was the opposite of

19 GSPK: I. HA, Rep. 77, Ministerium des Innern, Titl. 1021, Nr. 62, Bd. 2. Request sent by the Berlin Jewish *Gemeinde* to the Ministerium der geistlichen Angelegenheiten, 10.07.1852.

20 CAHJP: Moritz Stern Collection, P 17/573, p. 5.

21 Preußen. In: *Allgemeine Zeitung des Judenthums* (*AZdJ*) 19, 23.07.1855, p. 386; Preußen. In: *AZdJ* 19, 17.09.1855, pp. 486–487.

what the executive council envisioned. The renovation of the building was received so well by congregants that many desired further improvements on a large scale – especially as the enlargement failed to solve the persistent lack of space.[22]

In 1856, a year after the election of a new community council, the *Gemeinde* purchased the plot at Oranienburger Straße no. 30. In the following months, even before they had received official permission to build, the council asked Knoblauch – whose private home stood in the Oranienburger Straße, at no. 101 – to create a design. This suggests either that, after ten years of negotiations with the Prussian authorities, Jewish officials felt they were nearing a conclusion, or that they considered the available site too ideal to pass on, even if they had to wait for another ten years to lay the first stone. The lack of source material leaves this question unanswered, although the fact that Knoblauch began drawing so soon suggests that perhaps both factors played a role.

The location was indeed close to ideal. The Oranienburger Straße was one of the arteries of Berlin Mitte; although not upscale or particularly fashionable, it was a respectable street that contained low-built, two to three-story residential homes owned by lower to upper middle-class families. From the variety of possible sites, wrote Knoblauch's son in 1866, the Oranienburger Straße site had the "special advantage of circumstance" (*Umstand*), despite its "inconvenient shape for a monumental building."[23] It was situated in the center of the city's Jewish neighborhood: in the eastern corner of the plot stood the hospital, a number of smaller synagogues were in the immediate vicinity, most Jews resided in the area, and virtually all communal institutions – such as the rabbinate, the seminary, the orphanages, and Jewish schools – were nearby. Erecting a monumental synagogue anywhere else at this time would have been illogical.

While the choice of location was self-evident, the choice of architectural style was not. That the synagogue would be built according to a Moorish design was not a foregone conclusion. Indeed, Knoblauch's early sketches show variations of a highly classicist design, one that included a rather stiff facade with eight narrow pillars, rectangular arched windows, and a central entrance way featuring a modest tympanon and five steps. A massive dome was to crown the main prayer room, which contained two rows of circular windows to

22 Hammer-Schenk: Baugeschichte und Architektur der Neuen Synagoge, p. 44.

23 Gustav Knoblauch: Die neue Synagoge in Berlin. In: *Zeitschrift für Bauwesen* 16 (1866), pp. 3–6. This article was written by Eduard Knoblauch's son after the architect's death in 1865.

provide the interior with natural light. The architect's early proposals, however, highlighted two problems, the first of which concerned the oddly-shaped plot. It was a rectangular site with an unfavorable angle, which meant that the building's longitudinal axis had to turn into an east-west direction in order for worshippers to face Jerusalem. "It met the street at a crooked angle," explains Lothar Brieger, "and its borders were irregular due to the neighboring property that encroached upon it. These were restrictive problems for a monumental building."[24] Moreover, the street front was narrow while space further back widened, which complicated matters. Knoblauch's first drafts dealt insufficiently with these structural challenges and failed to maximize the use of space. A second problem involved the visibility of the building. Because the dome was located away from the main street facade, its visibility and that of the synagogue as a whole was reduced – a feature that we know Jewish officials disapproved of as they specified in a later design competition announcement that "the synagogue ha[d] to be visible and the building as well as the entrance ha[d] to clearly display their worthy purpose."[25] Whether the proposed classical style was a bone of contention is unclear; the building committee minutes have never been recovered. What we do know is that the community council "could not come to an agreement on the design and preferred to hear other options. [It therefore] decided to announce a public design competition."[26] A formal building committee was established under the chairmanship of Knoblauch, and the Architectural Society of Berlin was asked to act as judge to choose the most promising proposal. The decision to involve the Architectural Society in the process and to advertise an open competition in a well-known architectural journal indicates the extent to which synagogue building turned into a public affair.

A notice in the *Zeitschrift für Bauwesen* in 1857 listed the wishes of the building committee:

> The Jewish community in Berlin intends to build a synagogue at Oranienburger Straße 30 and offers a prize of 500, 300 and 200 thaler respectively for the three best design plans [...] Who will take charge of the building process is not determined by the prize-winning design. The main prayer room should not be positioned directly at the street, but should

24 Lothar Brieger: Die Neue Synagoge in Berlin. In: *Gemeindeblatt der jüdische Gemeinde zu Berlin* 37, 13.09.1936, p. 5.

25 Der Vorstand der jüdischen Gemeinde: Concurrenz-Eröffnung für Pläne zu einer neuen Synagoge in Berlin. In: *Zeitschrift für Bauwesen* 7 (1857), pp. 448–450, here p. 449.

26 Knoblauch: Die neue Synagoge in Berlin, p. 4.

> be reached through an enclosed entryway […] However, [one] should be able to identify the synagogue from the street.[27]

The building, the cost of which was not to exceed 125,000 thaler, was to provide seats for approximately 1,400 men and 800 women, as well as for sixty choir members positioned in the gallery. Knoblauch, enthusiastic about the project, remained a participant in the competition and submitted new designs. This time his drawings presented a building with Moorish overtones, a dramatically different type of synagogue than what he had envisioned earlier. It was a toned-down version of previous sketches that featured an intensely Oriental structure with an abundantly decorated exterior. They illustrate how Knoblauch played with the location of the dome; in one version he integrated it into the facade, while in another he placed it above the prayer room, situated away from the street front. The former was the basis for the final plan, although the intensity of its Oriental design was toned down even further. Some of the elaborate decorative details, for instance, were replaced with a simpler finish. The triple, narrow window-panes set back in a rectangular frame, too, softened the strong Oriental flavor, including instead hints of the local *Rundbogenstil* so typical of Karl Friedrich Schinkel. Construction began in May, 1859, and as the project progressed it became increasingly clear how seriously the building committee had underestimated the costs. The committee had specified in its initial announcement that the total expenditure was not to exceed 125,000 thaler, but two years later it had to adjust the numbers when the *Gemeinde* took out a construction loan of 300,000 thaler at 5 percent interest. Over the course of the 1860s expenses soared. Financial records show that in 1865 expenditures had reached nearly 650,000 thaler, an amount, assured Jewish officials, that would not increase any further.[28] However, when the building was finally finished, the total cost had reached 750,000 thaler, which made the Oranienburger Straße synagogue not merely the largest, but also the most expensive synagogue ever built.

The final structure, which had a depth of 308 feet, held 3,200 people. Its multi-colored brick front rose to 92 feet and was crowned by a spectacular 160-feet-high central dome with a Magen David at the top. The two side buildings, which featured narrow octagonal windowed turrets with Moorish decorative patterns, were topped with ribbed onion cupolas. The entrances

27 Der Vorstand der jüdischen Gemeinde: Concurrenz-Eröffnung für Pläne zu einer neuen Synagoge in Berlin, p. 448.

28 CAHJP: Jüdische Gemeinde Berlin – D/Be4/122: "An die verehrten Mitglieder unserer Gemeinde".

on each side provided access to the women's galleries. The central portion of the facade included three tall, arched windows, under which a triple-arched portal appeared, fronted by a low, largely ornamental iron balustrade. The portal led male worshippers to the dodecagonal first room, the design of which camouflaged the oblique angle in the ground plan and guided people effortlessly to the sanctuary. Knoblauch, who placed the great dome over this dodecagonal space, had found an elegant solution to one of the difficulties in the original design.

The ante-room, encircled by a ribbed vaulted ambulatory, provided access to the men's vestibule, to the floors upstairs, and to the sanctuary. Before one entered the latter, however, one had to pass through a second room, which was often used for weekday services. Once congregants stepped into the main synagogue they faced what few European Jews at that time had experienced, namely a magnificent space, 143 feet long and 126 feet wide, with a richly decorated vaulted ceiling, thousands of seats, an imposing apse that contained the ark and space for the choir, a ground floor adorned with mosaics, and large glass ceiling windows that allowed sunlight to descend directly on to the ark and the congregation. The galleries on the western side were two stories and were, together with those placed on the northern and southern walls, supported by slender, slate-colored iron pillars. The sophisticated lighting system, too, must have dazzled first-time visitors. The double windows allowed for the installation of gas lighting, a revolutionary system at the time, which supplied not merely light but also a warm, "magical" atmosphere during the evening hours.

The result of the *Gemeinde's* twenty-year quest for a new synagogue was a remarkable building that visually marked Mitte as the center of Jewish life in Berlin and that publicly announced the presence of a respectable Jewish community. In virtually every way, the building showcased the Jews' "worthiness" as *gebildete Bürger*, undermining the persistent stereotype of the "artless Jew" and his supposedly "uncultured" behavior. If the design attested to the Jews' architectural sophistication, the conspicuousness of the golden dome demanded that Berliners face the reality of a Jewish presence in their midst.

We know that many Christian contemporaries visited the new synagogue. They were curious about the new landmark that had taken seven years to be completed and that looked so different from anything they had seen before. Reporters described the building and the inaugural events in local newspapers; architectural theorists analyzed its interior and exterior design in building journals; and foreign visitors commented on the high level of decorum and religious reform, which struck many (especially foreign Jews) as excessive. In almost all of these accounts, the building proved to have an overwhelming effect on Christian observers. They were impressed with its magnitude, its advanced lighting system, its solemnity. The *National Zeitung*, for instance, stated that

> the new house of worship is the pride of the Jewish community of Berlin; but even more, it is an ornament to the city, one of the most remarkable creations of modern architecture in the Moorish style, and one of the most distinguished construction projects that the northern German royal capital has carried out in recent years.[29]

From an architectural perspective the synagogue was a grand success. A closer look at the discourse surrounding the building, however, reveals an ambiguous side to the positive reception. The language used to describe the synagogue, for instance, has both an inclusionary and exclusionary quality. Gentiles generally hailed the new addition to the urban scene and praised the Jews' architectural achievement, but they also viewed the synagogue as a verification of the Jews' perpetual difference. The building was exotic and magical, and therefore inherently un-German. The synagogue was a "fairy-tale building," wrote the *National Zeitung*, that "leads us into the fantastic wonder of modern Alhambra with all the thousand-fold magic of the Moorish style."[30] It was an aesthetic confirmation, initiated by the Berlin *Gemeinde* itself, that German Jews were not part of the *Volk*. The numerous references to the "magic" of the building suggest that gentiles perceived the scene as utterly foreign, as a fantasy. This was precisely what Jewish architects such as Edwin Oppler had been trying to avoid, namely the emerging reputation of synagogues – and Jews themselves – as a foreign element in the German national body. Oppler considered the "unrestrained fantasy" in synagogue architecture only justified when one wanted to make an "anti-Christian" statement, the last thing German Jews should do considering their still undetermined political status.[31] A Moorish style building thus sent the wrong message. The reality, after all, was that Christian society would not accept Jews who proclaimed themselves to be Germans but who represented themselves publicly as strangers.

29 *National Zeitung*, 06.09.1866, page number unknown.

30 The *National Zeitung*, *Vossische Zeitung*, and *Bauzeitung* all described the building as "magical" and "fantastic."

31 Harold Hammer-Schenk: Edwin Oppler's Theorie des Synagogenbaus. Emanzipationsversuch durch Architektur. In: *Hannoversche Geschichtsblätter* (1979), pp. 99–117, here p. 114.

Indeed, one might argue that Christian observers responded favorably to the Oranienburger Straße synagogue precisely because they perceived the Jews as different from themselves; stylistically the building met their expectations. Prevailing stereotypes about the Jews' character, after all, corresponded to those identified with Oriental architecture. In 1866, *Der Taunusbote* directly linked the Oriental design of the new building with the character of Arabs and Jews alike: "The fantasy of [Moorish] architecture is infinite, which is disruptive when one needs to include explicit forms. Herein lies the relationship of the Jewish character with that of the Arabs […] Their fantasy is drawn to the arbitrary, to the unrestrained, to fairy tales, something that is reflected in their architecture."[32] Both Jews and Arabs, claimed the author, were nomads, *semitische Gruppen* lacking a national style and so their capricious artistic expressions were but a natural outcome. The Berlin *Gemeinde* chose the Moorish style for their synagogue at a time when German society at large was trying to define "Germanness," when the qualities associated with the Oriental aesthetic – arbitrariness, leisure, decadence, irreligiosity – were precisely the ones furthest removed from the German ideal. Prussians could thus admire the architectural sophistication of this landmark, but it was an architecture that affirmed and reinforced the Jews' separation rather than their integration into German culture.

The new building also had its critics. An interesting, although not necessarily representative, case is that of Heinrich von Treitschke. Known for his zealous nationalism and anti-Jewish sentiments, the historian wrote to his wife that he saw the golden dome of the synagogue glimmering in the sunset while on his way home. He admitted to her that he found it "a beautiful building, immensely rich […] the architecture of which is so fine as this ugly, uninspiring style can be." It was indeed, wrote Treitschke, "the richest and largest of Berlin's 'churches'!"[33] Yet Treitschke could not associate the Jews' architectural display with religious respectability and cultural sophistication. Instead, the only way he knew how to interpret it was by placing the building in the historical context he had created for himself, which meant that the synagogue

32 The article from *Der Taunusbote* was reprinted in the *AZdJ*. See Über Bauwesen und Musik zu jüdischen gottesdienstlichen Zwecken. In: *AZdJ* 31, 01.01.1867, pp. 5–8. Eduard Knoblauch, too, proclaimed that he was designing a synagogue for the "große, national abgeschlossene Gemeinschaft," that large, nationally isolated community, the Jews. See L.P.: Carl Heinrich Eduard Knoblauch. In: *Zeitschrift für Praktische Baukunst* (1865), pp. 289–304, here p. 301.

33 Von Treitschke wrote this letter on April 28, 1871. Heinrich von Treitschke: *Deutsche Kämpfe, neue Folge: Schriften zur Tagespolitik*. Leipzig: Hirzel 1896, p. 321.

was a visual testimony to the Jews' growing power and wealth. In an essay entitled "Herr Graetz und sein Judentum" (1879), Treitschke concluded,

> if one notes the characteristic fact that the most beautiful and splendid house of worship in the German capital is a synagogue (which one cannot blame on the Jews but on the Christians), then it virtually cannot be denied that the Jews are more powerful in Germany than in any other Western European country.[34]

The implication was that if Christians allowed the Jews certain liberties, then the latter would exploit these liberties to the fullest – as the construction of this magnificent synagogue confirmed – at which point the Jews would reveal the extent of their power and influence. That synagogues were actually much smaller and more modest in places where the Jews enjoyed full civil rights, as in Amsterdam and London, and that the "power" of Berlin Jewry was quite minimal, did not enter Treitschke's mind.

The synagogue made a public statement in Berlin's cityscape, although not everyone interpreted that statement in the way that it was intended. The point, however, is that spatial concerns – including the debates over location, size, and visibility – contributed in significant ways to Jewish self-representation and to popular perceptions. Furthermore, the building's architecture played a more pronounced role in announcing the public face of Judaism than in cities west of Berlin, such as Amsterdam and London. The publication of a design competition in the *Zeitschrift für Bauwesen,* the decision to revise Knoblauch's initial drawings so as to make the golden dome more visible, the building's sheer size and prominent location, and the outspoken Oriental exterior were a conscious attempt on the part of the building committee to stake a claim to a permanent and conspicuous presence of Jews in the city. The structure invited a gentile gaze, it demanded a positive conversation on the Jews of Berlin. Their legal status, after all, was still a contested matter, as was their claim to membership in the German *Volksgemeinschaft.* In 1865, a year before the inauguration of the Oranienburger Straße synagogue, an editorial in the *Allgemeine Zeitung des Judenthums* stated that many contemporaries in Prussia "still found it impossible to think of the Jews as Germans":

> why shouldn't we tell the truth? Among the *Kulturvölker,* it is the Germans who continue to oppose our equality and it is in the German states that our emancipation is still unrealized […] Indeed, that so much is written and said about it here proves that in Germany we have to overcome the extraordinary in order for equality to be acknowledged […] In north-America, France, Holland, Belgium, England, Denmark, and Italy only little has

34 Von Treitschke is quoted in Simon Hermann: *The New Synagogue, Berlin: Past – Present – Future.* Berlin: Hentrich 1992, p.10.

> appeared in writing on this topic, but [legal emancipation] was implemented in only a short period of time.[35]

In order to overcome the extraordinary, the Jews of Berlin took an extraordinary approach by building the largest and most striking synagogue in the world. Seeking to explain Judaism to a non-Jewish audience, it presented Judaism as a civilized and respectable faith – one that stood in stark contrast to enduring stereotypes.[36] The organ, the fixed pews facing the altar, the sophisticated lighting system, the strictly enforced rules of decorum, and the overall spirit of *Bildung*, all elements that gentile observers could recognize and appreciate, demonstrated the Jews' cultivated behavior and fine taste. Most of all, the synagogue showcased the Jews' successful "regeneration" and "worthiness" as German citizens of the Jewish faith.

Whether monumentality was always an effective means of communication is up for debate. Some scholars have maintained that nineteenth-century synagogues, whether in France, Italy, Germany, or elsewhere, spoke the language of successful integration, but this assessment is too general. In different national and local contexts, synagogues told stories unique to their time and place. They were multivocal rather than univocal and included Jewish as well as non-Jewish voices. They also generated a multiplicity of interpretations with the public – interpretations that were not always positive and that echoed popular stereotypes. In making a public statement, synagogues were sometimes misunderstood or misinterpreted.

The inability to command interpretation exposes the inherent limitations of artistic expression. After all, architecture – all art – is anti-essentialist: meaning lies not in form itself and cannot be controlled or made foolproof. It is inherently situational, fluid, and produced by observers whose opinions are colored by politics, socioeconomic status, aesthetic tastes, and so forth. Moorish-inspired structures epitomized cultural sophistication to some, but pretentiousness and excessiveness to others; many German Christians read the Oranienburger Straße synagogue as a confirmation of the Jews' foreignness while their Jewish neighbors saw it as an opportunity for religious pluralism. In other words, there was not a single meaning to the phenomenon of monumental synagogues during the nineteenth century. Rather, as the German philosopher Hans Georg Gadamer remarked in his magnum opus,

35 Judenthum und Deutschthum. In: *AZdJ* 17, 25.04.1865, pp. 251–256, here p. 252.

36 Kalman P. Bland: *The Artless Jew: Medieval and Modern Affirmations and Denials of the Visual.* Princeton: Princeton UP 2000.

Wahrheit und Methode, "the discovery of the true meaning of a text or a work of art is never finished; it is in fact an infinite process [...] Religious structures embark on lives of their own, and engage in conversations of their own, over which their creators can exercise little or no restraint."[37] Gadamer would most likely suggest the interpretation presented here only adds to the multiplicity of meanings; another moment in the creation of interpretation.

37 Hans-Georg Gadamer: *Truth and Method.* London: Continuum 1975, p. 298.

The Emergence of the First European Jewish Metropolis in Warsaw, 1850–1880

François Guesnet

Around 1850, the Jews of Warsaw constituted a young community. The first cemetery had been founded just two generations ago by Shmuel Zbytkower, a wealthy army contractor and banker, on the east bank of the Vistula river due to settlement prohibitions in the Polish capital proper.[1] From a couple of thousand Jews living in the Praga suburbs and within the noble precincts, called *jurydiki*, exempt from the capital's *privilegium de non tolerandis judaeis*, the Warsaw Jewish community grew into a significant regional center with around forty thousand registered Jewish inhabitants in 1850. The communal leadership would be securely in the hands of the *Misnagdim*, the traditional rabbinical observant community. Their hegemony though was challenged by an ever growing Hasidic community and a small, but influential group of wealthy Jews – bankers, tax farmers, army contractors and industrialists – who would attempt to adapt the precepts of the German-Jewish reform to the realities of partitioned Poland. At the end of this period, Jewish Warsaw had grown into the largest Jewish settlement in the world, functioning according to its own unique set of rules.[2] In the course of one generation, between 1850 and

1 About the history of Jewish Warsaw see the survey by Antony Polonsky: Warsaw. In: *YIVO Encyclopedia on Jews in Eastern Europe*, ed. by Gershon Hundert, vol. 2. New Haven / London: Yale UP 2008, pp. 1993–2004. The most authoritative presentation remains the untranslated *opus maior* by Jacob Shatzky: *Geshikhte fun yidn in varshe*, 3 vols. New York: YIVO Institute for Jewish Research 1947–1953. About the founding of the first Jewish cemetery see Glenn Dynner: *Men of Silk. The Hasidic Conquest of Polish Jewish Society*. Oxford: Oxford UP 2006, esp. pp. 25–54, 89–116. Additional investigations into the history of Warsaw as a Jewish metropolis in Glenn Dynner / François Guesnet (eds): *Warsaw. The Jewish Metropolis: Studies in Honor of the 75th Birthday of Professor Antony Polonsky*. Boston / Leiden: Brill 2015.

2 This administrative entity had come into being as a result of the Congress of Vienna in 1815 and therefore was also known as Congress Poland, or *Kongresówka* in Polish.

1880, the number of registered inhabitants of Warsaw more than doubled, from around 150,000 to ca. 300,000.[3] In the same period of time, the number of Jews registered as inhabitants in the Polish capital grew threefold, from below 40,000 to more than 120,000. For much of this period, it formed the largest Jewish settlement in the world, and at the time, surpassed any other Jewish community of European diasporic history.

In the early stages of this dramatic demographic development, the increase in Jewish inhabitants originated above all from smaller towns and the countryside of the central Polish provinces. Later, a steady influx of Jews from the Tsarist Empire added to this internal process of urbanization. Already in the 1870s, observers stated that the Jews in Warsaw formed an agglomeration of co-existing distinct smaller units, defined by origin, religious persuasion, and cultural choices. These differences in identifications were less important for the emergence of this first Jewish metropolis in European Jewish history than the sheer size of these sub-units. Thus, the members of the various Hasidic communities present in Warsaw would not only identify as followers of these specific communities, but also as non-*Misnagdim*, adherents of traditional rabbinical Judaism, who for much of the 19th century probably still formed the majority of observant Warsaw Jewry. This conflict would lead to the well-known 'unholy alliance' between Hasidic Jews and the integrationist camp, joining forces to oust the Misnagdic chief rabbi Jakob Gesundheit in 1871. All Jews with a local or central Polish background would be much irritated by the growing number of Jews from the Russian Empire, the so-called Litvaks, distinguishing themselves through their considerable degree of linguistic acculturation to Russian culture, their political mobilization, social coherence and economic success. These various sub-units of Warsaw Jewry were in themselves sufficiently large to constitute viable sub-communities with a full set of religious, charitable and educational institutions, thus forming a complex system of co-existing networks. Demographic growth seemed to play a major role here – not only were all of these sub-communities fully functional independently, they also had to reckon with and recognize the presence of the large number of adherents of alternative Jewish cultural and religious choices, constituting the highly variegated Jewish presence in the Polish capital. This was certainly a place to 'break the cake of custom', as

3 For a table of the development of the Jewish population in Warsaw, see François Guesnet: *Polnische Juden im 19. Jahrhundert. Lebensbedingungen, Rechtsnormen und Organisation im Wandel.* Cologne / Vienna: Böhlau 1998, p. 34.

Robert Park famously defined the impact of the metropolis on its inhabitants.[4] However, in contrast to the assumption of a necessarily secularizing and modernizing process posited by Park, the metropolitan dialectics also allowed traditionalist Jewish communities to thrive, form new alliances and challenge competitors on a whole new level.

At the end of this period of Jewish metropolization, Warsaw no longer had a chief rabbinate, and the community board had been replaced by a so-called 'community administration' (Pol. *Zarząd Gminy*), controlled by Jewish integrationists (Pol. *postępowcy*). This façade institution had, however, no control over the most substantial needs of the vast majority of Warsaw Jewry, and a thriving, highly complex network of individual, associational, and administrative forms of support emerged. Another process culminated in 1881 as well: after numerous smaller incidents and minor riots, Catholic Poles went on a three-day rampage against their Jewish neighbours, much to the shock and dismay of the more enlightened members of the Polish and Jewish public, who had thought that the events of Southern Russia would not and could not occur in Poland.

This contribution will investigate three forms of encounters within metropolitan Jewish and non-Jewish spaces. First, I propose to understand the widespread practice of Torah processions as a tool of inner-Jewish cohesion. Secondly, I will investigate the encounter of Jewish and non-Jewish masses in the streets of Warsaw as a means of collective self-assertion in the multinational metropolis. Thirdly, I will invoke the parks of Warsaw and their use by Warsaw Jews to offer some insights into the realities of urban spaces that held out the promise of openness and neutrality, but which were nonetheless defined by complex modes of in- and exclusion. As in other cities around the world, synagogues and prayer houses mirrored the complex structure and practices of the Warsaw Jewish community. Applications were made to the authorities by individuals, and independently from the Synagogue Supervisory Board.[5] Their diversity reflected the metropolitan community, and congregations often served as institutional cores for the major religious, cultural and political identifications among Warsaw Jewry. This holds true for the dozens of associational prayer houses (for an example, see below), for the

4 Robert E. Park: Human Migration and the Marginal Man. In: *The American Journal of Sociology* 33 (1928), reprinted in Richard Sennett (ed.): *Classic Essays on the Culture of Cities*. Englewood Cliffs: Appleton Century Crofts 1969, pp. 131–142.

5 Guesnet: *Polnische Juden*, p. 397.

numerous prayer houses of the various Hasidic communities,[6] for the synagogue established by the small but assertive group of Jews from German lands establishing themselves during the Prussian rule 1796–1806,[7] for the so-called Polish Synagogue which in 1840 attempted to achieve the status of an independent community, as well as for the considerable number of Russian-Jewish prayer houses, some of which – towards the end of the period under consideration in this essay – would sign on to the early Zionist programme of *Hibat Tsion* (Hebr. Love of Zion),[8] and finally the Great Synagogue opened in 1879, the representative place of worship uniting the two – Polish and German – variants of opting for cultural integration, often mistakenly identified as community synagogue.[9]

Beyond these fixed places of worship, less perceptible and more transient expressions of Jewish religious life proceeded without significant interference from the authorities and created spaces of Jewish religious practice, some permanent, some temporary, which would integrate the emerging metropolitan community. Among the most notable were the processions to celebrate the completion of a new Torah scroll, for one of which we have an impressive description from the Polish press:

> The association of the local water carriers has its prayer room in the Grützhändler house on Nowowiniarska Street. It celebrated the completion of a Torah scroll yesterday. At eleven o'clock in the night, around fifteen thousand Jews paraded along the Nowowiniarska and the Swiętojerska Streets, went down the Nalewki, up to Franciszkańska Street and back to Nowowiniarska Street. The new Torah scroll was protected by a canopy. A dozen torch bearers preceded the parade, huge lanterns, flags and pennants accompanied it. Young men whistled in a harrowing way. Around twenty members of the association in outlandish disguise were on horseback, some of them wearing spooky masks.[10]

6 Dynner: *Men of Silk*, pp. 89–116.

7 Jürgen Hensel: Wie „deutsch" war die fortschrittliche jüdische Bourgeoisie im Königreich Polen? In: Hans Hecker / Walter Engel (eds): *Symbiose und Traditionsbruch. Deutsch-jüdische Wechselbeziehungen in Ostmittel- und Südosteuropa.* Essen: Klartext 2004, pp. 135–172.

8 Kronika. In: *Izraelita* 1 (1885), p. 4.

9 Aleksander Guterman: The Origins of the Great Synagogue in Warsaw on Tłomackie Street. In: Władysław Bartoszewski / Antony Polonsky (eds): *The Jews in Warsaw.* Oxford: Blackwell 1991, pp. 181–212.

10 Z miasta. In: *Kurjer Warszawski* 238 (18/30.12.1873), p. 512; for a later photograph of the prayer house see Eleonore Bergman: *'Nie masz bóżnicy powszechnej.' Synagogi i domy modlitwy w Warszawie od końca XVIII do początku XX wieku.* Warszawa: DiG 2007, p. 263. For an earlier example of how Jewish celebrations on occasion were highly visible and public events see Dynner: *Men of Silk*, pp. 83–85, discussing the wedding of the grand-son of the Seer of Lublin (Yaacov Yitshak Horowitz, 1745–1815) in the town of Żelechów in 1805.

This lively description captures the performative impact of such a parade: the nightly spectacle with lights, noise, disguises and horses would one the one hand mark a very special moment in the existence of a rather modest association. On the other hand, the parade would also serve to underline the association's place both in the Jewish community and in urban space. The route chosen for the parade would lead around two blocks in the very heart of the Jewish neighbourhood and demonstrate the claim of the water carriers as constituting part of this Jewish world. Even if the number given in the cited article is in all likelihood somewhat inflated, similar parades took place in Warsaw and other towns of the Kingdom on a regular basis, without being, it seems, hampered by the authorities.[11] They are documented for the whole period under consideration here, and demonstrate the appetite of members of religious associations to assert their status and place in the community publicly, ignoring the reservations repeatedly formulated by the Warsaw *Zarząd Gminy*.[12] A comparable leniency was demonstrated by the authorities throughout the period under consideration towards the founding of private religious primary schools (Hebr. *heder*). The obvious lack of political will to control the burgeoning multitude of private Jewish schools allowed such schools to satisfy the basic educational needs of the emerging, diverse Jewish metropolitan community. Although legislation concerning primary and secondary education in the Kingdom of Poland was highly regulated, Jewish private primary schools were never as closely monitored as, for example, Polish ones.[13] A survey in 1891 established that around 450 male and 376 female pupils attended the ten elementary schools established and supervised by the *Zarząd Gminy*, dwarfed by the more than twenty six thousand Jewish boys and girls attending private *heder* schools in Warsaw – hence, the officially recognized administration of the largest Jewish community in the world controlled just two or three percent of elementary schooling of Jewish children. The vast majority of Jewish children were taught privately without any administrative supervision to speak of – or, in the case of the

11 The description of another Torah procession in 1866 in Warsaw explains that "old people and children, men and women from far away and nearby places gathered" for the occasion, see Guesnet: *Polnische Juden*, p. 257. More parades were reported in 1877 and 1878, see Pogadanki. In: *Izraelita* 31 (1877), p. 245, and Kronika. In: *Izraelita* 32 (1877), p. 256, as well as Pogadanki. In: *Izraelita* 35 (1878), p. 281, and Pogadanki. In: *Izraelita* 47 (1878), p. 381.

12 Kronika. In: *Izraelita* 32 (1877), p. 259.

13 For the close supervision and oppressive regulation of Polish elementary education, especially after the January Uprising in 1863, see Ryszard Kucha: *Oświata elementarna w Królestwie Polskim w latach 1864–1914*. Lublin: Krajowa Agencja Prasowa 1982.

large segment of impoverished Jewish tradespeople, received no structured education at all.[14] Less transient, but still less visible than for example a synagogue were the Sabbath enclosures (*eruvin*) installed around Jewish neighbourhoods in Polish towns and cities, and also in Warsaw. Here, the attitude of the authorities seems to have been more strained. Although a ministerial order in 1860 allowed for the installation of *eruvin*, it also stipulated that local authorities should take care that these enclosures would "not offend other faith communities."[15] Repeated calls to dismantle these demarcations of Jewish space point to the fact that these restrictions were not, however, enforced.[16]

The formation of the metropolitan Jewish community in Warsaw was based on the extraordinary increase in the Jewish population and its growing diversity. Traditional charities as well as the state approved communal administration attempted to cater to the needs of this rapidly growing and diversifying Jewish metropolis, and failed. One reason for the failure of Jewish communal institutions to adapt to those changing needs was the overbearing administrative and police control of public life, the consequence of the Polish patriotic aspirations of the period that culminated in the January Uprising of 1863. There is no need to repeat the often and well told story of the short period of Polish-Jewish brotherhood in 1861, the limited but noticeable involvement of Jews in the January Uprising of 1863, this last attempt in the 19th century for a military reversal of Russian rule, as well as the emergence of a specifically Jewish thread in the 'organic work', and its attempt to invigorate Polish society through educational reform, social policy, and an advancement of Polish economic endeavours.[17] Rather, this last section proposes to investigate the role of public spaces in Warsaw in this tumultuous period as reflecting the emergence of a metropolitan Jewish community.

14 Kronika. In: *Izraelita* 19 (1891), p. 157. These numbers were based on official statistics, which means that the numbers of Jewish children attending schools outside the control of the *Zarząd* was probably significantly higher.

15 Jakob Kirszrot: *Prawa Żydów w Królestwie Polskim*. Warszawa: Nakład Zarządu Warszawskiej gminy starozakonnych 1917, p. 15.

16 In reaction to attacks on the *eruv* in a provincial town, the Warsaw head of police prohibited new enclosures in 1878. As these restrictive regulations were published on several occasions, the Jews of Warsaw seemingly did not fully comply, see Guesnet: *Polnische Juden*, p. 261.

17 A very short overview over this period in Antony Polonsky: *The Jews in Poland and Russia*, vol. 1: 1350–1881. Oxford / Portland: Littman 2010, pp. 314–321, and in more detail in Magdalena Opalski / Israel Bartal: *Poles and Jews: A Failed Brotherhood*. Hanover: UP of New England 1992, as well as the still essential Alina Cała: *Asymilacja Żydów w Królestwie Polskim, 1864–1897 postawy konflikty stereotypy*. Warszawa: Państwowy Instytut Wydawniczy 1989.

The so-called 'Jewish War' of 1859 offers a first occasion to investigate the role of urban space and the public sphere in this period. A review in the the *Gazeta Warszawska*, a leading Warsaw daily, of a violin recital triggered the affair. In it, the author claimed that the soloist, although of first class, had only a sparse public because she was not Jewish; thus, the Jewish public had not bothered to turn up.[18] This statement would then lead the author to racist and antisemitic statements of the crudest kind:

> As we can see, Ms Neruda [the violon soloist, F. G.] does not have the favours of a large coterie, thought to have musical taste and certainly making claims to it. She did not have the eagle's nose, the dark tone of the skin, the black hair and other characteristics of this non-Aryan tribe – she doesn't trill the *r*, her family name doesn't end on *berg*, *blatt*, *kranc*, *stern* or the like. Thus there's no reason for this mysterious coalition which has garnered the whole of Europe in general, and us in particular.[19]

The lengthy reflections which followed came to the conclusion that unfortunately, the Jews in Poland would not return to their homeland, and thus constituted a major problem for the Polish nation. A short period later, the editor of the *Gazeta Warszawska*, Antoni Lesznowski, made public the fact that he had received anonymous letters challenging the concert review, emphasising the contribution of the Jews to the Polish economy, culture, and society. Lesznowski also explained that he had handed over the letter to the police for investigation. This in turn lead to more accusations against him, some of which were formulated in a letter signed by members of the younger generation of Warsaw Jews who identified with the Polish cause and Polish culture. Lesznowski brought the authors to trial on charges of slander and libel, drawing further attention to the matter which was also intensely debated in the Polish emigration in Western Europe, with Joachim Lelewel (1786–1861), among the leading liberal thinkers in the emigration, devoting a long essay to the affair. Lesznowski's decision to go before a criminal court was considered by parts of the Polish public as un-patriotic – in any case, because of the

18 The balanced and most complete account of this episode in Kazimierz Bartoszewicz: *Wojna żydowska w roku 1859: początki asymilacji i antisemityzmu*. Warszawa: Gebethner i Wolff 1917. See also Artur Eisenbach: *The Emancipation of the Jews in Poland, 1780–1870*, ed. by Antony Polonsky. Oxford: Blackwell / Institute of Polish-Jewish Studies 1991, pp. 398, 420–421; Theodore R. Weeks: *From Assimilation to Antisemitism: the "Jewish Question" in Poland, 1850–1914*. DeKalb: Northern Illinois UP 2006, pp. 39–41.

19 Cited after Bartoszewicz: *Wojna żydowska*, pp. 37–38; for a recent republication of several central texts of this episode see François Guesnet: *Der Fremde als Nachbar. Polnische Texte zur jüdischen Präsenz. Texte seit 1800*. Frankfurt am Main: Suhrkamp 2009, pp. 127–155, here pp. 135–136.

January Uprising in 1863, it was never adjudicated.[20] The most important consequence of the affair would be the fact that Polish-Jewish relations as well as Jewish cultural choices would be part of public debate and perceptions.
This would be all the more important in the years to come, when political and cultural identifications were put on display in the context of the patriotic mobilization, the insurrectionist upheaval, but also in later years. Chief rabbi Dov Berush Meisel would very consciously involve himself in patriotic demonstrations, most famously joining the funeral of the victims of the police attack against a patriotic demonstration on March 2, 1861.[21] He also encouraged the singing of the Polish national anthem in synagogues, prompting the head of police to inform "Rabbi Meisels" that, "unless he stops the singing of the national hymn in the synagogues, he will shut them up."[22] Much less well known are later instances of Jews participating in patriotic demonstrations. Their reflection in the international press documents the relevance the contemporaries attached to these occurrences. On the occasion of the funeral of archbishop Melchior Fiałkowski (1778–1861), a correspondent of *The Times* observed that

> the foreign Consuls, English and French, took part in the sad ceremony, and joined it on the Saxon-place; as also the Protestant and Jewish congregations, with every symptom of profound and fervent sorrow. The body of the Archbishop was carried in turns by the clergy, the peasants, artisans, Government officials, students, and Jews.[23]

A remarkable lithograph of this funeral by the well-known painter and photographer Maksymilian Fajans (1827–1890), himself sympathetic to the Polish cause, highlights the prominent place of the Jewish representatives. A group of around six students is shown following directly behind the hearse with the archbishop's remains, themselves followed by a larger group of Jews headed by Dov Berush Meisels and the preacher of the so-called German synagogue on Daniłowiczowska Street, the young Dr. Markus Jastrow (1829–1890).[24]

20 *Sprawa żydowska w r. 1859, w liście do Ludwika Merzbacha*. Poznań: Merzbach 1860.

21 The painting of Aleksander Lesser, *The Funeral of the Five Victims of the Demonstration of 2 March 1861* (1866), today on display in the National Museum in Kraków, is the iconic expression of this episode.

22 Poland (from our own correspondent). In: *The London Times*, 23.07.1861. The correspondent further wrote that "the head of police does not threat to close the Catholic churches, in which the hymn is sung, [therefore] it has been hastiliy inferred that the Lieutenant-General attaches less importance to the prayer of a Christian than to that of a Jew."

23 (From a correspondent): State Affairs in Warsaw. In: *The London Times*, 24.10.1861.

24 Maksymilian Fajans: *Exportacya Zwłok nieodżałowanej pamięci Najdostojnieszego Arcybiskupa Metropolity ks Antoniego Melchiora Fijałkowskiego zmarłego w dniu 5 października 1861 r.*, in the collections of the National Library Warsaw, also accessible through http://polona.pl/item/854772/

In the following years, other funerals would be highly politicized events and occasions for the public display of political discontent, as in the case of the suicide in 1880 of Ignacy Neufeld, a young Jewish student who took his life in reaction to extremely harsh reprimands for the demonstration of Polish patriotic feelings. Also in this case, the fact that the funeral crossed religious boundaries seemed to define the participating communities themselves:

> Although he belonged to an Israelitish [sic] family, the funeral procession, led by a rabbi, was attended by a throng of at least 10,000 persons, consisting of both Poles and Jews, and including some of the most prominent citizens of both nationalities and confessions.[25]

The incident was also reported in the *New York Times*, with a stronger emphasis on the political implications:

> An immense crowd of about 10,000 persons accompanied him to his final resting-place; women sobbing, and cries of 'Down with the tyrant' were heard the whole way. Such a crowd has not been seen in the streets of Warsaw since 1863. The Police turned out in full force, the military being under arms the whole time in the barracks. The excitement is great and continues to increase.[26]

Of greater importance in the context of the emergence of a metropolitan Jewish community, however, would be crowds gathering for the funerals of the two most respected and admired religious authorities in the Polish capital in the period under consideration in this chapter: Yeshaya Muszkat, the rabbi and supreme judge of the Praga Jewish community, who died in 1868, and the Warsaw chief rabbi Dov Berush Meisels, who passed away in 1870. Their respective deaths would be momentous events in the history of the metropolitan community.

In the case of Muszkat, his demise would lead to the abolition of an independent *bet din* in this neighbourhood, which had been the site of the first Jewish cemetery in Warsaw. It also offered an opportunity to officially incorporate the Praga *Hevra kadisha* into the Burial Administration of Warsaw and spelled the end to the semi-autonomous existence of the Praga Jewish community.[27] His funeral was attended by many thousand Warsaw Jews, the first mass

(accessed 30.05.2014). About Rabbi Jastrow, who later became preacher in the synagogue on Tłomackie Street, see Guterman: The Origins, pp. 199, 202–206.

25 A Popular Demonstration in Warsaw. In: *The London Times*, 12.02.1880. See also Shatzky: *Geshikhte fun yidn in varshe*, vol. 3, p. 226.

26 Driven to Despair by Russian Injustice. In: *The New York Times*, 09.02.1880.

27 Guesnet: *Polnische Juden*, pp. 229, 391; both Ignacy Schiper: *Przyczynki do dziejów chasydyzmu w Polsce*, ed. by Zbigniew Targielski. Warszawa: Państwowe Wydawnictwo Naukowe 1992, p. 67, and Shatzky: *Geshikhte fun yidn in varshe*, vol. 1, p. 134, argued for such an exceptional status of the community in Warsaw-Praga.

funeral of many to follow. The contemporaries emphasised the exceptional number of people in attendance, bearing witness to the outstanding status of Muszkat, who could claim to have commanded respect among Misnagdic and Hasidic Jews alike.[28] About the funeral of Dov Ber Meisels, we read in *Der Israelit*, the lead publication of German observant Jews, published by Rabbi Lehmann:

> In accordance with strict Jewish observance, the funeral avoided any ostentation – nevertheless, it was an impressive event due to the formidable crowd it attracted. Not only the Jews of Warsaw, who form the largest community in Europe, attended the event, but many Christians from all walks of life. Meisels enjoyed the highest esteem, as a rabbi and as an individual, but also as a political personality [...] Due to his liberal outlooks and his Polish patriotism, the authorities did not trust him – and this distrust continued after his demise: The censor has forbidden to print any obituary in the local papers except for a short note about his passing away, and certainly no mentioning of the formidable funeral.[29]

These funerals seem to have been among the first public gatherings of very large numbers of Warsaw Jews in an explicitly Jewish context. The impact of such an encounter of huge Jewish crowds cannot be overstated, as they would have given a concrete experience of what Warsaw would be for the decades to come: the largest Jewish community in Europe, and for a considerable period of time, of the world. In the history of the community as a representative and administrative body of the Jews of Warsaw, it would be of equal relevance. Few later figures would command a cross-denominational respect comparable to that of these two leaders. Their demise would have a significant impact on the metropolitan rabbinate. Warsaw's rabbinical reach would expand to Praga, ending independent halakhic jurisdiction east of the Vistula. Furthermore, after the removal of Yaacov Gesundheit from his office as chief rabbi, the halakhic supervision in the Polish capital would rest with district rabbis who lacked authority over the whole of Warsaw. These subdivisions would be a reflection of the polycentric character of the emerging Jewish metropolis.

Torah processions, demonstrations, and funerals, which would make the presence of a large Jewish community visible, and which would insert this community into the social, cultural and political fabric of the capital, certainly contributed to a sense of identification and belonging to this place which was

28 Tsevi Falk Vinaver: Rusland. In: *Ha-Magid* 13 (1868), p. 100; Shatzky: *Geshikhte fun yidn in varshe*, vol. 1, p. 146.

29 Rußland. In: *Der Israelit* 9 (02.03.1870), p. 158.

Warsaw. This appropriation of the local space however had also an everyday dimension which would be based both in Jewish and in non-Jewish contexts. In order to illustrate how urban space needed to be negotiated between communities, but also between communities and the authorities, seemingly neutral urban spaces offer an appropriate perspective. More specifically, the use of urban parks, closely connected to the formation of the European metropolis as such, allows us to further understand the processes through which the Jewish community of Warsaw negotiated its place in the capital. The two most important green spaces in 19th century Warsaw, the Saxonian Garden (*Ogród Saski*) and the Krasinski Park (*Park Krasińskich*) were both situated in the immediate vicinity of the Jewish quarter. The realities and complexities of using these popular venues are well reflected in a letter to the German *Der Israelit*:

> The Saxonian Garden features an establishment for mineral waters, visited by thousands of patrons during summer. The police chief orders the Jews to enter the Garden only from the rear entrance of the park, and bans them to walk around during the drinking cure, although this is recommended therapy. The order does not explicitly target the Jews, it is claimed, but only the traditional [Jewish] dress […] The great majority of the Jews of Warsaw, even if they do not appreciate the generally accepted European dress, visit the Garden in appropriate, even elegant garments. These measures are dictated by the hatred of Jews alone. During the shortlived Wielopolski government [1861–1862, F. G.] such narrow-minded restrictions had disappeared, yet we find them again today.[30]

Thus, multiple objectives governed the use of recreational space in central Warsaw: From the point of view of the authorities, a modern institution like an urban park was incompatible with traditional Jewish dress, and over decades conflicts would erupt around the question whether Jews in non-European dress would be acceptable or not.[31] Water cures as an innovative form of healthcare, immensely popular among Jews and non-Jews alike, seemed to offer a counter-argument to a restrictive definition of acceptable dress, as healthcare would trump the narrow-minded argument of the head of police.

Russian administrators did not, however, have a monopoly on narrowmindedness. Also for integrationist Jews, the presence of traditional Jews in urban parks was difficult to stomach:

30 Rußland und Polen. In: *Der Israelit* 26 (26.06.1870), p. 491.

31 For the role of green urban spaces in the context of 'popular autocracy' in the imperial Russian context, see Boris Anan'ich / Alexander Kobak: St Petersburg and Green Space, 1850–2000: An Introduction. In Peter Clark (ed.): *The European City and Green Space. London, Stockholm, Helsinki and St Petersburg, 1850–2000*. Aldershot: Ashgate 2006, pp. 247–271, here p. 254.

> The observant middle classes, after some hesitations in the past years, also joined the event [a charitable fundraiser]. We were appalled by the boldness with which these visitors, dressed in their long garbs and accompanied by their wigwearing wives, moved through the Garden. Their loud babbling and shouting of repulsive names like Moyshe, Khaye, Gitle, with a loud voice, resonated with a hurtful echo in the hearts of the better educated patrons.[32]

Thus, the metropolitan Jewish community had to not only negotiate its own diversity, but negotiate cultural, behavioral and religious choices with the wider community as well. Also, modern recreational spaces like urban parks would not be neutral. They would be governed and policed by the same principles as the remainder of urban space. They would, however, offer new forms of engagement and interaction. The Krasinski Park in particular would become a frequent venue for Jewish charitable events, like a lottery for the *Dom Schronienia*, the almshouse supported by the whole of the Jewish community. The two central parks would remain venues for Jewish charitable events in the years to come, and a report about the coordinated distribution of cheap meals by competing observant and Russian-Jewish charities on the occasion of *Lag b'omer* in the year of crisis and revolution 1905 seems to indicate that at least in the area of charitable work, these urban spaces could claim to offer neutral grounds.[33]

Finally, the places and spaces of the rapidly growing Warsaw Jewish community needed to be negotiated not only within this community and with an authoritarian administration, but also with the non-Jewish, mostly Polish community in the capital. As is well known, the first large scale pogrom took place in Warsaw at the very end of the period under consideration in this chapter, on Christmas Day 1881. It seems that already earlier, the cohabitation of Jews and non-Jews had led to outbursts of violence. In one case, Jews celebrating the Feast of Tabernacles (Hebr. *sukkot*) were attacked in their hut:

> On the evening of Sukkot, cheery and even-minded Jewish families had sat down in their beautifully decorated huts, as a mob of around 50 Christians assaulted them and beat and kicked men, women, and children. The head of police in this 9th district angrily dismissed the complaint, claiming it to be a non-issue, as nobody had been killed [...] The very next day, uncouth youths attacked a Jewish funeral, but this time the perpetrators were arrested.[34]

32 Pogadanki. In: *Izraelita* 34 (1872), p. 274.

33 Odgłosy. In: *Izraelita* 20 (1905), p. 230.

34 Rußland. In: *Der Israelit* 44 (01.11.1871), p. 812.

It seems of relevance here that the 9th district – to the west of the Warsaw city center – had been at quite a distance from the Jewish neighbourhood, and reflects the reluctance of Poles to accept Jewish settlement beyond their traditional quarters.[35] A much more dramatic assertion of religious identification like the Torah procession discussed earlier seemed less of a challenge to the Christian population, as it happened in an undoubtedly Jewish neighbourhood – outside of the Jewish enclave, even a modest *sukkiyah* would constitute a provocation.

Conclusion

The third quarter of the 19th century was a crucial period in the emergence of the first Jewish metropolis in European diasporic history. The first reason is demographic – not only was Warsaw the location of the largest Jewish community in Europe, and for a number of years in the world – it was also a highly diverse community. More importantly, each subgroup would develop a strong sense of identity, contrasting its own religious and cultural choices with those of other Jews, and translating these distinctive characteristics into politics, socializing, *weltanschauung*, and, last but not least, community politics. This holds true for the Jews who came to Warsaw from German territories as well as from Lithuania or the Russian heartland, for the Misnagdim and the members of the numerous Hasidic communities. Jews with inclinations towards a reviewed aesthetic of dress, everyday life and religious ritual rejected the ways of old, while the period of patriotic mobilization in the 1860s witnessed the emergence of a Jewish romantic commitment to the idea of a Polish fatherland for Jews, as well. These differences notwithstanding, the Polish capital became a place where Jews would physically encounter their own community as a mass society, defining, marking and sometimes overwhelming public space. In the period under consideration, confident public events like demonstrations or funerals would be the occasions for a wholly new Jewish encounter – one of a metropolitan community.

35 This is also reflected in the animosities against Jews taking up residence in locations from which Jews had been excluded until the emancipation of 1862, leading to threats against houseowners letting to Jews, see Warschau. In: *Der Israelit* 37 (1862), p. 296.

Jewish Quarters as Urban Tableaux[1]

Eszter Gantner

At the beginning of the 2000s investors became interested in district 8, one of the internal districts of Budapest. District 8 – the so-called Belső-Erzsébet város [Internal Erzsébet town] – is situated on the Pest side of Budapest, in the vicinity of the inner city centre developed in the 19th century. Some of the buildings in the district were built even at the beginning of the 19th century. The architectural picture and structure of the quarter remained barely changed until 1989. After the political changes the quarter had been 'discovered' by real estate investors, because of its central location in the city.
2004 a civil group named PROTEST[2] established organised demonstrations against uncontrolled sale, demolition and building. As a result of the radical steps of this civil organisation a dialogue started in the media, which contributed to the fact that this part of the district became known as the Jewish quarter and determined the set of images associated with this phrase. Since 2002 the quarter has been under UNESCO protection, which clearly legitimated the outstanding cultural heritage of the Jewish quarter. In 2006 the PROTEST group initiated at ICOMOS inspections to be performed to determine how much the quarter, which had been declared a world heritage site,[3] was endangered by demolitions and property development.[4]

1 The text is a supplemented version of a previous article, published in: *Anthropological Journal of European Cultures* 23,2 (2014), pp. 11–25.

2 An NGO in Budapest founded in 2006.

3 http://www.international.icomos.org/risk/world_report/2006-2007/pdf/H@R_2006-2007_20_National_Report_Hungary.pdf (accessed 13.12.2012).

4 Plans were also prepared concerning the architectural reconsideration and revival of the heritage without further demolitions: among these the award-winning district development plan prepared for the 2005 EUROPAN competition also laid great emphasis on the Jewish cultural heritage within the quarter. http://www.europan.at/A_Europan8/www.europan.at/E8/index1fe1.html?idcatside=74 (accessed 13.12.2013).

In the debate arising in connection with the protection and architectural redefinition of the Jewish quarter one of the most significant break lines was represented by the discussion around the definition of the concept of the 'Jewish quarter'. The diversity of the possible answers threw light upon the fact that the interpretation and – consequently – the future of the Jewish quarter is a part of a much more complex process involving many participants, a process which is not exclusively determined by the architectural value of the buildings situated in the quarter.
On examining the special literature and research dealing with the cultural and architectural reconstruction of Jewish quarters there seems to exist some kind of consensus about what the phrase 'Jewish quarter' covers. In texts advertising the tourist signs of certain cities and also in the narrative of debates on architectural and heritage protection issues this phrase appears again and again. Sometimes it occurs in a historical dimension, sometimes it is associated with a shtetl-image, or in other cases it means the same as ghetto. Still, on comparing the various uses and interpretations of the phrase, there is certainly one common point: the 'Jewish nature', the Jewishness of the Jewish quarter is determined by the Jewish population (that used to exist or is presently existing), which is apparently different in appearance. To give some examples:

> […] In many towns and villages, numerous buildings still survive in the old Jewish quarters or ghettos, where Jews either chose or were compelled to live in medieval times or later.[5]
> […] compulsory residential quarter for Jews. […] Jewish Quarter is […] a residential area that evolves spontaneously.[6]
> […] traditional Jewish merchant quarter […] this quarter becomes the traditional residential area […] of one of the largest Jewish communities […].[7]

The definitions cited as examples presume the existence of a homogenous group that can be clearly distinguished in respect of its customs, life-style and appearance and leaves a specific material (visible) impression on a given part of the city. But how can the phrase 'Jewish quarter' be interpreted, when the Jewish community, which is different in 'appearance' and presumably in respect of its practices too (meaning a strictly religious community), does not leave clearly materialising impressions on the cityscape, as, for example, in Antwerp or Williamsburg or even in the London quarter called Finchley?

5 Ruth Ellen Gruber: *Jewish Heritage Travel: A Guide to Eastern Europe.* Washington: National Geographic 2007, p. 9.
6 *Encyclopaedia Judaica*, vol. 7. Jerusalem: Keter 1971, e.g. pp. 542–543.
7 http://www.ovasegyesulet.hu/ (accessed 13.01.2013).

Even the synagogues are hardly distinguishable, there are very few Hebrew words or signs in the streets, only the appearance of the residents (possibly) indicate that the quarter or certain streets are inhabited by a clearly identifiable group. What is the situation when although a large number of people declaring themselves Jews live in a certain area, this population is not distinguishable in any form, because they have a secular, cultural or other type of relation to their Jewishness that they maintain at a certain level, in certain practices. But these attitudes are not decipherable by outsiders in the urban space, and these maintained identities do not leave an impression on the given part of the city either. An example of this may be district 13 in Budapest called Újlipótváros or Berlin Charlottenburg[8], where the large secular Jewish population cannot be seen from the 'outside', only people within the group are aware of it, so the populated area becomes a type of 'Jewish area' only for them.

How can the phrase Jewish quarter be interpreted – and this may be one of the most common phenomena in the towns and cities of continental Europe (first of all in its post-socialist part) – when a significant Jewish community does not exist anymore, but its memory and architectural heritage, that is the 'material impression', has remained in the city? Or when the by-gone presence is only preserved in the memory of the city, but the buildings themselves do not exist anymore (e.g. the Scheunenviertel in Berlin)? In the context of the issues raised above the following basic question occurs: What makes the Jewish quarter still Jewish – or in other words: 'What makes a well-defined territory, predominantly inhabited by Jews, Jewish?'[9]

The questions are not new; there is a continuous interest in the revitalizing process of formal Jewish quarters. Since the early 2000s the ongoing 'disneyfication'[10] of these urban areas is a phenomenon reflected upon especially in the field of Jewish studies. Ruth Ellen Gruber has been continuously analysing the process of revitalisation from ethnological perspectives.[11] The

8 Alina Gromova: *Generation »koscher light«. Urbane Räume und Praxen junger russischsprachiger Juden in Berlin.* Bielefeld: Transcript 2013.

9 Julia Brauch / Anna Lipphardt / Alexandra Nocke: Exploring Jewish Space. An Approach. In: Iid. (eds): *Jewish Topographies.* New York: Ashgate 2008, pp. 2–23, here p. 18.

10 Iris Weiss: Jewish Disneyland: Die Aneignung und Enteignung des Jüdischen. In: *haGalil*, April 2001. http://www.hagalil. com/golem/diaspora/disneyland-d.htm (accessed 12.01.2014).

11 Ruth Ellen Gruber: Beyond Virtually Jewish… Balancing the Real, the Surreal and Real Imaginary Places. In: Monika Murzyn-Kupisz / Jacek Purchla (eds): *Reclaiming Memory. Urban Regeneration in the Historic Jewish Quarters of Central European Cities.* Krakow: International Culture Center 2009, pp. 63–81; Ead.: *Virtually Jewish. Reinventing Jewish Culture in Europe.* Los Angeles: University of California Press 2002.

publication *Reclaiming Memory*[12] reflects on the concrete practices, strategies and agents of the revitalisiation of Jewish quarters in the former socialist countries in manifold ways. In that context Ruth Ellen Gruber and Magdalena Waligórska emphasise the role of 'imaginary' and visibility in the process of revitalisation as well. But the reconstruction of these sites in relation and in the context of general processes like 'competition of the cities'[13] or *Erinnerungskultur*[14] is less discussed yet. Also the images themselves, used in the revitalisation or re-imaginering of the Jewishness of these sites, have rarely been researched.

In this context the paper concentrates first of all on the 'external' (i.e. non-Jewish) reading, on the images present in this reading which are called in this study 'urban tableaux', as they seem to play a dominant role in the contemporary interpretation and revitalisation of Jewish quarters.

Erinnerungskultur in the Urban Space

Erinnerungskultur

In the past few decades cultural studies, memory and memorialization have come to serve as key terms in investigating questions of knowledge and memory production, and have spurred a new interdisciplinary exchange between social science, cultural studies and neuroscience practitioners. In history, the forms, functions, as well as changes in approaches to collective memory have drawn particular attention.[15] The historian Hans-Günter Hockerts defined the term *Erinnerungskultur* as "a loose, umbrella term intended for the general public that encompasses the totality of the indefinite and academic use of history."[16] In contrast, the anthropologist Sharon Macdonald has

12 Murzyn-Kupisz / Purchla (eds): *Reclaiming Memory.*

13 Annika Mattisek: Städte als Gegenstände und Schauplätze hegemonialer Kämpfe. In: *Bildpunkt. Zeitschrift der IG Bildende Kunst*, Summer 2009. http://www.igbildendekunst.at/bildpunkt/2009/symbolischebarrikaden/mattissek.htm (accessed 12.01.2014).

14 In the frame of this article, the term *Erinnerungskultur* – translated as culture of remembrance – describes the assemblage of practices and strategies of various agents shaping the commemoration of the Holocaust and National Socialism in the urban public space.

15 Tillmann Robbe: *Historische Forschung und Geschichtsvermittlung. Erinnerungsorte in der deutschsprachigen Geschichtswissenschaft.* Göttingen: V&R Unipress 2009.

16 Hans Günter Hockerts: Zugänge zur Zeitgeschichte: Primärerfahrung, Erinnerungskultur, Geschichtswissenschaft. In: Konrad H. Jarausch / Martin Sabrow (eds): *Verletztes Gedächtnis. Erinnerungskultur und Zeitgeschichte im Konflikt.* Frankfurt am Main: Campus 2002, pp. 39–73, here p. 41: "einen lockeren Sammelbegriff für die Gesamtheit des nicht spezifisch wissenschaftlichen Gebrauchs der Geschichte für die Öffentlichkeit."

described *Erinnerungskultur* as a space in which history manifests itself, both discursively and normatively, as "heritage"[17], or as the interaction between material traces of the past and symbolic practices of the present. Thus *Erinnerungskulturen* always reflect a process of public negotiation, struggling with conflicts present in bringing together individual experience and collective memory, and politically normative and socially desirable commemoration of popular narratives and critical presentations of history.[18]

The Holocaust and the assumption of responsibility for its memory by European countries constitute the lynchpin of Diana Pinto's notion of Jewish space.[19] In her article, she introduced the term 'Jewish space' that motivates this volume, as well as 'voluntarily Jewish', which describes the construction of identity free of external prescription. Pinto situates Jewish space in the context of the *Erinnerungspolitik*[20] European democracies engaged in during the 1980s, at which time Holocaust memorialization began to assume an institutional form through the establishment of Jewish museums, research institutes, and exhibits. Jewish space is a consequence of these memory practices and the product of the *Erinnerungspolitik*, which she explicates in announcing its arrival:

> There is now a new cultural and social phenomenon: the creation of a 'Jewish space' inside each European nation with a significant history of Jewish life. The first is the gradual integration of the Holocaust into each country's understanding of its national history and into twentieth-century history in general. And the second is the revival of 'positive Judaism'.[21]

Her work emerges from a phase of the *Erinnerungskultur* that dates to the early 1980s, and which has been referred to as the period of *Vergangenheitsbewahrung*,

17 Sharon Macdonald: *Difficult Heritage. Negotiating the Nazi Past in Nuremberg and Beyond.* New York: Routledge 2009.

18 Robert Bohn / Christoph Cornelißen / Karl Christian Lammers (eds): *Vergangenheitspolitik und Erinnerungskulturen im Schatten des Zweiten Weltkriegs. Deutschland und Skandinavien seit 1945.* Essen: Klartext 2008.

19 Diana Pinto: The Third Pillar? Toward a European Jewish Identity. In: András Kovács (ed.): *Jewish Studies at the CEU: Yearbook I. (Public lectures 1996–1999).* Budapest: CEU 1996, pp. 177–199.

20 *Erinnerungspolitik* and *Erinnerungskultur* represent a complex of political, social and cultural – particularly, of course, historical – factors that relate to the memory and memorialization of the Holocaust. The former emphasizes their political dimensions and the latter focuses on their cultural ones.

21 Diana Pinto: *A New Jewish Identity for Post-1989 Europe.* London: Institute for Jewish Policy Research 1996. http://www.jpr.org.uk/Reports/CS_Reports/PP_no_1_1996/index.htm (accessed 08.02.2014).

i.e. conservation of the past.[22] Aleida Assmann elaborates that this phase is identified by the reproduction of the means of remembering. In a paradoxical manner, the establishment of new and additional museums, memorials, dedicated archives and research institutes reinforce the institutionalization of memory, and through these exercises of political power and influence, normative understandings of the past. More recently, numerous individual projects and initiatives (for example, the *Stolperstein* project)[23] constitute a new development and represent an expansion of the established body of stakeholders in the field of memory and memorialization. These actors, from municipalities to independent artist and citizen groups, have influenced the form and trajectory of the *Erinnerungskultur* as well as the work of academic research and state-supported institutions.

Since the 1980s remembrance policy has also left visible, physical, built traces in the urban spaces. If no monument or museum was built, then the Jewish architectural heritage was upgraded or changed its function, as a result of which for example a deserted synagogue was converted into a research centre or museum.[24] By now the different forms of remembrance policy manifested in the urban space cannot be separated any more from the architectural heritage in European cities. Several different types of spaces are projected onto each other and onto the Jewish architectural heritage, including the constructed and built spaces of remembrance and the constructed Jewish cultural spaces. Presumed Jewish quarters, synagogues, ritual baths and cemeteries form the basis of this process.

The Urban Space

During the process of globalisation, cities and metropolises have come into the foreground all over the world. These metropolises, and large cities that regard themselves as such, define themselves as 'world cities'[25] and compete with each other in the fields of economy, culture and tourism. European cities similarly to their Asian or South American competitors are all

22 Aleida Assman: Wendepunkte der deutschen Erinnerungsgeschichte. In: Ute Frevert (ed.): *Geschichtsvergessenheit – Geschichtsversessenheit*. Stuttgart: DVA 1999, pp. 42–50, here p. 45.

23 http://www.stolpersteine.com/ (accessed 14.02.2013).

24 For example the Rashi House in Worms, Germany. http://www.worms.de/englisch/tourismus/sehenswuerdigkeiten/juedisches_worms.php?navid=23&fileSsi=/deutsch/tourismus/sehenswuerdigkeiten/juedisches_worms.php&navid=52; http://www.europan.at/A_Europan8/www.europan.at/E8/index1fe1.html?idcatside=74 (accessed 16.12.2013).

25 Ulf Hannerz: The Cultural Role of World Cities. In: Anthony F. Katsuyoshi (ed.): *Humanising the City? Social Contexts of Urban Life at the Turn of the Millenium*. Edinburgh: Edinburgh UP 1993, pp. 67–84.

participants in this process. The way the individual cities present their ethnic and cultural diversity plays an outstanding role in the competition. This diversity and its efficient representation is a capital[26] (a part of symbolic economy), as it radiates an image of the city with the help of which it can gain concrete economic advantages, such as for example increasing tourism, attracting creative industries, promoting capital flow. As a condition of being successful in the competition the cities have realised 'self-culturalisation' in order to be able to define their individuality and specific features more favourably,[27] among other reasons. All this is manifested in renovating and reinterpreting city quarters, supporting events, creating an individual image and marketing cultural – first of all – architectural values. Cities consciously build up their presumed specific features and communicate them to the world, creating by this a city-brand, similarly to product marketing.[28] Such a city-brand profits both from creating museum quarters and from reconstructing ethnic quarters. This phenomenon and the fact that culture has become a resource, has been the subject of discourses in the field of social and cultural sciences for several decades. In accordance with this, in contemporary city research there are two analytic approaches dealing with the phenomenon outlined above: one of them defines the urban space as a stage, on which cultural diversity and social differences are not simply present but are represented again and again in the most different forms;[29] the other interpretation puts the discursive changing of cityscapes[30] in the centre, and this change is influenced by political, economic and city-planning factors. In both analytic approaches the concept of urbanity plays a central role in a certain sense of ethnical-cultural diversity,[31] and also as a representation strategy, as ethnic diversity is regarded

26 Sharon Zukin: *The Culture of the Cities*. New York: Blackwell 1996.

27 Andreas Reckwitz: Die Selbstkulturalisierung der Stadt. Zur Transformation moderner Urbanität in der „Creative City". In: *Mittelweg 36* 18,2 (2009), pp. 2–43; Gerhard Mahnken: Public Branding und Wissen: Zum Entstehungsprozess einer metropolitanen Raummarke am Fallbeispiel Berlin-Brandenburg. In: Ulf Matthiesen (ed.): *Zur Koevaluation von Raum und Wissen. Analysen und Plädoyers für eine wissensbasierte Stadtpolitik*. Wiesbaden: VS 2009, pp. 235–254.

28 Ingo Balderjahn: Markenführung für Städte und Regionen. In: Manfred Bruhn (ed.): *Handbuch Markenführung*, Bd. 3. Wiesbaden: Gabler 2004, pp. 2357–2374.

29 Wolfgang Kaschuba: Zwischen Niemandsland und Residenz: Die Neukodierung öffentlichen Raumes in Berlin. In: *SRL-Mitteilungen für Stadt-, Regional- und Landesplanung*, 3/2000, pp. 5–7.

30 Annika Mattisek: Städte als Gegenstände und Schauplätze hegemonialer Kämpfe. In: *Bildpunkt. Zeitschrift der IG Bildende Kunst*, Summer 2009. http://www.igbildendekunst.at/bildpunkt/2009/symbolischebarrikaden/mattissek.htm (accessed 13.01.2014).

31 Gisela Welz: *Inszenierungen kultureller Vielfalt*. Frankfurt am Main / New York / Berlin: Akademie 1996.

as a strategic factor, with the help of which a city can become more attractive for global tourism and capital flow.[32] This phenomenon can be described with the term 'ethnic representation'.[33] This term relates to a complex symbolic and political strategic repertoire, which contains forms of ethnic self-representation that can be used for political purposes. Subcultures and self-representations are becoming part of the cityscapes more emphatically, and at the same time they also reflect the new discursive context of the cities.[34] In this explicitly performative urban self-representation ethnic presence plays a dominant role, and the participants can easily be identified in this process: entrepreneurs, city politicians, artists and tourists, who, via their everyday cultural and symbolic practices, all contribute to the materialisation and symbolisation of ethnic-cultural diversity and in creating local features.[35]

The processes outlined above, specifically in connection with Jewish heritage and Jewish quarters, are manifested on the internet in the form of advertisements in which the city brand appears as an ethnic product: '*Jewish Budapest*' or '*Jewish Berlin*' or '*Jewish Prague*'. The buildings that have remained here and still bear visible and specific features, the visible forms of *Erinnerungspolitik* (e.g. memorial tablets) and the 'Jewish' images subsisting on different discourses all serve both historic-authentic and exotic-ethnic expectations in the urban environment. The labels such as: '*Jewish Berlin*', '*Jewish Budapest*', '*Jewish Paris*', etc. are *products* of the cities' symbolic topography and map, which again are the results of both the practice of remembering the Jewish community and Jewish life of the given city and the practice of facing the Holocaust.

'Jewish Quarters' as Urban Tableaux?

When browsing the web sites of Toledo[36] and Córdoba[37] the word 'Judería' appears among the first pieces of information. Both towns list their former Medieval Jewish quarter and synagogue – of the few synagogues that have remained in Spain – among their main sights. After 1490 these buildings were used as churches, and then in the last decade of the 20th century the original

32 Zukin: *The Culture of the Cities.*

33 Kaschuba: Zwischen Niemandsland und Residenz.

34 Annika Mattisek: *Die neoliberale Stadt. Diskursive Repräsentationen am Stadtmarketing deutscher Großstädte.* Bielefeld: Transcript 2008.

35 Ulf Hannerz: *Transnational Connections: Culture, People, Places.* London: Routledge 1996; Thomas Biskup / Marc Schallenberg (eds): *Selling Berlin – Imagebildung und Stadtmarketing von der preußischen Residenz bis zur Bundeshauptstadt.* Stuttgart: Steiner 2008.

36 http://www.toledosefarad.org/JUDERIA/lajuderia.php (accessed 20.12.2013).

37 http://www.andalucia.com/cities/cordoba/juderia.htm (accessed 20.12.2013).

synagogue parts were revealed and made into museums. There is no Jewish community in either of these towns, so the built Jewish heritage is completely managed by the municipalities of the two towns. At the same time when the medieval Jewish heritage was upgraded, the image appearing on the sites was created by branding and by the economic needs of the towns – attracting as many visitors as possible in the present case – and the services offered in association with the image.

Most of the European towns that have Jewish quarters do not have a significant Jewish community. In many towns the everyday experience of Jews and non-Jews living together has become eclipsed or is not present in any form other than historic records; groups of images – *tableaux* – containing remembrance-knowledge fractures and splinters have remained. The images themselves, on what in this case the imaginary of Jewishness draws, are *results* of, as the art historian Hans Belting puts it: "pure personal or collective symbolization".[38]

In this study the application of the concept *urban tableaux* helps to describe the process of *imagineering*[39] *Jewishness* in relation to architectural heritage. *Urban tableaux* are the assemblages of those *results* referring to Jews in the urban context that are used as a pool to create and re-create something called 'Jewish'. This is the end product of the process of imagineering and the *results* of the *tableaux* can be used ad libitum.[40]

In the case of Toledo and Cordoba the characteristics occur by mentioning the medieval 'glorious' past, the richness of medieval Jewish culture and outstanding Jewish personalities, who by now have become organic parts of the town image. There is no living community having its own reading and identities, so there is nothing to remark upon, and the Jewish past of these towns can be remodelled, interpreted or used without any possible 'control'. Cities with a larger Jewish community, such as Paris, Berlin, London or Budapest, are in a more complex situation. In most of them there are both architectural impressions and Jewish communities with plural identities, at the same time the Jewishness *imagineered* by the given city is also present, and it appears in the city branding too.[41]

38 Hans Belting: *Bild-Anthropologie. Entwürfe für eine Bildwissenschaft.* Munich: Beck 2001, p. 11.

39 Rolf Lindner: The Imaginary of the City. In: Internationales Forschungszentrum Kulturwissenschaften (ed.): *The Contemporary Study of Culture.* Wien: Bundesministerium für Wissenschaft und Verkehr 2003, pp. 289–294.

40 A similar process is described in the concept of "urban Imagineering" by Alexa Färber in: Alexa Färber (ed.): *Hotel Berlin. Formen urbaner Mobilität und Verortung.* Berlin: Lit 2005.

41 http://www.budapest.com/city_guide/culture/jewish_budapest.en.html (accessed 20.01.2014).

Paris/Marais

Today the Marais in Paris – which also consists of myths constructed alongside historical facts and architectural impressions – is not the home of the Jewish community – which, we have to emphasise again, is plural in Paris too –, but the image and content of this urban space is determined first of all by the gay subculture. Still, the Jewish Paris commonplace concentrates on the Marais. Michel Laguerre[42], in his work analysing European Jewish quarters describes the Jewish quarter in Paris as a living quarter, identifying the quarter itself with the Jewish population living there, although the Marais does not have a significant Jewish population any more. First of all the Marais appears on the different websites as the display of an imagined Jewish existence, where especially the presence of the Jewish cuisine is conspicuous (falafel, kosher confectionery).[43] At the same time, among the average buildings of the 19th arrondissement a Jewish quarter develops through the specific use of space of religious Jewish life, invisibly to those who are unable to decipher the presence of these people. The synagogues cannot be seen. Nor can be other elements of the infrastructure, such as the mikveh or the Jewish school. Yet, Jewish religious life still takes place here. And then we have not mentioned the scenes of secular French Jewish life, or the urban spaces of the Sephardic Jews, which are not related to the Marais and are not regarded as a Jewish quarter by anyone.

Krakow/Kazimierz

> Jewish life in Krakow, nearly extinguished by the Nazis, was driven underground in the communist era. Kazimierz, where Schindler's List was filmed, was a neglected and underpopulated district under communism. In recent years it has been transformed into one of the hippest parts of the city. […] Jewishness has been adopted as a selling point, almost a badge of cool, in a way that is sometimes tasteless. Converted golf carts tout for tourist custom with awnings displaying the itinerary: "Auschwitz, Schindler's factory, Jewish quarter." […] There have been complaints over a "Jewish-themed" restaurant that displays a page of the Torah on its wall […].[44]

The above citation appeared in the *Guardian* two years ago and clearly describes the process of the construction of the quarter's 'Jewishness'. Kazimierz is

42 Michel Laguerre: *Global Neighbourhoods – Jewish Quarters in Paris, London, and Berlin.* New York: State University of New York Press 2008.

43 www.parislemarais.com (accessed 20.01.2014).

44 Jeevan Vasagar/Juilan Borger: A Jewish Renaissance in Poland. In: *The Guardian*, 07.04.2011. http://www.guardian.co.uk/world/2011/apr/07/jewish-renaissance-poland (accessed 20.03.2013).

one of the mostly researched quarters, as the richness of academic publication shows.[45] If we analyse the programmes of the Jewish Culture Festival over several years, the following images appear: Klezmer, Galicia, Hasidism, Kabbala, Yiddish, Jewish Food and the quarter itself with the synagogue, the cemeteries and the ghetto. On the basis of the images the commonplace of a bygone 'desired' past takes shape: the vanished Eastern European Jewish culture. These are sellable images (*results*) that could be deciphered by everyone.

By now among the supporters and sponsors of the festivals there are the Polish ministry of Tourism and the Municipality of Krakow too, making it clear that the festival with its own imagined/constructed Jewish participants represents a *selling point* in the marketability of the city. The example of Krakow perfectly indicates the intertwining of the physical space, the constructed space retouched with ethnic/religious culture and remembrance policy, and the urban economic interests.

For years numerous European cities have been organising 'Jewish' themed festivals similar to the one in Krakow[46] on the basis of almost the same script. The majority of these festivals feed from and reflect on the past communicating specific knowledge and notions about the Jewry. On the one hand the festivals strengthen the images and expectations in the non-Jewish environment and, on the other hand, they reduce the present-day European Jewish existence and culture to these images, neglecting its variety and richness.

On the basis of our analyses to date[47] this tableaux is formed by the Holocaust, the Yiddishkeit and the commonplace of happy peacetime. In Europe today there is no Jewish cultural festival that does not include aspects of the Holocaust, the Hasidic Jewry or of melancholic yearning for the idealised coexistence of Jews and non-Jews at the turn of the century for the past 'happy peacetime'. Of these three, it is perhaps the Holocaust that demands the least explanation.[48] The 'happy peacetime' in the festival programmes may mean sightseeing, a theatre play or book presentation.

45 For example, Jurgita Šiaučūnaitė-Verbickienė / Larisa Lempertienė (eds): *Jewish Space in Central and Eastern Europe: Day-to-Day History*. Newcastle: Cambridge Scholars 2007; Murczyn-Kupisz / Purchla (eds): *Reclaiming Memory*.

46 http://jewish-heritage-travel.blogspot.de/2012/03/jewish-culture-and-other-festivals-in.html (accessed 30.03.2015).

47 Eszter Gantner / Mátyás Kovács: Altering Alternatives: Mapping Jewish Subcultures in Budapest. In: Brauch / Lipphardt / Nocke (eds): *Jewish Topographies*, pp. 210–221.

48 Since 1990 the reflection on the Holocaust became part of the self-determination and public role-undertaking of all social groups and political forces that identify themselves as being democratic.

Therefore it is (not) surprising that the Krakow festival[49] uses the commonplace of Yiddishkeit. Yiddishkeit as a commonplace primarily means the (false) revival, the replaying of the memory and customs of the Eastern European Hasidic Jewry obliterated in the Second World War.
The majority of the festivals are organised and sponsored by the cities – for example, in Berlin the annual Jewish cultural festival was founded by the city leadership – and is generally headed by the appointed art director. Certainly further empirical research is needed on these *tableaux* and on their possible changes in the future. But for the moment, these homogenous images of Jewish quarters hide the heterogeneity of formal and present Jewish life and culture in these cities. As an exception the Budapest Negyed6/Negyed7 festival[50] could be mentioned, which was founded by a young Jewish NGO, Marom, in 2010. The festival consciously breaks away from the mentioned 'triangle' of images projected on the city's Jewish heritage. Although the Jewish cultural space created by Marom during the festival days deals with and is based on the architectural sites as well, but at the same time in an exchange with them. It also reflects on their pasts and present, on their various dwellers and inhabitants with diverse private histories. The festival also reinterprets various elements of the Jewish tradition in accordance with the contemporary, generational demands offering for a wider audience a view into a lively, vibrant and *existing* urban Jewish culture.[51]

Berlin / Spandauer Vorstadt / Scheunenviertel

In Berlin the designation *jüdisches Viertel* (Jewish quarter) even to this day relates to the area behind Alexanderplatz, where Jewish refugees arrived at the end of the First World War primarily from civil war-stricken Russia and the Ukraine, and from the eastern parts of the disintegrating Habsburg Empire.[52] The majority of them intended to stay in Berlin just for one or two months hoping for emigration, therefore choosing the cheap accommodation behind Alexanderplatz they moved to Scheunenviertel, which was fixed in the memory of the city as an Eastern European ghetto. After the Second World

49 More detailed analysis in Gruber: Beyond Virtually Jewish, pp. 63–68.

50 http://negyed6negyed7.com (accessed 10.01.2014).

51 In the case of Budapest a further research is needed with a special focus on the possible interaction between the growing antisemitic public political discourse and the fate of the Jewish tangible heritage.

52 Tobias Brinkmann : Topographien der Migration. Jüdische Durchwanderung in Berlin nach 1918. In: Dan Diner (ed.): *Synchrone Welten. Zeitenräume jüdischer Geschichte.* Göttingen: Vandenhoeck & Ruprecht 2005, pp. 175–199.

War the majority of the buildings here were demolished, so today their presence can only be found in the literature. Irrespective of this, Scheunenviertel lives on in the consciousness of Berlin as a Jewish quarter: in this part of the city there are tours organised for tourists, literature readings are held, a culture industry has been established around the remaining buildings and one or two streets built on Jewish heritage: the restaurants bear Jewish-sounding names, a klezmer music centre and a Yiddish theatre have been established in the quarter. In this way, the Eastern European Yiddishkeit space, Scheunenviertel, standing in the focus of Berlin's constructed Jewish past (the entire architecture of which does not actually exist today as it was demolished after 1945) is recreating itself from the memories of Eastern European Jewish refugees and shtetl-dreams. Scheunenviertel appears on many tourism websites as Berlin's Jewish quarter;[53] moreover, the sociologist Michel Laguerre devoted a separate section to it.[54] In these cases the image of a former Jewish Quarter is 'materially' projected onto another city quarter containing Jewish tangible heritage: the Spandauer Vorstadt.

However, the interviews with the various stakeholders in Berlin paint a completely different picture of the city's Jewish quarter – showing the possibility of various forms of interpretation and the *elasticity* of the term 'Jewish quarter'.

The following excerpts are from qualitative interviews led during the spring of 2011 in Berlin with the following partners[55]: director of the Jewish Museum, owner of the company milk&honey tours, an employee of the Visit Berlin marketing agency and two journalists at the most important city event magazines: *TIP* and *Zitty*.

> Does Berlin have a Jewish quarter?
> Apart from the historical dimension I don't really see it that way. I myself live at Nordbahnhof, and the Spandauer Vorstadt [historic center] was a kind of Jewish quarter; [today] with the Beth Cafe and the Leo-Baeck-Haus, and you see a reflection of Jewish life there, that the police are always guarding the buildings. But I don't really consider that a Jewish quarter, but rather more of a 're-initiation', a re-institutionalisation, which I can't experience in my everyday life […]
> So I would say no […] I would make a differentiation. Tourists would think that there is. I of course know that there isn't one, or in the form in which it's depicted, perhaps it existed in the Middle Ages. There always was an area to which Jews were drawn, the

53 For example: http://www.touristeye.com/Scheunenviertel-Jewish-Quarter-Berlin-p-18181 (accessed 20.01.2013).

54 Laguerre: *Global Neighbourhoods*, pp. 37–61.

55 The interview partners asked to be quoted anonymously.

> Bayerische Viertel or some such. A Jewish quarter must have had cultural institutions, like a theater, and stores to supply it. The Spandauer Vorstadt [historic center] was once a beggars' quarter, and for that reason Jews were at that time also residents there. So naturally as a tourist you still find traces of Jewish life, but no longer on the scale that tourists would like. It's similar to what you find with regards to the Nazi period… But there aren't the real centers of power from the Nazi period, or a ghetto in the sense of a medieval quarter. The Jüdenhof [a residential complex dating to the Middle Ages] no longer exists in Berlin…
> Do you believe that there's a 'Jewish' element in Berlin's urban image, meaning that the city in some form uses what is 'Jewish' to appeal to tourists or to promote itself?
> Definitely. I do think that this historical dimension of Berlin, that it is indeed a line with which to reel in tourists. The other is the party aspect of the city. We once did a survey, why tourists come, and we learned that tourists, particularly international ones, were familiar with city's history, that is the fall of the Wall and Berlin of the 20s, also the Nazi period, meaning the historical Berlin. And Berlin markets itself as a 'historic' city, you need only to look at how well history exhibits here do […] And the fact is that Berlin was the launching point for the Nazi's reign of terror, which is repeatedly portrayed in Hollywood productions and has penetrated the furthest corner of the earth, which of course is important, so that people go and see the places themselves, where these horrors came from. That will then be incorporated into a tourist's itinerary. People go from Potsdamer Platz and the Holocaust Memorial to Checkpoint Charlie, and they have covered a good deal of historical sites. It shows people's need to really visit the places where things took place.

The process outlined above, specifically in connection with Jewish heritage and Jewish quarters, is manifested on the internet in the form of advertisements in which the city brand appears as an ethnic product: *Jewish Budapest* or *Jewish Berlin.* The buildings that have remained here and still bear visible and specific features, the visible forms of remembrance policy (e. g. memorial tablets) and the 'Jewish' images subsisting on different discourses all serve both historic-authentic and exotic-ethnic expectations in the urban environment. The Jewish quarters in Budapest and Berlin, as well as in Paris and in many other cities, have become a brand, a brand that now has a fixed set of 'images' of 'Jewishness'.

Interestingly enough, these urban *tableaux* seem to contain similar *images* although the current cities have different histories and traditions. These 'travelling images' include the nostalgic look on the destroyed Eastern European Jewish culture and the use of this culture as a kind of pool for 'Jewishness' is still characteristic. This phenomenon was described already during the 1990s,[56] but seemingly it became a fixed *tableau*, not disappearing with time. It appears

56 Gruber: *Virtually Jewish*; Murzyn-Kupisz / Purchla (eds): *Reclaiming Memory*; Šiaučūnaitė-Verbickienė / Lempertienė (eds): *Jewish Space in Central and Eastern Europe.*

for example in the form of the small wooden figures of a traditionally looking Jew in the shop at the entrance of the Dohány synagogue in Budapest. The image of the 'shtetl', 'mixed' with the 'Holocaust', especially in Berlin and added with a certain 'quantity' of the melancholic, nostalgic cohabitation of Jews and non-Jews during idealized times of peace at the turn of the century are the essence of the 'fixed' homogenous images of Jewishness and Jewish quarters.

But the last interview quote refers also to something else, namely to that special role that the Holocaust plays in the construction of the Berlin Jewish space/quarter. Berlin is home to the country's largest Jewish community of some ten thousand people. This multi-identity, strongly post-Soviet community creates its own spaces in a city where the constructed Jewish space does not only include the non-existent ex-Jewish quarter (Scheunenviertel), but also the Jewish Museum and the Holocaust Memorial.

The Jewish quarter, Jewish Berlin has become a brand, which now has a fixed 'image' and constructed canon. Those personalities, those architectural and other memorials that belong to this canon were established over the course of the past decade. All this can be traced from the appearance of tourism, the catalogues, the thematic tours offered in the city. Present-day Jewish life in the city is not a part of this canon, which, apart from one or two momentary media inspections, is not influenced by the large number of the Israeli population (for the time being).[57] Naturally there are Israeli participants in the Jewish cultural festival (primarily music events),[58] but due to the political tensions linked to Israel and probably with consideration of the large Muslim minority, these seem to be somewhat hidden. At the same time present-day Jewish culture is becoming increasingly synonymous with Israel (which the festival reflects perfectly: the majority of the events look into the past, and the present, in other words present-day Jewish life and culture, is embodied by Israeli artists and productions).

Conclusions

This study – a snapshot – intended to analyze the role of the images, first of all the *tableaux* – assemblages of images – used in the revitalization of a Jewish tangible heritage – especially of Jewish quarters. These images seem to play an essential role in the contemporary interpretation and revitalization

57 http://www.dw.de/unkosher-jewish-night-takes-berlin-by-storm/a-15987608 (accessed 20.12.2012).

58 http://www.juedische-kulturtage.org/ (accessed 20.12.2012).

of the 'Jewishness' of the Jewish quarters. On the basis of the processes and examples outlined in the article it seems that the 'Jewish' nature and the ethno-cultural character of the Jewish architectural heritage remaining in European cities are primarily determined by the external economic, commemoration politics and city marketing actors. The space created in this way has been and is created in a well-coded way around the architectural heritage characteristic of the given culture. The once functional buildings (synagogue, mikveh, etc.), the knowledge relating to them, the fact that they played an important role in the life of a community, as well as the image set related to the community legitimise and ensure the authenticity of the ethno-cultural space constructed around them – Jewishness in the present case. This, however, leaves the existence/non-existence of the given community completely out of consideration, and 'arbitrarily' communicates a very homogenous picture of the given culture put together from discretionally selected elements, not reflecting its possible diversity and self-definition. Therefore, the practices of *Erinnerungskultur* manifested in the urban space and the 'images of Jewishness' constructed in the various discourses satisfy the demand for both the historic-authentic and for the exotic-ethic producing urban *tableaux*. All other possible interpretations, images, details become marginal as opposed to the governing marketable construction and in this way Jewish culture and heritage of the cities are simplified into just an exotic piece of history.

Imperial, Ethnic and Local (Non-)Jewish Space in the Cities of Imperial Russia

Alexis Hofmeister

Shtetl, Ghetto and Lost Paradise. Looking Back at the Russian Empire as a (Non-)Jewish Space

Space is among the most basic human experiences as is time. While geography is also concerned with human movement in time, history is also concerned with human movements through space.[1] Given the fact that the historical narration of the Jewish historical experience is still dominated by the idea that the catechism of Judaism is its calendar,[2] every effort to establish a more balanced view is worth considering. It has been suggested that it is more promising to look for experiences of space and place instead of its pure description and to research the ambivalent and multifaceted space in between Jews and

1 Wolfgang Kaschuba: *Die Überwindung der Distanz. Zeit und Raum in der europäischen Moderne*. Frankfurt am Main: Fischer 2004, pp. 13–28; Sylvie Anne Goldberg: *Le clepsydre. Essai sur la pluralité des temps dans le judaïsme*. Paris: Michel 2000.

2 A thought, attributed to Samson Raphael Hirsch (1808–1888), a leading neo-orthodox rabbi from Germany. Samson Raphael Hirsch: *Gesammelte Schriften*, vol. 1. Frankfurt am Main: Kauffmann 1902, p. 1. The opinion that the documentation of spatial aspects of Jewish history was simply lacking or at least sparsely documented was voiced by the eminent scholar of Jewish literature and German reform rabbi Leopold Zunz (1794–1886). In an introduction to the 1841 edition of the travelogues of Benjamin of Tudela (12th cent.) he states that "no branch of knowledge appears to be cultivated more scantily, or to be less known than that of geography." Yet Zunz explicitly excludes the knowledge of the Holy Land from his verdict and to the contrary cites an impressive list of texts from Jewish pen containing geographical details. Leopold Zunz: Essay on the Geographical Literature of the Jews from the Remotest Times to the year 1841. In: Adolf Asher (ed.): *The Itinary of Benjamin of Tudela*, vol. 2. London / Berlin: Asher 1841, pp. 230–317, here p. 230 (http://reader.digitale-sammlungen.de/de/fs1/object/display/bsb10239667_00012.html).

Gentiles rather than the well-known dichotomies of Jewish and Non-Jewish spaces.[3]

> When I was a little girl, the world was divided into two parts; namely, Polotzk, the place where I lived, and a strange land called Russia. All the little girls I knew lived in Polotzk, with their fathers and mothers and friends. Russia was the place where one's father went on business. It was so far off, and so many bad things happened there, that one's mother and grandmother and grown-up aunts cried at the railroad station, and one was expected to be sad and quiet for the rest of the day, when the father departed for Russia.[4]

This significant spatial marking of the world of a Jewish child is to be found in the autobiography of Mary [Ma(rya)she] Antin (1881–1949), published 1912 in Boston. It is an example for a narrative understanding of the "Old Home" in Russia which was widely shared among a certain generation of Jewish migrants to the Americas.[5] Its influence was even felt in the field of historiography of East European Jewry.[6] A hypothesis to start with is that the experience of topographic mobility of the Jewish population in the Russian empire had an impact on the description of imperial space and its respective hierarchies. As the quote from the autobiography of a migrant as prominent as Mary Antin shows, this relation made itself felt with respect to several interrelated layers. The simple dichotomy of the home of the Antins and the seemingly far-away and strange land called Russia creates a distance between the real places of Jewish life and the empire as the space of Jewish economic activity. The imperial territory looms here as a space of possibilities – where mostly bad things are happening to Jews. Antin's narrative takes Polotsk as a place out of the imperial landscape to which it politically belonged since the first partition of Poland in 1772.[7] Different experiences might have

3 Anna Lipphardt / Julia Brauch / Alexandra Nocke: Exploring Jewish Space. An Approach. In: Iid. (eds): *Jewish Topographies: Visions of Space, Traditions of Place (Heritage, Culture, Identity).* Aldershot / Burlington: Ashgate 2008, pp. 1–23, here p. 16.

4 Mary Antin: *The Promised Land.* Boston: Houghton Mifflin 1912, p. 1. A digital copy of the text is available via the North American Immigrant Letter, Diaries and Oral Histories Database: http://alexanderstreet.com/products/north-american-immigrant-letters-diaries-and-oral-histories.

5 Frank Wolff: The Home that Never Was. Rethinking Space and Memory in Late Nineteenth and Twentieth Century Jewish History. In: *Historical Social Research* 38,3 (2013), pp. 197–215.

6 Steven J. Zipperstein: Shtetl There and Here. Imagining Russia in America. In: Steven J. Zipperstein: *Imagining Russian Jewry. Memory, History, Identity.* Seattle / London: University of Washington Press 1999, pp. 15–39; Olga Litvak: You Can Take the Historian out of the Pale but Can You Take the Pale out of the Historian? New Trends in the Study of Russian Jewry. In: *AJS Review* 27 (2003), pp. 301–311.

7 Polotsk. In: *Evreĭskaia Ėntsiklopediia. Svod znaniĭ o evreĭstve i ego kul'ture v proshlom i nastojashchem.* Sankt Peterburg: Obshch. dlia Nauchnych Evreĭskich Izd. 1913 [reprint: Moscow: terra 1991], vol. 12, pp. 696–698; Stefan Rohdewald: *„Vom Polocker Venedig". Kollektives Handeln sozialer Gruppen einer Stadt zwischen Ost- und Mitteleuropa.* Stuttgart: Steiner 2005.

contributed to this narration of the Jewish and non-Jewish world as completely divided and segregated spaces. Men and women followed different paths of economic activity – a fact which also had a spatial aspect.[8] While women according to Mary Antin took care of the Jewish house, men had to look for their business outside of the Jewish home. This might not have been the general experience of the ordinary Jewish family in Russia, where many woman did take care for the household as well as for the economic needs of the whole family.[9] To the difference between feminine and masculine perspectives one has to add the weight of the retrospective view from the other side of the Atlantic. As a result the essential differences between here and there, between once and now, between one ethnic group and others are strengthened. The conflicts and complex contradictions of Jewish life shrank to a simple woodcut-like picture showing the Russian empire as a space Jews were reluctant to discover and travelled to only with a heavy heart. For the Jewish migrants to North America this picture holds a certain truth in it. Even if they did not cross the Atlantic because of personal experiences with anti-Jewish violence, their image of Russia was shaped by a clear-cut division of Jewish and non-Jewish spaces.[10] While Russia under the *ancien régime* became a non-Jewish – and almost inhuman space – places like Polotsk as did *shtetlach* [small towns] elsewhere became a lost paradise. Nevertheless, the successful migrant Mary Antin, who wrote from a geographical as well as from a

8 The feminine perspective on the difference between the Jewish home in a small town and the Russian metropolis depends of course on the social position of the author. While Pauline Wengeroff's memories in this regard resemble the dichotomist view of Mary Antin, women like Anna P. Vygodskaja (1868–1943), Deborah Baron (1887–1956) and Ita Kalish (1903–1994) saw their going to the big cities as part of their emancipation from the grip of family and tradition. Pauline Wengeroff: *Memoiren einer Grossmutter. Bilder aus der Kulturgeschichte der Juden Russlands im 19. Jahrhundert.* 2 vols., 2nd ed. Berlin: Poppelauer 1913; Ead.: *Memoirs of a Grandmother. Scenes from the Cultural History of the Jews of Russia in the Nineteenth Century*, ed. by Shulamit S. Magnus, 2 vols., Stanford: Stanford UP 2010, 2015; Anna Pavlovna Vygodskaia: *Story of a Life. Memoirs of a Young Jewish Woman in the Russian Empire*, ed. by Eugene M. Avrutin / Robert H. Greene. DeKalb: Northern Illinois UP 2012; Ita Kalish: *A rebishe heym in amoliken poyln.* Tel Aviv: J.L. Peretz 1963 [Warsaw: Gmina Wyznaniowa Żydowska 2009]; Ruth Adler: Dvora Baron. Daughter of the Shtetl. In: Judith R. Baskin (ed.): *Women of the Word: Jewish Women and Jewish Writing.* Detroit: Wayne State UP 1994, pp. 91–110. See also the memoirs of the daughter of Simon Dubnow (1860–1941), Sophia Dubnova-Erlikh: *Bread and Matzoth*, trans. from the Russian by Alan Shaw. Tenafly, NJ: Hermitage 2005.

9 Shaul Stampfer: How Jewish Society Adapted to Change in Male/Female Relationship in 19th/early 20th Century Eastern Europe. In: Rivkah T. Blau (ed.): *Gender Relationships in Marriage and Out.* New York: Scharf Publ. Trust of the Yeshiva UP 2007, pp. 65–83.

10 Shaul Stampfer: Patterns of Internal Jewish Migration in the Russian Empire. In: Ya'acov Roi (ed.): *Jews and Jewish Life in Russia and the Soviet Union.* Ilford / Portland: Frank Cass 1995, pp. 28–47, here p. 42.

chronological distance about her life in the Russian empire speaks also about a room-in-between the Jewish *shtetl* and Russia proper:

> After a while there came to my knowledge the existence of another division, a region intermediate between Polotzk and Russia. It seemed there was a place called Vitebsk, and one called Vilna, and Riga, and some others. From those places came photographs of uncles and cousins one had never seen, and letters, and sometimes the uncles themselves. These uncles were just like people in Polotzk; the people in Russia, one understood, were very different. [...] How I wanted to see Russia! But very few people went there. When people went to Russia it was a sign of trouble; either they could not make a living at home, or they were drafted for the army, or they had a lawsuit. No, nobody went to Russia for pleasure. Why, in Russia lived the Czar, and a great many cruel people; and in Russia were the dreadful prisons from which people never came back. [...] It seemed there were certain places in Russia – St. Petersburg, and Moscow, and Kiev – where my father or my uncle or my neighbour must never come at all, no matter what important things invited them. The police would seize them and send them back to Polotzk, like wicked criminals, although they had never done any wrong. [...] So there was a fence around Polotzk, after all. The world was divided into Jews and Gentiles.[11]

According to Israel Bartal three factors were responsible for such an ahistorical image of the life of the Jewish population at the Western border of the Russian empire like Antin's: the minimizing or neglect of the influence of Polish Aristocratic culture, the leveling of the differences between metropolis and small town, the overemphasizing of the difference between the Jewish life in the small towns – the famous *shtetl* – on the one hand and the life in their Gentile neighborhood on the other.[12] Nostalgic pictures of bygone days in the "old Jewish home" in Eastern Europe fulfilled a vital function in the narrative of loss and sorrow after the total annihilation of Jewish life in Eastern Europe during the Shoah.[13] On the other hand the doomed and forsaken Jewish space is mostly neglected in the story of the Jewish success. In this perspective Jews had to abandon the space of the *shtetl* in favor of social

11 Antin: *The Promised Land*, pp. 1–5.

12 Israel Bartal: Imagined Geography. The Shtetl. Myth and Reality. In: Stephen T. Katz (ed.): *The Shtetl. New Evaluations*. New York / London: New York UP 2007, pp. 179–192, here p. 186. In an ironic twist the original account of the migration of Mary Antin was published under the title *From Plotzk to Boston*. As Plotzk at that time was a Polish city the author was thus polonised. Mary Antin: Preface to the Second Edition. In: Mary Antin: *From Plotzk to Boston*. 2nd ed. Boston: W. B. Clarke 1899, pp. 16–17.

13 We find tendencies of an ahistorical *shtetl*-nostalgia in post-war America at the beginning of the Cold War in Mark Zborowski / Elizabeth Herzog: *Life is With People. The Jewish Little-town of Eastern Europe*. New York: International UP 1952. For a solid contextualization of this classic, read the introduction by Barbara Kirshenblatt-Gimblett to the new edition New York: Schocken 1995, pp. ix–xlviii.

mobility in the big cities of the Russian empire, the United States or Western Europe. Particularly because of their success the 20th century became the *Jewish Century* – as it was labeled by Yuri Slezkine. According to Slezkine Jews had the inherent ability to think and act as non-attached and de-territorialized Mercurians in a capitalist-bourgeois turned world.[14] That is why they could turn their back to the *shtetl*. Until today a historiography which clings at nationally and linguistically defined units has to come to terms with the sheer number of the Jewish overseas migration from Eastern Europe, which counted for almost two million people from 1881 to 1914.[15] East European and North-American perspective were only brought together recently.[16] The individual migratory direction resulted from the influence of several and often contradicting exterior forces. The collective movement took shape in the form of a wandering into the nearest city and from there to a greater city and finally to metropolises like Warsaw, Odessa or Kiev. Another and much bigger step was made by those who left the Jewish pale of settlement (*cherta evreĭskoĭ osedlosti*) or Russia altogether and went to St. Petersburg and Moscow or to Buenos Aires, New York, London or Johannesburg.[17] The most popular direction of migration inside the Jewish pale of settlement went along a Northwest-Southeast-axis.[18] In combination the rapid demographic growth and the large currents of Jewish migration lead to a significant shift of the geographical centers of Jewish settlement in the world. If at the beginning

14 Yuri Slezkine: *The Jewish Century*. Princeton / Oxford: Princeton UP 2004, pp. 4–39.

15 Two classic papers are still recommended read: Simon Kuznets: Immigration of the Russian Jews to the United States. Background and Structure. In: *Perspectives in American History* 9 (1975), pp. 35–124, again in: Stephanie Lo / E. Glen Weyl (eds): *Comparative Perspectives on Jewish Migration*. New Brunswick: Transaction 2012, pp. 143–232; Arcadius Kahan: Economic Opportunities and Some Pilgrim's Progress: Jewish Immigrants from Eastern Europe in the United States, 1890–1914. In: *Journal of Economic History* 38,1 (1978), pp. 235–251, again in: Roger Weiss (ed.): *Essays in Jewish Social and Economic History*. Chicago: University of Chicago Press 1986, pp. 101–117.

16 Anna Lipphardt: *Vilne. Die Juden aus Vilnius nach dem Holocaust. Eine transnationale Beziehungsgeschichte*. Paderborn: Schöningh 2010; Rebecca Kobrin: *Jewish Bialystok and Its Diaspora*. Bloomington: Indiana UP 2010; Frank Wolff: *Neue Welten in der Neuen Welt. Die transnationale Geschichte des Allgemeinen Jüdischen Arbeiterbundes 1897–1947*. Köln: Böhlau 2014.

17 Shaul Stampfer: The Geographic Background of East European Jewish Migration to the United States before World War I. In: Ira A. Glazier / Luigi de Rosa (eds): *Migration across Time and Nations. Population Mobility in Historical Contexts*. New York: Holmes & Meier 1986, pp. 220–230; Yvonne Kleinmann: Zur Genese jüdischer Gemeinden in russischen Großstädten 1840–1900. Innovative Entwürfe und beharrliche Tradition. In: *Aschkenas* 17 (2007), pp. 55–74; Frank Wolff: Global Walls and Global Movement: New Destinations in Jewish Migration 1918–1939. In: *East European Jewish Affairs* 44,3 (2014), pp. 187–204.

18 Stampfer: Patterns of Internal Jewish Migration, p. 29.

of the 20th century about 80 % of Ashkenazi Jews lived in Central and Eastern Europe, the respective numbers dropped significantly until they reached about 50 % at the beginning of the 20th century. Around 1900, 10 % of the Jewish population in the world lived in Western Europe, about a quarter in the United States. Beginning with the First World War and accelerated by the abolition of all restrictions of topographical mobility inside Russia by the February Revolution of 1917 a Jewish migration towards the Russian interior took place. Its cultural implications were expressed with the greeting: "Next year in Moscow!" which resembled the traditional greeting at Pesach: "Next year in Jerusalem!"[19] The space of the Russian interior which was remembered by Mary Antin as non-Jewish and un-Jewish became the living place of many Jews. When the poet Osip Mandelstam (1891–1938) remembered his childhood in imperial St. Petersburg he was already living in Moscow. But in contrast to Antin he did not seem to identify with small-town Jewry, neither in his childhood nor later on. The Judaic chaos seemed to be everywhere around him and around the imperial city: "All the elegant mirage of Petersburg was merely a dream, a brilliant covering thrown over an abyss, while round about there sprawled the chaos of Judaism – not a motherland, not a house, not a heart, but precisely a chaos."[20]

We can reconstruct space through communication and the writing and reading about a particular space plays a prominent role as it does in the memories of Mary Antin or Osip Mandelstam. It certainly fulfils an important function in the process of memory.[21] Space and the experience of spatial change do serve as occasion of memory as many autobiographical texts show. If Russia is invoked as a non-Jewish space it serves as a negative background for the positively associated and newly acquired home of America. That the invocation of Russia as a Jewish space depended largely on the perceived readership of a text is demonstrated by the fact that the German translation of Mary Antin memories was published under the title: "From the Ghetto into the promised land."[22] The ghetto to the German reader was in a twofold

19 Gabriele Freitag: *Nächstes Jahr in Moskau! Die Zuwanderung von Juden in die sowjetische Metropole 1917–1932*. Göttingen: Vandenhoeck & Ruprecht 2004.

20 Osip Mandelstam: *The Noise of Time: The Prose of Osip Mandelstam*, trans. from the Russian by Clarence Brown. San Francisco: North Point 1986, p. 77.

21 Marc Redepenning: Eine selbst erzeugte Überraschung: Zur Renaissance von Raum als Selbstbeschreibungsformel der Gesellschaft. In: Jörg Döring / Tristan Thielmann (eds): *Spatial Turn. Das Raumparadigma in den Kultur- und Sozialwissenschaften*. Bielefeld: Transcript 2008, pp. 317–340, here pp. 329–334.

22 Mary Antin: *Vom Ghetto ins Land der Verheißung*, trans. from the English by Marguerite Steindorff / Ulrich Steindorff. Stuttgart: Robert Lutz 1913 (http://sammlungen.ub.uni-frankfurt.de/urn/urn:nbn:de:hebis:30:1-174572).

sense a place beyond his own experience and nevertheless a familiar place of the "other" – be it the Jew in general or the East European Jew or the pious Jew of "yesterday".[23] A particular literature of the ghetto had explained its mores to him and brought ethnographic details close to non-Jewish and Jewish readers alike.[24] Besides that the ghetto was the place where the East European or Russian Jew was from, it was evident that he had to travel westward to shake off the heavy yoke of its traditions to become a member of the civilized tribe.[25] Even thinkers like Ahad Ha'am (1856–1927) could not free their rhetoric of the powerful image of the walled ghetto.[26] It was only the modern city in its ambivalence as a non-Jewish as well as a Jewish place that was invoked as an anti-*shtetl* or for that sake an anti-ghetto.[27] It will suffice to cite the example of a young Hershel Baraznik (later Henry E. Burroughs) who came from the Volhynian *shtetl* Kashoffka (Kashivka) to the port-city of Odessa with the highest expectations and was bitterly disappointed. In his memoirs, published about 25 years later in Boston, he described his feelings as a ten year old boy:

> My visions of what Odessa must be were so extravagant that when we entered the suburbs and I saw real houses and streets I was disappointed for a moment, but not for long. […] The domes and pillars of the cathedrals were, indeed, vermilion and blue and gold. Naval officers more resplendent than the army officers or the Cossacks strode through the streets, which were unbelievably broad and swept as clean as a floor on the eve of Passover. […] Among the crowds I kept seeing men who looked like pictures of the Tsar and only with difficulty restrained myself from asking if the Tsar were really there. The streets were shaded by magnificent trees and the parks filled with shrubs and flowers. Everyone was busy and happy as we drove from the station toward the hotel. […].[28]

23 Steven E. Aschheim: *Brothers and Strangers. The East European Jew in German and German-Jewish Consciousness.* Madison: University of Wisconsin Press 1982.

24 Kristiane Gerhardt: Vom Raum zur Geschichte. ‚Ghetto' als Metapher historischer Grenzziehung im 19. Jahrhundert. In: *Pardes* 17 (2011): Ghetto: Räume und Grenzen im Judentum, pp. 19–34. (http://opus.kobv.de/ubp/volltexte/2011/4938/pdf/pardes17.pdf).

25 For the respective narratives Jakob Fromer (ed.): *Salomon Maimons Lebensgeschichte.* München: Georg Müller 1911 (https://archive.org/details/salomonmaimonsle00maim); Jakob Fromer: *Vom Ghetto zur modernen Kultur. Eine Lebensgeschichte.* Charlottenburg: Selbstverlag 1906.

26 Sheila E. Jelen / Michael P. Kramer / L. Scott Lerner (eds): *Modern Jewish Literatures: Intersections and Boundaries.* Philadelphia: University of Pennsylvania Press 2011, pp. 1–10. For Ahad Ha'am: Achad-Haam: Nachahmung und Assimilation. In: Id.: *Am Scheidewege*, vol. 1, trans. from the Hebrew by Israel Friedlaender. Berlin: Jüdischer Verlag 1913, pp. 225–239.

27 John D. Klier: A Port, Not a Shtetl. Reflections on the Distinctiveness of Odessa. In: *Jewish Culture and History* 4,2 (2001), pp. 173–178.

28 Harry E. Burroughs: *Tale of a Vanished Land. Memories of a Childhood in Old Russia.* Boston: Houghton & Mifflin 1930, pp. 253–254.

Alas, one moment of brute force, enacted on the open street destroyed all of Hersh Baraznik's illusions:

> As the cab turned, I caught a glimpse of a side-street and saw a crowd of men, evidently Jews, running in a body toward a goal I could not see. They were all dressed in blood-stained aprons and had long knives in their hands. Wikos said at once that they were butchers. From another direction came a mob of Russian laborers with long hair and canvas blouses, bearing spades, clubs and guns in their hand. The Jewish butchers, cornered in an alley, turned around to fight and I saw the knives gleam, the clubs swinging, men fall and bleed, others run. The police stood calmly at their posts, as if the affair was none of their business.[29]

The *city of god* – as Baraznik called it – no longer was a paradise. After the shock of the pogrom fight another misfortune happened to him. At the water closet of the hotel he lost his leather belt – one of his most precious belongings. Odessa – symbol of the modern way of life and its civilizing achievements – came to be the place he disliked most: "I began to hate Odessa thoroughly and to feel a twinge of that distaste for modern conveniences which Schloime Gimbel, the Framingham junk man, has retained through thirty-five years in America."[30] Whereas the question if Imperial Russia could possibly become a home for its Jews is debated nowadays among historians, Odessa as modern cities in general seemingly never became a home to Hersh Baraznik.[31] The answers to this question differed among Jews themselves according to their status at the time of the respective memory as well as according to their social belonging in late Imperial Russia and not the least according to their gender role.[32]

29 Burroughs: *Tale of a Vanished Land*, pp. 253–254

30 Ibid., p. 257.

31 Kerstin Armborst-Weihs: Historiographie. Das Russische Reich als historischer Ort des Judentums. In: Michal Kümper (ed.): *Makom: Orte und Räume im Judentum. Real – Abstrakt – Imaginär.* Hildesheim: Olms 2007, pp. 95–105; Kenneth B. Moss: At Home in Imperial Russian Modernity – Except When They Weren't: New Histories of Russian and East European Jews, 1881–1914. In: *The Journal of Modern History* 84,2 (2012), pp. 401–452.

32 For the changing perception of Russia as an "Old Home", see Frank Wolff: The Home that Never Was. The problem of divergent memories is addressed in Mordechai Zalkin: Wilno / Vilnius / Vilne: Whose City Is It Anyway? In: Richard I. Cohen / Jonathan Frankel / Stefani Hoffmann (eds): *Insiders and Outsiders. Dilemmas of East European Jewry.* Oxford / Portland: Littmann Library of Jewish Civilization 2010, pp. 221–230; Janis Augsburger: Die Mythen von Vilnius. Von den Schwierigkeiten Pluralität zu erinnern. In: Esther Kilchmann / Zaal Andronikashvili (eds): *Topographien pluraler Kulturen. Europa vom Osten her gesehen.* Berlin: Kadmos 2011, pp. 243–268; Martin Schulze Wessel / Ekaterina Makhotina: Einleitung. In: Martin Schulze Wessel / Irene Götz / Ekaterina Makhotina (eds): *Vilnius. Geschichte und Gedächtnis einer Stadt zwischen den Kulturen.* Frankfurt am Main: Campus 2010, pp. 9–24.

Jewish and non-Jewish Space in the Cities of the Late Russian Empire

A systematic overview of the history of particularly Jewish spatial experiences in the Russian realm is lacking although this picture is about to change.[33] In general there are three main fields were the historicity of spatial perceptions have become particularly obvious: the history of Jewish migration, the history of the *shtetl* as a living as well as a memorial space and the history of pogroms as a history of the fight over public space. Having said this I do not intend to neglect that there are other very promising fields as the history of Jewish housing or the history of the contested urban space where a lot of new insights are to be gained.[34] I take it as granted here that cities are not a priori shared spaces of communication and mutual comprehension.[35]

For the sake of an overview I propose to group Central and East European cities according to the demographic profile of their Jewish population: a) historical cities from the Middle Ages like Prague, Lemberg (Lvóv), Kiev and Vilna which in the 19th century attracted Jewish migrants as administrative and cultural centers but less so because of their meaning for industrialization which more or less was a secondary effect of their administrative, infrastructural and cultural function; b) port-cities and border-towns, some of them founded as late as in the 18th century with free-port charters like Salonika, Odessa, Trieste and Brody with a secondary industrialization that functioned genuinely as points of trade and commerce while also fulfilling administrative

33 For efforts to historicize the *shtetl*: Chae-Ran Y. Freeze / Jay M. Harris (eds): *Everyday Jewish Life in Imperial Russia, Select Documents, 1772–1914*. Waltham: Brandeis UP 2013; Jeffrey Shandler: *Shtetl: A Vernacular Intellectual History*. New Brunswick: Rutgers UP 2014; Yohanan Petrovsky-Shtern: *The Golden Age Shtetl: A New History of Jewish Life in East Europe*. Princeton / Oxford: Princeton UP 2014.

34 For the history of Jewish housing: Alla Sokolova: Shtetl Houses and Synagogues: From the History of Architecture to Stories about Architectural Monuments. In: Aliza Cohen-Mushlin (ed.): *Jewish Architecture in Europe*. Petersburg: Imhof 2010, pp. 159–173; Barbara E. Mann: Bayit. In: Ead.: *Space and Place in Jewish Studies*. New Brunswick: Rutgers UP 2010, pp. 81–97. For the history of Jews in urban space: Lois C. Dubin: *The Port Jews of Habsburg Trieste. Absolutist Politics and Enlightenment Culture*. Stanford: Stanford UP 1999; Jörg Gebhard: *Lublin. Eine polnische Stadt im Hinterhof der Moderne (1815–1914)*. Köln / Weimar / Wien: Böhlau 2006, pp. 104–126; Natan Meir: *Kiev, Jewish Metropolis: A History, 1859–1914*. Bloomington: Indiana UP 2010; Amelia M. Glaser: *Jews and Ukrainians in Russia's Literary Borderlands. From the Shtetl to the Petersburg Bookshop*. Evanston: Northwestern UP 2012; Börries Kuzmany: *Brody. Eine galizische Grenzstadt im langen 19. Jahrhundert*. Wien / Köln / Weimar: Böhlau 2011; Steven J. Zipperstein: *The Jews of Odessa: A Cultural History, 1794–1881*. Stanford: Stanford UP 1986; Oleg Gubar': *Ocherki ranneĭ istorii evreev Odessy*. Odessa: VMV 2013.

35 Martina Löw: Städte als sich unterscheidende Erfahrungsräume. Grundlagen für eine sinnverstehende Stadtsoziologie. In: Heike Hermann (ed.): *Die Besonderheit des Städtischen: Entwicklungslinien der Stadt(soziologie)*. Wiesbaden: VS 2011, pp. 49–67.

and cultural tasks which attracted huge numbers of seasonal workers and migrants but also served as hubs of migratory transit; c) heavily industrialized points of settlement of much more recent origin like Yuzouvka (Donetsk), Ekaterinoslav (Dnepropetrovsk) and Lodz (Łódź) whose former regional meaning for trade and commerce was outnumbered by the almost towering dominance of their industrial output.[36] These places attracted Jewish as well as non-Jewish migrants in great numbers. The Jewish communities in cities with the demographic profile of the first type usually had old and conservative Jewish communities while the Jewish elite in the port and merchant cities was more open to change and to a significant extent adopted the life-style and values of their non-Jewish bourgeois environment. A similar kind of adoption was practiced by the mostly ordinary Jews in the industrial places of the third type. Jews there could seldom maintain their traditions at all, while ethnic strife and social conflict was shaping their identity. Of all places the merchant cities seemed to have come closest to the ideal of the city as a shared place common to all inhabitants. The following three examples from the late Russian empire illustrate this rather sketchy typology.

Kiev was almost a Russian speaking city around 1900. It incorporated nearly thousand years of history of Orthodox Christendom and St.-Vladimir-University was bearing the name of its holy patron. The city was the residence of a Governor-General and fulfilled important functions as a center of commerce and trade. Russian military personal, pilgrims, merchants and students contributed to the strength of the Russian element.[37] The Ukrainian speakers counted for less than half of the population. Between 1874 and 1897 their share fell unto a quarter.[38] The step-by-step industrialization of Kiev depended on migrants. The majority of them came from not-so-far-away places situated in the surroundings of the city which were mostly Ukrainian

36 This model is used according to Rainer Lindner: *Unternehmer und Stadt in der Ukraine*. Konstanz: Universitätsverlag 2006, pp. 39–85. See also Steven L. Guthier: Ukrainian Cities during the Revolution and the Interwar Era. In: Ivan L. Rudnytsky (ed.); *Rethinking Ukrainian History*. Edmonton: Canadian Institute of Ukrainian Studies, The University of Alberta 1981, pp. 156–179, here p. 157; Bohdan Krawchenko: *Social Change and National Consciousness in Twentieth Century Ukraine*. New York: St. Martin's 1985.

37 Natan Meir: Jews, Ukrainians, and Russians in Kiev: Intergroup Relations in Late Imperial Associational Life. In: *Slavic Review* 65,3 (2006), pp. 475–501.

38 Michael F. Hamm: *Kiev: A Portrait, 1800–1917*. Princeton: Princeton UP 1993, pp. 98–103. Affiliation according to language in Kiev 1897 (Russian: 54,20 %; Ukrainian: 22,23 %; Yiddish; 12,08 %; Polish: 6,69 %) according to Henning Bauer / Andreas Kappeler / Brigitte Roth (eds): *Die Nationalitäten des Russischen Reiches in der Volkszählung von 1897*. Stuttgart: Steiner 1988, vol. B, p. 398.

speaking. Russian and to a lesser extent Jewish entrepreneurs dominated the economic life of Kiev. While they were split up among ethnic lines their common economic and social interests expressed itself in the field of sociability. Ethnic and social conflict among the lower classes resulted in violence during political crises.[39] During the pogroms of 1881 and 1905 this violence was directed at the Jewish population. Kiev saw the short lived attempts to erect a Ukrainian nation-state in the turmoil of the Russian Revolution and the years of the Civil War 1917–1921.[40] While there was a fair share of Ukrainian-Jewish cooperation during this period it soon became to be memorized as a period of bloodshed and inter-ethnic conflict because of the anti-Jewish pogroms perpetrated by Ukrainian troops of the Directorate as well as by the Whites.

Odessa's port was one of the most important reloading points of the Russian empire. But the dynamic port city, founded 1794 by Catherine the Great, was much more than a center of trade and commerce. In 1865 a university was opened.[41] The social life of the multi-ethnic city was colorful and its cultural events were not only frequented by military officials, merchants, priests and professors. Students and craftsmen participated as well. Even in the last third of the 19th century when the promise of social ascent was no more valid the city attracted a large share of the migrants. Social conflicts increased and the bloody pogroms of 1881 seemed to repeat a pattern which could have been observed in 1821, 1859 and 1871.[42] A pogrom-like situation arose again in the first days of October 1905 when the news of the granting of a parliament (*Duma*) triggered a hitherto unseen street violence against Jewish shops and lives. The experience of the modern yet mundane city shaped two political

39 For the seemingly clear cut division between them and us in the social fabric of late Imperial Kiev: Lazar M. Kaganovich: *Pamiatnie zapiski rabochego, komunista-bolshevika, profsojuznogo, partiĭnogo i sovetsko-gosudarstvennogo rabotnika.* Moscow: Vagrius 1997, p. 61; Matthias Vetter: Lasar M. Kaganowitsch 1893–1991: Eine biographische Skizze. In: *Zeitgeschichte* 22,1–2 (1995), pp. 46–61.

40 Henry Abramson: *A Prayer for the Government. Ukrainians and Jews in Revolutionary Times, 1917–1920.* Cambridge, MA: Ukrainian Research Institute and Center for Jewish Studies, Harvard University 1999; Kenneth B. Moss: *Jewish Renaissance in the Russian Revolution.* Cambridge, MA: Harvard UP 2009.

41 Guido Hausmann: *Universität und städtische Gesellschaft in Odessa, 1865–1917. Soziale und nationale Selbstorganisation an der Peripherie des Zarenreiches.* Stuttgart: Steiner 1998, pp. 489–491.

42 Caroline Humphrey: Odessa: Pogroms in a Cosmopolitan City. In: Caroline Humphrey / Vera Skvirskaja (eds): *Post-Cosmopolitan Cities. Explorations of Urban Coexistence.* New York / Oxford: Berghahn Books 2012, pp. 17–64.

generations of young Jews.[43] The educated Jewish elite in the spirit of the European enlightenment since the first third of the 19th century had promoted students in Russian language. It is likely that even without the official restriction and final banning of the Ukrainian language the attraction of the Russian language would not have lost its appeal to Jews and Ukrainians alike.[44]
All in all the Ukrainian option was not very attractive for Odessa's Jews. Nevertheless it was Vladimir Jabotinsky (1880–1940), a secular Russophone Jew from Odessa who propagated the concept of a Jewish-Ukrainian rapprochement. At the beginning of the 20th century the young journalist became very well aware of the uneasy relation of the Jewish population towards Russian imperiality and Ukrainian nationality alike.[45] Jabotinsky acted not in a social vacuum. He was part and parcel of a self-conscious Jewish elite of the city whose ideal was a non-traditional but consciously Jewish Jewishness in a multi-ethnic environment.[46] Alas, the image of the city in Soviet and Post-Soviet times was much more shaped by the myth of Odessa's humorous underworld and its self-conscious Jewish share.[47]
In Ekaterinoslav social conflicts were fought with considerable ruthlessness; strikes and pogroms could be a daily event. Like Odessa Ekaterinoslav was founded by imperial decree. Her demographic growth resulted from migration from the more northern Ukrainian guberniyas and from the Russian center. It was a city of industry and workers, dependent not on a port but on iron and coal. With the exploration of these resources with the help of foreign investments at the last third of the 19th century the rapid industrialization

43 Steven J. Zipperstein: *Elusive Prophet. Ahad Ha'am and the Origins of Zionism.* London: Halban 1993, pp. 67–104, 170–257; Michael Stanislawski: *Zionism and the Fin de Siècle. Cosmopolitanism and Nationalism from Nordau to Jabotinsky.* Berkeley: University of California Press 2001, pp. 116–237.

44 Hausmann: *Universität und städtische Gesellschaft in Odessa, 1865–1917*, pp. 421–431.

45 Olga Andriewsky: Medved' iz berlogi: Vladimir Jabotinsky and the Ukrainian question, 1904–1914. In: *Harvard Ukrainian Studies* 14,3–4 (1990), pp. 249–267.

46 Sophie Dubnov-Erlich: *The Life and Work of S. M. Dubnow. Diaspora Nationalism and Jewish History*, trans. from the Russian by Judith Vowles. Bloomington: Indiana UP 1991, pp. 90–96.

47 Patricia Herlihy / Oleg Gubar: The Persuasive Power of the Odessa Myth. In: John Czaplicka / Nida Gekazis / Blair A. Ruble (eds): *Cities after the Fall of Communism. Reshaping Cultural Landscapes and European Identity.* Baltimore: Johns Hopkins UP 2009, pp. 137–165; Rebecca Jane Stanton: *Isaac Babel and the Self-Invention of Odessan Modernism.* Evanston: Northwestern UP 2012; Tanya Richardson: *Kaleidoscopic Odessa: History and Place in Contemporary Ukraine.* Toronto / Buffalo / London: University of Toronto Press 2008; Jarrod Tanny: *City of Rogues and Schnorrers. Russia's Jews and the Myth of Old Odessa.* Bloomington: Indiana UP 2011; Marina Sapritsky: Negotiating Cosmopolitanism: Migration, Religious Education and Shifting Jewish Orientations in Post-Soviet Odessa. In: Caroline Humphrey / Vera Skvirskaja (eds): *Post-Cosmopolitan Cities. Explorations of Urban Coexistence*, pp. 65–93.

of the Donbass-Dnepr-bend took off. Between 1885 and 1897 the population of Ekaterinoslav grew at a rate of 159% and at the end of this period it counted 112,000 inhabitants.[48] Annual growth was at about 8%. During the wave of anti-Jewish violence of 1881–1884 Ekaterinoslav saw one of the most brutal and devastating pogroms.[49] Besides a specific culture of violence among the local workers and socially declassified elements this might be attributed to a social imbalance of the city's population. Contrary to the situation in Odessa there were almost no public spaces outside the world of the huge enterprises. Students or academics had no influence on the workers; doctors and other professionals had to be afraid to become victims themselves during times of social crisis. While the middle and upper classes were very tiny groups, the quantitatively dominating lower classes were divided among themselves in many ethnic and social sub-groups. Conflicts of interest between strikers and strike breakers were solved by fists – especially ordinary and non-learned workers frequently attacked the city center and its Jewish population.[50]

Conclusion

Reading accounts of spatial experiences side by side with the results of socio-economic studies which map the urban space in late Imperial Russian cities helps to understand the interaction between Jews and Gentiles as well as its mental framing. It would in any case mean the revision of the notion of a particular segregated – inclusive as well as exclusive – Jewish space. Jews and non-Jews in the cities of Imperial Russia lived and worked side by side at certain spaces. At the same time they both created particular places of their own. How they conceptualized their regular toing and froing depended not the least on the spatial constitution of the urban spaces which seldom were understood as neutral. The imperial state as well as the urban populations at some moments joined forces but usually were engaged in conflicts

48 Lindner: *Unternehmer und Stadt in der Ukraine*, p. 71.

49 Charters Wynn: *Workers, Strikes, and Pogroms. The Donbass-Dnepr Bend in Late Imperial Russia, 1870–1905*. Princeton, N.J.: Princeton UP 1992, pp. 111–113, 192.

50 Gerald Surh: Ekaterinoslav City in 1905: Workers, Jews, and Violence. In: *International Labor and Working-Class History* 64 (2003), pp. 139–166. Ekaterinoslav – nowadays Dnepropetrovsk – today is called the "Jewish capital of the Ukraine". Andrij Portnov / Tetjana Portnova: Die "jüdische Hauptstadt der Ukraine". Erinnerung und Gegenwart in Dnipropetrovs'k. In: *Osteuropa* 62,10 (2012), pp. 25–40. The authors prepare a monographic account of the history of Ekaterinoslav – Dnepropetrovsk. See also: Aleksandr Bystriakov: *Evreĭ Ekaterinoslava – Dnepropetrovsk (XX vek)*. Dnepropetrovsk: ART-PRESS 2002.

over the meaning and functioning of urban space.[51] A balance of powers resulting in pockets of ethnically and politically neutral space therefore was brought about only temporarily. In that sense pockets of urban space at short moments of Russian Imperial history were the playground for experimenting with Jewish urbanity. Thus local space bought historical time.

51 Guido Hausmann (ed.): *Gesellschaft als staatliche Veranstaltung. Selbstverwaltung, Assoziierung und Geselligkeit in den Städten des ausgehenden Zarenreiches.* Göttingen: Vandenhoeck & Ruprecht 2002, pp. 13–28, 112–115, 156–166.

Mapping (Non-)Jewish Spaces of Memory, Narration and Representation

Gypsy Spaces and Jewish Spaces as Hyper-Liminal Spaces of Inversion

Longing for the Shtetl and the Gypsy Camp

Monica Rüthers

In the 1990s, Europeans developed shtetl nostalgia. There was a growing interest in Yiddish language and literature, Klezmer concerts and lectures on Chassidism. Former Jewish districts were rediscovered, synagogues renovated and Jewish museums opened. A survey mapping Jewish culture in Europe counted 28 festivals of Jewish culture between May 2000 and April 2001 in Poland, Belgium, Sweden and Italy alone.[1] In the mid-1990s, Diana Pinto observed that in Germany "non-Jews can embark on university degrees in Judaic studies confident of entering an expanding professional field" and that there were "in fact few countries in Europe today that do not choose to exploit the phenomenon of 'Jewish space' whether for noble or opportunistic reasons."[2] Pinto identified the Jewish spaces[3] as a major challenge: "How should Jews approach and intervene in Europe's growing Jewish Spaces, increasingly initiated, populated and even administered by non-Jews?"[4] She

1 Rebecca Schischa / Dina Berenstein: Mapping Jewish Culture in Europe Today: A Pilot Project: In: *JPR Report* 3 (2002). http://www.jpr.org.uk/Reports/JC_Reports/no_3_2002/index.htm (accessed 02.05.2013). – The author wishes to thank the anonymous reviewers for their helpful suggestions.

2 Diana Pinto: A New Jewish Identity for Post-1989 Europe. In: *JPR Policy Paper* 1 (1996), pp. 1–15, here p. 7.

3 In this article, 'Jewish spaces' denote spaces dedicated to Jewish culture such as museums, study courses, exhibitions, culture festivals or themed urban spaces. Ruth Ellen Gruber familiarized a broader public with these spaces with the concept of *virtually Jewish*. Ruth Ellen Gruber: *Virtually Jewish. Reinventing Jewish Culture in Europe*. Berkeley: University of California Press 2002.

4 Diana Pinto: *The Third Pillar? Toward a European Jewish Identity*. Budapest 1999, p. 11. http://web.ceu.hu/jewishstudies/pdf/01_pinto.pdf (accessed 14.05.2013).

regarded the Jewish spaces as a form of agora where debates would emerge and where Jews could obtain a high resonance.

At the same time as the Klezmer craze spread to Europe, Flamenco music – featured, for example, in Carlos Saura's musical film *Carmen* (ES 1983) – became popular. In 1987, the Gipsy Kings from Arles hit the international pop-charts with *Bamboleo*, and Goran Bregović started composing the music for the Gypsy films of Emir Kusturica. From the 1990s onwards, Roma musicians performed at a growing number of Gypsy music festivals. In the 2000s, DJ Shantel picked up on Balkan Pop and Gypsy Music and introduced them to the club scene. 'Gypsy' has been a fixture in fashion ever since the hippie movement. Gypsy romance held a space in European popular cultures in opera, novels and popular songs. It has been updated in the Romanian telenovela *The Heart of the Gypsy* (*Inima te Tigan*, Acasă TV, since 2007) and the British reality show *My Big Fat Gypsy Wedding* (Channel 4, since 2010). At the same time, one can observe a festivalization of Gypsy conventions such as Gypsy pilgrimages in France and Spain or Gypsy horse fairs in Britain. In their capacity as publicly accessible 'Gypsy camps', they are drawing an ever larger public. The festivalization of older events was paralleled by the emergence of Gypsy music festivals throughout Europe and the US. The upswing of Gypsy music was accompanied by films directed by Tony Gatlif, Emir Kusturica and Radu Mihaileănu.[5]

However, Gypsy spaces are not an established concept. Research on Gypsy music festivals has come close to exploring this notion,[6] as have studies on the circulation of Gypsy images in film and other media. To draw attention to Gypsy spaces as a concept, I published a book on the configurations of Jewish und Gypsy spaces, updating (visual) images of the Other and their position in the cultural topographies of Europe and its cultures of remembrance.[7] A subsequent article emphasized the empirical layout of the topic

5 In his motion pictures *Train de vie* (1998) and *Le Concert* (2009), Romanian director of Jewish origin Radu Mihaileănu ascribes extraordinary musical talent to Jews as well as Gypsies.

6 David Malvinni: *The Gypsy Caravan. From Real Roma to Imaginary Gypsies in Western Music and Film.* London / New York: Routledge 2004; Ursula Hemetek: Applied Ethnomusicology in the Process of the Political Recognition of a Minority: A Case Study of the Austrian Roma. In: *Yearbook for Traditional Music* 38 (2006), pp. 35–57; Carol Silverman: Trafficking in the Exotic with 'Gypsy' Music. Balkan Roma, Cosmopolitanism, and 'World Music' Festivals. In: Donna Buchanan (ed.): *Balkan Popular Culture and the Ottoman Ecumene: Music, Image, and Regional Political Discourse.* Lanham: Scarecrow 2007, pp. 335–364; Ioana Szeman: 'Gypsy Music' and Deejays. Orientalism, Balkanism, and Romani Musicians. In: *The Drama Review* 53,3 (2009), pp. 98–116.

7 Monica Rüthers: *Juden und Zigeuner im europäischen Geschichtstheater. "Jewish Spaces"/ "Gypsy Spaces" – Kazimierz und Saintes-Maries-de-la-Mer in der neuen Folklore Europas.* Bielefeld: Transcript 2012.

and further explored the particularities and different historical and cultural contexts of Jewish spaces in Central Europe and Gypsy spaces in the Mediterranean over the 20th Century.[8] In another article, I investigated the role of music, the assignation of special musical talents to Jews and Gypsies, and the contexts and implications of the festivalization of the two minorities since the 1990s.[9] In the present article, I take a comparative approach using spatial concepts to highlight the structural similarities of the spaces. What can we learn from the exploration of Gypsy spaces to achieve a better understanding of Jewish spaces?

The characteristics and functions of Jewish/Gypsy spaces cannot be investigated without looking at the larger historical context, i. e. raising the question of how specific spatial practices such as festivals are linked to major cultural shifts across Europe in the aftermath of the fall of the Iron Curtain. The growth of both Jewish and Gypsy cultural spaces parallel, and are an integral part of, a wider growth in the popularity of world cultures. This increased appreciation of minority cultures may well be stimulated by the emergence of multicultural societies in Europe. On the other hand, "imperial nostalgia" is involved.[10] My underlying thesis is that Gypsy and Jewish spaces share central features that reveal important aspects of the construction of non-Gypsy/non-Jewish identities. Fascination with the spaces is rooted more in an outside quest for identity than a genuine interest in the minorities. The two most famous events, the Kraków Jewish Culture Festival and the Gypsy pilgrimage to Saintes-Maries-de-la-Mer, shall provide a basis for comparison.

25 Years of Jewish Space in Kraków: An Assessment

The first Jewish Culture Festival in Kraków was organized in 1988 and focused on Yiddish films. In retrospect, one can distinguish three phases in the development of this particular Jewish space.[11] The first was the growing international success of the festival, fostered by the Klezmer revival and

8 Monica Rüthers: Jewish Spaces and Gypsy Spaces in the Cultural Topographies of a New Europe: Heritage Re-enactment as Political Folklore. In: *European Review of History* 20,4 (2013), pp. 671–695.

9 Monica Rüthers: Quand le Balkan Beat pompe et le klezmer gémit. Les festivals de musique gitane et juive. In : *Cahiers d'Ethnomusicologie* 27 (2014), pp. 203–224.

10 Renato Rosaldo: *Culture and Truth. The Remaking of Social Analysis.* Boston: Beacon 1989, pp. 68–87. For the shift of interest in minorities in the folk festival scene from decolonization to the European Other, see Laurent Aubert: *The Music of the Other. New Challenges for Ethnomusicology in a Global Age.* Aldershot: Ashgate 2009.

11 For a detailed history of the Jewish district, see Rüthers: *Juden und Zigeuner*, pp. 56–62.

the fall of the Iron Curtain. Following the shooting of Steven Spielberg's motion picture *Schindler's List* in 1993, Kazimierz became a tourist destination. 'Jewish' cafés, book stores, museums and souvenir markets flourished. Visitors were American heritage tourists and Western Europeans discovering the former socialist countries, youth tours from Israel visiting the nearby death camps and the Temple Synagogue, and Haredic Jews travelling to the grave of Rabbi Isserles. The non-Jewish locals discovered and appropriated Jewish history and culture as wood carvers, Klezmer musicians, café owners or tour organizers.[12] The few elderly Jews in Kraków lived apart from the tourist space. During the second phase, from the mid-1990s onwards, the festival grew, more tourists arrived, and Jewishness became an important brand. The organizers began to invite more Jewish musicians. Soon the very best of the international Klezmer scene met up in Kraków. Factors contributing to the success of Kazimierz were the proximity to Auschwitz, the filming locations and, most importantly, the old Jewish quarter that lent a sense of 'authenticity' to the festival.[13] Musicians described the atmosphere that emanated from the old buildings as 'magical'.[14] The scope of the program was expanded. The Holocaust, commemorated at the beginning, disappeared behind the sepia-coloured pictures of the traditional Jew and the shtetl. The concept of Jewish spaces spread throughout Central European cities such as Prague, Budapest and Berlin. This sparked the interest of the media and academics. At the same time, Judaism was re-imported from the U.S., mainly through the Lauder foundation and the American Jewish Joint Distribution Committee.[15] The third phase began in the mid-2000s, when reflexivity set in. In Poland, the books of Jan T. Gross on Polish-Jewish relations had a great impact. As European Judaism regenerated, young Polish Jews discovered their own ways

12 Erica Lehrer: Repopulating Jewish Poland. In: *Polin. Studies in Polish Jewry* 16 (2003), pp. 335–355; Magdalena Waligórska: Jewish Heritage Production and Historical Jewish Spaces: A Case Study of Kraków and Berlin. In: Jurgita *Šiaučiūnaitė-Verbickienė* / Larisa *Lempertienė (eds)*: *Jewish Space in Central and Eastern Europe: Day-to-Day History.* Newcastle: Cambridge Scholars 2007, pp. 225–250, here p. 229; Ruth Ellen Gruber: The Kraków Jewish Culture Festival. In: *Polin. Studies in Polish Jewry* 16 (2003), pp. 357–367, here pp. 361–363.

13 On authenticity in tourism, see Dean MacCannell: *The Tourist: A New Theory of the Leisure Class.* New York: Schocken 1976.

14 Gruber: Kraków Jewish Culture Festival, pp. 361–363; Waligórska: Jewish Heritage Production, p. 229.

15 See the documentary of Australian director Nolan Menachemson, *POLAND'S NEW JEWS* (The NRS Group, 2001). Transcripts of the Interviews to be found on http://polandsnewjews.nrsgroup.com.au/ (accessed 02.03.2013).

of being Jewish and Polish at the same time.[16] They also started to attend the festival. Today, the programme includes interactive events such as musical workshops, cooking, Yiddish language courses and lectures on recent research on Polish-Jewish relations.[17] The musical performances range from cantors in the Temple Synagogue to traditional Klezmer, pop, fusion and jam sessions. The grand finale concert draws a public of around 15,000 and is broadcast live on Polish television.

Jewish spaces[18] in general and Kazimierz[19] in particular have been researched since the mid-1990s. At the same time, a polemical debate on 'Jewish spaces without Jews' and a 'Jewish Disneyland' emerged in the media.[20] However, the Jewish spaces without Jews increasingly became populated by Jews as tourists as well as performers. After the collapse of the socialist regimes, European Jewry grew in strength. The Jewish Culture Festival has become part of Jewish cultural life. Since 2005, there has been a new trend towards a multicultural opening of Jewish spaces. With the help of EU funding, they were transformed into zones of intercultural contact by inviting Roma or Palestinian musicians.[21] Meanwhile, the Jewish district has come to sport a

16 Pinto: The Third Pillar; on Polish-Jewish identities see Claire Rosenson: Polish Jewish Institutions in Transition: Personalities over Process. In: Zvi Gitelman / Barry Kosmin / András Kovács (ed.): *New Jewish Identities: Contemporary Europe and Beyond.* Budapest: Central Europe UP 2003, pp. 263–289.

17 Magdalena Waligórska: Kleznetworks, the Transnational and the Local Dimension of Jewish Culture Festivals. In: Petra Ernst / Gerald Lamprecht (eds): *Jewish Spaces. Die Kategorie Raum im Kontext kultureller Identitäten.* Innsbruck / Wien / Bozen: StudienVerlag 2010, pp. 137–156, here p. 145.

18 *Šiaučiūnaitė Verbickienė / Lempertienė (eds)*: *Jewish Space in Central and Eastern Europe*; Monika Murzyn-Kupisz / Jacek Purchla (eds): *Reclaiming Memory. Urban Regeneration in the Historic Jewish Quarters in Central Europe.* Kraków: International Cultural Centre 2009; Ernst / Lamprecht (eds): *Jewish Spaces*; Anna Lipphardt / Julia Brauch / Alexandra Nocke (eds): *Jewish Topographies. Visions of Space, Traditions of Place.* Aldershot / Hampshire: Ashgate 2008.

19 Jack Kugelmass / Annamaria Orla–Bukowska: "If You Build it They Will Come": Recreating an Historic Jewish District in Post–Communist Kraków. In: *City & Society* 10,1 (1998), pp. 315–353; Gruber: Kraków Jewish Culture Festival; Lehrer: Repopulating Jewish Poland; Waligórska: Jewish Heritage Production; Magdalena Waligórska: A Goy Fiddler on the Roof. How the Non-Jewish Participants of the Klezmer Revival in Kraków Negotiate Their Polish Identity in a Confrontation with Jewishness. In: *Polish Sociological Review* 152,4 (2005), pp. 367–382.

20 Iris Weiss: Jewish Disneyland – die Aneignung und Enteignung des "Jüdischen". In: GOLEM 3 (2002); Henryk M. Broder: Reise nach Zydoland. In: *Spiegel Online*, 05.04.2006. http://www.spiegel.de/kultur/gesellschaft/juden-in-krakau-reise-nach-zydoland-a-409793.html (accessed 16.05.2013).

21 Magdalena Waligórska: Spotlight on the Unseen: The Rediscovery of Little Jerusalem. In: Murzyn-Kupisz / Purchla (eds): *Reclaiming Memory*, pp. 99–116; on integration see http://www.theothereuropeans.eu/6-0-About-the-band.html (accessed 30.05.2013).

multicultural nightlife. Nevertheless, the Jewish community of Kraków has remained small, numbering only around 200 members. It is still only during the festival days that Jewish life thrives in Kraków. Despite the new reflexivity, the commercialization of Jewishness and the expansion of Jewish-theme cafés in Poland continue.[22]

Saintes-Maries-de-la-Mer

Every year on the 24th and 25th of May, the annual pilgrimage of Travellers to Saintes-Maries-de-la-Mer known as *la Fête des Gitans* – the Gypsy festival – takes place.[23] Gypsies of all kinds meet up with thousands of tourists and natives in the town. Circles of vans and trailers in the parking lots around the village and the *Marché des Gitans* complete the picture. On May 24th, the statue of Sara the Black, patron saint of the Travellers, is carried to the sea by a small group of *Gitans* who lead a colourful procession, chanting and praying. A priest saying prayers of intercession into an electric bullhorn walks with them. They are escorted by *Gardians* (cowboys) on their white horses and *Arlésiennes*, local women in traditional costumes. Countless onlookers line up in the streets and on the beach. The horsemen lead the small procession through the crowd towards the sea, where the bearers of the statue go into the water with the saint to wet her feet. Vigils are held in the crypt of the medieval church; weddings and baptisms are celebrated during the festivities. Everyone is dressed up, mostly Gypsy or Camargue style.

Despite the spectacular character of the event and its being mentioned in every tourist guide on Southern France, there is little literature on the historical, intercultural and heritage aspects of the Gypsy pilgrimage to Saintes-Maries-de-la-Mer.[24] However, since the pilgrimage has been a tourist destination since the early 20th century, there are a number of travelogues.[25] These were

22 On newly created traditions and encodings in the 20-year history of virtually Jewish spaces, see Ruth Ellen Gruber: Beyond Virtually Jewish: New Authenticities and Real Imaginary Spaces in Europe. In: *Jewish Quarterly Review* 99,4 (2009), pp. 487–504.

23 The author attended the pilgrimage in 2004, 2007, 2009 and 2012.

24 Ina-Maria Greverus / Heinz Schilling (eds): *Zigeuner und Wir*. Frankfurt am Main: Institut für Kulturanthropologie und Europäische Ethnologie 1979; Marc Bordigoni: Le 'pèlerinage des Gitans', entre foi, tradition et tourisme. In: *Ethnologie française* 32,3 (2002), pp. 489–501; Eric Wiley: Romani Performance and Heritage Tourism: The Pilgrimage of the Gypsies at Les Saintes-Maries-de-la-Mer. In: *The Drama Review* 49,2 (2005), pp. 135–158.

25 Jean-Louis Vaudoyer: *Les Stes Maries de la Mer*. Paris: Émile-Paul Frères 1927.

written by artists,[26] *Romani Rai's* (non-Gypsies who were accepted as friends by Gypsies)[27] or authors of travel literature.
The original Maria pilgrimage is based on the Catholic tradition according to which Marie-Jacobé and Marie-Salomé Christianized the Provence. A legend from the 11th century describes Sara as the servant of Martha of Bethany. Together with the Marias, she fled Palestine by ship around 50 AD during one of the first persecutions of Christians and landed in Saintes-Maries-de-la-Mer. The local Maria pilgrimage only became a Gypsy pilgrimage at the end of the 19th century, when visitors from Paris discovered 'Gypsies' among the harvest helpers attending. Gypsies aroused interest as exotic figures in magazines, on postcards and in paintings.[28] At the same time, rural traditions and folklore were promoted by intellectuals and patrons in the context of the emerging nation state. In 1895, the local historian Marquis Folco de Baroncelli-Javon (1869–1943) settled in the Camargue as a bull breeder.[29] He attended the regional folklore festivals and began to organize performances. The blossoming of local folklore fostered the emerging tourism.[30]
The charm of the 'Gypsy camp' has attracted artists and non-conformists since the 1920s. In 1935, Baroncelli proposed adding a procession for the officially non-canonized Sara to the May festivities to the Catholic Bishop. The new ritual known as the *Procession des Gitans* created an attractive event for tourists. Folco de Baroncelli himself accompanied the first procession with his mounted *Gardians*. From 1942 to 1946, 6,500 Gypsies were detained in 30 camps in occupied France, five of them in the *zone libre*. The labour camp of Saliers in the Camargue was designed in 1942 as a model 'Gypsy village'. Due to poor organization and neglect, the 300 inmates suffered from hunger and diseases.[31] Following an Allied bomb raid in 1944, the camp was dissolved. After 1945, French Travellers continued to work in the traditional economic

26 Cuno Fischer: *Schicksal der Zigeuner: Vorurteil und Wirklichkeit, dargestellt am Beispiel der ‚Gitans'*. Nürnberg: Glock & Lutz 1968.

27 Walter Starkie: *Auf Zigeunerspuren: Von Magie und Musik, Spiel und Kult der Zigeuner in Geschichte und Gegenwart*. Munich: Hanser 1957; Maurice Colinon: *Les Saintes Maries de la Mer ou les pèlerins du clair de lune*. Paris: S.O.S. 1975; Pierre Derlon: *Unter Hexen und Zauberern. Die geheimen Traditionen der Zigeuner*. Basel: Sphinx 1976.

28 Anton Holzer: Faszination und Abscheu. Die fotografische Erfindung der ‚Zigeuner'. In: *Fotogeschichte* 110 (2008), pp. 45–56.

29 Robert Zaretsky: *Cock & Bull Stories, Folco Baroncelli and the Invention of the Camargue*. Lincoln: University of Nebraska Press 2004.

30 Bordigoni: Le 'pèlerinage des Gitans'.

31 Emmanuel Filhol / Marie-Christine Hubert (eds): *Les Tsiganes en France: un sort à part (1939–1946)*. Paris: Perrin 2009.

niches: as craftsmen, in the carnie business or as stall owners at markets and antiques dealers. They also resumed the pilgrimage to Saintes.
During the 1950s and 1960s, the *Fête des Gitans* was mainly regional and attracted a few artists, photographers and writers. Their works made the pilgrimage better known. In the 1960s, the wild Camargue and the Gypsy pilgrimage became a destination for hippies and bohemians. With the development of mass tourism and mobility, the public came to Saintes-Maries-de-la-Mer in greater numbers in the 1970s. Since the 1980s, signs of festivalization became manifest. Safety concerns increased with the growing number of tourists and coincided with the gentrification of the village. The Camargue was branded 'Gypsy', while the Gypsies were driven from the village: the authorities set up large parking lots on the outskirts and assigned the *Gitans* to camping spaces there. The 'Gypsy market' was moved from the streets to the central square next to the town hall. The former entanglement of the village and camp gave way to a spatial separation. The village became a stage where the *Gitans* go to perform their Gypsyness. The role of VIPs in Saintes is interesting: Manitas de Plata and the Gipsy Kings became internationally known in the 1960s and the 1980s and attend the pilgrimage every year. Pépé LeFleur for many years led the procession. These popular musicians and performers are important role models for young *Gitans*. They are also figureheads of the pilgrimage, which is an important and rare opportunity for the *Gitans* to present their culture in an accepted context. They perform as pilgrims, musicians and Gypsies. To them, the public display of their culture, the folklore show, is an integral part of their culture.[32] The procession merges elements of religious ritual with those of performance, enactment and local folklore. The image created is an important economic factor for both the *Gitans* and the Camarguais. Guardians, Arlésiennes, ministers and the tourist office create it together with the *Gitans*. Restaurants offer *soirées Gitanes* (mostly with non-Gypsy musicians) throughout the season. The Gipsy Kings operate a theme park, *El Patio*. *Roulottes de tsiganes*, wooden Gypsy wagons, are on offer as guest rooms at bed-and-breakfast inns. The tourists are attracted by themed environments in which 'real Gypsies' appear and perform, but would never visit actual *Gitan* neighbourhoods in nearby Perpignan, Montpellier or Barcelona.

32 Monika Heilmann / Birgit Rambalski: Die Folkloreschau ist Kultur! Beobachtungen bei Touristen und Zigeunern. In: Greverus / Schilling (eds): *Zigeuner und Wir*, pp. 101–111, here p. 104.

Borderlands and Festivals as Liminal Spaces

The 'magical' aura of Kraków's old Jewish district has already been mentioned, and no festival of Gypsy music can possibly compete with the 'authenticity' granted by a 'traditional Gypsy pilgrimage' featuring a black Sara being carried to the sea under the glaring sun of the 'wild Camargue'. Edward Bruner has pointed out the importance of the narratives created to invest tourist spaces with meaning.[33] An important element in the narratives surrounding the festivals and the pilgrimage is the promise of an extraordinary experience. The significance of the historical site distinguishes these events from other festivals. By accessing and updating traditional clichés, tourist narratives aim at emotions. In both Kraków and Saintes, they accumulate layers of significance by referring to notions, spaces and events that are each marked by certain characteristics or overtones of *liminality*.[34] Signifiers of liminality are: transcending boundaries, a state of social and cultural flux, on the threshold, "betwixt-and-between", a spontaneous feeling of togetherness (termed *communitas* by Victor Turner)[35], as well as ambiguity. The question is whether these signifiers of liminality indicate real liminality and thus a cultural process, or whether they remain superficial, encapsulated in the event, thus fixating rather than changing cultures.

The most successful Jewish and Gypsy spaces are situated in the Mediterranean and in Central Europe. Both are liminal zones where Europe meets its exotic Other.[36] Such spaces have been conceptualized as borderlands,[37] contact zones[38] and tourist border zones.[39] Mary Louise Pratt defined contact

33 Edward M. Bruner: *Culture on Tour. Ethnographies of Travel.* Chicago / London: University of Chicago Press 2004, p. 22.

34 Victor Turner developed the concept of liminality from the late 1960s to his death in 1983. His first studies on liminality drew strongly on Arnold van Gennep's three phases of the rites of passage. See the chapters "Betwixt and Between: The Liminal Period in *Rites de Passage*" in Victor Turner: *The Forest of Symbols: Aspects of Ndembu Ritual.* Ithaca: Cornell UP 1967, pp. 93–11.

35 On "Liminality and Communitas" see Victor Turner: *The Ritual Process. Structure and Anti-Structure.* London: Routledge 1969, pp. 94–130, and "Passages, Margins, and Poverty: Religious Symbols of Communitas" in Victor Turner: *Dramas, Fields, and Metaphors.* Ithaca: Cornell UP 1974, pp. 231–271.

36 Julie Scott: Imagining the Mediterranean. In: *Journal of Mediterranean Studies* 15,2 (2005), pp. 219–243, here p. 226; Jacques LeRider: Mitteleuropa as a Lieu de Mémoire. In: Astrid Erll / Ansgar Nünning (eds): *Media and Cultural Memory / Medien und kulturelle Erinnerung.* Berlin / New York: de Gruyter 2008, pp. 37–46.

37 Rosaldo: *Culture and Truth,* pp. 207–208.

38 Marie Louise Pratt: Arts of the Contact Zone. In: *Profession* (1991), pp. 33–40.

39 Bruner: *Culture on Tour.*

zones as "social spaces, where cultures meet, clash and grapple with each other, often in contexts of highly asymmetrical relations of power, such as colonialism, slavery, or their aftermaths as they are lived out in many parts of the world today."[40] In Renato Rosaldo's opinion, borderlands "should be regarded not as analytically empty transitional zones but as sites of creative cultural production".[41]

Central Europe has been described as a nostalgically glorified place of yearning.[42] Jews have been constructed as Central Europeans, as symbols of the civilized multiculturalism of Central European urban topography. Gypsies are viewed as extremely poor illiterate nomads with no European heritage. In the 1990s, Roma had to fight for citizenship in the post-socialist countries. Jews could choose between several citizenships. Belly dancers are a fixture at Gypsy culture festivals, and although Roma have been living in Europe since the Middle Ages, they are constructed as immigrants: "in the EU discourse, as well as in the academic literature, hinting to the origin of 'Gypsies' in India has regularly been the starting point of narration on this group".[43] The mental map of Europe appears as a hologram: from the Jewish viewpoint, the Bucovina or the Carpathian mountains are situated in Central Europe. Looking from the Gypsy/Roma viewpoint, the same areas jump to the east and thus to the margins of Europe.

The Camargue is situated at the southern edge of Europe, in the exotic and separatist Mediterranean borderlands. Tourism is a field for the "production of the Mediterranean",[44] and Baroncelli surely knew how to tell his story. Out of an insect-plagued swamp, he created a mythical scenery of untouched nature harbouring wild horses and free people. In the accounts of visitors, the Gypsy camps on the parking grounds are vividly described as picturesque places of reckless freedom where monkeys clamber up caravans. Barbeques conjure up impressions of Gypsy camp fires. Stories of knifings evoke the hot-blooded Gypsy defending his honour. Descriptions of fortune-tellers, of bright-eyed children in rags and of beautiful young girls in colourful dresses

40 Marie Louise Pratt: *Imperial Eyes. Travel, Writing and Transculturation.* London: Routledge 1992, p. 7.

41 Rosaldo: *Culture and Truth*, p. 208.

42 LeRider: Mitteleuropa as a Lieu de Mémoire, p. 42.

43 Kathrin Simhandl: Beyond Boundaries? Comparing the Construction of the Political Categories 'Gypsies' and 'Roma' Before and After EU Enlargement. In: Nando Sigona / Nidhi Trehan (eds): *Romani Politics in Contemporary Europe. Poverty, Ethnic Mobilization, and the Neoliberal Order.* London / New York: Palgrave Macmillan 2009, pp. 72–93, here p. 79.

44 Scott: Imagining the Mediterranean, p. 224.

fuel magical, exotic and erotic fantasies. Clichés are organized around the oppositions of speaking and being silent, dancing and fighting, rags and eccentric outfits, illiteracy and magic powers, good and bad magic. These dichotomies determine the oscillating status of Gypsies as marginal men, dwellers of the borderlands.[45]

The tourist border zones Ed Bruner investigated as spaces of cultural production[46] are populated by largely homogeneous tour groups, (postcolonial) local organizers and small groups of indigenous locals performing their 'traditional culture' shows conceived especially for tourists. In both Saintes and Kraków, one can try to distinguish between locals, visitors and 'visited' minorities (Jews or Gypsies), but none of the groups is homogeneous, and the boundaries are blurred. Yet the term 'tourist border zones' applies well, since locals and visitors mingle with exotic minorities in a controlled environment. Both festivals are associated with rituals and have strong religious connotations that grant them a transcendent and thus liminal character. In terms of festival typology, the two events are of the carnival-like and participative type, marked by spontaneous elements such as street music.[47] Different folklores meet; dressing up is a common feature. The festive mood is enhanced by music and dancing. In addition, Kazimierz and Saintes powerfully evoke 'lost' or otherwise inaccessible social spaces: they promise access to the shtetl and the Gypsy camp, thus transgressing boundaries.

It seems that the capacity of Kraków and the Camargue as *lieux de mémoire*[48] is also of importance. In *lieux de mémoire*, which are defined by their alleged importance for a (imagined) community, layers of different meanings are superimposed, obliterating boundaries of time and space as well as social boundaries.

The events take place in picturesque historical urban settings. Postmodern urban spaces have been recognized as performative spaces where cultures are in flux.[49] Increasing mobility and the lucrative touristic branch of city

45 On the concepts of marginal and frontier men, see Robert E. Park: Human Migration and the Marginal Man. In: *American Journal of Sociology* 33,6 (1928), pp. 881–893; Anne Norton: *Reflections on Political Identity*. Baltimore: Johns Hopkins UP 1988, pp. 53–58. The concepts are discussed in Rüthers: *Juden und Zigeuner*, pp. 49–52.

46 Bruner: *Culture on Tour*, p. 193.

47 Owe Ronström: Concerts and Festivals: Public Performances of Folk Music in Sweden. In: *The World of Music* 43,2/3 (2001), pp. 49–65, here pp. 57–58.

48 Pierre Nora (ed.): *Les lieux de mémoire*, 3 vols. Paris: Gallimard 1984–1992.

49 Regina Bittner: Die Stadt als Event. In: Ead. (ed.): *Die Stadt als Event. Zur Konstruktion urbaner Erlebnisräume*. Frankfurt am Main / New York: Campus 2001, pp. 14–23; Regina Bormann: Urbane Erlebnisräume als Zonen des Liminoiden. In: Ibid., pp. 99–108.

travelling have turned urban spaces into 'experimental spaces'. Festivals and other events attract the public. Festivals are known to create liminal spaces. On the one hand, they transform urban spaces into the likenesses of longed-for places and "parcels of simulated happiness".[50] On the other hand, people can re-conceive imagined communities in such open spaces – there is a large range of genres for such metasocial performances.[51] As collective creations, festivals, like other urban experiential spaces serve to create community and thus 'identities'. They achieve this by addressing the public on an emotional level. Liminal spaces are part of a concept that depicts the dynamics of social life. This develops in a continual process of negotiating cultural meanings and social contexts.[52]

In short, the promoters heighten the promise of a transformative experience by building up layers of liminality: the festivals take place in European borderlands and on historically meaningful sites, lending them a 'magical' aura. Jews and Gypsies are exoticized as marginal people out of time, pre-modern and archaic. They are nomads and as such at home nowhere yet everywhere. In addition to the festive mood of the events, the music and spiritual elements, the narratives create a promise of hyper-liminality. An account published in 1965 reads:

> In the moonlight you hear the sound of guitars and violins. From several directions unfamiliar rhythms mix. Hands clap, heels pound. Hips, hands and feet of the dancers merely hint at hardly perceptible movements. Like golden blind worms, arms wind in the light of the glowing charcoals. The rhythms become faster. Eyes shine from the dark. The fever mounts. At dawn the dancing ends in wild ecstasy.[53]

The actual experiences do not always live up to the expectations. Complaints about the loss of authenticity and the increasing numbers of ignorant tourists have been part of the narratives since the 1920s.[54] Others must see their wishes fulfilled since many visitors come regularly. The promise of liminality however only extends to individual experience. It does not include social change. Thus, 'Gypsyness' becomes a vehicle for self-awareness.[55]

50 Bittner: Die Stadt als Event, pp. 15, 17.

51 Victor Turner: *From Ritual to Theatre. The Human Seriousness of Play*. New York: Performing Arts 1982.

52 Bormann: Urbane Erlebnisräume, p. 102.

53 Marie Raymonde Delorme: *La Camargue. Mariage de la mer, de la terre et du ciel.* Verviers: Gérard 1965, p. 166.

54 Vaudoyer: *Les Stes Maries de la Mer*, p. 47.

55 Szeman comes to similar conclusions for the Gypsy music business and points to the fact that imitation and appropriation turn the Gypsy into a mere "vehicle for entering the exotic *Balkans*" (Szeman: 'Gypsy Music' and Deejays, p. 100).

Social inversion is a common feature of carnival-like and participative festivals.[56] Public festivities grant minorities the opportunity to congregate in great numbers, but also to present themselves to the public. Young Jewish Poles come to the festival because the usual relationship between minority and majority is inverted: in festival-time Kazimierz, Jewish Poles are proud to wear a kippa and to belong to a transnational community. The Gypsy pilgrimage to Saintes also creates a space of inversion:

> In either case, at church as well as on the street corner, the gypsy king, finally, rightfully, takes the place of the gypsy pariah. For an hour or for an evening, for two days of truce and recovered friendship, the grievances of the unloved are heard. And once more, at this magic moment, the miracle of Saintes-Maries-de-la-Mer unfolds.[57]

However, this possibility is limited in time and space. Spaces of inversion represent an exceptional state that confirms rather than challenges the prevailing social order. So it seems that the very existence of Jewish and Gypsy spaces is proof of the marginal or precarious status of these minorities. Festivals, pilgrimages and markets only offer the opportunity to negotiate this status. Outside the festival spaces, multiple choices of secular, symbolic or cultural Judaism became available for Central European Jews. Roma and other Gypsies however are only accepted into the larger society as performers, artists and musicians. Jews are other Europeans, whereas Gypsies are non-European Others.

Conclusion

The festivals in Kraków and Saintes-Maries-de-la-Mer attract a large public because they are carefully honed into tourist spaces. Both focus on diasporic minorities that are seen as being able to perceive themselves as transnational groups. This turns them into a projection screen for the hyper-mobile postmodern elites who like to think of themselves as 'global nomads'. So, on the one hand, Jews and Gypsies are viewed as hyper-modern, while on the other they appear to 'Europeans' as the inner Orientals, as pre-modern and archaic, as 'nests of tradition', bound to religion and occultism. In both cases, they are 'marginal men'.

In the themed spaces, Jews and Gypsies evoke clichés: music and dancing, caravans, campfires and fortune-telling. Jews are pictured in traditional garb and as shtetl dwellers. The Jewish space of Kazimierz sports themed cafés and Klezmer concerts; Jewish heritage is appropriated as part of Polish history.

56 Aubert: *The Music of the Other*, p. 27.

57 Colinon: *Les Saintes Maries de la Mer*, p. 35 (transl. MR).

The Camargue is branded as 'Gypsy'. In tourist and festival spaces, the Other is exoticized and invested with certain meanings and properties.

Jews and Gypsies are represented in a space out of time and remote from everyday routine. Local folklore is tuned to tourist economies. The procession of *Sara-la-Kâli* combines the popular perception of the Gypsy, the tradition of the *Gitans* and the *Gardians* on their horses. *Santons* (Provençal cradle figures made of ceramics) can be purchased in the form of horse-drawn Gypsy wagons and their romantically idealized dwellers. In Kraków, wooden figurines of 'traditional Jews' are on sale.[58] The Other is appropriated and transformed into a small object, a souvenir to be sold to tourists for individual consumption. Jews and Gypsies have become kitsch.[59] As spaces of inversion, the festival and the pilgrimage call integration into doubt.

The comparison with Gypsy spaces enables a new, more theoretical approach to Jewish spaces. When perceived as tourist spaces related to tourist economies, the exoticization of Jews appears in a new light. The significance of historical place is obvious when festivals on historical sites are compared to festivals elsewhere. It also becomes evident that claiming authenticity and liminality are common features suggesting that the festivals have more to do with some quest for identity than with a genuine interest in the minorities other than as mystic frontier people. The heavily clichéd Jewish and Gypsy spaces are part of European popular cultures. Images, narratives and fetishes circulate between souvenir stands, films, festivals, magazines, travelogues and other media. But they are part of the Jewish and Gypsy cultures as well.

The comparative approach raises a lot more questions than it is possible to answer without in-depth research. Are the reasons for the simultaneous fascination with Jews and Gypsies part of one major quest (e.g. for a new European identity) or are they driven by separate interests? What are the attitudes of the locals towards the minorities and the public festivities? And what are the functions of the festivals for the Jewish and *Gitan* participants? Actually, it is much easier to answer these questions for the Jewish than for the Gypsy side. Gypsies are not represented in the scholarly community, and there are no written accounts from the *Gitano* point of view. When asked by outsiders, members of the group usually feed back the known narratives to researchers or journalists. The near invisibility of Gypsy spaces parallels the general asymmetry concerning Jews and Gypsies in research as well as in European commemorative cultures.

58 Lehrer: Repopulating Jewish Poland.

59 Susan Stewart: *On Longing. Narratives of the Miniature, the Gigantic, the Souvenir, the Collection.* Durham: Duke UP 1993, pp. 145–151, 167.

In the Cellars and Attics of Memory

Mapping Jewish and Non-Jewish Spaces in Contemporary Poland

Magdalena Waligórska

Given that pre-Second World War Poland was home to the biggest Jewish community in Europe, not only are the material vestiges of Jewish culture ubiquitous there, interwoven into the fabric of both Polish cities and the countryside, but also the category of 'the Jewish space' appears particularly laden with sometimes conflicting meanings. Often derelict, forgotten or adapted for new purposes, historic Jewish districts, synagogues or cemeteries in contemporary Poland might be read both as symbols of centuries-long Jewish presence and testimonies of the Jewish annihilation. While Poland as a geographic space is often regarded by foreign Jews and framed by Holocaust tourism primarily as the site of the Holocaust that is tinged with death, actual spaces of Jewish life and death might or might not be identifiable as Jewish in the minds of Poles who inhabit/encounter them. Their Jewish history is often unknown, repressed or overwritten by new meanings and functions they perform: synagogues put to a new use, such as a former prayer house in Kraków used as a disco, or the synagogue in Poznań converted into a swimming pool, are just two examples of hundreds of other such 'overwritten' Jewish spaces.[1] In many locations, Jewish spaces are defined just by their absence: demolished synagogues and cemeteries razed to the ground, like the

1 Many of them have been photographed by Wojciech Wilczyk, whose pictures and commentaries can be found in *Niewinne oko nie istnieje / There Is No Such Thing as an Innocent Eye*. Warsaw: Museum of the History of Polish Jews 2009; as well as by Chris Schwarz, whose photographs accompany Jonathan Webber: *Rediscovering Traces of Memory: The Jewish Heritage of Polish Galicia*. Bloomington: Indiana UP 2009.

one in Szczecin, might be commemorated in the urban space with plaques or symbolic monuments, but are gaps and scars rather than spaces that are meaningful for social interactions.

On the other hand, in the past two decades many of the historic Jewish sites in Poland, particularly in the urban centres, have undergone revitalisation. The renovated Cracovian Tempel and Kupa Synagogues, or the White Stork Synagogue in Wrocław, are perhaps the most spectacular examples. But apart from restoring the former function and appearance of Jewish sites, and 'over-writing' the history of their non-Jewish use (and sometimes abuse) with a layer of Jewish significance again, the recent years have also seen the emergence of entirely new Jewish spaces and attempts at reconstructing the destroyed historic sites, at least virtually.

Thus, next to new Jewish cultural institutions, museums (the most notable of them being the Museum of the History of Polish Jews in Warsaw), Jewish festivals or community centres opening in Poland, we have also seen attempts at 'retrieving' landmarks of Polish-Jewish architecture using digital and experimental media to offer contemporaries a glimpse into the already non-existing Jewish spaces. Notable examples of such projects are the 3D model of the Jewish district in Lublin launched by the Teatr NN/Brama Grodzka association, or the virtual model of the Great Synagogue of Warsaw destroyed by the Nazis in 1943, which is currently being created by the Museum of the History of Polish Jews in Warsaw.[2] The "Gwoździec Re!construction" project (2011–2012) pursued a similar goal, taking the idea of reconstruction a step further. Using the materials, tools and building techniques of the period, professional craftsmen and volunteers made a replica of the 18th century Gwoździec synagogue roof, including the rich polychromies in its interior. The structure is part of the core exhibition of the Museum of the History of Polish Jews in Warsaw, which opened in October 2014.[3]

With the wealth of these new initiatives devoted to commemorating, revitalising or creating new Jewish spaces in Poland the question of renegotiating the topographies of 'Jewish' and 'non-Jewish' spaces becomes particularly salient. Given that both Jewish and non-Jewish spaces as a category can only be defined vis-à-vis or in opposition to something denoted as 'non-Jewish' or

2 A virtual model of the Jewish district in Lublin is available online at http://teatrnn.pl/przewodniki/makieta/xxw_old (accessed 01.09.2013).

3 For more information about the Gwoździec project of the Museum of the History of Polish Jews, see http://www.jewishmuseum.org.pl/pl/node/616, and http://gwozdziec.tumblr.com/history (accessed 04.09.2013).

'Jewish', respectively, they imply boundaries, tensions and potentially also conflicts that play out in public spaces. The present essay examines the troubled relation of Jewish spaces and non-Jewish spaces in the urban context, although similar phenomena of "overwriting" and appropriating Jewish spaces have also been taking place in rural areas of Poland.[4] It is, however, Jewish sites in the larger cities such as Warsaw, Kraków, Łódź and Wrocław that, thanks to Jewish heritage tourism and local Jewish culture festivals, have emerged as the most visible and paradigmatic (but also contended) Jewish spaces. This essay addresses the way local actors define the boundaries and negotiate the new functions of formerly Jewish sites in contemporary Poland, looking in particular at the case of the Jewish district of Kraków – Kazimierz as a space where the 'rediscovery' of the Jewish space triggered a wave of counter-narratives that put its more recent non-Jewish history into the limelight.

Before we move on to the particularities of the case at hand it will be useful, however, to review some of the current debates that addressed the role of the Jewish space in the Polish collective memory. Interestingly, much of this exchange was spurred by artists who, inspired by Jewish sites, made a crucial contribution to the discussion on the status of Jewish heritage in Poland and the Polish topography of memory more generally.

Mapping the Jewish Spaces in Poland after 1989

In the past two decades, Jewish spaces in Poland have attracted the attention of numerous scholars as well as photographers, artists, writers and, last but not least, tour operators. While some cherished the pre-WWII Jewish landscape in Poland as preserved in old photographs, postcards or memoirs, others documented the current revitalization of Jewish material heritage or pictured its neglect.[5] In the past ten years, a plethora of new publications

4 One of the most well-known and probably best-researched cases is the little town of Jedwabne, site of the infamous pogrom of 1941 orchestrated by local Poles. Anna Bikont, in the "Postscriptum" to her seminal study *My z Jedwabnego*. Wołowiec: Czarne 2012, pp. 545–549, addresses the "overwriting" of Jewish space and the memory of the pogrom in the public space.

5 Monika Krajewska: *Czas kamieni*. Warsaw: Interpress 1982, was the first photo album dedicated to Jewish spaces – in this case cemeteries – in post-war Poland and one of the first publications on Jewish heritage in post-Holocaust Poland. In the last decades, both the reprints of old photographs and new albums dedicated to Jewish sites have proliferated. Among the notable publications which used archival images of Jewish spaces in Poland are: *A World before a Catastrophe*. Kraków: International Cultural Centre 2007; Eugeniusz Duda / Marek Sosenko (eds): *Old Jewish Postcards*. Kraków: Muzeum Historyczne Miasta Krakowa 1997; Ulrike Grossarth (ed.): *Stefan Kiełsznia. Ulica Nowa 3: Zdjęcia lubelskiej dzielnicy żydowskiej z lat 30*. Leipzig:

dedicated to Jewish spaces emerged, from travel diaries and Jewish legends to Jewish-themed guidebooks (e.g. for the Jewish Kraków, Łódź or Kielce) to crime novels set in the pre-war Jewish milieu.[6] This heightened interest in Jewish spaces both in academic and popular writings is correlated with the broader phenomenon of the discovery of Jewish heritage in Poland and the memory debates that have been occupying Poles for the last two decades.[7]

Spector 2011. A unique ethnography of a Polish Jewish space is also the illustrated memoir of Mayer Kirshenblatt by Mayer Kirshenblatt / Barbara Kirshenblatt-Gimblett: *They Called Me Mayer July: Painted Memories of a Jewish Childhood in Poland Before the Holocaust.* Berkeley: University of California Press 2007. Interestingly, some pre-WWII documentations of Jewish spaces, such as Majer Balaban's history of Jewish Lublin with drawings by Karlrich Henker from 1919, have been reprinted in their original layout; see *Die Judenstadt von Lublin.* Lublin: Brama Grodzka / Teatr NN 2012. Memoirs, or even anthologies of texts about Jewish spaces, are yet another genre; see Władysław Bartoszewski / Marek Edelman: *I była dzielnica żydowska w Warszawie.* Warszawa: PWN 2010. A powerful document of the neglect of Jewish spaces in Poland is Artur Żmijewski's photo-project Cmentarz wojenny wieś Skłoby – Cmentarz żydowski Szydłowiec. In: Joanna Tokarska-Bakir (ed.): *PL: Tożsamość wyobrażona.* Warszawa: Czarna Owca 2013, pp. 280–340. Recently we have also seen a number of scholarly analyses of the history, neglect and regeneration of Jewish spaces in Poland and Eastern Europe more generally; for example, Monika A. Murzyn: *Kazimierz: The Central European Experience of Urban Regeneration.* Kraków: International Cultural Centre 2006; Jurgita Siauciunaite-Verbickiene / Larisa Lempertiene (eds): *Jewish Space in Central and Eastern Europe: Day-to-Day History.* Newcastle: Cambridge Scholars 2007; Monika Murzyn-Kupisz / Jacek Purchla (eds): *Reclaiming Memory. Urban Regeneration in the Historic Jewish Quarters of Central European Cities.* Kraków: International Cultural Centre 2009.

6 For urban legends of Jewish spaces, see Henryk Halkowski: *Żydowski Kraków: Legendy i ludzie.* Kraków: Austeria 2009; Jaroslaw Knap: *Magiczny Kazimierz.* Kraków: Krakowska Grupa Multimedialna 2005; for guidebooks on Jewish spaces in Poland, see, among others, Agnieszka Sabor: *Sztetl: Śladami żydowskich miasteczek.* Kraków: Austeria 2005; Eugeniusz Duda: *Żydowski Kraków: Przewodnik po zabytkach i miejscach pamięci.* Kraków: vis-a-vis 2010; Marek Maciągowski: *Przewodnik po żydowskich Kielcach.* Kraków: Austeria 2008; Joanna Podolska: *Łódź żydowska: spacerownik.* Łódź: Agora 2009; for Jewish-themed urban crime novels, see Paweł Jaszczuk: *Foresta Umbra.* Poznań: Rebis 2004; Konrad Lewandowski: *Perkalowy dybuk.* Wrocław: Wydawnictwo Dolnośląskie 2009; Małgorzata Kuźmińska / Michał Kuźmiński: *Sekret Kroke.* Warszawa: Świat Książki 2009; Zygmunt Miłoszewski: *Ziarno prawdy.* Warszawa: WAB 2011. See also Magdalena Waligórska: The Jewish-Style Whodunit in Contemporary Poland and Germany. In: *East European Jewish Affairs* 3,2 (2013), pp. 143–161.

7 It is impossible to list the massive amount of publications that have addressed the questions of Polish-Jewish history and memory in the past twenty years. Much of the debate, however, was triggered by Jan T. Gross's *Neighbors.* Princeton: Princeton UP 2001, which brought the events of the pogrom in Jedwabne in 1941 to popular attention, and *Fear.* Princeton: Princeton UP 2006, which focused on the pogrom in Kielce in 1946. The debate initiated by these publications concerned to a large extent the question of Polish complicity in anti-Jewish violence and was followed by many other path-breaking publications, such as Barbara Engelking: *Szanowny Panie Gistapo: Donosy do władz niemieckich w Warszawie i okolicach w latach 1940–1941.* Warszawa: Stowarzyszenie Centrum Badań nad Zagładą Żydów 2003; Barbara Engelking: *Jest*

Jewish spaces thus became the subject of debate but also its venue. A number of Polish artists have used historic Jewish spaces to offer alternative means to commemorate Jews and critically comment on Polish-Jewish relations. One of the best-known such interventions, and perhaps the most successfully incorporated into the urban landscape, was Joanna Rajkowska's project *Pozdrowienia z Alej Jerozolimskich* (*Greetings from Jerusalem Avenue*) in Warsaw. In 2002, the artist placed a 15-meter-high artificial palm tree at the roundabout of Warsaw's Aleje Jerozolimskie to remind Varsovians, with this playful allusion to Jerusalem, of Warsaw's once-vibrant Jewish life. Art projects referencing Jewish spaces have often been controversial. Wilhelm Sasnal, a prominent contemporary Polish painter, who in 2001 pictured a scene from Art Spiegelman's celebrated comic book *Maus* on a wall in Bielsko-Biała (where one of the events pictured by Spiegelman actually took place), raised controversies because he posed questions about the Polish complicity in reporting hidden Jews to Nazi authorities. To be sure, in the past twenty years, Jewish spaces in Poland have not only become objects of nostalgia and commodification, but also important topoi in art, literature and commemoration culture.[8]

But against this background of the new fascination with Jewish spaces per se, many artists and scholars have also addressed the sometimes conflicting topographies of Jewish and non-Jewish spaces. American historian Michael Meng, in his *Shattered Spaces*, looked at how Jewish sites after the Second World War fell prey to changing paradigms of memory and political instrumentalization. Erased and forgotten in the aftermath of the Holocaust to be slowly rediscovered in the 1970s, the restored Jewish spaces have finally come to be used as a visible proof of what Meng terms "redemptive cosmopolitanism" – "a performative embrace of the Jewish past that celebrates the liberal, democratic nation-state rather than thinking critically about its past and present failures."[9] If Jewish spaces in post-1945 Poland have been overwritten with non-Jewish use, their recent restoration also has implications for the 'non-Jewish space' in that it serves for the construction of a new self-understanding of a nation that wishes to see itself as multicultural and tolerant.

taki piękny słoneczny dzień: Losy Żydów szukających ratunku na wsi polskiej 1942–1945. Warszawa: Stowarzyszenie Centrum Badań nad Zagładą Żydów 2011; Jan Grabowski: *Judenjagd: polowanie na Żydów 1942–1945.* Warszawa: Stowarzyszenie Centrum Badań nad Zagładą Żydów 2011; and many others.

8 See also Erica Lehrer / Magdalena Waligórska: Cur(at)ing History. New Genre Art Interventions and the Polish-Jewish Past. In: *East European Politics and Societies* 27,3 (2013), pp. 510–544.

9 Michael Meng: *Shattered Spaces. Encountering Jewish Ruins in Postwar Germany and Poland.* Cambridge: Harvard UP 2011, p. 250.

If the voices of historians have been crucial in this recent debate on Jewish and non-Jewish topographies, so have been the voices of photographers. Notable in this respect are the works of Chris Schwarz with his *Rediscovering Traces of Memory* (2009), Wojciech Wilczyk's *There Is No Such Thing as an Innocent Eye* (2009), Elżbieta Janicka's *Festung Warschau* (2011) and Łukasz Baksik's *Matzevot for Everyday Use* (2013). These four remarkable albums not only provide a poignant commentary on the use and abuse of Jewish spaces in present-day Poland, but also significantly contribute to the scholarly debate about the Polish landscape of memory and the politics of commemoration.

British photographer Chris Schwarz, founder of the Galicia Jewish Museum in Kraków, collected his photographs of Jewish sites while travelling extensively through the region of Galicia in southern Poland. Picturing not only derelict synagogues, cemeteries, and sites of Nazi atrocities, but also the ways local people engaged with and commemorated the Jewish past, Schwarz's photographs, accompanied by captions by the British social anthropologist Jonathan Webber, convey a sense of absence and also address the question of how Poles *respond* to abandoned Jewish spaces. Picturing antisemitic graffiti, the desecration of Jewish tombstones or profane uses of synagogue buildings, Schwarz's photographs document the status of the abandoned Jewish heritage in Poland as a thorn in the eye to those who, like the vandals that scratched the word "Poland" across the fresco of a Star of David in the synagogue of Dąbrowa Tarnowska, would like to see Jewish spaces effaced by the hegemonic Polishness.[10] But at the same time, Schwarz also shows places where the boundary between the Jewish space and non-Jewish space becomes more blurred, such as the Christian tombstone with the sign of a menorah in the town of Tuchów, erected by a Holocaust survivor for the woman who had rescued her life.[11]

Wojciech Wilczyk and Łukasz Baksik engage with Jewish spaces which have been overgrown with new significance in the Polish landscape. Over 300 photographs of Polish synagogues gathered in Wilczyk's album take us on a tour of the Polish countryside, where sacral Jewish spaces today house a pub, a funeral services company, a metal scrap yard and a cinema.[12] Baksik's photographs of Jewish tombstones recycled by local Poles as building material are even more disturbing. Jewish material culture is here stripped of its original

10 Jonathan Webber / Chris Schwarz: *Rediscovering Traces of Memory. The Jewish Heritage of Polish Galicia.* Bloomington: Indiana UP 2009, p. 33.

11 Ibid., p. 112.

12 Wilczyk: *Niewinne oko nie istnieje / There Is No Such Thing as an Innocent Eye.*

meaning and function, literally overwritten and degraded to the role of raw material which is up for grabs. The space of a Jewish cemetery is assimilated here into the space of a non-Jewish household. A more radical metamorphosis is hardly imaginable.[13]

The single biggest site of such overwriting is, however, the Jewish ghetto of Warsaw. In the passionate and truly eye-opening photo-essay by Elżbieta Janicka, we encounter not only the new city built upon the ruins of the old, but also a large-scale attempt at overlaying the spaces of Jewish suffering and resistance with a plethora of commemorative sites dedicated to the Polish war losses. Author and literary scholar Bożena Keff, in her introduction to Janicka's walking-tour companion to Warsaw, speaks of the "re-writing of history" which "expunges the heterogeneous and the alien, that is Jewish, elements" from the cityscape.[14] Janicka pictures how Polish non-Jewish memory invades the most symbolic of Jewish spaces – the area of the Warsaw Ghetto – filling the urban space with plaques, monuments, memorial stones and shrines devoted to the non-Jewish heroes of the Warsaw Uprising of 1944, but also spatially unrelated events, such as the Battle of Monte Cassino (1944), or the assassination of Catholic priest, Jerzy Popiełuszko, by the Communist secret police in 1984. Janicka pictures the historic Jewish space as colonized by the current Polish politics of memory and made almost invisible under the layers of rival commemoration projects.

The tense coexistence of the Jewish past and the non-Jewish present in Muranów, a district built on the rubble of the ghetto, is also the subject of Beata Chomątowska's *Stacja Muranów*. In this ethnography of rebuilding and forgetting, Chomątowska addresses the question of how Poles developed new emotional links to Muranów after 1945 and how the quarter's Jewish past haunts them today. Research by social psychologists carried out in Muranów indicates the long-time effects of 'overwriting' Jewish spaces in Poland: legends of Jewish ghosts and hidden Jewish treasures circulate among the inhabitants of the former ghetto, some of whom feel they infringe on the space of Jewish death.[15] Trauma lingers in such overwritten Jewish/non-Jewish spaces.

13 Łukasz Baksik: *Macewy codziennego użytku / Matzevot for Everyday Use*. Wołowiec: Czarne 2013.

14 Bożena Keff: Trup, Horror, Obczyzna. In: Elżbieta Janicka: *Festung Warschau*. Warszawa: Wydawnictwo Krytyki Politycznej 2011, pp. 10–11.

15 Beata Chomątowska: *Stacja Muranów*. Wołowiec: Czarne 2012, pp. 332–348.

A Tale of Two Cities

Kraków's Jewish district of Kazimierz could arguably serve as a counterpoint to many other overwritten Jewish spaces in Poland. As one of the best-preserved Jewish quarters in the country, it has witnessed a growing influx of tourists and undergone an intensive revitalization over the past two decades. Enjoying the status of a UNESCO World Heritage site and popularized by the annual Jewish festival, Kazimierz features in the public perception as a Jewish space par excellence. Yet, at the same time, the recent Jewish heritage boom that took place there has also inspired counter-narratives which focused on Kazimierz's post-1945 *non-Jewish* history.

Kazimierz has been a space of Jewish settlement since the Middle Ages. Home to outstanding Jewish scholars and containing some of the most important monuments of Jewish sacral architecture in Poland, Kazimierz played the role of the centre of Jewish life in Kraków until 1941, when the Jewish population was forced into a ghetto in the neighbouring district of Podgórze.[16] After the Holocaust, Kazimierz never regained the character of a bustling Jewish district again, although it still hosted a significant Jewish community shortly after the Second World War. In the aftermath of the Holocaust, however, as most of the surviving Jews had emigrated when prompted by post-war pogroms and, finally, the antisemitic purges of 1968, Kazimierz fell into disrepair and became a socially deprived area. The Jewish material heritage of the district, though still visible, did not have much significance for its new inhabitants. This was to change only in the 1990s, after the systemic change brought new opportunities to the tourist market and Steven Spielberg immortalized Kazimierz in his *Schindler's List* (1993).

The rebirth of Kazimierz after 1989 has been the focus of many scholarly analyses.[17] One of the questions that have occupied the observers of the

16 For the history of the Jewish Kazimierz, see Majer Bałaban: *Historja Żydów w Krakowie i na Kazimierzu 1304–1868* [1931]. Kraków: Krajowa Agencja Wydawnicza 1991; Michal Galas / Antony Polonsky (eds): *POLIN: Studies in Polish Jewry*, vol. 23: Jews in Kraków. Oxford: Littman Library of Jewish Civilization 2010; Katarzyna Zimmerer: *Zamordowany świat: Losy Żydów w Krakowie 1939–1945*. Kraków: Wydawnictwo Literackie 2004; International Cultural Centre (ed.): *A World Before a Catastrophe: Kraków's Jews Between the Wars*. Kraków: International Cultural Centre 2007; Barbara Zbroja: *Miasto umarłych. Architektura publiczna Żydowskiej Gminy Wyznaniowej w Krakowie w latach 1868–1939*. Kraków: WAM 2005; Henryk Halkowski: *Żydowski Kraków. Legendy i ludzie*. Kraków: Austeria 2009.

17 On the revitalization of Kazimierz after 1989 see especially Murzyn: *Kazimierz. The Central European Experience of Urban Regeneration*. On the broader phenomenon of Jewish heritage revival in Central Europe, see Ruth E. Gruber: *Virtually Jewish. Reinventing Jewish Culture in Europe*. Berkeley: University of California Press 2002; Erica Lehrer: *Jewish Poland Revisited. Heritage*

Jewish heritage revival in Kazimierz was the one of the consequences of the rediscovery of Jewish heritage for the actual urban spaces and their inhabitants. With the rise of Jewish heritage tourism and an unprecedented surge of interest in Jewish culture, the district's transformation came to be considered as paradigmatic for the new role that Jewish heritage came to play in Central Europe.[18] Monika Murzyn, who examined the economic development of the Jewish district in the 1990s and the early 2000s, noted that in 1994–2004, while Kazimierz was becoming a trendy destination for tourists and a hot spot of Kraków's nightlife, the number of restaurants, bars and cafes more than tripled.[19] The gentrification that followed to a certain extent fed on the picturesque and film-set-like poverty of the quarter, but led to the exclusion and increasing alienation of the local inhabitants, who were being gradually pushed out of their tenement houses that were now converted into hotels and restaurants.[20]

The radical change in the functions of the district triggered a reaction from the local inhabitants. In 2002, they wrote a letter to the district authorities complaining about the "scandalous expansion" of pubs and cafés in Kazimierz. Some of the tenants reacted even more radically, throwing potatoes at the pub customers from their windows.[21] That started a wider debate that also enquired into the role of the Jewish heritage revival in the rampant gentrification of the district. One of the newspaper reports commenting on the developments in Kazimierz opened with the heading *The Invasion of Klezmorim.*[22] The Jewish cultural revival personified by klezmer musicians thus turned into shorthand for the commodification processes in Kazimierz.

The role of Jewish-style restaurants and cafes and the success of the annual summer Jewish Culture Festival for the gentrification of the district soon became a topic for the media. Janusz Makuch, head of the Jewish festival, also

Tourism in Unquiet Places. Bloomington: Indiana UP 2013; Magdalena Waligórska: *Klezmer's Afterlife. An Ethnography of the Jewish Music Revival in Poland and Germany.* Oxford: Oxford UP 2013.

18 Murzyn-Kupisz / Purchla (eds): *Reclaiming Memory.*

19 Monika Murzyn: 'Winners' and 'Losers' in the Game. The Social Dimension of Urban Regeneration in the Kazimierz Quarter in Krakow. In: György Enyedi / Zoltan Kovacs (eds): *Social Change and Social Sustainability in Historical Urban Centers. The Case of Central Europe.* Pécs: Hungarian Academy of Sciences 2006, pp. 81–106.

20 Ibid., p. 90.

21 Renata Radłowska: Kazimierz. Protesty przeciwko rewitalizacji. Woleli plac martwy. In: *Gazeta Wyborcza*, 08.07.2002, p. 3.

22 Wojciech Orliński: Szanuj menela swego. Duży Format. In: *Gazeta Wyborcza*, 30.06.2008, pp. 2–4.

took a position in this debate, expressing his regret that the tourist infrastructure developing in the district threatened the aura of this historic space.

> This place is selling itself like a prostitute! It has turned into the biggest beer-drinking site in Kraków. Unfortunately, I am partially responsible for that, because it all started with the festival. Kazimierz became famous all over the world and people started coming here. Hundreds of pubs opened and the real ambience of this place has been trampled down.[23]

The discussion about Kazimierz became a debate about the legitimate and illegitimate uses of a space loaded with conflicting memories and myths. The symbolic character that the district has for Jews, and the fears of the non-Jewish tenants of being driven out by allegedly Jewish investors, added a new edge to the exchange. After a noisy rock concert organised in Szeroka Street, the central square of the Jewish district, the owner of one of the Jewish-style restaurants and a publishing house specializing in Jewish heritage, Wojciech Ornat, protested in a press interview in 2004 against defiling the memory of Jews. The concert, staged near two synagogues and a cemetery, appeared to him as a profanation of a space that should be dedicated to the preservation of Jewish heritage. In his opinion, opening the Jewish district to all kinds of cultural activities triggered a "Huns' invasion" that endangered the Jewish character of the space.[24]

His plea triggered a fierce reaction from the newspaper's forum. One of the readers accused an undefined Jewish group of monopolising the space of Kazimierz:

> Don't they mind the exhaust fumes, dozens of coaches and the houses being sold and turned into well-prospering hotels for rich Western tourists? A group of people is appropriating the rights to decide about something that is a common cultural good, and there are not even enough of them to say Kaddish when necessary.[25]

The comment, which implicitly identifies Jews as the main agents of gentrification, also reveals the local fears that the tiny Jewish minority in Kraków might assume full control over the quarter, an idea that echoes antisemitic rhetoric about Jewish territorialisation. Restitution of Jewish property, targeted revitalization and the intensification of Jewish heritage tourism in the

23 Janusz Makuch cit. in Renata Radłowska / Elżbieta Niemczura: Kazimierz. Reaktywacja. In: *Gazeta Wyborcza Kraków*, 23.06.2003, p. 1.

24 Wojciech Ornat cit. in Rafał Romanowski / Seweryn Blumsztajn: Jak grać na Szerokiej. Najazd Hunów. Pod rozwagę. In: *Gazeta Wyborcza Kraków*, 24.09.2004, p. 1.

25 "Czunia" cit. in: Co wolno, a czego nie na Szerokiej. In: *Gazeta Wyborcza Kraków*, 25.09.2004, p. 2.

past two decades meant a profound change both to the local economy and memoryscape. And as the forgotten or repressed stories of historic others were suddenly gaining saliency, a new wave of nostalgia about the post-1945 *non-Jewish* Kazimierz became more and more prominent.

In 2003, a local newspaper launched a series of reportages about the present-day inhabitants of Kazimierz and opened an Internet forum for those who felt nostalgic for the olden days in the district. "My Beloved Kazimierz and the Ghosts of the Past" soon beat all records in popularity.[26] In the accounts collected in the forum, Kazimierz of the post-war era was populated with noble drunkards and culturally aware prostitutes who contributed to the dark but inspiring atmosphere of the district. The sense of equality and fraternity in this narrative stands in clear opposition to the disintegration of the local communal bonds and evictions brought about by the recent gentrification. One of the inhabitants interviewed by the local newspaper recounted:

> All Kraków used to call us the people from the margin, saying that we were just drunkards, pimps, thieves and whores. But we would queue for hours to get the tickets for a theatre play! The queue was sometimes 150 meter long… and all of them queued: the drunkards and the down-and-outs, the decent and the honest, and the indecent and the dishonest. When finally seated in the theatre, everybody was equal. They were all people of Kazimierz who came for a bit of culture.[27]

Access to culture, indeed, seems to be an important motif in these accounts and the presence of renowned artists among Kazimierz's post-1945 inhabitants feeds its new myth. In the early 1960s, local authorities offered three houses in the centre of the Jewish district to Cracovian artists. A number of well-known painters, writers, architects and musicians moved into this 'colony', among them the composer Krzysztof Penderecki. His sister, Barbara, recollects the proletarian Kazimierz as a sinister but artist-friendly environment:

> I moved into Szeroka Street in 1962. Frankly speaking, I was afraid to live here. One heard about the district's terrible reputation, about the "lumpenproletariat." In the beginning I was paralyzed with fear, but it turned out that our neighbours were entirely harmless […] They used to say about the people from Kazimierz that they were the most uncultured ones in Kraków, but as soon as they saw us on the other end of the street, they would

26 The forum still exists and, as of 2014, has more than 1,800 entries. http://forum.gazeta.pl/forum/w,61,852367,,Kazimierz_moj_ulubiony_i_te_duchy_przeszlosci.html?s=18&v=2 (accessed 13.03.2014).

27 Renata Radłowska: Kazimierz. Reaktywacja. Dlaczego tu mieszkają, dlaczego odchodzą? Nasze ulice pustych domów. In: *Gazeta Wyborcza Kraków*, 27.06.2003, p. 7.

immediately take their hands out of their pockets as a sign of respect. Possibly they felt honoured by having artists as neighbours.[28]

Stories about the proletarian Kazimierz have inspired guidebooks[29] and street festivals – in particular the Festival of Soup (2002–2010), annually opened in Plac Nowy by the Queen of Kazimierz (in private, the owner of a local liquor store) – but the myth also reverberated in the local music scene. The highly acclaimed musical *Pan Kazimierz* (*Mr. Kazimierz*), based on the post-1945 urban legends from the district, featured songs about local thieves and alcoholics and an accompanying CD included a map of Kazimierz marking the sites mentioned in the songs. One of them, *Cztery piweczka i flaszeczka* (*Four Beers and a Bottle of Booze*) by Michał Zabłocki, pictures the homely atmosphere of Kazimierz's underworld and lists the grievances of local people:

Po małym piwku z samego rana Kaziu ruskiego wzniósł szampana. Aż się truskawki uśmiechnęli Co tu leżeli od niedzieli,	A morning beer and some Russian champagne revives our debate like a breeze of fresh air,
Temat się zdarzył polityczny, Że lepiej było za komuny. Człowiek nie robił i się liczył, A teraz liczą się fortuny [...] Mocno pod wieczór przyjeżdża Stacha W przy-ubrudzonych nieco łachach, Mówi, że flaszki nie przywiozła, Ale przywiozła mięso z kozła. Koźlę już skwierczy, smaku nabiera, Stacha sie zawsze jednak przyda. Ślinka nam leci jak cholera. Dziś pogadamy se o Żydach.[30]	Communism was better, but that changed quick you could be someone and work just a bit now only money can do the trick [...] Stacha arrives late with her clothes not so neat She's got no booze, but a pound of goat's meat cooking our dinner, we chill and schmooze once we fill our stomachs, we'll talk about the Jews.

This slightly picaresque ballad captures two key motifs of the recent nostalgia for post-war Kazimierz. One of them is the disenchantment with the systemic transformation in Poland and a resulting longing for the Communist past. The other is the memory of the previous inhabitants of Kazimierz, the

28 Barbara Penderecka cit. in Renata Radłowska: Kazimierz. Reaktywacja: na takich sąsiadów czekam. In: *Gazeta Wyborcza*, 09.07.2003.

29 For example, Jarosław Knap: *Magiczny Kazimierz*. Kraków: Krakowska Grupa Multimedialna 2005, pp. 15–29.

30 Liner notes to *Pan Kazimierz*. Poemat 2008, p. 16. A free translation into English by the author.

Jews, who are here, rather disconcertingly, brought in conjunction with an overt, be it humorous, critique of capitalism. Even though the contents of the ominous conversation "about the Jews" remain unspecified, the context of the song brings to mind conspiracy theories rather than warm-hearted reminiscing. To be sure, the place of Jews in this new narrative of Kazimierz is an ambiguous one.

Cellars and Attics

In her pioneering study of Kazimierz, Monika Murzyn noted that for many inhabitants the history of the district begins only after the war, and the Jewish past of the neighbourhood is removed from their perception of the place.[31] The narratives of the proletarian Kazimierz demonstrate it well. While the range of non-Jewish reactions to Jewish spaces in Poland is certainly wide, ranging from erasure and overwriting to rediscovery and embrace, the alternative narratives of the proletarian Kazimierz point to one more mode of negotiating non-Jewish spaces vis-à-vis historic Jewish spaces: that of creating narrative exits from history, which Michel de Certeau metaphorically termed "cellars and attics."[32]

The way humans generate the 'identity' of the spaces they inhabit, believed de Certeau, is via stories they tell about them. Given that stories pertaining to one space can be many, these narratives are often internally conflicting and full of oppositions. Their heterogeneous nature, however, allows the creation of cellar-like and attic-like spaces which have their particular function as "storage sites", or points of entrance and exit:

> It is through the opportunity they afford of storing up pregnant silences and inarticulate stories – or rather through their ability to create cellars and attics everywhere – that local legends [...] create exits, ways of leaving and re-entering, and thus habitable spaces.[33]

Legends of spaces, like palimpsests, are fragmented and incompatible with each other but allow us to see different meanings that various groups attach to places. They can also reveal how we create exits from unwanted narratives and how we shape the "invented tradition" of spaces.[34] In the words of Yi-Fu

31 Monika A. Murzyn: *Kazimierz. Środkowoeuropejskie doświadczenie rewitalizacji*. Kraków: Międzynarodowe Centrum Kultury 2006.

32 Michel de Certeau: Practices of Space. In: Marshall Blonsky (ed.): *On Signs*. Baltimore: Johns Hopkins UP 1985, pp. 122–145, here p. 142.

33 Ibid.

34 Eric J. Hobsbawm: *The Invention of Tradition*. Cambridge: Cambridge UP 2008.

Tuan, one of the first scholars who brought the dimension of space to the attention of historians:

> [A] city does not become historic merely because it has occupied the same site for a long time. Past events make no impact on the present unless they are memorialised in history books, monuments, pageants, and solemn and jovial festivities that are recognised to be part of an ongoing tradition.[35]

In other words, if the spatial environment is only "a scaffold to which we attach meanings,"[36] legends of space and their local enactments give the final shape to that which we could call the identity of space.

If places are created in the act of seeing, as was postulated by Tuan, there are as many places as there are actors, perspectives and representations that define them.[37] Taking this principle seriously means that historic Jewish spaces can simultaneously be seen as Jewish or non-Jewish depending on the eye of the beholder. Geographical spaces, especially cities, often exist in the public imagination in many different images. Cities are "porous", in the words of Svetlana Boym, built of "layers of time and history".[38] The porous character of the city endows it, as Karl Schlögel put it, with "a bewildering simultaneity of times".[39] Even different variant names of one place (e.g. Kraków, Krakau, Kroke) evoke different periods or traditions in the history of the place and can conjure rival narratives.

Designating urban spaces as Jewish or non-Jewish in post-Holocaust Europe, however, has a particular weight. Before 1939 every fourth inhabitant of Kraków was Jewish. Today the Jewish community consists of less than 200 members. Many of the Holocaust survivors who returned to Kraków after the war emigrated after a pogrom that took place in Kazimierz in the summer of 1945.[40] The antisemitic purges of 1968 marked the final Jewish exodus, leaving Poland almost entirely deprived of its Jewish minority. Given the dimensions of Jewish presence in pre-war Poland and the circumstances that accompanied the 'disappearance' of Jews from Poland, including

35 Yi-Fu Tuan: *Space and Place. The Perspective of Experience.* London: Edward Arnold 1977, p. 174.

36 Kevin Lynch: *What Time Is This Place?* Cambridge, MA: MIT Press 1993, p. 241.

37 Karl Schlögel: *Im Raume lesen wir die Zeit.* Munich: Hanser 2003; Tuan: *Space and Place*, p. 161.

38 Svetlana Boym: *The Future of Nostalgia.* New York: Basic Books 2001, pp. 76–77.

39 In the original: "Die Stadt ist […] das verwirrende Nebeneinander der Zeiten" (Schlögel: *Im Raume lesen wir die Zeit*, p. 307).

40 Anna Cichopek: *Pogrom Żydów w Krakowie 11 sierpnia 1945 r.* Warszawa: Żydowski Instytut Historyczny 2000.

appropriation and redistribution of Jewish property as well as post-war acts of anti-Jewish violence, narratives of space that create exits from the Jewish past into alternative pasts might also be ways of soothing the collective sense of anxiety about the dark chapters in the history of Polish-Jewish relations. Urban myths celebrating the times of post-1945 non-Jewish presence in formerly Jewish spaces appeal to a certain nostalgia for the Communist era that has found its niche in contemporary Polish popular culture. Their focus on remembering this more recent layer of Polish history, however, obscures other, darker strata that rest beneath. The "inarticulate stories" stored in these narrative cellars and attics may not even concern Jews; they are stories about us, Poles, our amnesia and our role in appropriating and overwriting Jewish spaces – stories we are only slowly beginning to confront.

Between Poetics and Politics

The Eruv and the Wall in Recent Contemporary Artistic Imagination

Diana I. Popescu

> Something there is that doesn't love a wall […]
> Good fences make good neighbours
>
> (Robert Frost: *The Mending Wall*)[1]

The historically prevailing eruv of the Jewish diasporic experience and the historically recent separation wall that divides the West Bank landscape undoubtedly constitute the most radically opposed constructions of Jewish territoriality. These Jewish "fences" are fickle, inconsistent and misleading as they exclude and include simultaneously. The eruv and the wall function on rhetorical registers that show a deeply ambivalent way of relating to space and the other. These unlikely characters of the Jewish collective space have recently been critically examined by contemporary artists.

This article engages with several artworks that shed light upon the contradictory nature of the two spatial markers, and the ways in which they allow and block contact with the other. While American Jewish artist Ben Schachter's delicate thread-on-paper maps of sixteen eruvin (2010) and Sophie Calle's *L'Erouv de Jérusalem* (1996) deal with the poetics of the eruv as a way of reflecting upon the possibilities it offers in understanding Jewish/non-Jewish relationships in the diaspora, art dealing with the presence and politics of the wall such as Ravit Cohen Gat and Moshe Gerstel's installation *Next Year in Jerusalem* (2005) and Eyal Weizman's maps – part of the group project *Borderlinedisorder* (2002) – turn the wall against itself, utilising it as a canvas or

1 Robert Frost: *Complete Poems*. London: Jonathan Cape 1955.

background for acts of protest and, thereby, undermining its presence. The above-mentioned artworks shall serve as a starting point to reflect upon how, by means of art, the eruv's fragile presence is made more visible, whilst the wall's visibility is further obscured and its physicality diminished. This essay argues that the two phenomena carry a Janus face since both the eruv and the wall are steeped in ambivalence. It further raises the question of the societal significance of art in producing a critical awareness that can be integrated within collective consciousness. Art shows its influence over collective thinking in the course of a long temporal framework. This essay does not claim to gauge this impact. It rather suggests that artistic reflections upon spatial practices matter because they ask us to look anew at old practices, and through observation, reach a deeper level of understanding of what they reveal about us, contemporary audiences.

The Poetics of the Eruv

A symbolic Jewish enclosure composed of a fishing line strung between the tops of electric poles and other available constructions in the urban landscape, the eruv enhances the observation of Sabbath without transgressing the prohibition against carrying objects outside of the household. The eruvs' (or eruvin) raison d'être is to extend private space and offer the possibility to practice and affirm belief within a predominantly non-Jewish space. The eruv, thus, transforms space into a private dwelling where activities that one could undertake only within one's home are allowed and encouraged. In this way, the injunction against carrying no longer contravenes with the biblical command that the Sabbath be a "joy".[2] The discourse of the eruv established by Talmudic law for practical reasons, has more recently been discussed within an art historical context. Because of its symbolic vocabulary, the eruv has become associated with conceptual art. Hence, argues Joshua J. Friedman, "a thin string stretching down and across city streets, high above the traffic, jumping from telephone pole to lamp-post to fence, an eruv always has the air of an art installation".[3]

The art hidden within the eruv's fragile materiality is readily observed by art historian Margaret Olin, who defines the eruv as "the architecture's

2 Margaret Olin: Introduction: The Poetics of the Eruv. In: *Images. Journal of Jewish Art and Visual Culture* 5,1 (2011): Vizualizing the Eruv, pp. 3–13, here p. 3.

3 Joshua J. Friedman: String Theory. In: *Tabletmag*, 14.05.2010. http://www.tabletmag.com/jewish-arts-and-culture/33656/string-theory (accessed 12.06.2013).

minimum"[4], since the transformation of a city's neighbourhood into a courtyard for Sabbath often involves little more than "the reinterpretation of an existing structure as a gate, or a doorway"[5]. Sometimes a simple addition can cause a redefinition of space. In contemporary times, explains Olin:

> Natural boundaries such as a shoreline or a slight depression in the earth and artificial boundaries such as fences or utility wires must all be redefined as interconnecting gates, and attain a complete and unbroken courtyard that takes into account traffic and pedestrian patterns and the routes of freeways and other major roads and plazas.[6]

The eruv's "small vocabulary", as Olin calls it, serves primarily as a camouflage, keeping the eruv from intruding into the urban setting. Even users of the eruv can miss it, and need maps to avoid straying outside its barely visible boundaries. The eruv's balance between visibility and invisibility has been viewed as a barometer that registers the nature of Jewish/non-Jewish relations and Jewish interrelations.[7] This almost invisible boundary can conjure up very different reactions on the part of non-Jewish neighbours, as it oftentimes becomes a powerful symbol of tolerance and multiculturality, but also the site of inter-ethnic disputes and bitter controversies.[8] Indeed, some argue that the interest in camouflaging the eruv suggests the potential divisiveness of this seemingly innocent construction. The eruv reveals the vulnerability and fragility of a relationship with a non-Jewish space where Jews thread on a fine line between cohabitation and ethnic and religious tension.

More importantly, the eruv is an act of imagination, if not resourcefulness. "Given enough string and enough poles, and with a little creative use of existing walls, cliffs, and rivers, you can tie a circle round pretty much any place and call it an eruv", explains Landsman, the protagonist of Michael Chabon's novel *The Yiddish Policemen's Union*.[9] The eruv, in this context, transcends the rabbinical discourse from which it originates, and becomes a trope, a metaphor for Jewish mobility. Through the power of imagination and make-belief, the eruv "transforms any space into place" and invites one to feel at

4 Olin: Introduction, pp. 5–6.

5 Ibid., p. 6.

6 Ibid.

7 Charlotte Elisheva Fonrobert: The Political Symbolism of Eruv. In: *Jewish Social Studies* 11,3 (2005), pp. 9–35.

8 See public debates about the eruv in north London in the 1990s, and internal disputes arising between Orthodox Jews and secular Jews on the eruv in Jerusalem in Michele Rapoport: Creating Place, Creating Community: The Intangible Boundaries of the Jewish Eruv. In: *Environment and Planning D: Society and Space* 29,5 (2011), pp. 891–904.

9 Michael Chabon: *The Yiddish Policemen's Union*. London: Fourth Estate 2007, p. 25.

home, argues Barbara E. Mann.[10] Its appeal for artists lies predominantly in the ambiguity between its materiality and potentiality as a concept. As Mann explains, "the eruv is virtual, symbolic, and invisible as well as three-dimensional, material, spatial and urban".[11] The eruv's minimalist language has been by now explored by conceptual artists among them Mel Alexenberg, Avner Bar-Hama, Daniel Bauer, Sophie Calle, Alan Cohen, Elliot Malkin, Shirin Neshat, Ellen Rothenberg, Ben Schachter, and Suzanne Silver gathered under the auspices of several art galleries at Yale University, School of Art. Three distinct exhibitions explore the eruv's multiple facets, namely *This Token Partnership: The Materiality of a Jewish Spatial Practice*, investigating the eruv as an "urban bricolage", *Israel: Gated Community* for which the eruv evinces contrasting positions on the Israeli-Palestinian conflict, and *Internal Borders* exploring the internalization of external borders in Israel and Iran. Curated by Margaret Olin, they form the ground-breaking project called *Shaping Community: Poetics and Politics of the Eruv* (2012),[12] and accompanied by the volume *Visualizing the Eruv* (2011)[13] they advance the scholarship on the eruv making apparent the unbounded potential of this concept as an artistic trope.

Walking as a Way of Intimately Knowing the Eruv

In *Sixteen Eruvin I've walked through* American artist Ben Schachter brings into sight, using blue thread stitched into white paper, filled in with white acrylic paint, the outlines of the eruv-bounded Jewish neighbourhoods that he has walked through. The drawings on white watercolour paper are pierced by blue thread that draws the shape of the eruv. "The interior of the eruv is itself painted white, only slightly distinguished by a cool white impasto", describes art critic Richard Mcbee.[14] Choosing this technique, the artist emphasizes the close resemblance of the eruv to an abstract drawing. "As a contemporary artist, I see these structures as drawing in space", confesses the artist.[15] Schachter's drawings, I would argue, are in fact portraits of the eruvin, making apparent a multitude of shapes and even personalities embodied by

10 Barbara E. Mann: *Space and Place in Jewish Studies*. New Brunswick: Rutgers UP 2012, p. 138.

11 Ibid.

12 See brief description of each project on http://www.yale.edu/ism/eruv/ (accessed 12.06.2013).

13 Olin: Introduction, p. 3.

14 Richard McBee: Rabbinic Drawing in Space. In: *Contemporary Jewish Art*, 07.11.2008. http://richardmcbee.com/writings/contemporary-jewish-art/item/rabbinic-drawing-in-space (accessed 15.06.2013).

15 Ben Schachter cit. in ibid.

eruvin and born out of their interaction with space. Schachter is especially interested in capturing the ways in which the eruv infiltrates the architectural landscape by showing great sensitivity to its characteristics. His eruvin are described by Olin as "emulations of emulations".[16]

A myriad of shapes are created each representing the geography of eruvin in places such as Jerusalem, Venice, Philadelphia, Johannesburg, Boston, East Brunswick, New Brunswick, or New Haven. The Venice Eruv from 2007, for example, shows the canals that must be navigated as city streets pass over water and under buildings. It includes the Jewish historical ghetto and extends as far as Piazza San Marco. Schachter's maps reveal the eruvin in their abstract dimension which emulates the geographical structure of the cities that host them. This is especially evident for the Manhattan Eruv that imitates the rectangular, grid like layout of the city and its streets. Through these emulations, the artist invokes the eruv's sensitivity to the urban landscape that it traverses and unifies. It explores, as Schachter confesses, "the rigor and delicacy of an eruv's regulation but also the ingenuity it requires".[17]

Seen in their totality, these eruvin, I argue, testify to Jewish ingenuity in the use of space. More than emulations, they show an ability to select particular attributes of space, incorporate certain landmarks and negotiate the use of space in a manner that is mutually convenient to all parties involved. The irregular shape of the eruvin, always surprising, reveals acts of negotiating space by establishing the position of the eruv in relation to many factors among them the geography of the space, the presence of natural obstacles, the need to ask permission from local authorities and city councils to use the public space. Each inch of space has to be negotiated and well-considered. Furthermore, Schachter evokes the eruv, with its alembicated and complicated shape, as a practice of the diaspora. The barely visible, highly permeable boundaries of the eruv that symbolically come to life only one day every week, are open and shared by any group, and, in my opinion, represent the "kindest" form of appropriating the land, as it leads to spiritual empowerment, rather than a territorial possession. The eruv functions on an imaginary level and its power is activated by ways of belief, rather than national enforcement. The delicacy with which the eruv integrates the natural landscape and weaves through it, creating a complete enclosure, is further mirrored in the technique Schachter uses and in the chosen materials, paper and line. Paper

16 Olin: Introduction, p. 8.

17 Ben Schachter: The Eruv: Urban Drawing and Assemblage. In: *Images. Journal of Jewish Art and Visual Culture* 5,1 (2011): Vizualizing the Eruv, pp. 44–51, here p. 45.

can easily tear just as the symbolic empty walls of the eruv can fall apart. The immateriality of the eruv is thus made visible. What become strikingly apparent are the contours of the eruvin. Oftentimes intentionally hidden, the eruvin remain unseen to the unknowledgeable passer-by or the non-believer. The act of identifying the eruv, without use of maps, can be a challenge even for the most experienced ones. The ability to see and thus come to know the eruv requires intense observation, search and determination. Mapping out the eruvin, by means of walking, Schachter actively performs and embodies them. As he aims to identify delicate boundaries, the artist also activates the eruvin. By walking and discovering the boundaries of the eruv, one gets to intimately know the eruv's inner workings. The one who walks in search of the eruv not only becomes aware of the subtle characteristics of landscape, and its discrete changes in shape and meaning, but walking, one may argue, is a way of taking possession of the eruv, embodying it, and hence making its presence more visible. It also implies appropriating some of its characteristics, such as a sensitivity to the surroundings and consequently a better knowledge of what it means to share and negotiate space with someone else. The fragility of the eruv in diaspora does not only speak of the fragile relationship with the non-Jews, but could be seen in more positive terms, as a form of negotiation that ultimately leads to co-habitation – which should be understood in this context as gaining a better understanding of the boundaries of the other, and how one can interact within a shared space in a manner that is not imposing or forceful. This subtlety contributes to the eruv's integrity and power. Indeed, the concept of the eruv – can be taken as a model – a metaphor for a co-habitation of space, which does not carry the brutal markings of national possession, but is activated by means of imagination.

Remembering as a Way of Inhabiting the Eruv

French artist Sophie Calle, much like Schachter, has been intrigued by the eruv's potential as a concept. In her installation from 1996 called *L'Erouv de Jérusalem*, Calle makes transparent another quality of the eruv, namely its capacity to transform public space into a private dwelling. The artist, well-known for her inventive ways of testing the limits of the private self, addresses the concept of eruv as a manifestation of the private. Calle shows how memory plays a crucial role in making a shared collective space feel private. Interested in how space gains personal significance and comes to define one's identity, Calle asked fourteen inhabitants of Jerusalem, Israelis and Palestinians, to take her to a public site and share with her events that made these seemingly ordinary spaces gain personal significance. Her photographs of the sites alongside the corresponding texts – transcriptions of excerpts from the interviews – were installed on a large table on which a map of Jerusalem had been placed. On the walls of the gallery, Calle hung photographs of electric poles to which wires were attached in order to evoke an eruv. The stories that transform the public site into private spaces for these particular individuals are, as one might expect, varied. Whereas some are politically charged, others hold a deep personal significance. These collected narratives reveal the complexities and contradictions that accompany notions of territory and the other. What all stories have in common is the understanding of a boundary not as a limitation, but as a meeting point with the other, a place of transformation in the form of an exchange, but also growth, rather than only a form of separation. A woman recounts, not without a degree of nostalgia, memories from when she was a teenager. Her special place is a bench on which a boy from her neighbourhood she was in love with used to sit. On this bench facing her flat's windows, the boy whose name she did not even know, had often sat in silence awaiting her response. She could not gather enough courage to speak to him. She recalls after having not seen him for a few months,

> During the Six Day War, I was very worried, I thought about him all the time. And then one day, I went out, there he was on the bench. Only the silence was too loud. I could not talk to him. I did not have the courage. I was afraid that it does not work, and then my parents always said: do not talk to men, do not … I never said anything. Now it's over, I forgot. But I still see this separation, the boundary between the bed and the window.[18]

For others spaces become places containing memories of trauma. In 1961 another interviewee, then a seven year old kid had been hit and dragged by bus number 18 for six metres. He had lost his leg. For many years returning to the site of trauma seemed impossible. He confesses:

> For years, I vowed never to get on the bus 18 and I stood by my vow for some time. But one day the need took precedence over the will. Many years have passed since then, [now] I take this street almost every day and I can never help but remember. Strangely, I think that this piece of road belongs to me. A part of my body remained here. At the top of the number 67 Boulevard Herzog.[19]

The space where the traumatic event took place becomes a memory site that this interviewee is unable to let go of. It is the reminder of an intervention

18 Text translated from French by the author, retrieved from *L'Erouv de Jérusalem*. http://www.erudit.org/culture/cvphoto1383919/cvphoto1072402/20985ac.pdf (accessed 15.06.2013).
19 Ibid.

that had changed his life in a drastic way. No matter the time elapsed, the site still has the force of pulling him back in the past. In this case, one comes face to face with trauma as the most extreme form of othering. Space and memory become intricately bound together. The frontier, as a meeting point with the "other" and the complex emotions it generates, is invoked by yet another interviewee who recalls his/her arrival in Jerusalem and the first impressions of the landscape as follows:

> When I first arrived in Jerusalem in 1959, there was just one hotel isolated on top of this hill. The Diplomat hotel was truly the last stop. Beyond it there was nothing, but the very nothing was extremely powerful. It was a frontier not to be crossed. An invisible barrier much more intense than the real one on Jaffa Street with its wall. On the other side there was the other territory, the other culture, the other destiny, the other history. [...] All it would take was running down the slope and, somewhere between this side and the other, jumping into a minefield. This pull towards the void lasted half a second. But I felt the frontier and I still feel it today. You have the impression that in the air there are vertical rays of steam floating upwards. It is still there, this invisible thing in the middle of the valley.[20]

It appears that for this allegedly Israeli interviewee, the political meaning assigned to a space is equally powerful as the existence of a concrete wall. Other stories make apparent how the lives of both Israeli and Palestinian interviewees are defined by impassable borders, signalled by nearly invisible, ostensibly open, yet fully internalized borders. What lies outside is un-safe and alien. Hence, any attempt to move outside of one's self-imposed borders is threatening as the above-mentioned interviewee recalls. The pull towards the void stands as a metaphor for the proximity to the "other"; perhaps the only experience that can give a sense of who the "other" is. Indeed here, one might well argue, the "other" can be both the Israeli and the Palestinian. Having to face the other's history, culture, or destiny is seen by both sides as a daunting boundary. The ambiguity as to who is the "other" of these brief stories is maintained throughout Calle's installation. The borders of the eruv make these ambiguities even more apparent. What prevails, as a common characteristic to all stories, is the ways in which Calle's interlocutors, by acts of remembering, make space a less alienating concept. Space becomes a place where something happened. Through the interviewees' ability to remember, these spaces gain significance as memory sites. Calle's installation shows how memories, no matter whom they belong to are localised within and inhabit a space. The eruv is not only a border. It also means "mixture" or "partnership".

20 *L'Erouv de Jérusalem.*

Calle alludes to eruv as a partnership in the way in which both Israelis and Palestinians inherently relate to outer surroundings as not only repositories of memories, but also of their former selves. No matter how diverse these experiences may be, the fact that all happen in the space of the city of Jerusalem point to the palimpsest-like nature of space enclosing multiple narratives and to the key role played by memory and remembering as a way of turning space into place and home.

Both Schachter and Calle celebrate the concept of eruv for its multifaceted meaning and potential to raise universal questions on human relationship with space. While for Schachter the focus is on the interplay allowed by the eruv between visible and invisible borders, Calle's preoccupation lies with the relationship between memory and space and the intimate character space takes as the dwelling place of memories. The concept of eruv dealt with by both artists is reminiscent of the notion that boundaries are not a limiting force, but a creative one.[21] To quote Heidegger, "a boundary is not that at which something stops but, as the Greeks recognised, the boundary is that from which something begins its presencing".[22] The poetics of the eruv lies in its potential to bring forth a whole array of new beginnings – whether in the form of a conversation, a negotiation, an invitation to respond to the other, or as a means to understand deeply intimate connections with space. The creative force of the eruv is recognised by the artists themselves. Inspired by its illusory shape and meaning, they delve deeper and bring to the surface another way of looking at the eruv. Beyond its religious purpose, it is the potential of the eruv as an art form, its aesthetics that is brought to the surface. The territory shaped by the eruv is an aesthetic space as much as a religious or social one. Its presence does not block the horizon, to refer to Heidegger's note, but marks the beginning of something new, a new form of "presencing", or inhabiting space.

Similar functions are manifest by the "wall" in the sense that it too catalyses the artists' imagination. It too presents an illusory shape with its swerving, inconsistent and shifting shape very visible in some areas, and practically absent, replaced by barbed wire in others. The wall too, beyond its political and military role to divide, conquer and oppress also means protection and safety for others. For artists, the wall is most often a blank canvas on which they can project a meaning different than that given by those who erected

21 Rapoport: Creating Place, Creating Community, p. 896.

22 Martin Heidegger: Building, Dwelling, Thinking. In: Id.: *Poetry, Language, Thought*, transl. from the German by Albert Hofstader. London: Harper & Row 1971, pp. 141–161, here p. 154.

it. Unsurprisingly, the wall does not invite artists to meditate on the poetics of space, but rather prompts an art of protest, where poetics is replaced with politics. In the hands of art, the dual nature of the eruv and the wall – both spatial demarcations that simultaneously include and exclude – can be observed in a clearer light. In the case of the wall, the poetical aspect loses grounds to the political, and calls forth not the subtleties of conceptual art, but the socially-driven protest art.

The Politics of the Wall

Unlike the eruv's long-lasting existence, the wall[23] is a new manifestation of Jewish spatial practice. Ninety per cent of West Bank wall is composed of an elaborate network of barriers, rolls of barbed wire, and trenches as well as high-tech motion-detection systems, and, like the eruv, it uses the geography of the land to incorporate natural boundaries; while the remaining ten per cent consist of an eight meter high concrete fence. Its construction began in 2002 after a series of devastating attacks against Israeli citizens. The 670 km long wall, the security or anti-terror fence as it is called by Israelis, or the "Apartheid wall", known by the Palestinians, encircles the West Bank with sections around Jerusalem, blocking off Bethlehem and Ramallah. This border's ambivalence is reflected by the many different meanings it carries. While a means of ensuring safety for the majority of Israelis, for others including some Israeli academics and artists the wall is a symbol of the brutal Israeli policy of discrimination against Palestinians. There have been many symbolic attempts to dismantle the wall mostly made apparent on the wall itself. Labelled as "the largest protest banner in the world", it is a site of many graffiti works especially those of British street artist, Bansky.[24] His series of murals on the Palestinian side of the wall use the concrete slabs as a canvas to protest against the wall's very existence. His painted images of escape and

23 This spatial demarcation is known by many names, separation barrier is the most politically correct terminology, for the purposes of this article, I will use "the wall" for its historical echoes with the Berlin wall which had been used by many artists as a canvas to convey their protest, much alike the West bank wall is used today.

24 See William Parry: *Against the Wall: The Art of Resistance in Palestine.* Chicago: Chicago Review Press 2011; Talia H. Moscovitz: *Through the Wall: The West Bank Wall as Global Canvas*, Honors Junior/Senior projects, Northeastern University, Boston, January 2007, see http://iris.lib.neu.edu/cgi/viewcontent.cgi?article=1028&context=honors_projects (accessed 15.06.2013); Hugh Lovatt: *The Aesthetics of Space: West Bank Graffiti and Global Artists*, thesis at School of Oriental and African Studies, University of London, 2010. http://academia.edu/935825/The_Aesthetics_of_Space_West_Bank_Graffiti_and_Global_Artists (accessed 15.06.2013).

freedom include scissors cutting the wall, windows that open up to an idyllic landscape, or a girl floating by clutching balloons. Even though intended to increase awareness of how the separation has deeply affected the lives of Palestinians, Bansky's images were received with mixed feelings on the part of some Palestinians, who saw it as a way of effacing the ugliness of the wall, by painting beautiful pictures.[25] In stark contrast, the practice of beautifying and thus concealing the wall's existence by means of graffiti art has been encouraged on the Israeli side too. The paintings on the wall in the Gilo neighbourhood of Jerusalem come to mind. Shlomo Brosh, the initiator of the project, from the Jerusalem Municipality explained that "the idea was to make the walls transparent", "if they have forced us to shield ourselves, then we decided that at least we wouldn't give up the landscape that used to be there."[26] There have been many other attempts by Israeli authorities to make the wall "less visually troubling" by downplaying its size, or by painting picturesque images. These initiatives have been countered by other artistic projects aiming not to hide the wall by covering it in beautiful pictures, but to denounce it and make it disappear completely from the landscape. Among practices of resistance against separation one can include the weekly demonstrations in the village of Bil'in. These creative forms of protest became the subject of an art exhibition at the Minshar Gallery in Tel Aviv in 2006.[27] Another attempt to make the wall disappear was promoted by a group of twenty Israeli and Palestinian artists, also known as "artists without walls". Their intention was to create a "forum for dialogue between individuals engaged in all fields of art and culture [...] through nonviolent and creative actions".[28] Galit Eilat, one of its members, installed on both sides of the wall in the Abu Dis neighbourhood in Jerusalem, two cameras each filming what was happening on the other side of the wall. The material recorded on the Israeli side was projected for several hours on the Palestinian side of the wall and vice-versa. In this manner, the boundaries imposed by the wall disintegrated. The materiality of the wall had symbolically vanished giving viewers on each side of the wall full access, as if by means of a window, to the view that was blocked. However,

25 See Ronen Eidelman: The Separation Wall in Palestine: Artists Love to Hate It. In: Begum Ozden Firat / Aylin Kuryel (eds): *Cultural Activism: Practices, Dilemmas and Possibilities*. Amsterdam: Rodopi 2011, pp. 95–115.

26 Cit. in ibid., p. 97.

27 Ibid., pp. 101–103.

28 See full statement of this artistic movement against the wall on http://osaarchivum.org/galeria/the_divide/chapter19.html (accessed 15.06.2013).

one is well-aware that opening a window into the wall is not enough, since the goal, as stated by the artists without walls "is to do away with the wall altogether". They describe the wall as:

> merely an expression, in a concrete form, of what is already there, a high degree of segregation and wish for separation, a mentality, a feeling which is widely present in the public [...] so to work against the wall means [...] changing the mentality [...] the question is what it means to work against it, in both publics, both the Palestinian and the Israeli [...] it means to know that public, and to know how to bring the issue of non-separation in a way that still moves them.[29]

Another initiative against the wall was the collective project titled *Three Cities against the Wall Ramallah/Tel Aviv/New York* held simultaneously in these cities in 2005. The aim of the project was to "establish a foundation for building a community of artists across borders, and to demonstrate, through a combined effort, their opposition to injustice and oppression on moral and ethical grounds".[30] Israeli artists Ravit Cohen Gat and Moshe Gerstel placed a white couch in front of the West Bank wall aiming to reinforce the dichotomy between the safety and comfort represented by the couch and the insecurity and fear symbolised by the wall. This work called *Next Year in Jerusalem*, employs the phrase that ends the Passover *seder*, to express how the longing for a lost home and for a sense of belonging is made increasingly unattainable through the presence of the wall.[31] Whereas the afore-mentioned point to the wish to tear the wall apart by invoking affect and emotions, Eyal Weizman's approach is more analytical and didactic, showing how the wall reinforces a discourse of power entrapped in its obsession with territoriality and borders. Architect and academic Eyal Weizman's series of maps were an essential part of the exhibition *Borderlinedisorder*, representing Israel at the Architecture Biennale in Venice 2002. Maps are a traditional means by which a nation visualizes its place in the space it inhabits. When there is no political consensus in regard to owned territories, the maps that nations in conflict produce remain an issue of permanent reinterpretation and are only able to reflect individual zones of conflict. Through the national practice of binding identity to a place,

29 Statement by artists without walls. http://contemporary-anarchist.blogspot.co.uk/2007/02/three-cities-against-wall.html (accessed 15.06.2013).

30 Members of this project are also associated with the activist groups the Israeli Coalition against the Wall, Taayush and Anarchists against the Wall. These groups participate in protests and projects, both in Israel and Palestine, against the construction of the Wall and the occupation, including protests where there have been many victims, Palestinian, Israeli, and international. See full statement on http://www.abcnorio.org/againstthewall/ (accessed 16.06.2013).

31 See Moscovitz: *Through the Wall*, pp. 36–39.

what David Campbell refers to as ontopology (ontos – being, topos – space), a "nationalist imaginary" is made possible which requires:

> the expulsion from the domestic space of all that comes to be regarded as alien, foreign and dangerous. The nationalist imaginary thus demands a violent relationship with the other. Given that all forms of community are bounded to at least some extent, no form of community is going to be totally free of such violence.[32]

The territorial demarcation of identity is an inherently violent practice because it demands the repression or exclusion of the other. This is clearly the logic of both Israeli and Palestinian nationalism animated by different narratives of authentic belongings to the same territory. In Weizman's maps one can visualize this violent relationship with the other. Colour blue stands for the Israeli settlements and brown for the Palestinians ones, whereas military camps are marked with red. Due to its monumental size, the map is reminiscent of a graffiti work. The blown up cartographic image depicts the Israeli-Palestinian terrain as a patchwork territory in a dynamic process of change, dissemination and fragmentation.[33] It shows the "permanent reordering of boundaries, a perpetual disorder of borderlines".[34] In the West Bank, patches of Israeli land are encircled by Palestinian land and vice-versa, making it impossible to draw a clear and continuous border or distinction between the two. Weizman's map admits to the "failure" of mapping, and to the impossibility of dividing territory into space which clearly aligns with one identity or another. The map also speaks of the politics of architecture, namely, the relation between political power and the organisation of space.

These power relations are further reflected in the way in which the wall does not form a continuous and contiguous line, but curls around itself so that it creates islands and archipelagos reflecting a system of separation. Hence, the wall is a manifestation of top-down state power whose route is constantly transformed so as to respond to the position of the settlements. The fluctuation in the path of the wall further reflects the changes in Israeli politics. Compromises from NGOs on the political right or left are thus reflected in

32 David Campbell: *National Deconstruction: Violence, Identity, and Justice in Bosnia.* Minneapolis: University of Minnesota Press 1998, p. 13.

33 Several images of the map can be accessed on http://www.efrat-kowalsky.co.il/project/borderlinedisorder-8th-architecture-biennale/ (accessed 16.06.2013).

34 See description in exhibition catalogue Severino Faccin (ed.): *The Promise. The Land. Jewish-Israeli Artists in Relation to Politics and Society.* Linz: O.K. Center for Contemporary Art Upper Austria 2003, pp. 18–19.

the path that the wall takes.[35] The resulting flexibility of the wall's path does not count as a benign category, but in fact shows how occupation functions. Rather than the conclusive division between two nations across a boundary line, the organisation of the West Bank's wall has created multiple separations, provisional boundaries, which relate to each other through surveillance and control. Hence, in Weizman's maps, the wall makes visible the politics of occupation; it becomes a tool used to illustrate the violent nature of the relationship with the other.

Conclusion

The discussed artistic projects fulfil several functions: to make visible how these spatial demarcations function, what they produce and how they change human relationships and dynamics; to reflect upon their aesthetics and ethics; and ultimately to make apparent the highly ambivalent and complex reactions and sentiments these borders, visible or not, continue to provoke. The eyesore of the Israeli-Palestinian landscape, the wall seems the eruv's utmost alter-ego. On the other hand, the eruv still creates boundaries, even if they are internalised or on the verge of the invisible. It allows the existence of a degree of reciprocity through the fact that the other agrees with the symbolic interaction realised through the eruv. Unlike the eruv, the visibility of the wall is uncontested. But how alienating are the borders that the eruv and the wall draw between communities? Certainly both are markers that foreground alterity but also enable constructions of identities and shape identity politics. And, both show flexibility and mutability. Unlike the flexibility shown by the eruv in the unobtrusive manner in which it relates to space, the wall has a different kind of flexibility which reflects state sovereignty and power politics. Both propose a form of separation from the other, however, their manifestation and the inter-ethnic dynamic they unfold differs. While the eruv proposes a seemingly non-invasive separation, the wall becomes a site of irreconcilable division and conflict. Admitting to their contradictory effect brings no resolution. The eruv and the wall ultimately point to the spectrum of Jewish conceptualisations of space and of identity, and the complex collective story of the Jewish relationship with space. Both remain ambivalent concepts, and because of this, continue to capture the imagination of artists and contemporary audiences.

35 Argument suggested by Eyal Weizman in his contributions for opendemocracy, on http://www.opendemocracy.net/conflict-politicsverticality/issue.jsp (accessed 17.06.2013).

Locating Jewish Identities in Naomi Alderman's *Disobedience*

Martin Kindermann

In tandem with Edward Soja's call for a reconsideration of our notions of space in 1989, the representation of space and its various narrative implications have received an increasing amount of attention within literary scholarship.[1] Space can no longer be conceived as a container or a simple stage on which narrated events take their course, but rather, the relationality of the spatial network is now foregrounded. Further, as a result of the emergence of the modern metropolis, urban space has become one of the most crucial topoi of the literary representation of human experience. Through the immediate encounter of various historical, cultural and social frames, the city can be regarded as the central location for negotiating as well as articulating different interests and concepts of identity. With regard to the topic under discussion here – Jewish and non-Jewish spaces – the city maps out a broad scope of attempts to articulate Jewishness. For my analysis of Naomi Alderman's novel *Disobedience*[2] it is nonetheless necessary to readjust the semantic implications of the said opposition to some extent. Not only do we need to distinguish Jewish from non-Jewish spaces, but we furthermore need to differentiate between secular Jewish spaces, orthodox spaces, spaces of Progressive Judaism, and spaces of Conservative Judaism.[3]

1 Edward Soja: *Postmodern Geographies. The Reassertion of Space in Critical Social Theory.* London: Verso 1989.

2 Naomi Alderman: *Disobedience.* London: Penguin 2007.

3 Although for the sake of my argument this distinction can be narrowed down to a differentiation between the orthodox spaces of Krushka's congregation and spaces beyond this narrow frame.

Alderman's novel, which is set in an orthodox community in London's Hendon district, is based on a close intertwinement of urban space and strategies for articulating identity, both individually as well as collectively. The border between different semantic subspaces, or different neighbourhoods (and their specific social and historical layers), is central to the novel's attempt to represent cultural and social diversity. As articulation of the self is inevitably linked to notions of the other, the negotiation of spaces perceived as 'home' and those constructed as a 'location of otherness' is important to the discussion of urban space in the context of the literary representation of Jewish identity.

In comparison with academic discourse on the American-Jewish novel, British-Jewish writing has received much less attention despite its place in British culture for more than one hundred years. However, during the past two decades this situation has slowly begun to change: on the one hand, prize-winning texts such as *Disobedience*, Howard Jacobson's *The Finkler Question* or Linda Grant's *When I Lived in Modern Times* – to name but a few – clearly hint at a growing public interest in Jewish authors and their work; on the other hand, authors themselves have become more confident in articulating and negotiating Jewish identities. Nevertheless, specific analyses of texts are still scarce and most publications take an introductory approach to the topic. With regard to Alderman's novel, however, Donald Weber has previously stressed the author's confident approach to representing the polyvalence of British-Jewish identities and furthermore has shown how Alderman employs the notion of hybridity when it comes to the self-fashioning of a contemporary Jewish identity.[4] The text is part of a new strain in British-Jewish writing, which raises a new Jewish voice that no longer aims at a mediating position towards a non-Jewish readership. On the contrary, texts like Alderman's focus on the intercultural semantic locations of Jewish identity within the polyvalent framework of the city.

My analysis of the text aims at further exploring this diversity in connection to its representation of urban space. I will show that the novel's narrative design constructs a spatiality that strongly relies on relationality; space becomes an active agent in the process of narration through highlighting the hybrid formation of Jewish identities and relating them to the polyvalence of the spatial

4 Donald Weber: Anglo-Jewish Literature Raises Its Voice, 2011. http://www.jbooks.com/interviews/index/IP_Weber_English_Prn.htm (accessed 13.05.2013); Donald Weber: Unorthodox Desires, 2011. http://jbooks.com/fiction/index/FI_Weber_Alderman_Prn.htm (accessed 13.05.2013).

network. Herein is mobility of crucial importance: the location of the narrating voice within the narrated world, the characters' movements through the city, and the positioning of the self with regard to the constructed other are integral to my reading of the text. In a first step I will thus focus on the literary representation of space in general to establish key concepts for my analysis, where I emphasise the notion of the border as a vital constituent of the spatial network. In a second step I outline the semantic implications constructed by the text and their connection to notions of Jewish identities. In a third step I take mobility in urban space and narrative mobility into consideration to explore processes of intertwinement with regard to the constitution of Jewish spaces. Finally, I will focus on re-evaluations of spatial oppositions, which are brought about by the various movements between orthodox and non-orthodox, Jewish and non-Jewish spaces. Nevertheless, first some brief remarks on the relationality of space are necessary.

Representing Urban Space and the Semantic Border

The geographer Doreen Massey has outlined three basic propositions which any analysis of space needs to consider:[5] firstly, space has to be characterised as a relational network constituted through various interactions. Any notion which perceives space as a container or stage is unable to capture its historical or social layers as well as the performative shaping of space through the location of objects and bodies. Secondly, space is constituted through multiple heterogeneous relations; it is the product of various polyvalent relations that, via interpreting the spatial network, provide us with options to locate ourselves semantically and spatially with regard to our surroundings. And thirdly, space should not be perceived as static, but "it is always in the process of being made. It is never finished; never closed"[6]. Therefore space and time cannot be regarded as oppositional but as intertwined, because the one cannot be described properly without involving the other. The notion of space as a static container, independent from the dynamics of ongoing processes of locations, thus has to be discarded in favour of a relational concept that understands space as construed through time. Space is constituted by actions and movements, which clearly highlight the importance of time, as the relational network is constantly arranged and rearranged.

5 Doreen Massey: *For Space*. London: SAGE 2005, p. 9.

6 Ibid.

Any notion of space needs to consider social and historical layers, which are, on the one hand, inscribed into the spatial network, while simultaneously, on the other hand, they are amongst its vital constituents. Michel de Certeau, who emphasises the constructedness of space, has foregrounded the importance of social relations in the process of spatial constitution, arguing that space evolves through time as result of performative acts.[7] The city therefore is not just a stage where historical events unfold or individuals articulate identities, but the very processes of self-formation and self-location are part of the constant shaping of the relational network.

Consequently, literary space should by no means be understood as a mere replica of the world we inhabit. Each and every representation of space in literature constructs individual intra-textual networks of relations; processes of meaning-making, inherent to aesthetic representation in general, constitute further semantic layers that enrich the spatial framework. As space is constituted by mobility, literary space likewise depends on a mobile point of view, which allows for a depiction of the relational network that is able to capture its complexity. Thus, London in Alderman's novel is certainly not merely a simple mimesis of the modern metropolis. Rather, the novel stresses semantic layers and foregrounds certain elements of the spatial and semantic framework which are essential constituents of the process of aesthetic communication.

According to Jurij Lotman movement in the semantic framework of literary texts is of crucial importance: in works of literature the border as well as the available options for crossing semantic and spatial boundaries, and thus relocating oneself anew, are essential to the process of communicating meaning. Therefore texts construct interrelated semantic fields based on relevant discourses, and mobility between these fields is vital to the construction of the narrative sujet as well as to processes of meaning-making. Lotman's model of the *semiosphere* describes semiotic processes between semantic spheres with a special focus on the periphery as a location of dynamic processes that prompt hybridisation, as the penetration of semantic content leads to polyvalent meanings. Hence, literary space presents itself as a complex network of intertwined semantic spheres, each of which is open and limited at the same time. Because of its asymmetric structure with a core, which can be described as relatively stable, and a highly fluid periphery, outside and inside overlap and bring about translations from one semantic code to another. Through these

7 Michel de Certeau: *The Practice of Everyday Life*, transl. from the French by Steven Rendall. Berkeley / Los Angeles / London: University of California Press 1988, p. 117.

dynamics new information – the hybrid – is generated through constitutional processes of interpenetration.

These processes find their location within the semantic border between semiospheres. The border is thus a space of constant mutual interpenetration and constitutes a space of multiple meanings: "Just as in mathematics the border represents a multiplicity of points, belonging simultaneously to both the internal and external space [...]".[8] Through options of movement with regard to the border characters locate themselves in relation to the narrative sujet of a text within its various semantic subspheres, depending on their ability to cross the border or even locate themselves within the semiotic boundaries. Being thus located in a space of multiple meanings, such a character "belongs to two worlds, operates as a kind of interpreter, settling in the territorial periphery, on the boundary [...]".[9] And it is exactly this mode of heightened spatial and semantic mobility as well as competence that is of crucial importance in my analysis of characters such as Ronit Krushka and Esti Kuperman.

Constructing Polyvalence

The novel's main protagonists, Ronit and Esti, both struggle to locate polyvalent identities within and with regard to the orthodox Jewish space of Hendon. Being British, Jewish, homosexual, orthodox and secular, these two women have to incorporate polyvalent facets into their staging of Jewish identity, which situates them at the border between various semantic and spatial fields. Whereas Ronit, daughter and only child of a recently deceased and highly distinguished orthodox rabbi, left the community in her adolescence, her former lover Esti remains in Hendon and marries Dovid, Ronit's cousin and Rav Krushka's designated successor. Living in New York, Ronit stresses secular elements of Jewish identity-designs in a place "where everyone's Jewish anyway"[10]. Her father's death brings Ronit back to London where she is not only confronted with memories of a secluded childhood but is also forced to re-evaluate her notions of orthodoxy. American Judaism therefore appears in stark contrast to the Anglo-Jewish community (which the narrative voices depict as Haredi, equating orthodoxy with Judaism as a whole): Ronit's narrative portrays the Jews of the US metropolis as outspoken, publicly discernible

8 Jurij M. Lotman: On the Semiosphere, transl. from the Russian by Wilma Clark. In: *Sign System Studies* 33,1 (2005), pp. 205–229, here pp. 208–209.

9 Ibid., p. 211.

10 Alderman: *Disobedience*, p. 12.

and engaged in constant discussion about their notions of Jewish identity, whereas British Jews seem to be secluded and mute.

Esti, who knows perfectly well that she will only ever be attracted to women, stays in Hendon and marries Dovid, a sensitive disciple of Krushka's. Her decision to lead a religious life requires the repression of her sexual desire and condemns her to a life of silence. But her love for Ronit remains present in the community's collective memory, meaning that Esti's social location is precarious. Ronit's return confronts Esti with her own hybridity and furthermore brings about an articulation of sexual desire, as Esti believes she is still in love with Ronit. Just as Ronit has to evaluate spatialised memory when she manages her parents' estate (her mother died when Ronit was four years old), Esti's identity is likewise negotiated in strong connection to the relational network of space.

The novel's representation of polyvalent notions of both space and identity is mirrored in the narrative situation itself: the text is mediated through at least three distinguishable narrative voices. Each of the thirteen chapters is introduced by a quote from canonical religious texts which is expounded by what I consider the first narrative voice: a non-diegetic voice that interprets the quotes and thereby shows considerable scholarship in the readings of the passages. Ronit's first person narrative forms another voice, which by turns, in dialog with a third, non-diegetic voice relates the actual plot. The confrontation of these last two voices in contradictory representations of events often highlights perceptual conflicts as well as multiple ways to derive meaning from experience. The interpretations of the canonical quotes provide thematic introductions to the chapters and thus comment on the plotlines narrated by the other two voices. Narrating through multiple, often disagreeing voices constructs a mobile point of view, which illustrates the crucial importance of mobility within the semantic and spatial framework designed by the text.

Deconstructing Bi-spatiality

A bi-spatial division can be considered pivotal to Ronit's initial representation of urban space, although the semantic frame outside Hendon is seldom more than a counter-space to the orthodox semiosphere of Krushka's community.[11] New York City is from Ronit's point of view everything London is not:

11 As a counter-space I consider a space that is constituted solely in opposition to the semantic layers of another space. Ronit's narrative excludes orthodox spaces in New York (e.g. Crown Heights); therefore it can be considered to be constructed in semantic dependence to Hendon's religious sphere.

whereas she repeatedly equates London with silence and seclusion, which she associates with orthodoxy as a whole, Jews in New York represent cultural and social diversity. At second glance though, this diversity is based on a roughly modelled counter-notion to Ronit's understanding of the Hendon community:

> Because in Hendon there are plenty of people just dying to explain the meaning of life to you. I guess that's true in New York too, but in New York everyone seems to disagree with everyone else about what the meaning of life *is*. In Hendon, at least the Hendon I grew up in, everything faced in one direction.[12]

Ronit blends two seemingly conflicting designs of Jewish identity onto the spatial framework, so that Hendon, and thus British Jews in general, appear to be close-minded, isolated and silent, whereas Jews in New York secure public visibility through mobility and outspokenness. In Hendon the whole public discursive dimension of Jewish identity seems to disappear:

> But you don't get the vast participation in the cultural and intellectual life of the country of people who want to talk about, write about, think about Jewish things. And who know, confidently, that people who aren't Jewish will be interested in what they have to say too. […] There's a vicious circle here, in which the Jewish fear of being noticed and the natural British reticence interact. They feed off each other so that British Jews cannot speak, cannot be seen, value *absolute invisibility* above all other virtues.[13]

Obviously, Ronit construes Hendon as an enclosed space by constructing a semantic counter-space in New York, wherein orthodoxy simply disappears. Through this Ronit is able to see New York as merely secular space in a way that Haredi Judaism seems to belong to Hendon only. Therefore she can regard the handing out of orthodox brochures or lectures on her father's books in New York as an intrusion into the secular semiosphere of the city. Thus she negates any religious elements of Jewishness in New York, so that the city becomes a Jewish space that is at the same time not Jewish at all.

The non-diegetic narrative voice, too, constructs Jewish identity in relation to urban space, as the village atmosphere of Hendon is stressed through highlighting the specific orthodox character of the neighbourhood, which the text associates with a shtetl:

> Hendon is a village. It exists within a city, one of the greatest in the world. It has links to this city, people travel to and fro between them. But it is a village. […] Though there is a wider world, in Hendon all that is needful has been provided: Torah-true schools and

12 Alderman: *Disobedience*, p. 30.

13 Ibid., pp. 54–55.

> kosher shops and synagogues and mikvahs and business which are closed on the Sabbath and match-makers and burial societies.[14]

The seclusion of Hendon is further linked to a constant longing for the other place inherent to existence in galut. The construction of a collective memory space that articulates the absence of the anticipated re-location in a messianic context generates an imaginary homeland, which seems to contain the longed for return and at the same time stresses its impossibility. The text therewith links spatial belonging to the act of narration, which is itself an irrevocable part of the constitution of memory. As George Steiner puts it: "The text is home, each commentary a return"[15]. Belonging is construed in relation to the text, the holy text as well as the textuality of cultural memory, so that the act of referencing constitutes a comment that enables access to the imaginary homeland. However, the elusiveness of such a location strongly affects the process of locating the self within the spatial and semantic framework of the actual place of residence:

> We who live in Hendon now like to imagine ourselves elsewhere. We carry our homeland on our backs, unpacking it where we find ourselves, never too thoroughly or too well, for we will have to pack it up again one day. Hendon does not exist; it is only where we are, which is the least of all ways to describe us.[16]

Physical location seems to be of minor importance because of the emotionally charged place of belonging constructed through collective memory. Herein the non-diegetic voice raises the question of belonging, which was already voiced by Ronit in a secular context with regard to New York and Hendon, only this time from an orthodox point of view that understands each location in galut as fleeting and temporary.

Jewish spaces outside Krushka's community, in contrast to the polyvalent and multi-facetted design of the orthodox semiosphere of this congregation, are depicted rather superficially. Neither Ronit nor Esti consider Progressive or Conservative Judaism as alternatives to orthodoxy's harsh take on homosexuality. In similar fashion the text just roughly hints at Jewish spaces outside the small Hendon congregation. After the week of mourning for Krushka comes to an end Jewish newspapers cover the Rav's death in articles and obituaries:

14 Alderman: *Disobedience*, p. 123.

15 George Steiner: Our Homeland, the Text (1985). In: George Steiner: *No Passion Spent. Essays 1978–1996*. London / Boston: Faber & Faber 1996, pp. 304–327, here p. 307.

16 Alderman: *Disobedience*, p. 216.

> The *Jewish Chronicle* carried a half-page obituary, recording the events of the man's life. Its tone was slightly overenthusiastic, its detail a little hazy. The *Jewish Tribune*, a publication more certain in its convictions, printed a glowing and fulsome account of the Rav's achievements […].[17]

Through media coverage in two newspapers the diversity of Jewish spaces is hinted at and commented on by the narrative voice: the obituary in the *Jewish Chronicle* is shown to be unreliable because it reports that "the Rav had left no children"[18]. While the *Jewish Tribune*, a Haredi newspaper, seems to have stronger ties to the congregation. Its hyperbolic statement that Krushka "was without doubt already supping at the table of the righteous in the world to come"[19] is questioned by the narrative voice via its direct narrative link to the *Chronicle's* false information, and thus, the narrative voice renounces both accounts.

The text further uses reactions to Krushka's death within Hendon's Jewish population as a means to depict its diversity, and the implication of the event greatly varies with regard to the Rav's impact on the different congregations:

> In Hendon, the end of the mourning week passed almost without note for members of other synagogues and congregations. The death had been felt a little among the congregants of the shtiebels, those small, hidden synagogues formed in hollowed-out houses or unused offices. […] The worshippers at the larger synagogues, housed in suburban culs-de-sac […] read the *Chronicle* and shrugged or sighed or turned the page. And the young men and women of the 'alternative' services held in draughty halls, bound together by earnest debate and accompanied by monthly vegetarian dinner? It would be too far to say that they rejoiced. Let us say instead that, in so far as they were aware of the Rav, they felt only a slight sense of relief at the removal of an element which was neither liberal nor modern and, therefore, was without merit.[20]

The depiction constitutes a narrative movement through Hendon, starting out at the centre of the orthodox sphere (and its shtiebels), i. e., the communities closest to Krushka's congregation, towards the alternative services, resulting in a comment on the Rav's worthlessness to a liberal and modern Jewish life. Although the narration concentrates on Krushka's congregation, the congregations addressed are located in urban space, so that the Jewish space of Hendon is revealed as a polyvalent network consisting of multiple distinct notions of Judaism. Through this narrative focus the secluded

17 Ibid., p. 124.
18 Ibid.
19 Ibid.
20 Ibid., pp. 124–125.

character of the community often foregrounded in Ronit's narrative thread is incorporated into the narrative design of the non-diegetic voice.

In similar fashion, as with the depiction of New York City as a counter-space to Hendon, the various Jewish spaces of London represent a roughly modelled exterior to Krushka's community. Nevertheless, by outlining the polyvalence of Hendon as a Jewish space, however superficially, the text forms a counter-narrative to Ronit, who characterises Hendon first and foremost as homogenous. The more complex picture of the intertwinement of different Jewish spaces that is established at the end of the novel – when Esti and Dovid lead a congregation together – is therefore already hinted at in this rough outline of Jewish diversity.

Mobile Locations

Mobility, narrative as well as semantic, represents a vital means of exploring the relational network and the constantly reformulating semantic implications attributed to urban space during the act of narration. Moving through the city becomes a way of interpreting the framework. Such movements are further stressed through narrative strategies that employ a mobile point of view as location with regard to the sujet. Hence I will first consider actual movement in urban space before analysing semantic movement and, finally, I will briefly outline how a mobile point of view is essential to the depiction of the hybridity and polyvalence of Jewish spaces.

The mutual interpenetration of different spatial and semantic structures is apparent in the contrast between two London neighbourhoods, Camden Town and Hendon, from Esti's point of view; neighbourhoods which reveal dissimilarity but are also shown to be closely linked. Herein the dynamics at the border between semiospheres are represented in the context of Esti's journey: to avoid her neighbours' prying eyes she travels to Camden to buy a pregnancy test. The coming Shabbat dominates the portrayal of urban space, as Esti's temporal perspective is projected onto the city. Thus her religious experience of time and space is used to capture processes of interpenetration between secular and religious spaces. Consequently, the narrative flow is repeatedly disrupted by exact information on the time span left until the beginning of Shabbat. As Esti rides the tube, rhythmic sounds of the train, her counting of the days since her last menstruation and the narrator's counting of minutes until Shabbat form the background of her journey from the seemingly secluded Hendon to lively Camden Town.

The neighbourhood itself is depicted from Esti's character perspective. Initially it appears to be one further counter-space to the orthodox sphere of Krushka's community. Seen through Esti's eyes the Camden Town Underground station is an overwhelming, even destabilising experience:

> Camden sweated. It was loud. It smelled. Esti stood outside the station simply looking, her bag clutched tight against her body. A thin young man, whose chest read 'Screw the people', was leaning against the railing, eating a jacket potato from a plastic container. [...] The world spun. Esti wondered if she was about to faint. The shops and people began to merge into a distorted inner-ear judder. Everything became suddenly upside-down, inside-out. Bingle-mingle.[21]

Esti's crossing of the border between orthodox and secular space locates the character in a polyvalent subspace, which is highly fluid and dynamic and where Esti's own semantic framework no longer seems valid. To Esti urban space outside the stringent order of orthodoxy lacks orientation, is chaotic and resists attempts to derive meaning from the network. It becomes obvious that her journey is not only a movement between different neighbourhoods but also an articulation of narrative mobility that questions the semantic attributions that have been previously established. The contrast between these spaces is intensified with regard to Shabbat:

> Camden would not cease at 6.18 p.m., the streets would not become quiet, the people still. These people had not prepared for the Sabbath, they did not hear the sound of Friday in their skulls. [...] She wondered now if this was how Ronit felt in New York, without lines and demarcations, without order and sense, without an anchor. A thing to be both feared and desired.[22]

The encounter of semiospheres gives rise to reflections concerning the constructed other: being dislocated in Camden Esti begins to ponder Ronit's life in New York, which, from Esti's point of view, is also devoid of the order and security attributed to Hendon. Consequently, the exterior of Esti's familiar space remains ambivalent: although it clearly appeals to Esti, a sense of danger is still imminent to it. Esti's movement at once highlights the polyvalent constitution of space and its semantic attributions. She perceives Camden in terms of otherness but her experience also voices a fascination for the diversity of the neighbourhood. She connects this experience to her former lover, so that the space of the cultural other is not just forbidding but also becomes the location of hidden promise and unarticulated desire.

21 Alderman: *Disobedience*, pp. 169–170.

22 Ibid., p. 170.

Back in Hendon the opposition of secular and orthodox space is once more foregrounded, as the coming peace and quiet of Shabbat are manifested in urban space:

> A certain ripeness had fallen over the blue of the sky. The leaves of the apple trees, the red-tiled roofs, the parked cars, the roads all exhaled, saying, we are done, for this week our work is completed. They settled into the earth, allowing themselves to sag.[23]

The urban network becomes an agent, as space itself is preparing for Shabbat. The narrative focuses on religious semantic layers and thus the dynamic processes that constitute space seem to slow down for the day of rest.

Although Esti's social location in the community should be a central one (after all she is the wife of Krushka's designated successor), her love affair with Ronit brings her to the periphery of the semiosphere. At first the text takes up a character perspective, using the point of view of the congregation's collective memory: "It was understood that all was not well with Esti Kuperman, that there was some problem there, some trouble"[24]. The reason for Esti's precarious position in the social framework is unknown but the congregation's stance towards her is neither questioned nor explained by the text.

The introduction of Esti links her peripheral position within the community to the peripheral position of women in orthodox space: she sits in the women's gallery, which is a spatial articulation of the orthodox exclusion of women from religious practices in the synagogue.[25] But even at this point the text connects the double confinement of Esti – as woman in the gallery and as homosexual subject in the orthodox semiosphere – to special competences of perceiving and interpreting space: the elevated position of the gallery provides Esti with a vertical view on space, which, according to de Certeau, is linked to the point of view of the designer.

> [The bird's eye view of the elevated position] transforms the bewitching world by which one was 'possessed' into a text that lies before one's eyes. It allows one to read it, to be a solar Eye, looking down like a god.[26]

23 Alderman: *Disobedience*, p. 175.

24 Ibid., p. 3.

25 The women's gallery can be understood as a Foucauldian heterotopy, as an excluding confinement of the constructed other, Michel Foucault: *Die Heterotopien. Der utopische Körper. Zwei Radiovorträge*, transl. from the French by Michael Bischoff. Frankfurt am Main: Suhrkamp 2005, pp. 19–20.

26 De Certeau: *Everyday Life*, p. 92.

Through Esti's eyes the text decodes the picture of the men's section from above, drawing on her knowledge of space, as she is able to assign meaning to the colours of the men's kippot:

> Over time the hats and kippot had become individual to her, each blotch of colour representing a different personality. There was Hartog, the president of the board, […] walking up and down even while the prayers continued […]. There was Levitsky, the synagogue treasurer, swaying in a nervous pecking motion as he prayed. There was Kirschbaum, one of the executive officers, leaning against the wall and constantly dozing off and waking with a jerk.[27]

The narrative voice employs the character perspective of Esti to introduce members of the synagogue board, articulating variance, as different movements in space imply different attitudes ascribed to the characters.

The narrative foregrounds Esti's heightened spatial competence not only in its use of her point of view from the gallery but also in her being able to permeate space mentally as well as semantically. Thus the synagogue to Esti is not just a space of exclusion, rather her intense connection to the synagogue stresses her confident location within the religious semiosphere:

> Esti spread her mind wider and wider around the synagogue until she inhabited every space of it in her slow breathing. She was in the puckered ceiling plaster and the tired blue carpet, in the grilles that covered the windows, in the red plastic of the chairs, in the electric wires within the walls and in the throat pulse of every man and woman. She breathed and felt the synagogue inhale and exhale with her.[28]

Esti and the synagogue become one up to a point when she seems to inhabit the building and the located bodies alike.[29] Through this, the synagogue, and thus religious space, and Esti are linked to a degree that the community's attitude towards her is unable to question her self-location within the orthodox semiosphere. Her mental mobility further represents an appropriation of semantic space that is openly articulated when Esti challenges Krushka's last Dvar Torah in front of the Bimah. Here she claims space next to her husband, not only confidently re-locating herself as a woman in the men's section but also claiming leadership along with her husband. This claim rearranges the orthodox semiosphere and is simultaneously grounded upon Esti's strong rooting in religious space.

27 Alderman: *Disobedience*, p. 5.

28 Ibid., p. 103.

29 The mental expansion of the character into space constructs an intertextual intertwinement with Virginia Woolf's *Mrs Dalloway*, where the occupying of urban space is used to articulate questions of belonging and female self-location with regard to urban space.

Besides her semantic and spatial movement, the text also uses Esti's character perspective to stress the diversity of orthodox space, an ambivalence that is initially negated by Ronit. Esti's search for her former lover in the synagogue draws on the polyvalence of the relational network:

> She moved around the rims of the gallery, resting near the corners of the ceiling [...]. She knew what she was looking for. She allowed herself time to find it, among the sincere prayer and the insincere, among the worries and regrets and dedication and boredom and confusion and disapproval of the women. [...] I am sitting next to Ronit and her warm body is beside me as it always used to be[30]

Mobility makes Esti become aware of the variance of orthodox space and is furthermore, as she searches explicitly for Ronit's body, an articulation of sexual desire, which Esti publicly negates according to Krushka's advice. Therefore it is not surprising that Esti's final claim for religious authority is linked to an articulation of homosexual identity.

How vital the act of relating to the semantic layers of space, and thereby forming them, is to the characters becomes furthermore obvious when Ronit administers her parents' estate. In search for her mother's Shabbat candlesticks Ronit is confronted with narratives of family memory. In the course of this process her bi-spatial notion of Jewish space as well as her reserved relationship to her own family and orthodoxy are questioned. Her seemingly coherent notion of the past thus gives way to a polyvalent and therefore much more complex understanding of family relationships, religion and semantic locations within urban space.

Initially Ronit construes her own childhood first and foremost in terms of exclusion, e.g., as a girl in an orthodox home who was forbidden to study Torah. Her father's library consequently represents a space of rejection and disappointment. The history of the house has inscribed itself on Ronit's body, as a piece of bark from a tree nearby remains under her skin after she tripped over its root at the age of thirteen: "Not just any tree root; the tree root. The tree root that is part of me"[31]. The confrontation with memory space through objects like Ronit's Kiddush cup and especially her mother's candlesticks initiates a renegotiation of the past which allows for a more complex view on family space and, in a figurative sense, on orthodoxy. Intimate moments like her parents laughing together or the lighting of the candles on Shabbat become more and more important. Thus a seemingly coherent interpretation

30 Alderman: *Disobedience*, pp. 103–104.

31 Ibid., p. 72.

of orthodox space is deconstructed, because both poles – intimacy and exclusion – intertwine and give rise to a fragmented and hybrid notion of the past that contains multiple narratives. The gap between father and daughter is finally bridged when Ronit discovers that her father left the candlesticks with Esti, in case Ronit would want them. So Krushka, usually so reserved, shows some kind of insight into Ronit's psyche, securing her the only item she would long for – the memory object which also links father and daughter in grief for the deceased mother and wife – and thus also securing the reestablishment of an emotional connection between the generations.
Therefore Ronit's movement through Hendon also constitutes a semantic remodelling of implications inscribed into the spatial framework, which can be perceived as an act of simultaneously forming space and memory. Moreover, through evaluating her semantic location with regard to the memory space of her family home, Ronit readjusts her self-location towards the semiosphere of orthodoxy. Herein she articulates her own hybrid positioning in Jewish space and in addition highlights the polyvalent construction of identity in general. Ronit's being at once orthodox, secular, Jewish, American and British makes her feel dislocated in London as well as in New York:

> I'm an oddity. I know it. Even in New York, where everyone's just a little bit Jewish, I don't make much sense. The Orthodox world is tight […]. People from my background just *don't* leap the tracks, go and bat for the other team. Except when they do.[32]

Ronit questions coherent notions of Jewish identity that assume themselves unaffected by space, wholly reliant on what one could call a semantic subspace relocated in the cultural layers of collective memory that bring forth a stable, unchanging identity design. Space thus pervades the self and engages in the shaping of the construction of the semantic network as well as the formation of a hybrid identity.

> There is a myth – many of us believe it – that we are wanderers, unaffected by the place in which we live, hearkening only to the commandments of the Lord. It's a lie. These British Jews were British – they shuffled awkwardly, looked at their feet and drank tea.[33]

Thus the question of belonging is finally linked to the performative construction of the self. Identity therefore is no longer unchangeable but overcomes the clear-cut separation of being British and Jewish as well as the apparently

32 Ibid., p. 228.
33 Ibid., p. 247.

impenetrable separation construed between orthodox and secular semantic spaces.

As already outlined above, Esti's claim on narrative and interpretive authority is closely linked to mobility within the orthodox semiosphere. She literally takes up space within the synagogue as she delivers her speech during Krushka's hesped, the eulogy service, when she locates her homosexual identity in relation to Krushka's interpretation of the parashah *Bereshit.* Although her staying with her husband does not constitute a complete break, her decision is nevertheless based on affection for Dovid rather than on mere obedience. As she repeatedly stresses her right to disobey – which is underlined by the interpreting narrative voice's comment on Ya'akov wrestling the angel – her decision is negotiated in the context of the constant conflict of individual and mitsvot, through which her deep rooting in the religious semiosphere is additionally accentuated. Esti's coming out is linked to her claim on religious authority, as she challenges the Rav's interpretation of her desire with regard to the value of silence. Therefore the text does not solve the opposition of Esti's homosexual and orthodox self-fashioning, rather the narrative stresses Esti's decision. Instead of mending the ruptured self, her self-location inside the orthodox semiosphere can only highlight the fragmented character of Esti's identity design because of her polyvalent positioning with regard to the community as well as to the spatial and semantic framework. Thus by claiming space in the synagogue Esti also claims semantic space within Hendon and thus consciously takes up a complex and polyvalent position in the relational network.

Locating Diversity

Alderman's text confronts different semantic layers attributed to space in the process of locating the self within the city in relation to the various semantic implications inherent to urban space. Thereby the text underlines the dynamic processes taking place in its constitution by focusing on areas of intertwinement and hybridity. From this we can see that Jewish spaces do not exist as static distinct spatial entities but are polyvalent and dynamic: the novel portrays the diversity of Jewish spaces and, at the same time, foregrounds the intertwinement of Jewish and non-Jewish spaces. To accomplish this, it stresses locations within semantic and spatial borders, as here dynamics of negotiating spatial and cultural belonging become clearly visible. The novel thus deconstructs coherent notions of space and identity alike.

Consequently, the initial confrontation of Hendon and its various counterparts, which gives rise to a bi-spatial notion of space, is discarded in favour of a much more complex picture of both space and identity. Not only does the mediation through three different voices, which render distinct and often conflicting points of view visible in the narrative design, bring about a polyphonic portrayal, but by using mobility between semantic and spatial sub-structures (such as orthodox spaces and secular spaces) the text also foregrounds the importance of mobility when it comes to experiencing space and attributing meaning to the spatial network. As outlined by Massey, space does not exist in opposition to time but is strongly intertwined with temporal layers and cannot be construed as static. London is thus a hybrid network with multiple polyvalent layers in which Jewish and non-Jewish spaces as well as orthodox and non-orthodox spaces exist in a state of constant interchange. Space in Alderman's novel is an active part of the process of narration and it is through space that cultural and semantic boundaries are constantly questioned.

The novel focuses on semiotic dynamics taking place at the border between semantic fields and it is through these dynamics that processes of hybridisation give rise to questions that relate different notions of Jewish identity and attempts at self-location to the spatial network. The point of view within the dynamic network of space is shown to be of crucial importance to the semantic location: initially, orthodox space appears to be the only Jewish space but in the course of the narration this notion gives way to a far more complex vision on Jewish spaces. Through negotiating strategies of self-location and spatial semantics the novel highlights dynamic processes of intertwinement and interpenetration that clearly point to a relational understanding of identity. Consequently, space and identity as portrayed by the narrative are often ambiguous, multi-facetted and fragmented. The constitution of Jewish spaces thus relies on the protagonists' acts of locating themselves within the relational network. Here, the novel stresses the importance of self-locations that are able to draw on mobility rather than on a negation of dynamic processes. Urban space and the relationship between equivocally interpreted Jewish spaces are revealed as a complex network, which in the act of narration is experienced from multiple points of view. Therein the diversity of Judaism as well as the polyvalence of (Jewish) identity and urban space is highlighted, which gives rise to a multitude of interpretations of Jewishness. Each of these stresses new semantic attributions and interpretative layers, the intertwinement of which is explored and negotiated in the course of narration.

Epilogue

‘Jewish Quarter’ and ‘Kosher Light’
On the ‘Migrantisation’ of Jewish Urban Space

Wolfgang Kaschuba

The following fact appears before us today with shocking clarity: around eighty years ago, the synagogues in Germany and Berlin were burning. In this memorial year of 2015, numerous events, projects, and exhibitions are invoking these events and the subsequent Holocaust – a tribute that is almost taken for granted in a German capital that has consciously placed Holocaust memorialization at its historical and physical center as a visible testament to German guilt, thereby inscribing an unforgettable symbolic reminder of that guilt into German collective memory.

The purpose of these events is to draw attention to the dramatic, self-inflicted loss this city suffered during its years of barbarism: the loss of its humanity, as testified to by the loss of its Jewish citizens and their Berliner history and culture. For pre-1933 Berlin had been shaped by Jewish traditions and the Jewish investment in German culture to a degree that few other European capitals can match.

Only if this memory is kept alive; only if it remains visible behind the ‘dark’ wall in the history of Germany and Berlin, will the city’s newly-won ‘bright’ side – its image as an open and culturally tolerant metropolis – be truly experienced and confirmed in the present. Indeed, tolerance, as is known, can only be nourished on thoughtfulness, never on forgetfulness. This was and remains the promise of Germany after the Second World War.

This Berlin culture of memory seems to have seen to it that nothing be forgotten. The city landscape is pervaded by memorials and museums, memorial plaques and ‘stumbling stones’ that recall Jewish life and the Holocaust, lending the cityscape a thick, stony, commemorational texture. Countless publications and city-tours present Jewish quarters, communities, and individuals to locals and tourists alike as spaces and contours of a shared history. This special historicity of city culture and discourse is proudly presented to Jewish visitors from the Unites States or Israel as proof that, thanks to Berlin's new cultural diversity and appeal, this responsibility will never be neglected – for the sake of the city's past as well as present Jewish life.

Yet at second glance, it is also clear that precisely in this memorial year – seventy years after the end of World War II and the Holocaust – a caesura in memory politics is looming over Germany as well. This is particularly evident in cities like Berlin. Commemorations of the Holocaust rarely include witnesses, survivors, or members of the generation of the perpetrators, while the 'second generation' – which although born after the war, is nevertheless bound up in the same volume of collective memory – has long since lost its sway over the social discourse on German history.

At the same time, the binding force and influence of the 'German' memory-*topos*, which lies socio-biographically so far in the past, is clearly losing its grip on the younger generation. Unlike their parents, young adults today must 'immigrate' into this memorial landscape; that is, they must consciously choose to associate themselves with a historical space which, however, they no longer necessarily need to feel born into.

Many make this choice reluctantly, or not at all. Many were not even born in German territorial space, let alone under the shadow of its history; in order to be able to read and respect the past inscriptions of others, they first had to enroll themselves into a new society and city landscape – thereby breaking, generationally and socially, the strict 'morality' of collective memory in Germany, whose motto had been, 'Never forget!'. Above all, with Germany having become a society of immigrants, the old notion of a German ethnic binding force must necessarily fade away in proportion to that society's desire to avoid describing either itself or others in such ethnic, and therefore excluding, terms.

The creeping loss of memory surrounding the Holocaust is thus to some extent a cultural paradox of almost insoluble inner contradictions. If the notion of 'belonging' is no longer categorically and ethnically determined, becoming an open principle of social and national self-association, then the notion of 'collective memory' must also be further trans-nationalized and de-ethicized. Memory itself, by the same token, can no longer be 'social-morally' predetermined; as a result, the Holocaust loses its axiomatic moral effect. Whether or not some kind of 'ethical exception clause' can be formulated for it remains doubtful, at least in terms of the politics of memory.

Culturalization of the City Landscape

If we leave aside politically correct theory and examine instead the current urban practices in the Berlin cityscape, we will see that remembrance in 2015 indeed takes place within multiple, new cultural situations and social constellations of 'collective remembrance', which offer fewer common historical and moral denominators and seem to be drifting further and further apart. In retrospect, it can be said that after the gradual, hesitant recognition, during the 1950s, that Jewish life was attempting to re-establish itself in Germany; after the Holocaust was definitely incorporated into the German collective consciousness in the 1970s and 1980s; and after the 1990s, when Jewish history and life were finally declared a 'national heritage', the entire issue is still part of a general historical-cultural consciousness in Germany – a consciousness which, however, has long ceased to encompass everything and to apply to everyone. Rather, it has since become part of a confused situation in which collective memory becomes dramatically altered. Standard knowledge from high-school history class mixes with new images from TV-documentaries; motifs from fantasy films merge with information from websites, and religious myths melt together with common knowledge instilled by middle-class education.

This information, already largely detached from any concrete historical and intellectual context, becomes increasingly fragmented and variable; its information content is snapshot-like, fleeting and meant to shock and dazzle. This change has affected not only 'historically detached' youth cultures or 'historically amnesiac' rural communities, but has long ago reached groups at the center of educated middle-class society. Even among the middle-class, which at one time had been seen as enlightened, new and old forms of antisemitism, Islamophobia and other forms of xenophobia have long since resurfaced – as is shown by the Swiss referendum on banning minarets, the German debate over the headscarf, and the Danish discourses on immigration.

Another result of this shift has been the loss of the epistemic orders and hierarchies of our 'common sense'. Consequently, in the present, postmodern confusion of this new 'cultural memory', old Orientalist, antisemitic stereotypes stand side by side – often seemingly naturally – with trendy clichés about organic kosher food culture or the polyglot Jewish culture scene in Berlin. The historical roots, as well as the cultural meaning, of terms and images have become lost in an 'image reservoir' of fleeting motifs and photo-snippets that overlaps almost seamlessly with the digital space of the Internet, which absorbs millions of new images on a daily basis, without positioning them within a context of knowledge or memory, and thereby depriving them of 'meaning'.

In this way, our frameworks of collective and cultural memory tend to expand within these digital movements and frequently disappear within them. This development also resonates with changes occurring in our daily lives, in which physical and material space is encompassing ever new horizons as a result of its digital expansion and reinterpretation. The mass and force of global developments overwhelm us with their digitally manufactured simultaneity. Organization and navigation have become increasingly difficult: today, many young city dwellers can hardly read standard city maps anymore, having become prisoners of the urban navigation systems of their smartphone applications with their set direction commands. As a result, they can be said to be living, both cartographically and in terms of their everyday lives, in an urban 'tunnel system' – a metaphor that perfectly illustrates the present-day *condition urbaine.*

Yet it is common knowledge – in fact, a sort of open trade secret – that, since the deep urban crisis in the 1960s and 1970s, as cities threatened to collapse under the weight of production, traffic, pollution, and crime, there has been a constant promotion of the 'culturalization' of the city landscape. Culture – that is, a systematic arrangement of urban spaces and lifestyles that generate new appeal and cohesion – seemed capable of rescuing the cities, of keeping people in them. And it worked – surprisingly quickly and surprisingly well. It seems that since the 'museumization', 'festivalization' and 'eventization' of city culture that began in the mid-seventies – in other words, since museums and city history, music and literary festivals, theatre and art events, and penthouses in trendy neighborhoods have given inner-city areas a new structure and appeal – the 'exoticization' of urban culture has become the agenda. Things that are foreign, as well as those that are rendered foreign, seem to confirm to us that the 'world *in situ*' has now arrived in our big cities, which almost automatically gives rise to diversity and creativity, urbanity and metropolitan culture.

Today, the branding of big cities thus takes place largely via the staging and fitting out of the city landscape as a cultural 'theme park' in which 'self' and 'foreign' find themselves in constant contact and exchange. What is actually 'foreign' and 'one's own' is, however, negotiated anew in each case, based on a number of factors ranging from social to generational, ethnic to religious, and ethical to gender-related. Definite and unilateral self-associations to either high or low, global or local, Arab or 'German', mainstream or avant-garde culture have therefore become largely obsolete. For with or without Confucius, the way is always the goal: the discursive and symbolic battle over meanings and interpretations of cultural practices in the urban space *is* metropolitan, since culture can constantly re-invent itself in this way. And the metropolis aspires to be just such a 'laboratory' – one that facilitates and accommodates such experiments.

The Jewish Topos: The Old and New Exotic?

In this laboratory, almost everything is remixed and relabeled – that which is considered historically stable as well as taboo subjects such as the relationship between Jewish culture and urban society. At the onset of modernity, the image of the Jew stood, first and foremost, for the alien and sinister other. It signified an ethnic and religious minority that embodied the Eastern and the Semitic, and which was, consequently, socially segregated and culturally ex-territorialized in municipal 'Jewish quarters'. Then, with the advent of the European enlightenment, another image emerged alongside this one: that of a secular and bourgeois intellectual Jewry, which – although denied complete national integration on racist grounds – nonetheless became an undisputedly important bearer and shaper of urban enlightenment and intellectuality. This new image also provided key impetuses for the evolution of the urban avant-garde and Bohemia, whose members knew how to appreciate the sharp 'secular' intellectualism of their Jewish associates.

After the Holocaust, Germans had difficulty dealing with images of their Jewish 'neighbors' for several reasons: first, because hardly any of them remained; second, because one now had to be on guard against false habits and verbal expressions; and third, because of the Germans' evident irritation at the existence of 'new' German and Israeli Jews. The incident in which high-level German politicians congratulated Ignaz Bubis, the Chairman of the Central Council of Jews in Germany, on the speech given by 'his' head of state during Israeli President Ezer Weizman's visit to Germany in 1996 is a bitter illustration of such recent German-Jewish misunderstandings. In any case, one imagines Jewish life in Germany as urban only in those social spaces that had traditionally developed in a heterogeneous, anonymous and open manner.

This painstakingly re-established relationship between Jewish and urban cultures now seems to be drastically changing once again, as it is placed – within the scope of urban strategies of 'exoticization' – into spatial, commemorative, identity-related or imaginary frames. Jewish traditions and symbols can then be variously reinterpreted as urban life-styles or life-styles per se, depending on where the emphasis is placed – whether on the Holocaust or on religion, music or culinary culture; as a result, they become variants of ethnic-urban diversity. The context for this process of reinterpretation is created by cultural and imaginative upgrading processes which develop 'cultural diversity' further as urban capital, with the aim of staging it anew and capitalizing on it. In so doing, they attribute particular importance to 'ethnic' traditions and styles, spaces and themes. For 'ethnic' denotes something that is culturally different, alien, and therefore – above all in contemporary urban readings – 'exotic'; and vice-versa: 'Exoticization' in urban space inevitably implies making something 'other' and 'foreign' – since the foreign alone awakens curiosity and promises authenticity.

Urban diversity thus comes to be conceived above all as a diversity of style and value that makes the Jewish *topos* appear 'stylish' – or to be more precise, makes it into a 'Jewish style'. The urban contexts make this cultural transformation easy, as the Jewish *topos*, in its various manifestations, has proven to be highly compatible with urban musical and culinary culture, as well as with discourses on value and style. Depending on the tone in question, it then 'decorates' each cityscape, from New York to Odessa, with variants of Jewish/Yiddish urban symbols and lifestyles.

These developments are clearly reflected in the cultural advertisements published in Berlin's program magazines and on the city's Internet sites, such as those announcing the 'Yiddish Swing Orchestra' or 'The Kosher Red Hots' who promise 'Klezmer Dance Music from Eastern Europe' and 'Spanish-flavoured Love Songs of the Sephardim'.[1] 'Jewish theatre' and 'Jewish art' happily invoke the notion of a symbolic capital of Jewish-cosmopolitan culture, while the classified ads for 'kosher lamps', 'kosher clocks', or 'kosher wine' serve a double need: they satisfy everyday demands relating to the management of the familiar and communal forms of Sabbath rest, as well as those of a life-style market in which 'things Jewish' have become accessories of creative interior design. In addition, Berlin offers special 'Old Jewish Quarter Walking Tours' that cater to specific historical and touristic demands.

Much of this resembles what is happening in other large cities that serve as role models – for example, London, where 'Jewish London' is promoted as a cultural product incorporating tradition, life-style, and events, much in the same vein as the Notting Hill 'Caribbean Festival' or 'Indian Area'. Paris even

1 Cf. http://www.kosherredhots.com (accessed 23.02.2015).

offers 'kosher' Chinese restaurants in the 'Pletzl'[2]; and in Cracow, the newly fashionable 'Kazimierz Jewish Town' markets itself, on its Internet site, as the 'equivalent of Soho, the Quartier Latin, and Greenwich Village' – and all this without a present-day Jewish population.[3] Commerce and capital too have long since become a part of this imaginative Jewish 'branding'. In the words of a young Jewish visitor, discussing a friend's experience in Berlin: "It is really hard for Georg to go to a Jewish disco. You have to look perfect there. If you wear a Gucci skirt, you can't wear a Chanel top with it. Otherwise it doesn't match, and you'll be told: that just doesn't work."[4]

It is significant that Jews themselves frequently experience this process of gradual re-contextualization and transformation of Jewish culture today as problematic. Indeed, they often feel irritated and instrumentalized:

> Meshugge parties are often attended by Israelis and interested non-Jews. There is lots of House music, mixed with Israeli music. Members of the Jewish community and their friends, on the other hand, tend to attend Sababba parties. Sababba is more mainstream; the music is more popular and occasionally includes Israeli Evergreens […]. For the Israelis living here, it is sort of like us going into a club and hearing Udo Jürgens & Co.[5]

Being style-conscious is everything, also as a performative display – one of the reasons why the American-initiated Heeb movement, which aims to extricate Jewish culture from its victim status, developed its multi-dimensional experimental forms, which now resonate in numerous cities, including Berlin.

Consequently, Jews themselves can also experiment with the possibilities – including the financial ones – of self-exoticization and self-ethnicization, in what can be described as a passage from the passive into the active mode, lending the Jewish *topos* new cultural leeway on the urban playing field. At the same time, this is, especially in Germany, a risky game, since through this stylization, the Jewish *topos* as a global-ethnic phenomenon loses its particular affiliation with the backdrop of German history. Here, certain historical-political and moral discourses in the 'German context' – that is, in the surrounding society – tend to disintegrate: If the 'particular Jewish *topos*' becomes a 'general ethnic *topos*', then the cautionary shadow of Holocaust commemoration grows ever weaker.

2 Cf. http://www.phylliscooks.com (accessed 23.02.2015).

3 Cf. http://www.krakow-info.com (accessed 23.02.2015).

4 Alina Gromova: *Generation 'koscher light'. Urbane Räume und Praxen junger russischsprachiger Juden in Berlin*. Bielefeld: Transcript 2013, p. 102.

5 Ibid., pp. 210–211.

In terms of its effects, therefore, this involvement of the Jewish *topos* in the process of urban gentrification is highly ambivalent. On the one hand, a sort of cultural valorization may emerge through exoticization. On the other hand, the symbolic 'expatriation' of Jewish culture from its developed German context leads to discrimination.

'Demystifying Label Terms: Kosher'

An interesting illustration of the stylistic appropriation of the Jewish *topos* is offered by contemporary culinary culture. The internet magazine *Bob's Red Mill*, in its advertisement for a 'kosher product line' entitled 'Demystifying Label Terms: Kosher', declares with superb candor:

> Today, these foods represent far more than adherence to religious laws: "kosher" means that the facility and the sources of the ingredients used meet strict quality and cleanliness standards. Muslims, vegans and those with severe dairy allergies can look to the kosher symbols as a way to navigate the label.[6]

With the symbolic asset of religious certification, kosher food is marketed to other religions, alternative palates as well as fashionable dining cultures that value pork-free, vegan, or organic food. This also applies to kosher wine, fish and much more, which are presented as especially healthy: "kosher" is "naturally – the healthier way of life."[7] According to another publication, Jewish cuisine also fosters communication by "breaking barriers and promoting dialogue."[8] Through a clever trick, the promised de-mystification of Jewish culture serves as a pretext for its re-mystification and branding. To go by these ads, then, 'Jewish food culture' lends itself, in a very specific way, to a process of urban ennoblement.

In any case, it can be generally said that today, we are experiencing a process of an ever-increasing 'moralization' of our life-styles – at least as regards those sections of the middle class that reject incessant consumption on political and/or ethical grounds. Here, considerations of the relations between global power and capital play as much a role as do ecological and organic production criteria or notions of 'Fair Trade' and global natural resources, or commons. Economy and consumption are also to be re-imagined and redefined in political and cultural categories. In this context, 'kosher' appears as a moral label as well, combining a politically correct historical attitude with the

6 http://www.bobsredmill.com (accessed 25.02.2015).

7 Ibid.

8 http://www.funkproductions.tv (accessed 25.02.2015).

dietary and environmental standards of contemporary food culture – contributing to an ennobled moral stance that is a clear point-scorer in life-style debates and cooking shows: the 'kosher-burger' from the 'Jewish snack-bar' is now more 'correct' and chic than the veggie-burger from McDonalds – especially in organic-fixated Germany and 'green' Berlin.

By way of illustration, consider the following dialogue between a young Jewish man in Berlin and his female friend. Young man: "My kitchen is kosher. I separate milk from meat." Friend: "Really? And do you also have two fridges?" "No, I can't afford that. I also only have one dish cloth. But I think that you should at least do what you can, otherwise the tradition gets completely lost." "I bet you are doing this to impress girls. They get impressed when you say you keep a kosher kitchen."[9] This little exchange demonstrates how all the factors discussed above in theory play out practically, in real-life: the exoticization and ethnicization, the marketing and life-styling of the 'kosher light' brand, and the transfering of all of these 'identity effects' onto the actor. These are indeed 'market features' in action…

Déjà-vu: Jewish Culture as 'Immigrant' Culture?

Nowadays, we are so used to the whiff of the exotic and authentic that almost everything that originates elsewhere is imbued with this scent, and becomes interesting for our urban cultural palate. The alternative milieus outdo each other in elevating and gentrifying this migrant character, which fosters the city's cultural diversity. All these reasons have led to the beginning of a conscious or unconscious 'migrantization' of the Jewish *topos*, in clubs, shops, pubs and at urban events – irrespective of whether the supposed "foreignness" attached to things Jewish is valued or rejected. In either case, the effect is the same: 'exoticization'. Similar tendencies are also discernible within certain Jewish urban discourses, where clear distinctions are drawn between 'classic' Berlin Jewry and 'foreign' – Russian or Middle Eastern – Jewish styles.

Two forms of 'migrantization' are entangled here: that imposed from within, and that from without. These effects are magnified by the fact that many antisemitic attacks – both severe and less severe – on supposed Jewish residents or tourists no longer originate uniquely in the 'German' milieu, but increasingly in the immigrant groups within German society. As a young Jewish man said of his experiences in certain districts of Berlin, where it is advisable to avoid wearing visible signs of Jewishness: "That antisemitism among

9 Gromova: *Generation 'koscher light'*, p. 244.

Arab youth is increasing, and that 'Jew' has become a curse-word in German schools, is another story […]. This is on my mind. I don't want it."[10]

These are just a few observations and reflections on how Jewish culture, collective memory, and city culture now seem to be tending towards a new confusion – and not only in Berlin. In the case of Berlin, and by extension, of Germany, the assessment that Holocaust memory maintains a clear place within the moral dictates of collective memory remains valid. This memory, however, has been losing its hold on and relevance for the younger and less 'German' generations of Germans, while at the same time, there appears to be a process of active re-contextualization and de-contextualization of the relevant memorial motifs – as when things Jewish are increasingly placed into everyday contexts such as local urban or architectural history, music or culinary culture. This may further encourage cultural linkage and trends toward normalization with regard to the politics of memory. Yet it also poses an inherent danger: that of the loss of the specificity of a unique cultural relationship – in the German-Jewish case, one that had been defined exclusively through the Holocaust and its memory.

This bond disintegrates the moment the debates between the *Diary of Anne Frank* and the historians cease to be accessible – whether associatively or in the sense of memory politics – to new groups and generations in Germany, and when, instead, Jewish culture becomes labeled in terms of Jewish quarters, Klezmer music and kosher-burgers, and incorporated into 'trendy' urban assemblages of 'ethnic' and 'migrant' event culture. Here, the *kippa* and kosher food contribute, much like the Muslim mosque or head-scarf, the Croatian grill-restaurant or Caribbean music, to the scenery of an urban ethnic 'interior decor'. In so doing, they generate 'ethnic' culture and traditions – whether actual or supposed – as a special symbolic asset which, much like art, promises 'authenticity' and which can now be produced, consumed and 'accumulated' at will in the form of practices, knowledge, objects, and style. This in turn means that the city-marketing that had been formerly achieved 'using' the Jewish *topos*, is now clearly tending toward the branding of Jewish objects or practices themselves – toward the promotion of what might be referred to as a historically unique 'kosher migrant culture'.

To what extent this rather ambivalent urban 'culturalization' of the Jewish *topos* will prove to be a helpful – or rather, a dangerous – 'normalization' of the relationship between urban culture and Jewish culture, remains to be seen. This will be among the more intriguing existential questions for history, society, and city politics in Europe in the coming years.

10 Gromova: *Generation 'koscher light'*, p. 233.